Software Configuration Management Handbook
Second Edition

For a listing of recent titles in the *Artech House Software Engineering Library,* turn to the back of this book.

Software Configuration Management Handbook
Second Edition

Alexis Leon

ARTECH HOUSE

BOSTON | LONDON

www.artechhouse.com

Library of Congress Cataloging-in-Publication Data
A catalog record of this book is available from the U.S. Library of Congress.

British Library Cataloguing in Publication Data
A catalog record of this book is available from the British Library.

Cover design by Igor Valdman

© 2005 ARTECH HOUSE, INC.
685 Canton Street
Norwood, MA 02062

International Standard Book Number: 978-1-58083-882-4

10 9 8 7 6 5 4 3 2

To my father, Leon Alexander, and my mother, Santhamma Leon,
for their love, encouragement, and support.

Contents

7   Configuration identification   89

17 Documentation management and control and product data management 255

18   SCM implementation   275

19 SCM operation and maintenance   303

20 SCM in special circumstances   317

Preface

Configuration management is the art of identifying, organizing, and controlling modifications to the software being built by a programming team. The goal is to maximize productivity by minimizing mistakes. Practicing configuration management in a software project has many benefits, including increased development productivity, better control over the project, better project management, reduction in errors and bugs, faster problem identification and bug fixes, and improved customer goodwill. But a single software configuration management (SCM) solution is not suited for all projects; in fact, each project is different, and although the core SCM objectives and functions remain the same, the SCM system has to be tailored for each project.

Today's software development environment is highly complex and sophisticated. Now a single product could be developed by more than one company. Even in the same company, the different subsystems of the same product or system could be developed by teams that are geographically dispersed. Managing these projects without any scientific tools will be inviting trouble that could result in costly product recalls or project failures. SCM is the ideal solution for managing the chaos and confusion of software development, because its primary objective is to bring in control to the development process.

In 1999, when I started out to write the first edition of this book (*A Guide to Software Configuration Management*), my objective was to write a simple, easy-to-read, and jargon-free book on SCM covering the basic concepts. The idea was to get the reader as quickly up to speed on the basics and key issues as possible. In the first edition, I tried to explain the entire SCM cycle—from identification to configuration control to status accounting to audits and reviews—in sufficient detail to allow the reader to thoroughly understand the scope and complexity of SCM without becoming overwhelmed. I also explained how to perform the various SCM tasks, such as preparing an SCM plan, selecting an SCM tool, and implementing an SCM system.

Since publication of the first edition in May 2000, I have received suggestions, questions, and comments from readers all around the world. From this feedback and from my own research, I have found out what features of the book were liked, what points needed improvement, in which areas more material and more coverage were required, and what other areas needed to be covered. Consequently, I set my goals higher for the second edition. My objective was to produce a revised, updated, and comprehensive book on SCM while maintaining all of the good aspects of the first edition. I wanted to write a book that will help readers understand the SCM fundamentals and then master the advanced topics as they advance in their careers. So the goal was to produce a book that started with the basics, explained the fundamentals, and proceeded to advanced topics—a complete reference. Because of the change in the scope and magnitude of the book, it was decided to rename the book as *Software Configuration Management Handbook (Second Edition)*.

This book is about the practice of the SCM discipline. This book starts with the basics—the definition of SCM, its objectives and functions—and explains SCM as it should be practiced in the software development process. The different phases in the software development life cycle and how SCM plays a role in each phase are discussed in detail. The pitfalls of the software development process and the need, importance, and benefits of SCM are covered in detail, and the common misconceptions about SCM are demystified. The basic SCM concepts such as baselines, versions, variants, delta storage, branching, merging, and releases are explained clearly. Then the book provides in-depth coverage of the four pillars of SCM: identification, control, status accounting, and audits.

Once readers are familiarized with basic terminology and concepts, the book exhaustively discusses the advanced topics, such as SCM implementation phases, build and release management, interface and subcontractor control, software libraries, SCM plans and guidelines for writing good SCM plans, SCM standards, role of SCM in software process improvement (SPI) models (e.g., CMM, CMMI, ISO SPICE, BOOTSTRAP, Trillium), SCM organization, documentation management and control (DMC), and product data management (PDM).

Then the book covers one of the most important aspects of software configuration management—SCM tools. Topics including SCM automation, advantages of SCM tools, and how to select the right tool are explained so readers can select the SCM tool that is best suited for their organization or project. A salient feature of this edition is the comprehensive coverage of the different activities required to plan, design, implement, operate, and maintain a good SCM system. The various activities such as SCM system design, tool selection, implementation, postimplementation activities, operation and maintenance of the SCM system, and how to perform SCM in different scenarios (e.g., very large projects, Web site management, distributed environments, integrated development environments) are given a thorough treatment.

The book has three appendices: SCM Resources on the Internet, SCM Bibliography, and SCM Glossary. The first two appendices will be of immense value for readers who want to further explore the new frontiers of

SCM. The third appendix will help readers when they encounter unfamiliar terms during the early chapters of the book.

One important aspect of this book is that it does not rely on any specific tool or standard for explaining the SCM concepts and techniques. In fact, one of the main objectives of this book is to give readers enough information about SCM, the mechanics of SCM, and SCM implementation without being tool and/or standard specific. The book gives information on how to select the right SCM tool for an organization or project and how to implement, manage, and maintain the tool so that the organization can reap the full benefits of SCM.

How to use this book

The chapters in this book are organized so that the concepts of SCM are developed from the ground up. Ideally, it should be read from start to finish, but such a reading plan will not suit many busy and advanced readers; therefore, I have tried to write individual chapters so they could be read on their own. If you come across a term that is not described in the chapter, you can look it up in the glossary and continue reading. Readers who are not familiar with SCM or who are novices in this profession should read the book from the beginning to get the most out of it.

Who should read this book?

This book is written for company managers who must support the SCM efforts, software project managers who must plan and design the SCM system for their projects, people who will implement the system, professionals who will manage and maintain the SCM system, and software developers, testers, quality assurance personnel, and all who will be affected by the SCM system. The style and approach of the book is intended to be practical rather than theoretical. It is written in an easy-to-understand and jargon-free style, so that it will become an invaluable tool in understanding the discipline of SCM and a useful guide in planning, designing, implementing, managing, and maintaining a good SCM system.

Acknowledgments

I am deeply grateful to all those people who helped me bring this book from idea to print:

I would like to express my gratitude to my reviewer, *Bruce Angstadt*, Independent SCM Consultant, for his comprehensive and thorough review of the manuscript and his amazing ability to end the review of each chapter on a pleasant note. His comments and suggestions have played a vital role in improving the organization, content, technical accuracy, and readability of the book.

I would like to thank *Mike Tarrani* for his suggestions and comments on how to improve this book.

I am grateful to my brother, *Mathews Leon*, for his suggestions, reviews, and comments and for helping me with the illustrations for the book.

Thanks to my father, *Leon Alexander*, and my mother, *Santhamma Leon*, for their love and support.

I would like to acknowledge the efforts of *Tim Pitts* and *Tiina Ruonamaa* of Artech House, for making writing this book a painless and pleasurable process. Thanks also to *Judi Stone* and *Kevin Danahy* for their efforts in making this project a success, and to the competent editorial staff, designers, and production team at Artech House, for their valuable contributions.

Very special thanks to *Patrick Egan* and the participants of the SCM discussion forums at *CM Crossroads* (*www.cmcrossroads.com*). I have gained a lot of knowledge and wisdom from your postings. It is a wonderful and continuous learning experience reading the posts. I wish all the members of CM Crossroads lots of success.

A lot of people have made valuable contributions to the discipline of software configuration management. These people, through their research, writings, preaching, and practice, have made the software community realize the importance and benefits of software configuration management. I salute those magnificent men and women for their efforts.

Finally, I would like to thank the readers of this book and wish them all the very best in their configuration management efforts.

—*Alexis Leon*

CHAPTER

1

Contents

Overview of software configuration management

1.1 Introduction

Computers and communication are becoming integral parts of our lives. A few decades ago, communication used to be between people—from one person to another. But now inanimate objects are getting into the act: books can tell cash registers how much they cost; identity cards can tell the door lock whether to open or not; automated guided vehicles can tell the host computer where they are in the shop floor and what they are carrying and when they will be free; missiles can compare the landscape with their own map and hit the target with pinpoint precision; and on the Internet people engage in lively chats and discussions and play games, even if they are physically in different continents.

The prime mover behind this digital revolution is computer software. Today software touches on and controls almost all aspects of our life: software makes us more efficient and productive, helps people learn and teach better, helps in making our homes, banks, and organizations more secure, helps doctors better diagnose diseases and find better treatments, and controls mission-critical applications and equipments. The list is endless.

As software becomes more prominent, the task of developing the software is becoming more difficult. Because software is used for critical applications and controlling sophisticated equipments and systems, even a small mistake or error can have catastrophic consequences. Today's software projects are becoming more complex in size, sophistication, and technologies used. Now most software products cater to millions of users, support different national languages, and come in different sizes and shapes (e.g., desktop, standard, professional, enterprise). For example, operating systems,

1

word processors, and even enterprise resource planning (ERP) packages support multiple languages and multiple currencies. Almost all application software products (such as word processors, ERP packages, and even SCM tools) support more than one hardware and/or software platform. For example, ERP systems can run on mainframes and client/server systems, different versions of Web browsers for the PC and Mac, and database management systems that run on MVS, UNIX, Windows NT, or Linux. The competition and the advancements in technology are driving the software vendors to include additional functionality and new features in their products just to stay in business.

In addition, users of software systems have matured, and the bugs and defects in a system are detected and publicized faster than ever—thanks to the Internet. In today's software development environment, where the communication facilities are advanced, the news that a software product is bad and has bugs can spread quickly. This is evident from the newsgroup postings and the news alerts that one gets so often nowadays. So if the company has to save face and prevent its market share from dropping, it has to provide the fixes and patches quickly. The time that a company gets to do damage control (i.e., find the cause of the bug, identify the problem area and fix the bug, ensure that the bug-fixing has not created additional bugs, do regression testing, and get the bug-fixed version of the software to the customer) is much less now than compared to the early days. Companies must react quickly in order to keep their reputations intact.

Thus, today's software development environment is complex and reaction or response times are short. Millions of software professionals around the world are developing complex software systems, which consist of a myriad of components, each of which evolves as it is developed and maintained. The task of managing a software project successfully and delivering a high-quality and defect-free product on time and without any cost overrun is nearly impossible. To survive in this brutally competitive world, organizations need some sort of mechanism to keep things under control or total chaos and confusion will result, which could lead to product or project failures and put the company out of business. A properly implemented software configuration management (SCM) system is such a mechanism that can help software development teams create top-quality software without chaos and confusion. According to Whitgift [1], SCM ensures that the development and evolution of the different components of a system are efficient and controlled, so that the individual components fit together as a coherent whole.

Software configuration management is a method of bringing control to the software development process. As Babich [2] has stated:

> On any team project, a certain degree of confusion is inevitable. The goal is to minimize the confusion so that more work can get done. The art of coordinating software development to minimize this particular type of confusion is called configuration management. Configuration management is the art of identifying, organizing and controlling modifications to the software

being built by a programming team. The goal is to maximize productivity by minimizing mistakes.

SCM is a process used for more efficiently developing and maintaining software, which is accomplished by improving accountability, reproducibility, traceability, and coordination. All of the processes of SCM, including the identification of configuration items, documentation of characteristics, and controlling change, are to ensure integrity, accountability, visibility, reproducibility, project coordination and traceability, and formal control of system and project evolution [3]. This chapter is intended as an introduction to the discipline of software configuration management.

1.2 Common SCM myths

A lot of myths surround the discipline and practice of software configuration management. People are often unwilling to adopt SCM because of these incorrect notions. In this section, we review some of the most common myths about SCM and try to demystify them.

1.2.1 SCM is a difficult, monotonous, and time-consuming activity

Properly implementing and managing an SCM system is not an easy task. During the early days of SCM, when all configuration management tasks had to be done manually, configuration management was a difficult, monotonous, and time-consuming activity. But even in those days, the benefits of having an SCM system far outweighed the difficulties. Today, with the availability of sophisticated SCM tools, managing an SCM system is a totally different ballgame. Today's SCM tools automate many of the repetitive, monotonous, and tedious SCM activities, thus making the practice of SCM a lot easier.

1.2.2 SCM is the responsibility of management

SCM is the responsibility of all people involved in the software development process. The company management is not responsible for the day-to-day operation of the SCM system. Their main job is to create an organizational environment in which SCM can thrive by giving SCM the full backing of management. They should also be involved in the development of SCM policies, usage guidelines, allocation of budget, tool selection, and appointment of competent professionals to implement and manage the SCM system. Only when the SCM team has the full backing and support of management will it be able to implement the system smoothly. Management should monitor the implementation and operation of the system, review the progress and status periodically, and take any necessary corrective actions as required. Management should also ensure that the SCM team gets the support and cooperation it needs from all departments.

1.2.3   SCM is just for developers

The software development team is one of the major users of the SCM system. These people benefit the most from a properly implemented SCM system. Problems such as missing source code, inability to find the latest
version of a file, corrected mistakes reappearing, programs that suddenly
stop working, and missing requirements can be avoided if a good SCM system is in place. But many developers see SCM as a waste of time and do it
just because they are forced to do it. This hostility toward SCM can be eliminated if developers are properly educated in SCM principles and made
aware of the benefits of an SCM system. With today's SCM tools, the level
of automation that can be achieved is phenomenal, and performing the
SCM activities is not difficult. Although one of the main beneficiaries of a
good SCM system is the development team, developers are not the only
people who benefit from SCM; the other beneficiaries include testers, quality assurance (QA) personnel, the maintenance team, and the support
team.

1.2.4   SCM is just for the SCM team

The days of full-fledged SCM teams are gone. Now SCM tools have replaced
humans in most areas and most SCM activities have been automated. Even
in cases and places when human intervention is required, the tools make
the job easier by automating the task, providing the relevant information
for better and faster decision making, and enabling better communication
among the people involved. Now the major tasks the SCM team has to perform include SCM plan preparation, tool selection, implementation and
operation, user training (on both SCM concepts and SCM tool operation),
change management, build and release management, audits and reviews,
and management reporting. To manage an efficient and effective SCM system that will help the organization to develop world-class software without
any problems, the SCM team needs the full support and cooperation of all
other departments, including developers, testers, QA personnel, the technical support team, management, and customers.

1.2.5   SCM is just for the maintenance and technical support team

Once the system is developed and tested, it is released to users. From this
point onward, the maintenance phase starts. Once people start using the
system, many errors that escaped the testing phase will be found. The users
might ask for new features and enhancements. The maintenance team must
attend to these requests and fix the bugs that are found. The jobs of the
maintenance and technical support teams will be a lot easier if the project
followed good SCM practices. The maintenance team can fix bugs quickly if
the SCM system documented the change history, build history, details of
bug fixes during development, and other such information. In addition,
managing and maintaining the different versions of the same product and

providing support to these different versions is not possible without an SCM system.

A good SCM system produces a record of the errors that occurred during development and how they were fixed. As the software continues in the maintenance phase, more problems and their solutions will be added to this record. This record of problems and solutions can help the technical support team avoid reinventing the wheel. If the project has not followed any SCM procedures, then maintaining the system can turn into one of the most difficult assignments software professionals can have. A good example of this situation is the Y2K projects, where people had to fix the problems in programs that were more than 20 to 30 years old, programs that had no documentation and that were developed without any programming standards and naming conventions. So for the effective and efficient functioning of the maintenance and technical support teams, a good SCM system should be in place from the beginning of the software development process and not at the beginning of the maintenance phase.

1.2.6   SCM slows down the software development process

Before the advent and popularity of SCM tools, SCM was a time-consuming process because almost all of the activities were performed manually. But even in those days, SCM was considered worth the effort because it saved a lot of time spent searching for missing files, fixing bugs that were already fixed, and troubleshooting problems caused by the use of incorrect versions. So even though SCM was a time-consuming process that slowed down the developers a little, the benefits far outweighed the costs. Today with the availability of excellent SCM tools, which automate almost all SCM functions, the practice of SCM is a lot easier. Therefore, the argument that SCM slows down the software development process or decreases the development productivity is totally absurd. In fact, in managing today's complex software projects, SCM is a must. Any organization that attempts to develop software products without a good SCM system will be shooting itself in the foot.

1.2.7   SCM is only needed to get certifications

It is true that a good SCM system is a must in order to obtain certifications such as ISO, CMM, and the like; but if SCM systems are implemented and managed just for the sake of getting the certification, then it is more likely that the systems will not deliver the expected results. The organization should create an environment or work culture that treats SCM as a fundamental necessity and not as a necessary evil to achieve some certification or to get a contract. The SCM system will not deliver its full potential if the people involved are doing the SCM activities only for the sake of doing it. In this aspect, training users about the benefits of SCM, SCM concepts, and efficient use of SCM tools is very important.

1.2.8   SCM tools will take care of everything

SCM tools have evolved over time and have now become sophisticated. Today's SCM tools automate most SCM activities and thus make the life of software users a lot easier. In many cases, the SCM tools are integrated into the development environment so that SCM becomes a part of the development process. But thinking that SCM tools will take care of everything can be a recipe for disaster. Many SCM activities, including change management, build and release management, and configuration audits, require human intervention and judgment. Although SCM tools make these jobs easier, there is no substitute for human intelligence and decision making. For example, an SCM tool can automate almost 80% of the change management process, but SCM personnel are needed to initiate a change request, to perform the impact analysis, and to decide when to incorporate the change.

1.2.9   One SCM tool will suit everyone

Hundreds of SCM tools are available in the marketplace. These tools differ in features, capabilities, size, functionality, price, technical support, customizability, and scalability. Organizations are also different from one another. Each has its own characteristics and identity. Assuming that one tool will be suited for all organizations is wrong. Selecting and purchasing an SCM tool without analyzing whether the tool is suited for the organization will have disastrous consequences. For an SCM implementation to be successful, the tool that is implemented should be compatible with organizational culture, practices, and procedures. So when purchasing an SCM tool, proper attention should be given to selecting the tool that is best suited for the organization.

1.2.10   SCM is expensive

SCM tools come in all shapes and sizes: some are free; some cost a small fortune; some perform rudimentary change management activities; and others cover the entire life cycle of the development process. Even though many free SCM tools are available, they have limited functionality, features, and technical support. Sophisticated, high-end SCM tools are expensive. An SCM system needs people to manage it. Thus implementing and managing an SCM system is an expensive affair, but these expenses should be weighed against the benefits of the SCM system. An efficient SCM system will increase the productivity of the human resources (e.g., developers, testers, QA personnel, auditors, managers), shorten development and change cycles, streamline software builds, reduce errors by automating the monotonous and repetitive tasks, speed up recovery to previous versions of software when errors are identified, enable the better management of projects by providing quality information, and improve customer satisfaction by resolving the bugs and problems quickly. When the benefits of the

SCM system are considered, it becomes evident that money spent on SCM is well spent, and the SCM system will pay for itself.

1.2.11   SCM is just for the source code

Many software professionals believe that configuration management is a solution suitable only for managing source code. This perception is far from the truth. Many of today's configuration management systems are capable of managing a wide variety of digital and electronic artifacts. As we look back on how this narrow-minded view of configuration management developed and why it still persists, there is no great mystery. First-generation configuration management systems were capable of versioning only ordinary text files and had self-limiting names such as Source Code Control System (SCCS). In fact, Microsoft's configuration management system still has such a name—Visual SourceSafe [4]. But configuration management has many other uses than just managing the source code. SCM can and should be used to manage all project artifacts, such as requirements, visual models, prototypes, executables or binaries, system files, libraries, documents, development tools, test scripts, and images.

1.2.12   SCM is change management and defect tracking

Change management and defect tracking are two major activities of SCM; however, other activities such as configuration identification, status accounting, and configuration audits are performed as well. So the notion that SCM is just change management and defect tracking is wrong. It is true that some tools available in the marketplace do nothing but change management and defect tracking. These tools help the project manager bring some amount of control to the development process. In many small projects, full-fledged SCM systems are not necessary because the cost of the system will not justify its purchase. So in these cases, a change management or defect tracking tool can be used efficiently to perform and automate the change management functions, while the other SCM activities are performed manually. But in the case of large, complex, and mission-critical projects, a simple change management tool will not be enough. In such cases, a full-fledged SCM tool—one that covers the entire functionality of SCM—should be used.

1.2.13   Software development can succeed without SCM

During the early days and sometimes even today, software development is done without SCM. Software development can sometimes succeed without SCM in the case of very small projects with small project teams, but today's software products are becoming more complex in size, sophistication, and technologies used. In addition, the different components of a software product are not necessarily built by a single group. This is the era of multisite, distributed development, where different components of a system are developed by different groups situated in different parts of the world. In such a scenario, managing a software project is a complex task. If proper control mechanisms and procedures are not in place, the software development can easily get out of control and projects can fail. The history of the software industry is full of such software disasters, and if one closely examines the major software failures, many could be attributed to the absence of an efficient SCM system.

1.3   A brief history of SCM

Configuration management has its origins in the manufacturing industry, more specifically in the U.S. defense industry. When the products that were developed were small and the product sophistication level was lower, the activities of product development and design change during the entire product life cycle could be managed by a single person or a group of close-knit people. But when the complexity of the products began to increase—as embodied by products such as fighter planes, tanks, and guns—it was impossible for a single person or group to maintain control over the design and production and, more important, the design changes. Moreover, the development of these products spanned many years and was handled by more than one person, so when control was transferred from one person to another, the associated information was lost, because no formal methods existed for documenting the design and the changes made to it.

In 1962, the U.S. Air Force responded to the control and communication problems in the design of its jet aircraft by authoring and publishing a standard for configuration management, AFSCM 375–1. This was the first standard in configuration management [5]. This standard was followed by many other standards, mainly from the U.S. military and the Department of Defense (the MIL and DoD standards).

As computers became popular, the importance of and focus on the software development industry began to increase. More people began to use computers and software products. Software systems made life easier by automating many tasks that had been done manually until then. As people got used to the convenience of the automated systems, they began to demand more features. The software development organizations were left with no choice as more players entered the market with newer and better products. Thus the computer programs became more complex in size (i.e., they are bigger than the earlier systems), sophistication (i.e., they are more complex and are used for mission-critical applications), and technologies used (i.e., today's applications use the latest technologies, such as workflow automation, groupware, Internet, and e-commerce). The size and the nature of the development teams have also changed. Now development teams consist of thousands of people from different cultural and social backgrounds, and the various subsystems of a system could easily be developed by different companies from around the world.

As computer programs became more complex and difficult to manage and as computer project teams became larger and more distributed, the problems that plagued the production engineers—such as inability of a single person to control and manage the development process, difficulty in managing change, communications breakdowns, and difficulty in transferring the knowledge when transferring responsibility—also began to appear in the software development processes. The U.S. Department of Defense and several international organizations, including IEEE, ANSI, and ISO, all started to address the problem of configuration management in the software development process, and all came out with their own standards. Among these, the most widely used standards are the ANSI/IEEE standards. More about the different standards is given in Chapter 12. Now SCM is accepted as a discipline and is practiced by most software organizations, if not all. Awareness about the need and importance of SCM is also increasing. Hundreds of tools and packages are available that help automate the SCM process and make the practice of SCM easier.

1.4   SCM: Concepts and definitions

Proper application of SCM is a key component in the development of quality software. Uncontrolled changes to the software under development are usually a significant cause of changes to a project's schedule and budget; unmanaged change is the largest single cause of failure to deliver systems on time and within budget.

Bersoff, Henderson, and Siegel [6] have defined SCM as the discipline of identifying the configuration of a system at discrete points in time for purposes of systematically controlling changes to this configuration and maintaining the integrity and traceability of this configuration throughout the system life cycle.

The IEEE [7] defines configuration management as a discipline applying technical and administrative direction and surveillance to identify and document the functional and physical characteristics of a configuration item, control changes to those characteristics, record and report change processing and implementation status, and verify compliance with specified requirements.

What does this definition mean? First, SCM is a discipline—one that applies technical and administrative direction and surveillance. The term *discipline* refers to a system of rules, so the practice of SCM cannot be done at the whims and fancies of individuals; it has to follow a set of rules. These rules are to be specified in a document called the *SCM plan* (discussed later in this chapter). The rules should be applied in a technical and administrative framework, and monitoring (surveillance) should be constant to ensure that the rules are followed. This means that SCM needs an organizational setup for carrying out the technical and administrative monitoring. SCM requires one group of people to carry out different SCM functions and another group to monitor that the SCM activities are performed according to the rules. The size and organizational structure of this group—the SCM organization or SCM team—will vary with the size and complexity of the projects.

Second, the SCM function should identify the configuration items and document their functional and physical characteristics. IEEE [7] defines a configuration item as an aggregation of hardware, software, or both that is designated for configuration management and treated as a single entity in the configuration management process. So the SCM discipline must identify the components (e.g., documentation, programs, functions, component libraries, data) of a software system. Then it should document the components' functional characteristics, such as what they are supposed to do, performance criteria, and features, as well as the physical characteristics, such as size, number of lines, number of modules, functions, and libraries.

Once the configuration items are identified and their characteristics are documented, the SCM system should control the changes to those characteristics. This means that once the SCM system is in place, any change to a configuration item should take place in a controlled way. Control does not mean prevention. It means that the SCM system should institute procedures that will enable people to request a change or an enhancement to a configuration item. Well-defined methods should be in place for evaluating these requests, studying the impact of each request on other configuration items, and then carrying out the changes if deemed appropriate. In other words, the SCM system should ensure that no changes are made to the configuration items without proper authorization.

Third, the SCM system should record the change management process and report it to all parties involved. This necessitates documentation of the change management process. The status of the change requests should be tracked and recorded from the point of origin until completion. Processes such as change requisition, evaluation, impact analysis, and decisions about whether to make the change or not should be documented and reported to all people involved.

Last, a mechanism should be used to verify that the system that is being developed and delivered is the one specified in the requirements definition and other related documents. In other words, the SCM system should ensure that what is developed and delivered is exactly what was required and specified. For this there should be some sort of an auditing or verification mechanism.

So, translated into plain English, SCM requires the components of a software system to be identified and their characteristics (both functional and physical) documented. Once this is done, any changes to these items should only be made through proper channels. This means that no one without proper authorization can make changes to an item. The entire process of change management should be documented and reported to all those involved. A mechanism should exist for checking and verifying that the system is being developed in accordance with the specifications.

IEEE [7] divides the SCM functions into the following four activities: configuration identification, configuration control, status accounting, and audits and reviews. *Configuration identification* is an element of configuration management, consisting of selecting the configuration items for a system and recording their functional and physical characteristics in technical documentation. *Configuration control* is the element of configuration management consisting of the evaluation, coordination, approval or disapproval, and implementation of changes to configuration items. *Status accounting* consists of recording and reporting information needed to manage a configuration efficiently. *Auditing* is carried out to ensure that the SCM system is functioning correctly and to ensure that the configuration has been tested to demonstrate that it meets its functional requirements and that it contains all deliverable entities. We will look at these four SCM functions in more detail in later chapters.

According to Davis [8], effective SCM is not just having a tool that records not only who made what change to the code or documentation and when but also the thoughtful creation of naming conventions, policies, and procedures to ensure that all relevant parties are involved in changes to the software. SCM is not just a set of standard practices that applies uniformly to all projects. SCM must be tailored to each project's characteristics, such as size of the project, volatility, development process, and extent of customer involvement. The best place to record how SCM should be performed for each project is in the *SCM plan*. The SCM plan documents what SCM activities are to be done, how they are to be done, who is responsible for doing specific activities, when they are to happen, and what resources are required. Chapter 14 details SCM plans, their organization, and contents

1.5   Importance of SCM

Poor configuration management or lack of it often causes the most frustrating software problems. Some examples of these problems are missing source code, changed component libraries, an inability to determine what happened to a particular program or data, an inability to track why, when, and who made a change, and difficulty in finding out why programs that were working suddenly stopped working. The problems are frustrating because they are difficult to fix, and they often occur at the worst possible times [9]. For example, a difficult bug that was fixed suddenly reappears, a program that was working mysteriously stops working, a developed and tested feature is missing, the updated version of the requirements document is not found, or the source code and the executable program are different versions. SCM helps reduce these problems by coordinating the work and effort of many different people working on a common project. SCM plays an important role in the software development process—analysis, design, development, testing, and maintenance—by ensuring (through configuration audits) that what was designed (as specified in the characteristics document) is what is built.

The key role of SCM is to control change activity so that problems (e.g., communications breakdown, shared data, simultaneous updates, multiple maintenance) can be avoided. This does not mean that all of the other SCM functions, such as configuration identification, status accounting, and configuration audits, are not important, because they are. Configuration identification should be performed well to manage the changes effectively. Status accounting information is used by project leaders and managers to keep the project under control. Configuration audits are required to ensure that what is specified is what is delivered. Even though we can consider configuration control (or change management) as the first among equals, the other functions are also vital for the efficient and effective functioning of SCM.

SCM is not easy; one has to do a lot of work to keep an SCM system in good shape, but the effort is worth it. Only when problems begin to crop up do users realize the importance of SCM, but by then it is too late and getting a project back on track can be a tedious task without SCM.

But for an SCM system to work, the people who are involved must be convinced of the importance and benefits of SCM. If SCM is done only for the sake of doing it, then it will fail to deliver on its promises. If SCM is done just to get some certification and not in its true spirit, then it will definitely fail. If SCM is treated as a management tool or a contractual obligation, it can easily become a bureaucratic roadblock that impedes the work [9]. Another point that should be noted here is that poor SCM practices tend to ripple throughout the entire organization, having an adverse effect on a large number of people and their work. Hence it is important to have a good SCM system. The presence of an SCM system that is planned poorly, implemented haphazardly, and practiced inefficiently will not improve a software development process but rather will create more problems than it solves. So the SCM system should be carefully designed, properly implemented, and practiced systematically and willingly.

1.6 Benefits of SCM

A properly designed and implemented SCM system has several benefits, including improved software development productivity, easier handling of software complexity, improved security, higher software reuse, lower software maintenance costs, better quality assurance, reduction of defects and bugs, faster problem identification and bug fixes, process-dependent development rather than person-dependent development, and assurance that the correct system is built. These benefits are discussed at length in Chapter 4.

1.7 Summary

If designed properly, implemented judiciously, and used efficiently, SCM systems will raise the productivity and profits of companies dramatically. For this to happen, the people who use the system should be educated on its potential benefits, capabilities, and ability to improve developmental productivity.

Many myths surround SCM. Many people consider it to be a bureaucratic process and additional work. These concerns were true to some extent in the case of manual SCM systems of the past, but today's SCM tools automate most SCM functions and make the practice of SCM easier and painless.

Poor SCM practices tend to ripple throughout the organization, having an adverse effect on a large number of people and their work, so it is important to have a good SCM system.

References

[1]   Whitgift, D., *Methods and Tools for Software Configuration Management*, Chichester, England: John Wiley & Sons, 1991.

[2]   Babich, W. A., *Software Configuration Management: Coordination for Team Productivity*, Boston, MA: Addison-Wesley, 1986.

[3]   Ben-Menachem, M., *Software Configuration Guidebook*, London: McGraw-Hill International, 1994.

[4]   Capasso, R., "Configuration Management—It's Not Just for Source Code," *The Rational Edge* (*www-106.ibm.com/developerworks/rational/library/content/ RationalEdge/feb01/ ConfigurationManagementFeb01.pdf*), 2001.

[5]   Berlack, H. R., *Software Configuration Management*, New York: John Wiley & Sons, 1992.

[6]   Bersoff, E. H., V. D. Henderson, and S. G. Siegel, *Software Configuration Management: An Investment in Product Integrity*, Englewood Cliffs, NJ: Prentice-Hall, 1980.

[7]   IEEE, *IEEE Standard Glossary of Software Engineering Terminology (IEEE Std-610– 1990)*, *IEEE Software Engineering Standards Collection (CD-ROM Edition)*, Piscataway, NJ: IEEE, 2003.

[8]   Davis, A. M., *201 Principles of Software Development*, New York: McGraw-Hill, 1995.

[9]   Humphrey, W. S., *Managing the Software Process*, New York: Addison-Wesley, 1989.

The software development process

2.1 Introduction

The software development process is that set of actions required to efficiently transform the user's need into an effective software solution. Efficiency means doing things in the right way, and effectiveness is doing the right things. So for the software development process to succeed, one not only has to do the right things but also do them in the right way.

Humphrey [1] defines the software development process as the set of tools, methods, and practices that we use to produce a software product. The software development process defines the activities required for building the software systems and incorporating the methods and practices to be adopted. It also includes the activities essential for planning the project, tracking its progress, and managing the complexities of building the software. Scientific software development—also known as software engineering—uses scientific and management techniques and productivity improvement tools for developing the software.

There is no universally accepted definition for software engineering. According to Jones [2], software engineering is a methodology that uses a set of recognized criteria (e.g., functionality, reliability, timeliness) and has its foundations in computer science, mathematics, engineering, and management. The practice of software engineering is a discipline, with a defined process for software development and maintenance. Software engineering aims at developing a full product that goes well beyond a small program and uses a set of tools and techniques to improve the productivity and quality of work.

So software engineering is not just programming; it is not development of a small program; it is the process of developing a software system or product. It demands management skills and communications ability. It requires analysis and design skills. It means following standards and procedures and working as a team.

Software engineering is not an art. A software engineer is constrained by user requirements, team decisions, and management instructions, and the software product is the fruit of the entire team's effort rather than the creation of an individual. The scope of software engineering also extends far beyond the development of the software product. It involves marketing, maintenance, and after-sales support. Just because the product you have developed is the best does not mean it is going to succeed. Discipline, teamwork, marketing, money management, planning, and many other nontechnical skills play a vital role in the success of a software product or system. Thus the objective of software engineering is not limited to the development of a high-quality product, but includes the tasks of successfully marketing and maintaining the product.

A software product starts its life as an idea or concept. Software can be of two types: generic products (those that are produced by a software development organization and are sold in the open market) and customized products (those that are developed to meet the specific needs of a customer). Examples of generic products (also known as shrink-wrapped products or packaged software or commercial off-the-shelf products) include word processors, electronic spreadsheets, database management systems, imaging tools, and web browsers. Customized products are developed for a specific person or organization to meet a specific need, such as computerization of bank operations, development of an airline or railway reservation system, or development of a software tool to accomplish a specific task (e.g., test data generation, code generation). In the case of generic products, the organization that develops the software controls the specification. In the case of custom products, the client or organization for which the product is being developed usually controls the specification. In other words, the characteristics and features of the generic products are market-driven (i.e., collected through market research, surveys, demos), whereas the client decides those of customized products.

Irrespective of the type of software product and the way in which the software product idea was conceptualized, the software product goes through a series of development phases. In most cases, the product's features and functions are specified, then designed and implemented. The product is then put into operation and, while it is operational, it is maintained. Finally, when the product's usefulness is over or when the product becomes obsolete, it is decommissioned. The series of steps through which the software product progresses (from conceptualization until retirement) is called the software development life cycle (SDLC).

2.2 Software development life cycle

Every software product has a lifetime—it starts its life as a response to a user's need or as a new product concept and ends up being obsolete. The life span of software systems varies from product to product. During its lifetime, the software goes through various phases.

The IEEE Standard Glossary of Software Engineering Terminology (IEEE Std-610-1990) defines the SDLC as the period of time that begins when a software product is conceived and ends when the software is no longer available for use. The SDLC typically includes a concept phase, requirements phase, design phase, implementation phase, test phase, installation and checkout phase, operation and maintenance phase, and sometimes, retirement phase [3].

Each software product passes through these stages, although the duration, sequence, number of iterations, and exact effect of each stage may vary. In other words, the life cycle of every software product is different. Some products will spend more years in the conceptual stage. There can be a variety of reasons for this variation: for example, the idea may not be technically feasible because of some hardware limitations, the product idea may not be economically feasible at that point in time, or the processing capability of the machines may not be good enough for the product to be commercially viable. Other products will be quickly designed and implemented and will spend more years in the maintenance phase, being modified repeatedly to fix the bugs (faults or errors) or to incorporate new features and functionality required by the users. In many cases, after many years of maintenance, a stage will be reached at which point it will be more cost effective to develop a completely new product rather than to attempt to maintain the current version yet again. So we have seen that every software product has a lifetime. Just like any other commercial product, it starts as someone's idea, need, or inspiration and ends up being obsolete, unsupported, and unused.

The different SDLC phases may overlap or be performed iteratively or be combined or omitted depending on the software development approach (model) used. Many theories and models have been advanced concerning how the software goes through these phases (and whether it goes through all of the phases). The most prominent process models are the waterfall model [3], spiral model [4], win-win spiral model [5], incremental model [6, 7, 8], operational model [9], transformational model [10, 11], joint application development (JAD) model [12], evolutionary development model [13], component assembly model [14], cleanroom software engineering [15], and concurrent development [16]. A detailed discussion of these models is beyond the scope of this book. The important point is that irrespective of the model chosen, they all go through the different life cycle phases (some models may not go through all of the phases), and the order in which a project moves forward through the different life cycle phases is determined by the process model.

Recent years have seen the emergence of several lightweight or agile process models. Agile proponents claim that the focal aspects of light and agile methods are simplicity and speed. In development work, accordingly, development groups concentrate only on the functions needed immediately, delivering them fast, collecting feedback, and reacting rapidly to business and technology changes. Agile software process models are characterized by the following attributes: they are incremental, cooperative, straightforward, and adaptive [17]. Incremental refers to small software releases, with rapid development cycles. Cooperative refers to a close customer and developer interaction. Straightforward implies that the method is easy to learn and modify and that it is sufficiently documented. Finally, adaptive refers to the ability to make and react to last-minute changes. These methodologies are mainly suitable for small projects that have small teams.

Some of the popular agile methods are extreme programming or XP [18, 19, 20], adaptive software development [21], the Crystal family of methodologies [22, 23, 24], dynamic systems development method [25, 26], feature-driven development [27], and Scrum [28, 29]. Although most of these models address certain aspects of SCM (e.g., the XP programming principles of collective code ownership, continuous integration, small releases, and refactoring have relations to SCM), none of them addresses the full functionality of SCM. The success of these projects lies in the fact that they are small and have a small team size. Also, these models and methodologies are still in their infancy and are still evolving. So one will have to wait and see how these agile methodologies will address the use of full-fledged configuration management systems.

2.3 SDLC phases

We have seen some of the popular SDLC models, but the purpose of this chapter is not to explore these life cycle models further. Software goes through certain phases before, during, and after the development process. We will look at those phases and examine each phase in detail. The when, why, and how of these phases are taken care of by the life cycle models. The various phases or steps in the SDLC are:

- Project start-up;
- Requirements analysis and requirements specification;
- Systems analysis;
- Systems design (high-level and low-level or detailed design);
- Development/coding and unit testing;
- System/integration testing;
- Acceptance testing;
- Implementation;
- Project windup;
- Maintenance;
- Retirement.

All of these phases will not be present in all projects. Also, all of the activities described in each phase will not be present in many projects. Depending on the size, nature, and complexity of the project, many of the activities and even some phases might not be present. Also, in many projects, the activities might be performed informally. For example, small projects will not have a detailed requirements definition document (RDD) or systems analysis document (SAD). Also, in many projects, the alpha and/ or beta testing phases could be absent.

The phases described in the following sections are for a fairly large project, but depending on the nature of the project and organizational policies, some of these phases might get clustered together, omitted, or practiced under a different name. Keeping this in mind, let's look at the different phases of software development in a little more detail.

2.3.1   Project start-up

The start-up phase is sort of a curtain raiser for the project. The project team is formed and the project leader is identified. The project is organized: modules are identified, key members are enlisted, and the people who will carry out the support functions, such as internal quality assurance and configuration management, are identified. The senior members of the project team sit down together and prepare the project plan to ensure completion of the project within the cost, time, and resource constraints based on the details available.

The main tasks in this phase are as follows:

▸ Study the project proposal and contract document (if it is a contracted work), estimation work papers, and other documents available.

▸ Obtain clarification on matters such as scope, contractual obligations, and client participation in the project, if required.

▸ Define the operational process for the project.

▸ Decide on the format and standards for documenting the project plan.

▸ Document the project plan per the chosen structure and format.

▸ Plan, design, and implement the SCM system.

This phase also sets up the hardware and software environment for the next phase, covering the hardware, system software, standards, and guidelines. The main tasks performed in this phase are as follows:

▸ Ensure that the environment defined in the project plan is still valid for the next phase and, if not, change it.

▸ For each resource that is defined as a part of the environment, check its availability. Requests are raised at this point to the respective support groups for supplying or arranging the required resources.

- Ensure that the required hardware and software are in place.

- Test the environment, if required.

- Obtain the working space, machines, and other infrastructure requirements for the team members.

- Add new procedures or modify current procedures to be followed by the team.

Most organizations will have their own software development standards and guidelines, and if the work is done for a particular client, the project will have to follow the standards of that company. In cases where project standards are not available, they must be developed and finalized during this phase. The standards for various phases include the following:

- Documentation standard for requirements definition document (RDD);

- Documentation standard for systems analysis document (SAD);

- Guidelines for various analysis techniques, such as data modeling and process modeling;

- Documentation standard for high-level design (HLD) document;

- Database and file design standards;

- Documentation standard for test plans and test specifications;

- Documentation standard for user documents;

- Documentation standard for low-level design (LLD) document;

- Documentation standard for unit test plans and specifications;

- Programming standards;

- Documentation standard for defect logs;

- System test plan standards;

- Test data preparation standards;

- Testing standards.

The SCM system is designed and implemented in this phase. Implementing the SCM system during the initial phase of the project has tremendous advantages because it will help get the maximum benefit from the system, and the SCM activities can be started from day one. The SCM system implementation involves several activities, such as system design, SCM plan preparation, SCM team organization, infrastructure setup, SCM team training, project team training, and system implementation.

One important task of the SCM system implementation is designing the SCM system and preparing the SCM plan. The project team leader and other members, such as representatives from the QA team and the SCM manager, sit together and design the SCM system and SCM procedures to be used in the project. The SCM manager is responsible for performing the SCM functions in the project. Sometimes the project leader will serve as the SCM manager, or in other cases a person will be designated for that post. If the company has a standard SCM plan, then that plan is tailored for the project. The proposed SCM system is documented in the SCM plan.

Each project is different and requires different approaches to SCM. The level of formalism, the number of procedures, the change control process, the SCM organizational structure, and other factors will vary depending on the size, nature, and complexity of the project. So for each project, the SCM implementation has to be done afresh. The organization may have many projects that already have SCM systems in place with the SCM tools already implemented. Even in those cases, however, the SCM system should be customized and a separate SCM plan prepared to suit the individual needs of the project. The presence of an established SCM system and tool will make things easier, because all the SCM system designers have to do is customize the existing procedures, practices, and guidelines for the current project. If the company is using enterprise-wide change management tools, then the tool infrastructure is already in place, but obtaining the tool support for the project, getting the workspaces and libraries allocated, and other tasks still need to be done.

The output of this phase is the project plan, SCM plan, and the standards for the next phases. This phase is usually done by a high-level team consisting of the project leader, management representatives, SCM manager, and support team representatives.

2.3.2 Requirements analysis and requirements specification

During this phase, user requirements are captured and documented and a detailed plan for the phase is prepared. The high-level activities for this phase are expanded so that each activity spans not more than one or two person-weeks. The dependencies among the various activities of this module are identified and the activities are scheduled. Plans for housekeeping activities such as backup and recovery and security are formulated. The resources required are estimated and the team members are allocated tasks.

One of the main tasks of this phase is understanding the current system (manual or computerized). This is not applicable for a new product development project where the task is understanding the functions the software is supposed to perform. The task should be undertaken with a view to examining its adequacy and identifying problem areas. The main tasks that are performed in this phase are understanding the current system by discussing it with the users and studying the documentation available. The main areas that are studied are organization objectives, activities, procedures, rules and standards, and files and interfaces.

Every existing system, whether manual or computerized, will have some problems or inadequacies. That is why it is being redesigned. Even if the system is functioning smoothly, there might be areas that could be improved. These existing problems, possibilities, and constraints are identified. The existing system, problems, and constraints are documented for future reference and the findings are discussed with the client or user.

The next step in this phase is the definition of the user requirements. The main activities performed in this phase are diagnosing existing problems and defining the user requirements. To do this, the context of the problems has to be understood, the scope of the problems has to be assessed, and the user requirements, application requirements, and information requirements have to be determined.

Once the user requirements have been defined, the next step is to prepare the RDD. Once the initial draft of the RDD is created, it is given to all of the parties of the software project—users, clients, the project team, and support functions. After incorporating suggestions from all groups, the final RDD is prepared. The output of this phase is the documentation of the existing system and the RDD. The requirements analysis and the preparation of the RDD are usually done by systems analysts in collaboration with users.

From this phase onward, the major SCM activities—configuration identification, change management and control, status accounting, configuration reviews, and audits—are performed. The different documents (e.g., standards, guidelines, SCM plan, project plan) that are identified as configuration items (CIs) are named, their physical and functional characteristics are recorded, and they are brought under the SCM control. The CIs in this phase will mainly contain the updated documents from the previous phase and the RDD. The RDD is usually put under configuration control. So once the final RDD is prepared, it is reviewed, approved, and a baseline is established. Normally, this is the first baseline and consists of the documents from the previous phase and the approved RDD. This baseline is known as the *functional* or *requirements baseline*. By establishing a baseline, the functional and other requirements described in the RDD become the explicit point of departure for software development, against which changes can be proposed, evaluated, implemented, and controlled. The requirements baseline is usually the first established baseline in the SCM process.

2.3.3   Systems analysis

In the systems analysis phase, the proposed system is defined after analyzing various alternatives. These are the main tasks performed in this phase:

- Study the approved RDD.

- Generate alternatives (solutions or designs) for the proposed system. To do this, one must access prior knowledge, customize candidate solutions, partition the system, and prototype the system if necessary.

- Evaluate alternatives. Perform impact or cost-benefit analyses for tangible costs (one-time and recurring costs, such as cost of the tools used in the project) and for intangible costs (procedural and personnel-related costs such as costs of training employees on tools to be used in the project).

‣ Select an alternative.

‣ Determine system requirements with respect to reliability, performance, security, backup and restore, error recovery, and other quality factors.

‣ Discuss the proposed system with the client.

In some cases, the project management may decide to develop a prototype of the system to demonstrate the understanding of the user requirements and the functionality that will be provided in the proposed system. Prototyping is required if a lack of clear understanding of the user requirements is considered a major risk in the project. The major activities in prototyping are as follows:

‣ Determine the objectives of the prototype. A prototype can be built to demonstrate an understanding of the existing system, functionality of the proposed system, data to be maintained, functions to be provided, data entry screens to be provided, inquiries and reports to be provided, and external interfaces to be provided.

‣ Decide on the type of prototype (i.e., whether it should be evolutionary or throwaway).

‣ Decide on the software and hardware platforms and the tools to be used for developing the prototype and then set up the environment.

‣ Build a prototype to meet the chosen objectives.

‣ Demonstrate the prototype to the client or users and obtain feedback. Incorporate suggestions for improvement.

Once the prototype is developed and the feedback is obtained, the next step is to prepare the systems analysis document, where the proposed system's functionality is documented. While preparing the SAD, a usability plan is also prepared when the system that is being built uses commercial off-the-shelf packages to perform some tasks in the system. The usability plan will compare the available packages and help identify the one that is best suited for the system in terms of cost effectiveness, amount of customization, and method of integration of the selected package into the software system. This plan is needed only if the system uses off-the-shelf packages.

During this phase, the project plan, SCM plan, and RDD are refined and updated based on the project progress and changes in the scope of the project. The output of the systems analysis phase is the prototype (if developed), the SAD, the usability plan, the updated project plan, the SCM plan, and the RDD. All documents except those produced in this phase are already under configuration control. So changes to them can be made only following the formal change management procedures. The documents produced during this phase are also brought under SCM control.

2.3.4 High-level design

In this phase, the system design objectives are defined. The following steps are carried out in order to properly design the system:

- Study the SAD and ensure that requirements are understood so that the HLD documents can be properly written.

- Understand the features and capabilities of the hardware and software environments in which the proposed system is to be implemented.

- Study standards and guidelines prepared for the HLD phase.

- Establish design objectives, constraints, and guidelines with respect to usability, user interface, performance (response time, memory, and throughput), reliability, design directives, and storage.

Sometimes a prototype is developed to demonstrate the user interface design, screens, navigation, and other features of the system. Developing a prototype in the HLD phase is required if the developers want to demonstrate to the user the design features of the system, such as system architecture, user interfaces, and system functionality. Sometimes a prototype is developed during the systems analysis phase to demonstrate an understanding of the user requirements and the functionality that will be provided in the proposed system. If such a prototype exists, then this prototype is refined during the HLD phase to demonstrate the user interface design, screens, navigation, and other features of the system.

In this phase, the system components such as modules, programs, functions, and routines are identified. The system components are identified hierarchically to the level required. The inputs and outputs of the system are defined, including menus, screens, navigation, levels of help and help screens, reports, error messages, and the user interface. The programs for each component are identified and classified as online/batch, reports, transactions, drivers, functions, libraries, and the like. The performance requirements for each component are established, and the components that can be reused are identified. The following items are produced as part of this exercise:

- System components list;
- User interface design;
- Programs and the interface definition between programs;
- Screens and report definitions;

‣ Screen navigation details;

‣ Help screens and messages.

The next step in this phase is to define the system architecture. The system architecture is established in terms of security, data access, communication, restart and recovery, audit, and user interface. The system architecture deals with issues such as whether the proposed system will be a client/server system, mainframe system, or geographically distributed system; what technology should be used; and how the communications network should be set up. The program dependencies and interfaces are identified, and the system architecture for each class of programs is finalized and documented.

Another task in this phase is the creation of a first-cut database and finalization of the database/file design. The database/file design is derived from a data model or data store identified during analysis, which should include content, access, and organization of the database/files. The contents of each of the tables/files in the database and the access path are defined. The necessary normalization of the database tables is performed to ensure processing efficiency. This step produces the database design document.

The final task in this phase is preparation of the HLD document as per documentation standards for HLD. The documents that have been prepared thus far, such as the design objectives document, the system architecture document, and the database design document, are used as the input for the HLD document. The system test plan is a part of the HLD document. So while the HLD is compiled, the system test plan (STP) and system test specification (STS) are also prepared, and they then form part of the HLD document. Preparation of the initial draft of user documents, such as the user manual, capabilities manual, and tutorials, is begun during this phase.

So this phase produces the following documents: high-level design (HLD) document, system test plan (STP), and system test specification (STS), and the initial draft of the user documents. All of the documents produced in this phase are reviewed and brought under SCM control. If changes are required for any of these items, then the change procedures are initiated and the changes are effected.

2.3.5 Low-level or detailed design

In this phase, the copy libraries, common routines, and program skeletons to be used are finalized. The HLD is analyzed to understand the system architecture, components, programs, and their interfaces. The standards prepared for the LLD phase are studied. The component libraries to be used for each of the programs in the system are identified, as are the common routines and the input and output for these common routines. If program skeletons or templates are to be used for various types of programs, then the scope and contents of such skeletons and templates are decided. The specifications for the component libraries, common routines, and skeletons are written.

The major task in this phase is to write the specification for each program in the system. Writing program specifications is essential for projects involving developments in procedural languages. For each program and reusable routine identified in the system, the program logic is determined; the structure chart is prepared (if necessary); the inputs, outputs, error messages, and help messages are finalized; and the program specification is prepared. As part of the program specification, the unit test specification (UTS) and unit test plan (UTP) are prepared.

The last step of this phase is preparation of the LLD document, consisting of program specifications for all programs, component libraries, skeletons, and templates of the system. All documents, specifications, and program templates produced during this phase are usually subject to configuration control.

At the end of this phase, the project plan is updated, and the RDD, SAD, HLD, STP, STS, and the user documents are refined based on the changes and additional information obtained during this phase. These changes are made following the change control procedures because these items are under configuration management, and hence unauthorized changes are not allowed.

The baseline that is established at the end of the design phase is usually called the *allocated* or *design baseline*. The allocated baseline contains the initial approved specifications that form the basis for the software development and testing. The allocated baseline represents the logical progression from the functional baseline and represents the link between the design process and the development process.

2.3.6 Coding and unit testing

During this phase, the programs, copy libraries, functions, and other program elements are coded (or generated) and tested (unit testing). The main people involved in this phase are the developers and programmers, analysts, the QA team, and testers. Out of all of the life cycle phases, this one involves the largest number of people. The SCM team is up and running and will be involved in activities such as change management and control, repository management, defect tracking, change request evaluation, and impact analysis. These are the major activities during this phase:

- Study the LLD document, test cases, and data.

- Include additional test cases if needed.

- Code the programs per the program specifications.

- If the evolutionary prototyping approach is followed, the prototype should be refined to yield the final code.

- Finalize all error and help messages.

- Conduct unit testing in accordance with the UTS.

- Record the test results.

- Log the following unit test errors: errors external to the program (where the error cannot be fixed in the program being tested), errors in the LLD and test specifications, errors caused by the standards adopted, and errors in the reused code.

- Diagnose and fix the errors.

- Update the defect logs.

- Initiate corrective action, as applicable. This might involve revisiting the earlier phases of the SDLC.

- Consolidate test results and findings and record them appropriately.

The output of this phase is the unit-tested programs, all of which (e.g., the source code, test scripts, test data, test results, the associated documentation, the change/problem reports) will be under SCM control. To make any changes to those items, formal change management process has to be followed. The developers will check-out and check-in programs, the change requests and problem reports will be initiated, the change management procedures (such as impact analysis and change control board meetings) will be at their peak, the project managers and leaders will be using the status accounting information to ensure that the project is on track and under control, and so on. The proper operation of the SCM system during this phase of the SDLC is of paramount importance to the project's success.

2.3.7 System testing

This phase is where the system testing or integration testing is carried out. The system test is done using the STP, STS, and system test data. Many companies also perform alpha and/or beta testing.

Alpha testing is done when the system or product has a lot of new, previously untested features. Because a lot of the functionality is untested, the development team might be uncomfortable proceeding with the final testing and release of the product until they get feedback from a limited number of users or customers. So the developers use the alpha testing primarily to evaluate the success or failure (or acceptance) of the new features that have been incorporated into the system.

Beta testing is required when the development team decides that some level of customer evaluation is needed before the final release of the product. In the case of beta testing, the developers are no longer looking for user inputs on functionality or features. The product has all of the functionality incorporated into it, so the development team will be looking for beta testers to uncover bugs and faults in the system. Unlike alpha testing, beta testing is done on a much larger scale (i.e., the number of people who do beta testing is much higher than that for alpha testing). Companies usually distribute beta releases free to people who have enrolled in the beta testing program, and in many cases beta versions are available for download from the company's Web site. New products will have alpha testing followed by beta testing. In the case of new versions of existing products, however, either alpha or beta testing is done.

The tasks in this phase are as follows:

› Carry out system tests according to the STP and STS. For alpha and beta testing, there are no test plans. In the case of alpha testing, testers evaluate the acceptability of the new features or functionality; in the case of beta testing, testers try to find bugs or problems in the product.

› Record the test results.

› Log the test errors.

› Diagnose and fix errors.

› Update the defect logs.

› Initiate corrective action as applicable. This might involve revisiting earlier phases of the SDLC.

› Perform regression testing.

› Consolidate and report test results and findings.

The major players involved in this phase are the QA team, testers, the development team (for bug/problem fixing), and the actual system users. If alpha and/or beta testing is used, then the number of people who will be testing the system will increase dramatically.

During this phase, the SCM team will have their hands full because they coordinate the change requests and problem reports and see to it that the changes are made according to the procedures and that all people concerned are aware of the changes. Once the project is successfully tested, the functional and physical configuration audits are performed to ensure that the final product is complete and satisfies the specifications. A baseline is established at this stage. This is called the *product baseline*. The product baseline represents the technical and support documentation that is established after successful completion of the functional configuration audit and physical configuration audit.

2.3.8   Acceptance testing

Acceptance testing is the formal testing that is conducted (usually by the user, client, or an authorized entity) to determine whether a system satisfies its acceptance criteria and to enable the customer to determine whether to accept the system. This phase is carried out only if the system is developed for a particular client or customer. In this phase, the project team prepares for the acceptance test by ensuring the availability and completeness of all work items needed for the acceptance test and populating the acceptance test data. The project team will assist the client or customer in acceptance testing, recording the errors found, and fixing them.

These are the main tasks in this phase:

- Provide support to the client in conducting the acceptance test.

- Ensure that documentation-related tests are also completed.

- Record acceptance test results.

- Log acceptance test errors.

- Diagnose and fix errors.

- Update the defect logs.

- Revisit earlier phases of the SDLC, as required, in order to fix errors.

- Perform regression testing.

- Prepare a report summarizing the test results. Highlight any disagreements.

2.3.9 Implementation

Once the integration, system, and acceptance (in some cases, alpha and beta testing) testing phases arecompleted, the software product or the system is turned over to the customers or clients or installed at the client site. The members of the development team will supervise the installation in the case of large projects. In the case of a shrink-wrapped project, the customer does the installation, and if problems are encountered, the vendor's technical support team is contacted. In the case of large projects, the installation team, in collaboration with the end users, installs the system and trains users in operating the system. Some amount of user training is necessary. Once the system is up and running and users are familiarized with the product, the implementation phase is finished. From that point onward, the maintenance team takes over and manages the technical support, product enhancements, error fixing, and other tasks.

2.3.10 Project windup

In this phase, project windup activities are completed. All of the resources acquired for the project are released. Here are the main activities in this phase:

- Carry out project-end appraisals.

- Release project team members and hardware and software resources.

▸ Return client-supplied products, if any.

▸ Ensure the availability of project documentation copies in the library.

2.3.11   Project maintenance

Once the system has been developed and tested, it is released to users. From this point onward, the maintenance phase starts. Once people start using the system, many errors that escaped testing will be found. The users might ask for new features and enhancements. The maintenance team must attend to these requests and fix the bugs that are found.

During the project maintenance stage, the full impact and usefulness of the SCM process can be felt. If the project was developed following a good SCM system, then all of the documentation, defect and defect-prevention details, help desks, and so forth will be available. All of the programs, technical documents, user documents, and the like will be readily available. There will not be any chaos and confusion. Everyone will know exactly where to look for items such as programs, libraries, documents, and change histories. Also, because the re-creation of any particular component or version could be done with high accuracy, the change management and problem-solving processes become much easier than without an SCM system. The jobs of the maintenance team and the technical support team are made a lot easier when the project has a good SCM system.

2.3.12   Retirement

The final phase in the life cycle of a software product or system is retirement. After many years of service, a stage is reached when any further maintenance would not be cost effective. This could happen because the proposed changes are so drastic that the whole design would have to be changed, and it would be cheaper to redesign and recode the entire product from scratch.

The other reason is that many changes may have been made to the original design that affect interdependencies that were inadvertently built into the product, so that there is a real danger that even a small change to one module will have a drastic effect on the functionality of the whole product. Yet another reason is that the documentation may not have been adequately maintained, thus increasing the risk of a regression fault to the point where it would be safer to recode than to maintain. Another reason for retiring a software product is that technological advancements have made the existing system obsolete. The hardware on which the product runs has to be replaced by a different (more powerful and less expensive) machine with a different operating system, and it is cheaper to rewrite from scratch than to modify the product. In each of these instances, the current product is retired, a new version is developed, and the life cycle continues.

During this phase, the SCM system for the project is also retired. Here one thing that should be remembered is that the SCM tools used are not retired. They will still be used by other projects. The SCM tool resources held by the project are released. The SCM system that was designed for the particular project and documented in the SCM plan is retired. The SCM team members and the maintenance and support team members are released to other projects. The records and documentation created during this project that have some value—either for legal reasons or as reference material—are retained as per the records retention policy specified in the

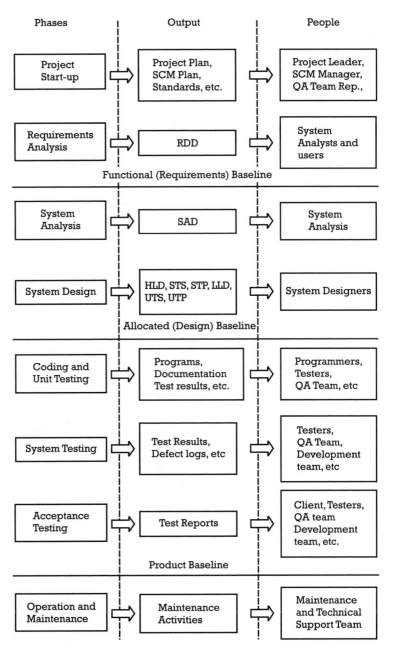

Figure 2.1   Life cycle phases and their relationship with SCM.

SCM plan. Usually they are archived and the unwanted documentation and records are disposed of.

True retirement (removal of the product) is a rare event that occurs when a product has outgrown its usefulness. The client organization no longer requires the functionality provided by the product, and it is finally removed from the computer on which it has been in operations mode for many years.

2.4 Summary

We have seen the various phases involved in the software development process. All of these phases may not be present in all of the projects, and as already mentioned, the order in which the various steps are executed will vary.

Some degree of overlap usually occurs between the various phases. The software life cycle model that is adopted will determine these variances. We have seen the various outputs of each phase and the role of SCM in the project life cycle. We also saw how and when the different SCM activities are performed in a project. These aspects are summarized in Figure 2.1.

References

[1] Humphrey, W. S., *Managing the Software Process*, New York: Addison-Wesley, 1989.

[2] Jones, G. W., *Software Engineering*, New York: John Wiley & Sons, 1990.

[3] Royce, W., "Managing the Development of Large Software Systems: Concepts and Techniques," *Proc. IEEE WESCON*, 1970.

[4] Boehm, B. W., "A Spiral Model for Software Development and Enhancement," *IEEE Computer*, Vol. 21, No. 5, 1988, pp. 61–72.

[5] Boehm, B. W., et al, "Using the Win-Win Spiral Model: A Case Study," *IEEE Computer*, Vol. 31, No. 7, 1988, pp. 33–44.

[6] McDermid, J. A., and P. Rook, "Software Development Process Models," in J. A. McDermid (ed.), *Software Engineer's Reference Book*, Boca Raton, FL: CRC Press, 1994, pp. 15.26–15.28.

[7] Brooks, F. P., "No Silver Bullet: Essence and Accidents of Software Engineering," *IEEE Computer*, Vol. 20, No. 4, 1987, pp. 10–19.

[8] Mill, H. D., "Top-Down Programming in Large Systems," in R. Rustin (ed.), *Debugging Techniques in Large Systems*, Englewood Cliffs, NJ: Prentice-Hall, 1971.

[9] Zave, P., "The Operational Versus Conventional Approach to Software Development," *Commun. ACM*, Vol. 27, No. 2, 1992, pp. 104–118.

[10] Balzer, R., Transformational Implementation: An Example, *IEEE Transactions on Software Engineering*, Vol. 7, No. 1, 1981, pp. 3–14.

[11] Balzer, R., "A 15 Year Perspective on Automatic Programming," *IEEE Transactions on Software Engineering*, Vol. 11, No. 11, 1985, pp. 1257–1268.

[12] Wood, J., and D. Silver, *Joint Application Development*, New York: John Wiley & Sons, Inc., 1995.

[13] Lehman, M. M., and L. Belady, *Program Evolution: Processes of Software Change*, London: Academic Press, 1985.

[14] Nierstrasz, O., Gibbs, S., and Tsichritzis, D., "Component-Oriented Software Development," *Commun. ACM*, Vol. 35, No. 9, 1992, pp. 160–165.

[15] Dyer, M., *The Cleanroom Approach to Quality Software Development*, New York: John Wiley & Sons, 1992.

[16] Aoyama, M., "Concurrent Development of Software Systems: A New Development Paradigm," *ACM SIGSOFT Software Engineering Notes*, Vol. 12, No. 4, 1987, pp. 20–24.

[17] Abraharnsson,P., et al, *Agile Software Development Methods: Review and Analysis*, Espoo, Finland: Technical Research Centre of Finland, VTT Publications, 2002.

[18] Beck, K., *Extreme Programming Explained: Embrace Change*, Boston, MA: Addison-Wesley, 2000.

[19] Beck, K., and M. Fowler, *Planning Extreme Programming*, Boston, MA: Addison-Wesley, 2000.

[20] Jeffries, R., A. Anderson, and C. Hendrickson, *Extreme Programming Installed*, Boston, MA: Addison-Wesley, 2000.

[21] Highsmith, J. A., *Adaptive Software Development: A Collaborative Approach to Managing Complex Systems*, New York: Dorset House Publishing, 2000.

[22] Cockburn, A., *Surviving Object-Oriented Projects: A Manager's Guide*, Vol. 5, Boston, MA: Addison Wesley Longman, 1998.

[23] Cockburn, A., *Writing Effective Use Cases: The Crystal Collection for Software Professionals*, Boston, MA: Addison-Wesley Professional, 2000.

[24] Cockburn, A., *Agile Software Development*, Boston, MA: Addison-Wesley, 2002.

[25] DSDM Consortium, *Dynamic Systems Development Method (Version 3)*, Ashford, England: DSDM Consortium, 1997.

[26] Stapleton, J., *Dynamic Systems Development Method: The Method in Practice*, Boston, MA: Addison Wesley, 1997.

[27] Palmer, S. R., and J. M. Felsing, *A Practical Guide to Feature-Driven Development*, Englewood Cliffs, NJ: Prentice Hall PTR, 2002.

[28] Rising, L., and N. S. Janoff, "The Scrum Software Development Process for Small Teams," *IEEE Software*, Vol. 17, No. 4, 2000, pp. 2–8.

[29] Schwaber, K., and M. Beedle, *Agile Software Development with SCRUM*, Englewood Cliffs, NJ: Prentice Hall, 2001

Selected bibliography

Behforooz, A., and F. J. Hudson, *Software Engineering Fundamentals*, New York: Oxford University Press, 1996.

Jones, G. W., *Software Engineering*, New York: John Wiley & Sons, 1990.

Marciniak, J. J., (ed.), *Encyclopedia of Software Engineering*, 2nd ed., New York: John Wiley & Sons, 2002.

Peters, J. F., and W. Pedrycz, *Software Engineering: An Engineering Approach*, New York: John Wiley & Sons, 2000.

Pfleeger, S. H., *Software Engineering: Theory and Practice*, 2nd ed., Upper Saddle River, NJ: Pearson Education, 2001.

Pressman, R. S., *A Manager's Guide to Software Engineering*, New York: McGraw-Hill, 1993.

Pressman, R. S., *Software Engineering: A Practitioner's Approach*, 5th ed., New York: McGraw-Hill, 2001.

Schach, S. R., *Software Engineering*, Boston, MA: Aksen Associates, Inc., 1990.

Shooman, M. L., *Software Engineering: Design, Reliability and Management*, New York: McGraw-Hill, 1983.

Sommerville, I., *Software Engineering*, 6th ed., Upper Saddle River, NJ: Pearson Education, 2001.

Pitfalls in the software development process

3.1 Introduction

The software development process is different from other production or manufacturing processes. According to Jones [1], software products are intangible, because there is no need for physical mechanisms, structures, or processes. Software engineers do not use most of the concepts familiar to traditional engineering, and their work is mostly independent of natural science. Also, software products are much more complex and sophisticated, thus requiring special care in conceptualizing, managing, organizing, and testing them. Software products are manufactured by a simple copying process, so almost all of the production effort is dedicated to design and development.

Because the software development process is different from regular industrial practice, normal rules of production or manufacturing do not apply here. For example, Brook's law [2] states that "Adding manpower to a late software project makes it later." It might sound strange, but it is true. If you calculate the time required to train the new people, the added communication channels because of the new people, and other related complexities, the project in question (the already late project) could be finished earlier if more people were not inducted. This is not true in a construction project, where additional labor can speed up the project.

So now that we have established that the software development process is different from the other manufacturing or production processes, we need to look at some of the problems that plague many a software project and that can result in time and cost overruns if corrective actions are not taken. The most frequent among these are the communications breakdown problem, shared data problem, multiple maintenance problem, and simultaneous update problem. In this chapter, we look at each of these problems in greater detail, because an understanding of these issues is crucial for realizing the importance of the configuration management function.

3.2   Communications breakdown problem

The era when a single person developed a software product is long gone. Today's software projects consist of teams with hundreds of members in different modules. The modules or subsystems of a project might be located in different continents and might very well include developers with different social, cultural, and educational backgrounds.

In a single-person project, communications breakdowns never occur. According to Rawlings [3]:

> When only one person is working on a project, that one person has a rather singular communication path with no need for interpretative cognition. The person has only him or herself to communicate with and, hopefully understands his or her own thought processes. When two people are working on the same project, there are now two communicators and two listeners with four potential communication paths. Not only is there a dramatic increase in the number of communication paths, there is also the problem of interpretative cognition, which now comes into play.

As more people are added to the project team, the total number of communication paths increases dramatically, as shown in Figure 3.1, and as the number of communication paths increases, the potential for communication errors also increases.

Interpretative cognition is a part of the process that occurs when two or more people communicate with one another. It is a measure of how much of a person's communication is understood by the other person or persons. You must have encountered situations in daily life when you said something and the listener understood something else, resulting in misunderstanding and confusion. In such cases, we say that the interpretative cognition did not work. When a person wants to communicate some idea, he or she must describe it using words, pictures, drawings, gestures, and so on. The person who is listening to this communication should see and hear the communication directed at him or her and should reconstruct the idea in his or her mind. If the two ideas are the same, then we say that the communication has been successful.

The complexity of this process increases as the idea that is communicated becomes more complicated or if the people who are involved are not familiar with one another's mannerisms and communication methods. Failing to understand a gesture or body language can convey the wrong meaning to the listener.

So in the case of large software projects, where complex and sophisticated systems are being developed, the ideas that are to be communicated

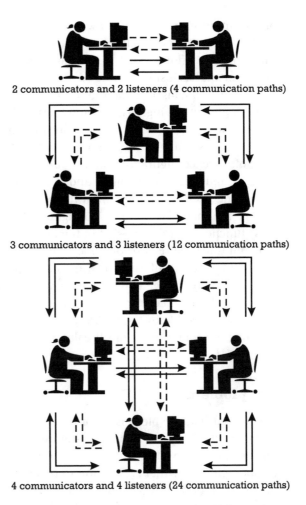

2 communicators and 2 listeners (4 communication paths)

3 communicators and 3 listeners (12 communication paths)

4 communicators and 4 listeners (24 communication paths)

Figure 3.1   Increase in number of communication paths with increasing team size.

are complex. Also, the project team may be working in different parts of the world, thus the chance to communicate face to face will be rare. Because of the different cultural and ethnic backgrounds of team members, the gestures, phrases, and colloquial usages will not be understood by all team members. So the lack of proper communication between team members or a communications breakdown can result in the failure of the project.

How do you control the communications and keep everyone informed about the tasks and activities that affect them? How will a project leader make sure that all team members are communicating with one another and that all people are aware of what is happening? How will the project leader ensure that the effort is not duplicated and the work of one person is not destroyed by another?

In the case of small projects, where the number of people involved is limited to two or three, effective communication is easier to establish. If the team members have been working together for awhile and are familiar with each others' communication patterns and work methods, then the chances of a communications breakdown and associated problems can be minimized, but not completely eliminated. Even in projects involving two or three people, efforts can be duplicated; one can overwrite the code the other person has just fixed, and so on.

If the problems just mentioned can happen in a small project, think about a project having, say, five modules and 100 members. It will be total chaos if some sort of control mechanism is not in place, and that control mechanism is configuration management.

Software configuration management helps prevent the communications breakdown by controlling and managing change. SCM ensures that if something is changed, then all of the people who need to know about the change are made aware of it. Configuration status accounting (CSA) is an SCM function that captures all of the activities in a project and keeps accurate and traceable records of these activities. CSA produces reports relating to various aspects of the software development process, such as items changed, who changed it, and why was it changed. The SCM database could also be queried using query languages for more specific information that is not available in the CSA reports. All of these tools go a long way in avoiding the communications breakdown problem.

3.3   Shared data problem

The shared data problem is a common source of trouble in any environment in which two or more programmers or programs share a common resource. It can be a function that is shared by two programmers. It can be a component library that is common to two programs. It can be a housekeeping program or an error-handling subroutine that is being used by all of the programs in the project. The trouble arises when one developer makes a change to any of the common or shared resources without telling others.

Consider two programmers, A and B, sharing a function (Figure 3.2). To improve functionality, programmer A makes some changes to the function. Programmer B is not aware of the change, but next time B tries to execute his program, it may "abend" or it may not function correctly depending on what changes A has made. B is completely unaware of the change made by

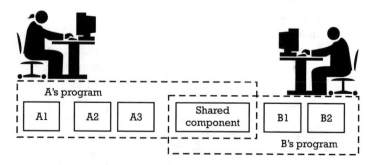

Figure 3.2   Shared data problem.

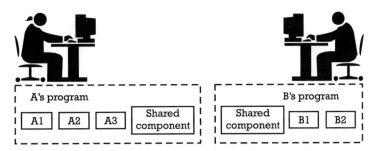

Figure 3.3 Shared data problem solved by using independent workspaces.

A to the function. He is amazed by the fact that the program that was working fine up to that point is suddenly not working. He can spend hours in debugging, but if he is not very lucky, he will never find the cause, because he has no reason to doubt the function, which is the real culprit. This type of situation occurs commonly in almost all projects on which more than one person is involved and in some cases in single-person projects too.

The software developers found a way to solve this problem: by creating separate and independent workspaces in which each programmer has her own copy of the resources she needs (Figure 3.3). In this situation, even if one programmer modifies the code of a shared resource, others are not affected because they are using separate copies of the same resource. But the solution given has one major drawback: It creates multiple copies of the same function or program throughout the project, which in most cases will not be identical. So a lot of space is wasted. But the real trouble is that this creates another problem—the multiple maintenance problem.

3.4 Multiple maintenance problem

This is a variation of the shared data problem. It occurs when there are multiple copies of the shared components in the system. The main problem created by having multiple copies is keeping track of them (Figure 3.4). How many copies of the function exist in the project? Which program uses

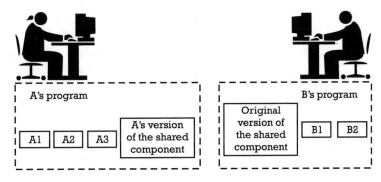

Figure 3.4 Multiple versions of the same component in use.

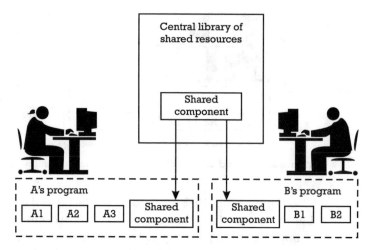

Figure 3.5   Solving the multiple maintenance problem using a central library.

which copy? How many copies are still in the original state? What changes were made? To which copies were those changes made? In the ideal situation, all copies across the system should be identical, but rarely is the situation ideal.

Suppose programmer A finds a bug and makes the necessary corrections to a function. It is her duty to inform all of the people who are using a copy of the function in question that she has made the change; otherwise, while she is using the bug-fixed version of the function, everyone else is using the one with the bug. When the time comes to integrate all of the common functions, the multiple copies will create problems for the programmers depending on which version of the function is actually used. So, if the new version—the one that is fixed—is used, then all programs that used the old version will be in trouble.

As with any problem, programmers found a way to solve the multiple maintenance problem too. They created centralized libraries (Figure 3.5).

The shared components were kept in a central location. The different programmers took the required resources from the central library. If a bug was discovered in a function, then the copy in the library was updated, so that it was available to all. These centralized libraries could be considered the predecessors of today's repositories.

There was a problem, however, with these shared libraries. There was no control over the changes made to a shared resource (e.g., program, function, specification) in the central library of shared components. Anyone could make a modification. There was also no formal mechanism for informing all users that a particular module or function had been changed, and there was no proper authority to decide whether a particular change was necessary or not. This lack of proper control mechanism led to another problem—the simultaneous update problem.

3.5 Simultaneous update problem

Consider this situation: Programmer A has found a bug and has fixed it. She copies the bug-fixed version to the central library, thus overwriting the existing copy. According to the procedure we saw in the previous section, this is how it should be done. That is, the changes are incorporated to the copy in the central library, where all of the shared resources are kept.

But what if programmer B also finds the same bug? He is not aware of the fact that A has found the bug and is fixing it or has already fixed it. He also fixes the bug and then copies the function to the library, thus overwriting the copy that was created by programmer A. So the work that was done by programmer A to fix the bug is lost.

This creates two major problems (Figure 3.6): (1) a lot of time and resources are wasted because two people, working in isolation, corrected the same mistake; and (2) different people will have different opinions about how to fix the same problem. Who will decide which option is the best and which one is to be used?

Now consider another variation (which is much more serious) of this problem: Programmer A finds a bug and fixes it. During the same time, programmer B finds a different bug and fixes it. But depending on which programmer updates the library copy last, the other programmer's work is lost, but both bug fixes are necessary and need to be incorporated into the function. This means that the uncontrolled and unmanaged functioning of these central libraries in which the shared resources are kept is not going to solve the problem. In other words, just by creating a repository of shared components and leaving it unmanaged and uncontrolled so that anyone can make changes to the items in the repository is not going to solve the problem.

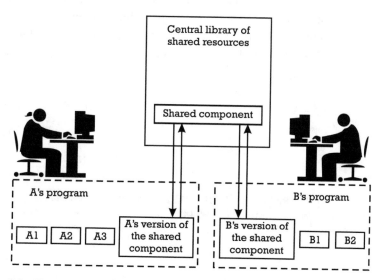

Figure 3.6 Simultaneous update problem.

SCM solves three problems mentioned previously—shared data problem, multiple maintenance problem, and simultaneous update problem—by enforcing formal change management and control procedures. Once an item is brought under SCM control, it is stored in a controlled library to which access is restricted. Developers cannot simply make changes to items—configuration items—in the controlled library. A change request has to be initiated, impact analysis has to be done, and the change has to be approved. Only when the change is approved will the item be released from the controlled library. Once the change has been made and tested, the item(s) has to be reviewed and approved before returning it back to the controlled library. Because developers cannot make changes to programs at will, the shared data problem is eliminated. Because there is only one library in which to keep the configuration items, and because only one person[1] can make changes to an item at a time, the multiple maintenance problem is also eliminated. Because access to the central library is controlled and formal change control procedures have to be followed to modify the items, the simultaneous problem is also eliminated.

3.6 Summary

We have seen the four major problems that create trouble in the software development process and that can drive programmers and developers crazy. Is there a solution to these problems? A good change management and control system can solve these problems and can bring discipline into the development process and improve the development productivity. A lot of time that would otherwise be spent on debugging and reworking can be saved. It is a well-known fact that the earlier defects are found, the easier and cheaper it is to solve them. In order to detect and solve the problems and to ensure that the solved problems are not recurring again, it is important to have a good SCM system in place from the beginning of the project.

References

[1]   Jones, G. W., *Software Engineering*, New York: John Wiley & Sons, 1990.

[2]   Brooks, F. P., *The Mythical Man-Month*, New York: Addison Wesley Longman, 1995.

[3]   Rawlings, J. H., *SCM for Network Development Environments*, New York: McGraw-Hill, 1994.

---

1. There are instances when more than one person needs to make changes to the same item, and SCM has ways to control such situations—branching and merging (see Chapter 5 for more details about this topic).

Need and importance of SCM

4.1   Introduction

In Chapter 1 we saw what SCM is; in Chapter 2 we got a brief introduction to the software development process and how the various SCM activities fit into the development process. In Chapter 3 we discussed some of the most common problems that plague the software development process. In this chapter, we look at why SCM is important and why it should be implemented in all software projects irrespective of their size (small, medium, large, or very large), complexity (simple or complex), and the stage (conceptual, design, development, testing, or maintenance) of the project.

4.2   Need for SCM

Here are just some of the reasons for implementing SCM:

- The nature of software products, projects, and development teams;

- Increased complexity of the software systems;

- Increased demand for software;

- The changing nature of software and need for change management.

4.2.1   The nature of software products, projects, and development teams

Software products have many different components in multiple versions and running on many different software and hardware platforms. The versions and variants are closely

43

interrelated, and if no control mechanism is in place, they can easily be modified, corrupted, or destroyed.

Software development projects are one of the most difficult types to manage. In a software project, everything from requirements to the development and installation environment is constantly changing. Users will modify the requirements they have given at the beginning of the project; programmers will make changes to code without letting other users of the same code know what they have done; the development environment might change as a result of some new developments in technology; the installation and operational environment can change because of some policy decisions by the customer or because of technological innovations or technological obsolescence; end users can vastly differ in their knowledge about the system they are going to use—the list of the difficulties in a software project is endless. To manage such a complex activity, the project manager needs tools to avoid chaos and confusion—tools that will ensure that the changes happen in an orderly and scientific manner, tools that prevent communications breakdown among the project stakeholders, tools that will alert the manager before something goes wrong (an early warning system), tools that will record everything so that when disaster strikes, troubleshooting is easier.

Today, most software products are developed by teams spread across the world and by people who have different social, educational, cultural, and ethnic backgrounds. The project manager needs a system to ensure that these teams can communicate smoothly without any misunderstandings. Also, employee turnover is a factor that troubles all projects. When an employee leaves a project, it takes a long time to recover from the loss because some portion of the project-specific knowledge is lost. If a system records what the employee did, how he or she did it, what tasks are left unfinished, and which other components are affected, then even if an employee leaves the project, someone else can take his or her place and pick up speed much faster because the new person has all of the details of the work that was done and is still to be done.

So it is clear that the special nature of software products, projects, and teams makes software development unique and complex. Attempting to succeed in such a venture without any tools or systems (such as SCM) is like attempting a tight-rope walk without any safety precautions. The most experienced and successful adventure sports personnel are the ones who do not make any compromises on taking safety measures and precautions. Similarly, more experienced and successful software project managers insist on scientific methods and tools for managing projects. Experience has taught them that the difference between a successful and failed project is the use of proper control mechanisms and scientific procedures.

4.2.2   Increased complexity and demand

Information technology is revolutionizing the way in which we live and work. It is changing all aspects of our lives and lifestyles. The digital revolution has given humankind the ability to treat information with mathematical precision, to transmit it at high accuracy, and to manipulate it at will. These capabilities are creating a whole world within and around the physical world.

The amount of information processing power that is available to humankind is increasing. Computers and communications are becoming integral parts of our lives. The driving force behind these advancements is computer software. Computer software is becoming more complex, and the amount of software being developed each year is increasing exponentially. Also, the software is being used to control a range of activities from mission-critical applications, such as controlling the operations of satellites and intercontinental ballistic missiles, managing the functioning of banks and hospitals, handling the airline and railway reservation systems, and so on, to performing mundane tasks such as operating a door-locking system or for desktop publishing.

Musa [1] estimates that the demand for software systems increases by 900% each decade. Boehm and Papaccio [2] predict that the expenditure on software development will increase by 200% each decade, whereas the productivity of software professionals increases by only 35%. So the gap between supply and demand is large. Software companies, nonsoftware organizations, and governmental agencies are producing hundreds of new applications and modifying thousands of existing ones every year. All of them are finding it difficult to develop high-quality software that they need on time and within budget.

Another aspect of software that has changed is its complexity. According to Jones [3], in the early days of software development, computer programs were typically less than 1,000 machine instructions in size, required only one programmer to write, seldom took more than a month to complete, and the entire development costs were often less than $5,000. Today, however, some of the large systems exceed 25 million source code statements, usually require thousands of programmers to write, can take more than five years to complete, and have development costs in the range of $500 million.

In the early days of software development, all of the parts or modules of a software system were developed in the same place, but the different components of today's complex software systems are not even built by the same organization. Many software systems are built jointly by different organizations working in different parts of the world. They may communicate via Internet, e-mail, or videoconferencing technologies. So in this distributed development environment where face-to-face communication is rare, managing and coordinating the development process is a difficult task.

This increasing demand for new software, the need to modify or maintain the existing software, the increasing complexity of the software development process, and the critical nature of the applications in which software is being used dictate that software development cannot be accomplished in the same way it was during the early days. As Jones [4] has stated:

Software has become the central component in many complex activities. For this reason, the challenge of producing it requires specialized and powerful techniques. It is not possible to rely on luck, guesswork and innate talent for dependable results.

We need scientific methods and techniques for developing software.

4.2.3 Changing nature of software and need for change management

Software systems are subject to constant changes—during design, during development, and even after development. The pioneering work in this area has been done by Lehman and Belady [5] and is detailed as a set of laws called Lehman's laws. According to Lehman's law of continuing change, any large software system that is being used will undergo continual change because the system's use will suggest additional functionality. It will change until it becomes more cost effective to rewrite it from scratch [6]. This means that the software will be subject to constant changes other than the bug fixes and defects that are already in the software and that will be detected during and after its development.

This is not all; the software system that is perfectly developed and that has met all requirements and passed all audits and reviews will also change. According to Lehman [7], even if a system were built in complete conformance to the requirements, the system would still evolve because the system is introduced into the real world, and the environment into which the system is introduced is subject to change. So in order to adapt to the changes in the environment in which the system works, it has to change. In other words, no matter how perfectly you built the system, it will have to be changed to meet the changes in the environment. So the only constant thing about software is change. If the changes are not managed, then they will lead to chaos and confusion. So a mechanism for managing the change and controlling it is required, and SCM is one such mechanism.

4.3   Benefits of SCM

We have seen the need for SCM. A well-designed and properly implemented SCM system will have a lot of benefits to developers, the organization, and customers. Some of the benefits of SCM are as follows:

- Improved organizational competitiveness;
- Better customer service and improved customer goodwill;
- Better return on investment;
- Improved management control over software development activities;
- Improved software development productivity;

- Easier handling of software complexity;

- Improved security;

- Higher software reuse;

- Lower software maintenance costs;

- Better quality assurance;

- Reduction of defects and bugs;

- Faster problem identification and bug fixes;

- Process-dependent development rather than person-dependent development;

- Assurance that the correct system was built.

4.3.1   Improved organizational competitiveness

Today's business environment is highly competitive. Organizations are fiercely competing with one another for market share. In this race to survive, only organizations that continuously improve their processes and implement and use scientific tools, techniques, and business practices will succeed. Software development is a process that has many pitfalls (as seen in Chapter 3) and many peculiarities (as mentioned in the beginning of this chapter). If not managed properly, the software development process can spiral out of control and can result in time and cost overruns and low-quality products. SCM is the discipline of controlling the chaos of the software development process by managing uncontrolled change and improving communication. SCM can improve the productivity of employees by reducing confusion, rework, and wasted effort. It can reduce the time-to-market and can help the organization produce high-quality products. Thus SCM can be used as a weapon to increase the organization's competitiveness. The difference between the market leader and an also-ran is often the presence of a good SCM system and an organizational culture that promotes effective use of the SCM system.

4.3.2   Better customer service and improved customer goodwill

Even though it is possible to drastically reduce the number of defects in a software product, it is impossible to completely eliminate all defects. Even if one manages to deliver a completely defect-free product to customers, there will be requests for enhancements. So once the product is released into the market, maintenance and technical support personnel should prepare to solve technical problems, incorporate enhancement requests, fix bugs, and so on. In order to make changes to the software (for incorporating new features or fixing bugs), the support team must identify the source of the bug or place where the enhancement is to be made. This process is made a lot easier if the organization has implemented a good SCM system from the beginning and followed the SCM procedures. Because the SCM system records all changes made to each and every configuration item, identifying the cause of a problem is easy. Because the SCM help desk contains a record of all known problems about the system and their solutions, troubleshooting is easier. Thus a good SCM system helps with quicker resolution of customer problems, thereby improving customer goodwill.

4.3.3 Better return on investment

A good SCM system automates the process of changing and deploying software applications. The SCM system helps in process improvement, process automation, communication, coordination, and change management and provides a better return on investment by:

- Reducing rework, wasted effort, and the number of errors;
- Shortening development and change cycles and reducing the time-to-market;
- Improving the quality of the products and reducing errors;
- Reducing the time to find and fix errors and bugs;
- Automating and streamlining build and release management;
- Increasing productivity for human resources throughout the organization.

4.3.4 Improved management control over software development activities

The SCM system improves communication in the software development project. The status accounting function provides the project and company management with up-to-the-minute information of what is happening in the project, so management can take proactive actions to keep the project on time and within schedule. The status accounting information also includes information about the quality of the software development (as indicated by the number of changes, problems, etc.) and process improvement (indicated by metrics such as average time to fix bugs, time spent on development, etc.) that will help management measure the status of the project and manage it better.

4.3.5 Improved software development productivity

In Chapter 3 we looked at the various problems—communications breakdown problem, shared data problem, multiple maintenance problem, and simultaneous update problem—that reduce the productivity of software professionals and result in wasted effort, duplicated effort, and a host of other complications.

If software development were carried out in an environment in which these problems did not occur, then productivity would naturally increase, because problems and mistakes would be reduced. For example, if the communication channels are well-defined and functioning smoothly, if changes are made in a controlled fashion, and if all team members are aware of how to handle changes (i.e., each team member knows what to do in order to change something), then a lot of time and effort can be saved. With an SCM system in place, developers have more time to develop software as opposed to looking for missing items, wasting time fixing bugs that have already been fixed, and solving problems caused by using different versions of the same code. This means a tremendous improvement in development productivity.

4.3.6   Easier handling of software complexity

We have seen that the software development activity is a complex process. The use of SCM in a software development project will equip all project stakeholders to better handle this complexity. SCM identifies all of the components or artifacts of a software project, captures its description and physical and functional characteristics, and scientifically and systematically classifies, categorizes, and names them. These components or configuration items are then stored in one or more protected environments so they are safe from unauthorized changes, corruptions, and even disasters. SCM tracks the progress of each component and alerts management of impending dangers, so preventive actions can be taken. Thus SCM acts as a management reporting tool that tells the project manager whether a project is on schedule or not. SCM also performs audits and reviews to ensure that the product that is being developed is exactly the same as the user requires (as specified in the requirements document). Thus SCM prevents chaos, confusion, rework, and wasted effort in a software development project by helping to make the complex task of software development a lot easier.

4.3.7   Improved security

SCM prevents unauthorized changes to the different components of the project. SCM achieves this security by placing the reviewed, approved, and baselined configuration items in controlled libraries to which access is restricted. SCM also maintains a change log (history of the evolution of the configuration item to its current state). This change log is kept along with the components and forms a valuable resource for troubleshooting problems, fixing bugs, and so on. Many SCM systems have off-site security vaults in which a copy of the latest version of the items in the controlled library is stored. These off-site vaults prevent data loss even in case of a disaster at the project site.

Employee turnover can seriously jeopardize project schedules because in most cases employees leave without transferring knowledge to their successors. Because the SCM system maintains records of all project-related activities performed by each team member, the new person can be brought up to speed with the help of the SCM logs and reports. Thus implementing an SCM system increases the level of security against potential losses, unauthorized changes, employee turnover, and disasters.

4.3.8 Higher software reuse

An SCM system maintains a record of the past (project history or change history), the present (project tracking and change logs), and the future (information about planned versions and variants). The components or artifacts of the project are classified, categorized, named, and stored so they can be easily identified and retrieved. These records help in a higher degree of software reuse, both for future versions and other projects.

4.3.9 Lower maintenance costs

When dealing with software costs, most people address only the short-term or visible costs such as the costs associated with design, development, and testing. But long-term costs are associated with system operation and maintenance that often constitute a large percentage (as high as 75%) of the total life cycle cost for a given system. Blanchard [8] called this the iceberg effect, in which the initial costs are the visible part of the iceberg—the tip of the iceberg—and the operational and maintenance costs (which amount to more than 75% of the total life cycle costs) are the submerged part of the iceberg. So the maintenance costs constitute a significant amount of a software system's total life cycle costs. Software maintenance is usually classified as follows:

- ▸ *Corrective maintenance*. Correct the mistakes that escaped the testing phase and are found during actual usage.

- ▸ *Adaptive maintenance*. Change the software to perform in a new environment or with some new interfaces.

- ▸ *Perfective maintenance*. Modify the software to include new functionality or additional features.

According to Lientz and Swanson [9], perfective maintenance costs account for 65% of costs; 18% are adaptive; and 17% are corrective. There are many reasons for the high maintenance costs irrespective of which class they fall into. The most important reason among these is the absence of a proper method for handling these maintenance issues. Almost all maintenance issues involve changing something, modifying the existing code, or adding new code to the existing system. The people who are supposed to do these activities should have a good understanding of what they have to do, how they have to do it, where they have to make the change or modifications, and what the impact of the change will be on other programs.

If the software was developed systematically, if the documentation is perfect, the changes made to the programs are recorded, and the program dependencies are defined, then the maintenance team's task is easy. So from the design stage onward, proper mechanisms, which ensure that the design and development are done in a systematic and controlled fashion, need to be in place. These control mechanisms play a vital role in reducing maintenance costs.

4.3.10 Better quality assurance

One of the main objectives of a quality assurance (QA) system is to prevent defects from occurring. In the past, when the concept of quality control (QC) was prevalent, the idea was to find defects once they had occurred. If we take the manufacturing industry as an example, the QC team was interested in finding defects before parts were shipped. So the QC team concentrated on the final inspection, with the objective that not even a single defective part got past the final inspection stage.

With the advent of the QA philosophy, the focus changed from the final inspection to the assembly line. The idea was to prevent the defects from occurring rather than to reject defective parts during final inspection. QA teams thus worked to identify the causes of the defects, why they were occurring, where they were occurring, when they were occurring, and how they were occurring.

This is also true in the case of software development. In the early days, the major thrust was given to finding the errors or bugs and fixing them before the product or system was delivered to the customer. No one really cared about the causes of these defects, how they originated, and so on. As long as they were found and fixed, life was good.

But the QC philosophy had a problem: it was costly. A lot of time and effort could be saved if the defects were detected early. But more important was that in the QC approach, because no one was looking into the causes of the defects, they remained undetected and reappeared in the next project. For example, suppose a defect was occurring because the programmer was not good at the CASE tool she was using to generate the code. So every time she generated new code, the same mistakes were repeated. But a causal analysis would have revealed this problem, and the programmer could be trained on the tool so the problem would not occur again. In order to do a causal analysis, one needs to have data, so there has to be a formal mechanism for problem reporting or defect logging and tracking.

4.3.11 Reduction of defects and bugs

Once you have a defect logging and tracking system in place, once the QA teams start looking into the causes of the problems and correcting them, once the checks and audits are made to ensure that the project standards and guidelines are followed, then the number of bugs and problems will be reduced. In most cases, the problems occur because the documentation is not in sync with the development, the RDD and SDD are not updated to reflect the latest changes, and different people are using different versions of the same program or function. In many projects, there are no formal mechanisms to find out which code belongs where and what changes were made and why and when, and so on. If the development process has a system that takes care of these types of issues, then the software development and maintenance processes will be easier.

4.3.12 Faster problem identification and bug fixes

In the usual system of testing, bugs are found and fixed, but if there is a mechanism for logging the bug/problem reports, categorizing them, analyzing the causes, and recording how the problem was solved, then much time can be saved the next time a similar bug or problem occurs. A lot of time and effort can be saved by not having to reinvent the wheel each and every time a bug or problem that has occurred in the past reappears.

Also, by recording the bugs, their causes, and the corrective actions, a knowledge base will be created that will grow with time and will be an invaluable resource for future tasks. When a problem is reported, the knowledge base can be searched for similar problems and, if one exists, the solution for the previous bug will help resolve the current problem faster. The knowledge base will grow in size and value as time goes on and as new problems and solutions are added to it. This also means that even when people who are working on a project leave, they leave behind the knowledge they have gained for others to use.

4.3.13 Process-dependent development rather than person-dependent development

In early days, when software projects were simple and small, the design and details of a project were often handled by a single individual. Even though projects have become larger and more complex, the dependency on the individual still exists. For example, in many projects, if you remove a few key people, the projects will come to a standstill, basically because the other team members do not have the whole picture of the project. There is no way they can have the whole picture because no documentation exists and, even if it does exist, it is often understood only by the people who wrote it. In many cases, these documents have not been updated and are not in sync with the system that is being developed.

This kind of dependency on people is dangerous. What happens if a key person leaves the company or is not able to work anymore? In such cases, the entire process of design and development has to start all over again, because no one knows what to do with the current system. Therefore, software engineering pioneers have always said that software development has to be process dependent, not people dependent.

Boehm [10] has said that talented people are the most important element in any software organization and that it is crucial to get the best people available. According to him, the better and more experienced they are, the better the chance of producing first-class results. But the problem with these geniuses is that their capability to work as a team, in most cases, will not be in the same class as their talent.

Software development has become too complex, and software systems are so huge that it is not possible for one individual to complete a project regardless of how talented he or she may be. To develop software systems success fully, even the best and most talented professionals need a structured and disciplined environment, which is conducive for teamwork and cooperative development. According to Humphrey [11]:

> Software organizations that do not establish these disciplines condemn their people to endless hours of repetitively solving technically trivial problems. There may be challenging work to do, but their time is consumed by mountains of uncontrolled detail. Unless these details are rigorously managed, the best people cannot be productive. First-class people are essential, but they need the support of an orderly process to do first-class work.

4.3.14 Assurance that the correct system has been built

Software development, as we have seen, starts with the requirements analysis. We have also seen that during the software development life cycle, the requirements will undergo many changes. So how do we make sure that the system that is being delivered to the customer is what the customer initially wanted and that it contains all of the changes that were suggested during the development period? In other words, how does the client or customer know that what he is getting is what he asked for?

There should be some sort of process for documenting the initial requirements and the changes made to them. There should also be some mechanism for checking or auditing the software system or product that is being delivered to the customer and certifying that the product satisfies the requirements. In other words, there should be a facility to conduct audits (or reviews) to ensure that what is developed and delivered is complete in all respects and is exactly what was specified.

4.4 Summary

We have seen that software systems are becoming more complex and sophisticated and are being used increasingly in mission-critical applications. We have also seen the changing nature of software and software development. Unless a system is used to manage and control change, it can lead to chaos and confusion, which can result in lowquality, lower productivity, and even the scrapping of a project. We saw why quality assurance is important and how it can help reduce bugs and maintenance costs. We also saw that we need a process-dependent system (as opposed to a person-dependent system) in order to be successful in the long run.

SCM is an ideal solution for the issues discussed and an excellent foundation from which other process improvement methodologies can be launched. SCM provides a mechanism for managing, documenting, controlling, and auditing change. So in today's complex software development environment, SCM is a must for all projects irrespective of their nature, size, and complexity, and it is better to have the SCM functions in place as early as possible. According to Davis [12], the SCM procedures should be designed and approved and recorded in a document—the SCM plan. This document should be written early in a project (as we have seen in Chapter 2, as early as the project start-up phase), and should typically be approved around the same time that the software requirements specifications are approved.

References

[1] Musa, J. D., "Software Engineering: The Future of a Profession," *IEEE Software*, Vol. 22, No. 1, 1985, pp. 55–62.

[2] Boehm, B. W., and P. N. Papaccio, "Understanding and Controlling Software Costs," *IEEE Trans. Software Engineering*, Vol. 14, No. 10, 1988, pp. 1462–1477.

[3] Jones, C. T., *Estimating Software Costs*, New York: McGraw-Hill, 1998.

[4] Jones, G. W., *Software Engineering*, New York: John Wiley & Sons, 1990.

[5] Lehman, M. M., and L. Belady, *Program Evolution: Processes of Software Change*, London: Academic Press, 1985.

[6] Lehman, M. M., and L. Belady, "A Model of Large Program Development," *IBM Syst. J.*, Vol. 15. No. 3, 1976, pp. 225–252.

[7] Lehman, M. M., "Software Engineering, the Software Process and Their Support," *Software Engineering J.*, Vol. 6, No. 5, 1991, pp. 243–258.

[8] Blanchard, B. S., *System Engineering Management*, New York: John Wiley & Sons, 1991.

[9] Lientz, B. P., and E. B. Swanson, *Software Maintenance Management*, Reading, MA: Addison-Wesley, 1980.

[10] Bohem, B. W., *Software Engineering Economics*, Englewood Cliffs, NJ: Prentice-Hall, 1981.

[11] Humphrey, W. S., *Managing the Software Process*, New York: Addison-Wesley, 1989.

[12] Davis, A. M., *201 Principles of Software Development*, New York: McGraw-Hill, 1995.

CHAPTER

5

Contents

SCM: Basic concepts

5.1 Introduction

Software configuration management is the set of activities that is performed throughout the project life cycle—from requirements analysis to maintenance. SCM is important because software is subject to constant change: software systems undergo changes when designed, when built, and even after being built. Uncontrolled and unmanaged change can create confusion and lead to communications breakdown problems, shared data problems, multiple maintenance problems, simultaneous update problems, and so on. So change has to be controlled and managed.

A software development project produces the following items:

- *Programs* (e.g., source code, object code, executable programs, component libraries, functions, subroutines);

- *Documentation* (e.g., requirements definition, systems analysis, systems design, high-level design, low-level design, test specifications, test plans, test scripts, installation manuals, release notes, user manuals);

- *Data* (test data and project data).

These items are collectively called a software configuration. IEEE [1] defines a software configuration as the functional and physical characteristics of the software as set forth in technical documentation or achieved in a product. The SCM system[1] identifies these items (the software items) and

---

1. SCM system means the tools, plans, and procedures as it is implemented in the project. It is the collection of all activities and personnel and other resources that performs SCM.

records their properties and relationships. This task would be easy if the items and the systems were not subject to change, but unfortunately that is not the case.

Changes can occur at any time. Bersoff's [2] first law of system engineering states that no matter where you are in the system life cycle, the system will change and the desire to change it will persist throughout the life cycle. So we have to deal with change, and SCM does that. But that is not the only thing SCM does; it also—through audits and reviews—ensures that the items that are being released satisfy the requirements that were set forth in the requirements and design documents.

So we can define SCM as the set of activities whose main purposes are to identify the configuration items (the items that are supposed to change or that will undergo change); find the properties, characteristics, and interdependencies of these items and record them; monitor these items; manage the changes made to these items; document and report the change process; and ensure that the items delivered are complete and satisfy all requirements.

5.2 Overview of SCM

To identify, control, and manage change, one must first identify which items in the project will be subject to change. So we must first identify the items that we plan to control and manage. These items are called, in the SCM terminology, configuration items. IEEE [1] defines configuration items as an aggregation of hardware, software, or both that is designated for configuration management and treated as a single entity in the configuration management process. It can be a program, a group of programs, a component library, a function, a subroutine, project documentation, a user manual, test plan, test data, project data, and so on. The SCM system is supposed to record the functional and physical properties (such as the features, what it is supposed to do, what performance criteria it is supposed to achieve, the size, lines of code, and so on) of these configuration items. Some examples of configuration items in a project follow:

- Project plan;
- SCM plan;
- Requirements definition document (RDD);
- Analysis, design, coding, testing, and auditing standards;
- System analysis document (SAD);
- System design document (SDD);
- Prototypes;

- High-level design (HLD) document;

- Low-level design (LLD) document;

- System test specifications;

- System test plan;

- Program source code;

- Object code and executable;

- Unit test specifications;

- Unit test plans;

- Database design documents;

- Test data;

- Project data;

- User manuals.

This list is by no means exhaustive. It varies from project to project. The designers of the SCM system for a particular project decide which items should be configuration items. The characteristics of each configuration item and their interdependencies with one another are recorded. Usually this information is recorded in what is called a *configuration management database* or the repositories in the case of SCM tools. We will learn more about the configuration management database later in this chapter.

Once the configuration items are identified and their characteristics are recorded, the next steps in SCM, as we saw in Chapter 1, are configuration control, status accounting, and configuration audits. We look briefly at these activities later in this chapter, but before we proceed, we should familiarize ourselves with some of the SCM terminology and concepts that we will be using in this book: baselines, deltas, versions, variants, branches, builds, releases, and so on.

5.3 Baselines

Baselines play an important role in managing change. During the software development process, the configuration items are developed. For example, design documents are created, programs are coded and tested, and user manuals are prepared. When a configuration item is complete, it is handed over to the configuration management team for safekeeping. The configuration management team will check whether the item that is given to them is complete (or contains all of the necessary components) per the SCM plan and place it in the controlled library. During specific points during the software development process, usually after the requirement phase, design phase, and release phase, the set of configuration items (CIs) under SCM control are formally designated as a baseline. So a baseline need not contain all of the items that are in the controlled library. Which items are to be included in a baseline is determined depending on the purpose for which the baseline is created. For example, a release baseline will contain only the CIs that are to be given to the customer.

There are two schools of thoughts regarding baselines: One suggests that the required CIs are placed into one of the different baselines, and the other proposes that a CI becomes its own baseline once it is given over to SCM for control. The problem with declaring any configured item as a baseline is that you lose the distinction between something that is merely checked in and when it becomes a part of some deliverable (such as the development, test, or deployed/release baselines). Just checking an artifact in may not even mean it gets included in a build. It may be an interim step as part of a parallel development effort, for example. A baseline does not represent simply any changed item, but rather a particular grouping of items at a specific point in time, for a given purpose.

Baseline is an SCM concept that helps control change. IEEE [1] defines baseline as a specification or product that has been formally reviewed and agreed on, which thereafter serves as the basis for further development and which can be changed only through formal change control procedures. So once a baseline is established, the CIs in the baseline can be changed only through a formal change management process. Pressman [3] compares the process of change management to a room with two doors: the IN and OUT doors. According to him, when an item has passed through the IN door—to the controlled environment—the item is brought under configuration control. Then the only way to make changes to the item is to get it out through the OUT door—using formal change management methods.

The baseline is the foundation for configuration management. The definition of SCM contains the concept of identifying the configuration—the functional and physical characteristics—of each CI at discrete points in time during the life cycle process. The configuration of software at a discrete point in time is known as a *baseline*. Each baseline serves as a point of departure or reference for the next development stage.

A software baseline is a set of software items formally designated and fixed at a specific time during the software life cycle. A baseline, together with all approved changes to the baseline, represents the current approved configuration. Usually, baselines are established after each life cycle phase at the completion of the formal review that ends the phase. Thus we have the requirements baseline, design baseline, product baseline, and so on, as we saw in Chapter 2.

A baseline provides the official standard or point of reference on which subsequent work is based and to which only authorized changes are made. After an initial baseline is established, every subsequent change made to the items is done using the configuration control process or, in other words, using formal change management procedures. Whenever an item is changed, all of the processes involved in making the change—change initiation to change requests[2] to change disposition and implementation—are recorded. Then the item being changed is reviewed and saved as a new version of the item. For all of these change management processes, the baseline serves as a reference point.

Baselines should be established at an early point in the project, but bringing all items under configuration control too early will impose unnecessary procedures and will slow the programmers' work. This is because before a software configuration item becomes part of a baseline, changes may be made to it quickly and informally. For example, consider a programmer developing a program: After he has completed coding, while doing the unit testing, the programmer stumbles on a better algorithm to accomplish some task in the program. Because the program is not part of a baseline, the programmer can make the necessary change to the program, recompile it, and continue with the testing. But if the same situation occurs after the program is checked in and/or has become part of a baseline, then the programmer will have to make a change request and follow the change management procedures to make the change.

So when should baselines be established? There are no hard-and-fast rules on this issue. It depends on the nature of the project and how the SCM system designers (the people who designed the SCM system and wrote the SCM plan) think. Establishing baselines involves a trade-off between imposing unnecessary procedures (thus reducing productivity) and letting things go uncontrolled (which will result in project failure). So these two factors should be kept in mind when deciding when to baseline. As long as programmers can work on individual modules with little interaction, a code baseline is not needed. As soon as integration begins, however, formal control is essential.

So before a configuration item becomes a controlled item, only informal change control[3] is applied. The developer of the item can make whatever changes are justified by project and technical requirements, as long as these changes do not conflict with the system requirements.[4] But once the object has undergone formal technical review and has been approved, a baseline is created. Once the configuration item becomes a baseline, project-level change control or formal change control is implemented.

Even though the most common baselines are the requirements, design, and product baselines, a baseline can be established whenever a need is felt.

---

2. Change request (CR) is a request to make a change or modification. A change request form (paper or electronic) is used to initiate a change and contains the details of the change, such as the name of the change originator, item to be changed, and other details of changes.

3. Informal change control is applicable when the developers can make change to their programs without following the SCM procedures. This is possible when the item has not been checked in and is not under SCM control.

4. the developer can find out whether the changes he makes to his program do not conflict with the system requirements by going through the system design specifications and high-level design documents. for example, in a program, whether the developer first calculates the tax and subtracts it from the earnings or multiplies the earnings with the (1-tax/100) does not conflict with the system requirements. the programmer makes this decision according to his idea about which is the best algorithm.

For example, many projects have many more baselines than the three mentioned previously. A new baseline is not necessarily established each time a CI is modified or added to the library. The number of baselines that a project has is determined by the SCM team, the project's needs, and what is advantageous to have. The information about when to create a baseline will be in the SCM plan.

You can have a baseline at the start of each phase, if you so choose. As for trade-offs, the only time there is a real need to establish a baseline is, if after it is done, a copy of the baseline leaves SCM control in some fashion (i.e., to a test lab or deployment)—that is the minimum for creating a baseline. You must know the set of software that starts a phase or is deployed so you know what changes should be made to it later. As for controlling the number of baselines is concerned, ask the following questions:

▸ What are the requirements from the customer vis-à-vis providing demonstrable progress reporting?

▸ What are the needs and requirements internal to your organization or project about status and/or progress reporting?

▸ What metrics do your customers, management, and project leadership need to see?

The answers to these questions can help you establish a baseline schedule.

5.4 Check-in and checkout

We have seen that once a CI is developed, reviewed, and approved, it is kept in a controlled library or repository. This process of reviewing, approving, and moving an item into the controlled environment is called *check-in*. Once an item is checked in, it becomes a controlled item and all change management procedures apply to it. It cannot be taken out and modified whenever a programmer feels like doing so, even if he or she is the author or developer of the item.

For making changes to an item that is in the controlled library, the change management process, which is discussed in detail in Chapter 8, must be followed (i.e., a change request has to be submitted, approved, and so on). Once the change request is approved, the configuration manager will copy the item (and other affected items, if any) from the controlled library so modifications can be made. This process is called *checkout*. Thus to make a change to an item that is under SCM control, it has to be checked out of the controlled library. After the changes are made, the item or items are again tested, reviewed, and if approved, they are again checked in to the controlled environment. The checkout/check-in process is shown in Figure 5.1. Today's SCM tools have made this whole process of check-in and checkout an easy task. Many tools allow programmers to work on the CIs

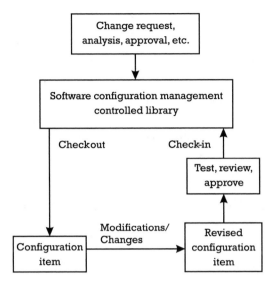

Figure 5.1   Check-in and checkout.

without physically checking out the items. Also, today's SCM tools allow more than one person to simultaneously work on the same CI (concurrent development). These facilities provided by modern SCM tools are discussed later in this chapter.

5.4.1   Versions and variants

During the software development life cycle, the configuration items evolve until they reach a state at which they meet the specifications. This is when the items are reviewed, approved, and moved into the controlled environment. But we have seen that the story does not end there. The item will undergo further changes (for various reasons such as defects and enhancements), and in order to make those changes, the change control procedures must be followed. The items have to be checked out, the changes implemented, tested, reviewed, approved, and again moved back to the controlled library. This change process produces a new version or revision of the item.

A *version* is an initial release or re-release of a CI. It is an instance of the system that differs in some way from the other instances. New versions of the system may have additional functionality or different functionality. Their performance characteristics may be different or they may be the result of fixing a bug that was found by the developer, tester, user, or customer.

Some versions can be functionally equivalent but may be designed for different hardware and/or software environments. In such cases, they are called *variants*. For example, two different instances of the same item, say, one for Windows and the other for Linux, can be called variants rather than different versions. Unlike a version, one variant of an item is in no sense an improvement on another variant.

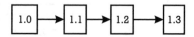

Figure 5.2   Version numbers.

As we have seen, the items once moved into the controlled environment can be changed only by using SCM change control methods. Each such change produces a revision or version. So each change to a controlled item produces a new version and except for the first, each version has a predecessor and except for the most recent, each version has a successor. The different versions of an item represent its history. It explains how an item got transformed or evolved from its initial form or stage to its current form. A new version of an item is usually created by checking out the most recent copy and making changes to it.

5.5   Parallel development and branching

So far we have seen that an item is checked out, changes are made, and then it is tested, reviewed, approved, and checked in. So the versions will form a linear line, as shown in Figure 5.2.

But in real life this linear development might not always be possible. In such cases, we use what is called a *branch*. Branches (Figure 5.3) are deviations from the main development line for an item. They are a convenient mechanism for allowing two or more people to work on the same item at the same time—parallel, concurrent development—perhaps for different goals. A common scenario is having one person working to add new features to the product, while a second is doing bug fixes on prior versions.

The version numbers of branches can be a little confusing, so they warrant a quick discussion. Version numbers on the main development line have only two parts—a major and minor number. Branches have four parts to their numbering scheme. The first two parts represent the point at which the branch splits off the main line. The third number indicates which of the many possible branches it is. For example, in Figure 5.3, we have only one branch originating from 1.3. As such, its numbering starts at 1.3.1.0 and proceeds from there. If a second branch is later formed from 1.3, its numbering will begin with 1.3.2.0, as shown in Figure 5.4.

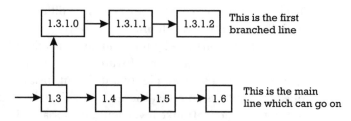

Figure 5.3   Branching for parallel development.

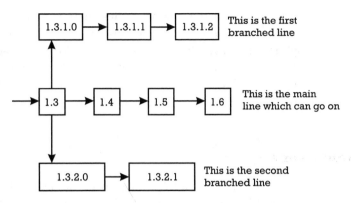

Figure 5.4 Multiple branches.

Branches can also extend from existing branches. For example, a branch can be formed from 1.3.1.1. This branch will have a six-part numbering scheme starting with 1.3.1.1.1.0, as shown in Figure 5.5. The first four parts represent the point at which the branch split off from the parent branch. The fifth number indicates which of the many possible branches it is. For example, in Figure 5.5, we have only one branch originating from 1.3.1.1. As such, its numbering starts at 1.3.1.1.1.0 and proceeds from there. If a second branch is later formed from 1.3.1.1, then its numbering will begin with 1.3.1.1.2.0.

Branches are often used as a temporary means of allowing parallel and concurrent development on a single file. Sooner or later, the edits made to the branched line must be incorporated into the main evolutionary line for the file. When doing this, the changes made by the different persons have to be merged. If the changes are made at different parts of the item, then the merge is an easy task, but if two people have changed the same lines of an item, then a decision has to be reached about how the merge is to take place. The person who does the merging should decide which one to keep and which one to discard. The SCM tools have automatic merging facilities that allow interactive merging, in which the tool will compare the changed

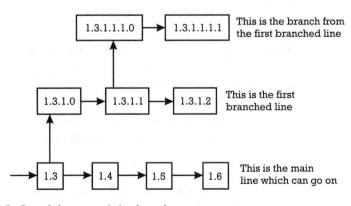

Figure 5.5 Branch from an existing branch.

portions of the two changed files to the original file (usually called the ancestor), and the user can choose which change to accept. In the author's opinion, however, it is always better to do an interactive or manual merge, because human judgment is better than the judgment afforded by the algorithms used by the tools. After the merge occurs, the branches have outlived their utility and no longer need to evolve separately.

5.6   Naming of versions

We have seen that all CIs have to be named and that the name has two parts: (1) a number part, which changes with each version, and (2) the name of the item, including the project, type, and other details. The names should be descriptive. For example, in a large project with many modules and subsystems, a simple name for a CI is not a good idea. In such cases, the name should have elements of the project, subsystem, module, and other components in it so that it can be easily identified with a project or subsystem. The number part of the name should be designed in such a way as to determine its relative position in the version hierarchy. For example, we have seen that the first version will be identified as 1.0, subsequent revisions 1.1, 1.2, 2.0, 2.1, and so on. A branch from version 1.1 will be identified as 1.1.1.0, and its subsequent versions 1.1.1.1, and so on. A second branch will be identified as 1.1.2.0 and so on.

5.7   Source and derived items

An item that is created from another item or set of items is called a *derived item*. The items from which a derived item is created are called *source items*. For example, an executable program is a derived item—an item that is derived from the source code using a compiler. In the case of derived items, the details, such as the list of source items used to derive the item, the tool or tools used to derive the item, and the environment in which the derivation was done, are important and should be documented. This information is important from the point of view of reproducibility and repeatability. For example, if you want to derive the particular version of a derived item, you will need all of the aforementioned information to do so. Also, if a problem is detected with a version of the derived item, then the following questions need to be answered to solve the problem:

- Which versions of which source elements (name and version of each source item) were used to build the item?

- Which tools were used for the process?

- What environmental variables and parameters (such as compile and link-edit options) were used by the tools while building the item?

These are the first questions that will have to be answered if a problem occurs, and a good SCM system should be able to provide the answers to these questions because these answers fully describe a derived item.

5.8 System building

System building is the process of combining "source" components of a system into components, which execute on a particular target configuration. The system or parts of it have to be rebuilt after every change in the "source." The following questions must be considered:

- Have all components that make up the system been included in the build instructions (dependencies resolved, include paths set, and so on), and do they have the proper version?

- Are all required ancillary files (data, documentation) available on the target machine?

- Are the required tools (e.g., the compiler or linker) available, and do they have the right version?

The system is built using a command file, which specifies the components of the system (both source and derived), their versions, their location in the controlled environment, the system-building tools (such as a compiler, linker, and so on), and their versions, the options, and environmental parameters that were set. In the IBM mainframe, this file is usually a JCL file; in UNIX it is a shell script; and in modern integrated development environments such as Visual C++ and Visual Basic it is a make file or project file. These command files are also configuration items and are necessary for reproduction of the particular configuration.

The build management facility of many SCM tools automates the process of constructing the software system and ensures that the systems are built completely and accurately at any time. These configuration builders save time, shorten build cycles, and eliminate build errors by providing repeatable, automated builds of the software development projects. In most cases, the system-building tools work with the version management tools and extract the correct versions of development objects from libraries. This simplifies the system-building process and eliminates errors when building complex versions on multiple operating systems.

5.9 Releases

A release consists of more than just the executable code. It includes installation files, data files, setup programs, and electronic and paper documentation. A system release is the set of items that is given to the customers. Each system release includes new functionality or features or some fixes for the faults found by customers, developers, or testers. Usually, there are more revisions of a system than system releases. Revisions or versions, as mentioned before, are created for internal use and may never be released to customers. For example, a revision may be created for testing.

When a release is produced (using the system-building process), it is important to record the environment in which it was produced: the operating system, versions of the components used, other parameters such as compile and link-edit options, and so on. This is important from the SCM point of view, because at a later stage, it might become necessary to reproduce the exact configuration that was released. For example, consider a bug that is discovered after the system is released. The easiest way to find the source of the problem is to find out what components were changed. The problem could be caused either by a bug in one of the changed components or by some environmental variables being changed (such as some compiler or linker options). So if we have a record of the components and the environmental details used for the release, it is easy to track the source of the defect. One merely needs to compare the details of the current release with the previous release and see what has been changed. So it is imperative that a proper mechanism to record the details of each and every release be instituted.

A release to a client or a *system release* should contain identifiers indicating the release or version number and should also include a release note containing the following information:

> Installation requirements, such as required operating system, memory, and processor specifications;

> How to install the system and how to test the system to ensure that the installation was successful;

> How to upgrade from an earlier version of the system;

> The key or serial number of the product, if such a number is required for installation;

> A list of known faults and limitations of the particular version of the system and a list of the faults that were fixed in the current release;

> New features introduced in the release;

> Instructions for contacting the supplier of the system for technical support or if problems arise.

Today, most of these activities, including the registration of the product, are done by installation programs, so release notes are not as important as they once were.

5.10 Deltas

In an ideal situation, all changes made to the CIs should be recorded, and all of the different versions of the items should be kept, because in a software system not all users will be using the latest version. So, even though the system may be in version 6.0, some users will still be using version 1.0 or 2.1. So configuration management systems should be able to produce the details of the latest as well as past versions and should be able to reproduce the components of every version. For example, years after a system is released, a request for a component in the first version can come up. Even if the system is currently in its seventh or eighth version, companies cannot ignore a client who still uses the initial version.

Ideally, copies of all versions should be kept in a repository, but this is not practical, because of the amount of disk space required. Instead, we create what is known as a *delta*. When a new version is created, the difference between the new and the previous version is called delta. So instead of storing full copies of all versions, one version and the deltas are stored, so that at any point in time the required version can be derived by applying the relevant deltas to the base version. The concept of deltas is shown in Figure 5.6.

Deltas are smaller than the source code of a system version, so the amount of disk space required for version management is greatly reduced. The two types of delta storage are forward deltas and reverse deltas, as shown in Figure 5.7.

The principle of forward delta storage is that the system maintains a complete copy of the original file. After this, whenever a new version is checked in, the two versions are compared and a delta report is produced. Then this delta report is stored instead of storing the full copy of the new version. Whenever the new version is required, the delta is applied to the original to get the new version.

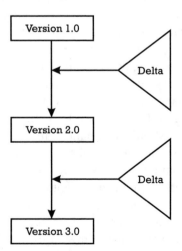

Figure 5.6 Use of deltas.

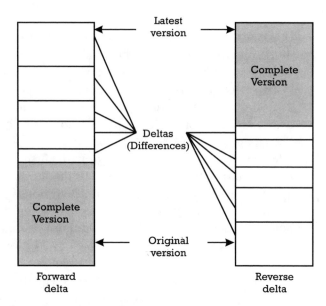

Figure 5.7   Forward and reverse deltas.

In the case of reverse delta storage, only the most recent version of the module is kept in the complete form. Whenever a new version is checked in, it is compared to the previous version and the delta is created. Then the previous version is deleted and the new version is stored.

The problem with forward delta storage is that as more revisions are added, more computation is required to obtain the latest revision. So the greater the number of revisions, the longer the retrieval time will be. This is because in the case of the forward delta, the change manager must always start with the original version and then apply the deltas one at a time to create the latest version. In the case of the reverse delta option, no computation is required to get the latest version, because it is stored in its full form.

Using deltas is a classical space versus time trade-off: deltas reduce the space consumed but increase access time. However, an SCM tool should impose as little delay as possible on programmers. Excessive delays discourage the use of version controls or induce programmers to take shortcuts that compromise system integrity.

The decision to go in for delta storage as opposed to storing copies of all versions should be made with respect to the amount of storage space required and the cost of storage and retrieval. With the cost of storage systems coming down, storing copies of all versions can be considered, thus eliminating the need for deltas. Another factor that decides whether to use delta storage is the accuracy in rebuilding the required versions using the deltas vis-à-vis the cost of storage and the time taken to retrieve an archived item from the backup mechanism. Whether to use delta storage or not is a subject of debate among SCM professionals. In the author's opinion, if the complete copies could be stored at a reasonable price and could be retrieved as fast as re-creating using the delta storage, then it is better to eliminate delta storage or limit it to text files.

The decision to use forward delta storage or reverse delta storage depends on the nature of the project. If the latest versions are more frequently required, then it is always better to use the reverse delta. In the real world, more than 75% of archive accesses are for the latest version, which explains the popularity of reverse delta storage among the change management tools. Many tools also offer the facility to use delta storage or keep the complete copies. So depending on the nature, size, and type of CIs in the project, administrators can select a method of their preference.

5.11   SCM database

We have seen that the properties, characteristics, and interdependencies of the CIs should be recorded in a database—the configuration management database. The configuration management database is used to record all relevant information related to configurations. The principal functions of such a database are to assist in assessing the impact of system changes and to provide information about the SCM process. The configuration management database, in addition to the details about the configuration items, contains information about change requests (which are also configuration items), their status, and information regarding the review and audit processes.

The contents and structure of the configuration management database should be defined during the SCM system design stage and should be documented in the SCM plan. In modern CASE environments, the configuration database is part of the system, and the details of the items are automatically recorded. In the case of manual SCM systems, the details have to be entered manually into the system. The system should have necessary precautions and safety mechanisms in place to prevent bypassing the procedures and thus corrupting the data and making it useless. If a CI is added without an entry in the database, then the integrity of the data in the database and the usefulness of the database are lost.

A configuration management database should be able to provide answers to queries such as these:

  ▸ What is the current configuration? What is its status?

  ▸ Which person has taken delivery of a particular version of the system?

  ▸ What hardware and operating system configurations are required to run a given system version?

  ▸ How many versions of a system have been created, and what were their creation dates?

▸ What changes have been made to the software, documentation, and other items in the project; who made them; and when were they made?

▸ Were the changes approved or just informally done?

▸ What versions of a system might be affected if a particular component is changed?

▸ How many change requests are pending on a particular item?

▸ How many reported faults exist in a particular version?

▸ Can the original be re-created from the changed version or the changed version from the original?

▸ Can I find out what happened to a specific item at some point in time, such as what changes were made to it and so on?

▸ Does the change that I make affect anyone else, or are anyone else's changes affecting my program?

With the increasing popularity of SCM tools, the necessity for a configuration database is decreasing. SCM tools have their own repositories in which they can store SCM-related information. The advantage of these systems is that SCM information is captured automatically as and when each activity is performed. So there is no need to enter details manually when a change request is initiated, when an item is released, when a change is made, and so on. This feature saves considerable time and effort and reduces the chance of creating errors that can occur during manual data entry. Also, with the facility to automatically capture the SCM information, such as when the activities happen, the SCM tool user has the ability to capture comprehensive SCM information without any additional effort.

5.12 SCM activities

Configuration identification, the first activity of configuration management, is the process of defining each baseline to be established during the software life cycle and describing the software configuration items and their documentation that make up each baseline. First, the software must be grouped into CIs. Once the CIs and their components have been selected, some way of designating the items must be developed, through a numbering and naming scheme that correlates the code and data items with their associated documentation. Finally, each CI must be described by the documentation in terms of its functional, performance, and physical characteristics.

Configuration control is the process of evaluating, coordinating, and deciding on the disposition of proposed changes to the CIs, and also includes implementing approved changes to baselined software and associated documentation. The change control process ensures that changes that have been initiated are classified and evaluated, approved or denied, and that those approved are implemented, documented, and verified.

Configuration status accounting is the process used to trace changes to the software. It ensures that status is recorded, monitored, and reported on both pending and completed actions affecting software baselines.

Configuration auditing is the process of verifying that a deliverable software baseline contains all of the items required for that delivery, and that these items have been verified to determine that they satisfy requirements.

We will examine these activities in greater detail in Chapters 7, 8, 9, and 10.

5.13 Summary

In this chapter, we studied the various configuration management concepts and learned SCM terminology. We learned about SCM activities and how they relate to one another. We gained an understanding of the fundamental concepts of SCM, such as versions, variants, branching, merging, deltas, system building, and releases.

References

[1] IEEE, *IEEE Standard Glossary of Software Engineering Terminology (IEEE Std-610–1990), IEEE Standards Collection (Software Engineering)*, Piscataway, NJ: IEEE, 1997.

[2] Bersoff, E. H., V. D. Henderson, and S. G. Siegel, *Software Configuration Management: An Investment in Product Integrity*, Englewood Cliffs, NJ: Prentice-Hall, 1980.

[3] Pressman, R. S., *Software Engineering: A Practitioner's Approach*, 5th ed., New York: McGraw-Hill, 2001.

Selected bibliography

Babich, W. A., *Software Configuration Management: Coordination for Team Productivity*, Boston, MA: Addison-Wesley, 1986.

Ben-Menachem, M., *Software Configuration Guidebook*, London: McGraw-Hill International, 1994.

Berlack, H. R., *Software Configuration Management*, New York: John Wiley & Sons, 1992.

CM Crossroads™: The Configuration Management Community (www.cmcrossroads.com).

Conradi, R. (ed.), *Software Configuration Management: ICSE'97 SCM-7 Workshop Proc.,* Berlin: Springer-Verlag, 1997.

IEEE Standards Collection, *Software Engineering,* New York: IEEE, 1997.

Magnusson, B. (ed.), *System Configuration Management: ECOOP'98 SCM-8 Symp. Proc.,* Berlin: Springer-Verlag, 1998.

Pressman, R. S., *Software Engineering: A Practitioner's Approach,* New York: McGraw-Hill, 1997.

Sommerville, I., *Software Engineering,* Reading, MA: Addison-Wesley, 1996.

Whitgift, D., *Methods and Tools for Software Configuration Management,* Chichester, England: John Wiley & Sons, 1991.

6

The different phases of SCM implementation

6.1 Introduction

We have seen that SCM is a set of activities that must be performed throughout the life cycle of the software system. Even though SCM activities can be initiated at any stage during a product's life cycle, it is better to have the SCM system in place from the beginning.

Company management should be convinced of the need for and importance of having an SCM system, preferably during the early stages of the project. Also, the people who will be using the system (e.g., developers, project leaders, QA team members, company management) should be made aware of the benefits of a good configuration management system. The benefits of SCM, as discussed in Chapter 4, could be used for this purpose.

SCM systems are capable of delivering dramatic productivity improvements, cost reductions, error/defect reductions, and more. They can improve customer goodwill, because the company will be able to provide customers with better-quality products and better technical support. By educating project personnel on the benefits and values of SCM, the myths about SCM, such as "SCM is nothing more than just additional documentation" and "SCM is additional work," are dispelled, and the need for SCM would become obvious. Also, today's SCM tools are so sophisticated and advanced that they make the whole process of performing SCM functions much easier than before.

There is a misconception that SCM is only for big companies and large projects. In the author's opinion, SCM should be implemented in all software projects—irrespective of the size of the project and organization—because change is inevitable in all projects, and unmanaged and uncontrolled change is trouble all the way. It is the author's experience that companies that use the scientific methods of software development from the beginning (i.e., even when they are small) have a workforce that is more willing and able to learn new technologies and adapt to changes and implement new procedures. The programmers and managers of these companies have gotten used to standard software engineering practices and procedures, and the work cultures of these companies evolve around these practices. New employees joining the company will also follow the procedures and methods, because peer pressure to do so will be high.

The advantage of this scenario is that the methodologies and procedures will produce dramatic results in such companies because people are doing things because they believe in them, not because they have to do them. For example, consider SCM: Everyone knows that SCM is not easy; it is difficult to keep a good SCM system (one that is efficient and effective) up and running, but the effort is worth it. If an SCM system is to become a success and deliver the promised results, the people who are involved have to be convinced of its worth. Just doing SCM for the sake of getting some certification will not produce the results that SCM is capable of achieving.

The purpose of this chapter is to explain the objectives and phases that make the life cycle of an SCM system from conception to retirement and how these events may be sequenced. The organizational culture and the nature of projects will differ from company to company. So two SCM implementations can never be identical; they will vary depending on the size, nature, and complexity of projects, development methodology, and organizational culture. The objectives, the different phases, the sequence of these phases, and other details of the SCM implementation will vary greatly from organization to organization.

It is important for company management, project leaders, consultants, developers, SCM personnel, and other stakeholders to have a good understanding of the large-scale conceptual picture of SCM and SCM implementation. Without the capability to understand the big picture, SCM practitioners can become lost. It is important to have a solid foundation for understanding the big picture so practitioners can understand the details of what they deal with on a day-to-day basis and how it relates to the rest of the project and affects the rest of the organization.

Two basic characteristics are common to all SCM implementation projects: objectives and phases (or events).

6.2   Objectives of SCM implementation

Objectives are the major high-level characteristics that can have a great impact on the success of an SCM project. The objectives include characteristics such as:

- Speed;

- Scope;

- Resources;

- Risk;

- Complexity;

- Benefits.

6.2.1   Speed

Speed of a project is directly related to the amount of time a company has before the completion of the SCM implementation or the amount of time the company would like to take for the implementation. The speed of the project in the context of this chapter is how much time the company would like to take in implementing the system. The amount of time the company actually takes may be dramatically different. The amount of time the company would like to take should be the figure used when developing a project plan.

6.2.2   Scope

The scope of the project includes all of the functional and technical characteristics that the company wants to implement. A company installing a full-fledged SCM system would have a much greater scope than a company installing a change management and defect tracking system.

6.2.3   Resources

Resources are everything that is needed to support the project, including people, hardware systems, software systems, technical support, and consultants. All of the different resources of an implementation have one thing in common—money.

6.2.4   Risk

The risk of a project impacts the overall success of the SCM implementation. Success is measured by factors such as overall user acceptance, return on investment (ROI), time to implement, and others. High-risk situations are less likely to possess these characteristics.

6.2.5   Complexity

Complexity is the degree of difficulty in implementing, operating, and maintaining the SCM system. Companies of different sizes, business environments, and organizational cultures have different levels of complexity. A multibillion-dollar corporation that has development sites and teams spread across the different parts of the world and working in different time zones is generally much more complex than a company with 50 employees occupying one geographic location.

6.2.6 Benefits

Benefits are the degree to which the company will utilize functionality of the SCM system for software development, maintenance, and other support activities. The SCM tools automate almost all aspects of the configuration management activities; they make the job of the developers, managers, and other stakeholders easy and improve the development productivity. To get the maximum benefit out of an SCM implementation, the system should be built around the software development process and organizational procedures followed by the organization. Better integration of the SCM system with the software development and maintenance process will result in high-quality products, reduction in number of defects, faster bug fixes, quicker incorporation of enhancements, and better customer service, which leads to improved customer satisfaction and goodwill. This will result in satisfied customers and improved brand image, which will lead to an increase in market share and profits.

Each of these objectives can be rated on a scale from low to high. Interrelationships exist between the different objectives. For example, companies that attempt to install an SCM system with low resources, high complexity, and at high speed would place themselves at high risk. Readjusting risk to a low value would cause other objectives to change their value based on other factors such as complexity. In addition to the interrelationships, various dependencies exist between the objectives. A good example of such a dependency is between speed and risk of the SCM implementation. A quickly implemented SCM system tends to be at higher risk than one implemented at a slower pace, taking the necessary precautions. When deciding on an SCM implementation plan, the various objectives, their interrelationships, and dependencies should be taken into consideration.

6.3 Different phases of SCM implementation

Like any project, SCM implementation goes through different phases. These phases are not clearly delineated, and in many cases one phase will start before the previous one is completed, but a logical order is followed. The logical order is the order in which the phases are listed. As mentioned, some overlap occurs between the phases, but the third phase cannot start before the second phase and so on. There are two ways to implement an SCM system in an organization: company-wide implementation (also known as the big-bang approach) and project-by-project implementation (incremental approach). Irrespective of whether an organization chooses the big-bang approach or incremental approach, the SCM implementation phases described in the next sections will have to be completed for each project because each project has its own peculiarities and needs. The advantage of the big-bang approach over the incremental approach is that many phases, such as training, tool selection, and tool implementation, could be done for all projects simultaneously, which can result in a reduction of the training and implementation expenses.

Do not confuse SCM implementation to the installation of the SCM tool. The SCM tool used for each project can be the same, but it does not need to be. Usually when an organization chooses an enterprise-wide configuration management (ECM) tool, all of the projects in the organization will use the same tool, but that may not always be the case. In such cases, tool implementation will be done only once, and as and when new projects are started, depending on the specific requirements of the project, the controlled libraries, workspaces, and so on are allocated.

One thing that should be remembered is that the SCM system is unique for each project; the phases described in this section will have to be repeated for each project (with perhaps the exception of tool installation). As time goes on and as most of the employees get trained in the SCM basics and SCM tool, the time and effort spent on training might come down, but new employees who join the organization will also have to be trained. Even in a given project, new team members need to be trained. Also, there will be product upgrades, new functionality in the new versions of the tools, new policies, new standards, regulations, and other changes. All of these changes will require training the employees who have already undergone the training. So as more employees get trained in SCM, the cost of training will come down, but training activities will have to be continued; training is a never-ending process. SCM tools will last several years and for many projects. The tools will be retired only when they become obsolete. More about this topic is given in the later section on SCM tool retirement.

One other thing that should be remembered is that each of the following phases discussed consists of many subphases or events. These events are discussed in later chapters. Some of these events are needs (requirements) analysis, request for information (RFI) and general research, ROI analysis, request for proposal (RFP), reference site examinations, hardware sizing, vendor site surveys, SCM tool selection, contract negotiations, customization decisions, documentation, end-user training, audits, performance measurements, and ongoing education and maintenance. Note that not all of the phases discussed in this chapter will be applicable in all cases. For example, in a small project for which a single person is responsible for SCM, there will not be an SCM team and SCM team training; or if the organization has already identified an SCM tool, then the preselection screening and tool evaluation phases (part of SCM system design) are not required.

The different phases of the SCM implementation are listed here and also illustrated in Figure 6.1:

1. SCM system design;

2. SCM plan preparation;

3. SCM team organization;

4. SCM infrastructure setup;

5. SCM team training;

6. Project team training;

7. SCM system implementation;

8. SCM system operation and maintenance (configuration identification, configuration control, configuration status accounting, and configuration audits);

9. Records retention;

10. SCM system retirement

The initial phases—from SCM system design up to SCM infrastructure setup—are performed by the SCM system design team with the help and support of company management. SCM team training is done jointly by the SCM design team and SCM experts (outside consultants or in-house experts). If SCM tools are used, then the training on those tools is given by the tool vendor's representatives or in-house tool experts.

The project team members are trained by the SCM team members, the design team members, the tool vendor's representatives, and the SCM experts. Here the role of the SCM experts and the SCM system design team members is to develop a loyalty among the employees for SCM. Because these people will be senior in the organizational hierarchy and have the necessary stature, they can convince people better than the SCM team members. So these top-level people should give their support, pledge their allegiance, and give an overview of SCM and its benefits to the employees. Training on the details and the day-to-day operational formalities can be handled by the SCM team members. The support and encouragement of top management and the full cooperation of all people involved are essential factors in the successful implementation and smooth functioning of any SCM system.

A question that naturally arises is that of how SCM team members and project team members can be trained on the SCM system before the system is implemented. That is, how can someone be trained on something that does not exist? Actually, the system exists, but it has yet to be implemented. The SCM system is designed, procedures are documented and defined in the SCM plan, and the tools that are going to be used are selected, purchased, and put in place. The SCM team and project team training takes place so that people can use the systems properly. So the main objective of the training is to establish the best practices and to convince users about the need for, importance of, and benefits of the SCM system—the one they are going to use.

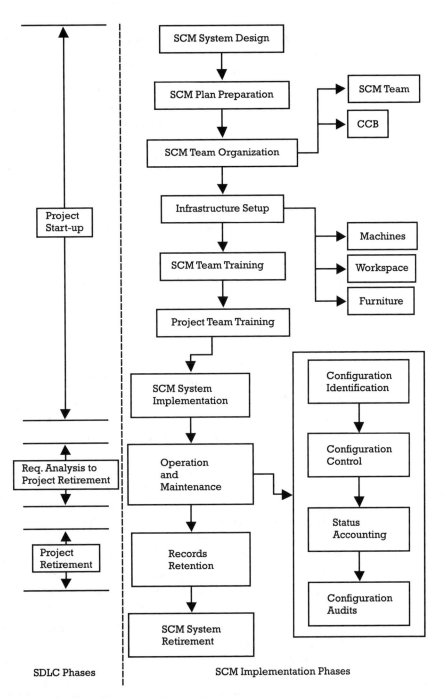

Figure 6.1   Different phases of SCM implementation.

The SCM system implementation phase involves the installation of the SCM tools and assigning duties and responsibilities. Once the tool and the necessary procedures are in place, the SCM team, developers, QA personnel, and other parties who will be using the system will use the system under the supervision of the consultants and tool vendor's representatives to iron out any problems that might arise and also to fine-tune the system. Once the problems are identified and solved and the system starts working smoothly, and the employees become confident about running the system, it is handed over to the employees. From this point onward, the operation and maintenance phase starts and will last until the system is retired.

Although the SCM implementation phases may seem linear and distinct from each other, in reality, throughout an actual implementation, the phases are fluid. In addition, the phases are repeated. For example, even the SCM plan can undergo changes. So if it is perceived that the current system needs changes, the changes are incorporated into the SCM plan, and if that change necessitates training, then that is done. Everyone involved in the SCM process is informed about the changes made to the SCM plan. The change management procedures are repeated many times—every time a change request is initiated. Status accounting, the function that records the happenings and reports the information, is a routine task. SCM audits and reviews are also done often depending on the criteria specified in the SCM plan.

We now look at each phase in some detail.

6.3.1   SCM system design

Once project management or company management decides to support SCM, the SCM system must be designed. If the company already practices SCM and already has guidelines, then the job is easy. The job of the designers is to tailor the company guidelines to suit the needs of the particular project.

Here one important thing to remember is that no two projects are the same. So even if the guidelines are taken from similar projects, it is necessary to customize them to suit the needs of the current project. The standards and guidelines must be customized depending on the nature of the project: some portions might need to be modified, some project-specific things might need to be added, and unwanted portions might need to be deleted. For example, if the guidelines talk about subcontractor control and the current project does not have any subcontracted items, then that section can be deleted.

The SCM system design team should include the project manager, the SCM team leader, and key personnel from the project team, QA department, andother areas. It is not a good idea to have too many people on the design team because this will only result in lowering the team's productivity. The responsibilities of the SCM design team include (but are not limited to):

- Developing the SCM system;

- Customizing the SCM system (if guidelines already exists);

- Preparing the SCM plan;

- Maintaining the SCM plan;

- Selecting the SCM team;

- Determining the constitution of the change control board (CCB).

If the company does not have any guidelines for the development of an SCM system, then SCM standards can be used, as discussed in Chapter 12. The design team defines the scope of the SCM system, what activities it will perform, how they will be performed, which activities will be automated, what tools will be used, what method will be used for version numbering, and how release management will be accomplished, among other tasks.

The SCM system design team also determines whether to use a manual system or tools, whether to make tools or buy them, and so on. If the decision is made to buy tools, then the team will evaluate the tools available in the market and select the tool that is best suited to the company's needs.

The team also decides the composition of the SCM team. Team size varies depending on the nature and size of the project. Large projects will have a full-fledged team with many people, whereas a small project may have a team a single person or a person working part-time. The design team also determines the constitution of the change control board (CCB) and defines guidelines for its functioning.

Once all issues regarding the SCM system have been finalized, the details are documented. This document is called the SCM plan.

6.3.2 SCM plan preparation

As we have seen, the SCM system design team decides on the particulars of the SCM system to be used. Once the system details are finalized, the decisions and procedures have to be documented. This document is called the SCM plan. The idea behind the SCM plan is to ensure that all SCM team members and the project team are aware of the procedures and the duties and responsibilities that each individual is supposed to carry out. The plan will also tell team members what resources are to be used and how they are to be used. It acts as a guideline in the resolution of conflicts. According to the IEEE [1], the SCM plan should contain the following sections: Introduction, Management, Activities, Schedules, Resources, and Plan Maintenance. We were introduced to SCM plans in Chapter 1, and we will look at them again in more detail in Chapter 15.

The SCM design team will prepare the plan and distribute it among the members. This document forms the basis for SCM training. The plan also contains a section that lists the procedures required to keep it up-to-date. So the plan is constantly reviewed and any required changes are made to it.

The SCM plan is also placed under configuration control, which happens once the plan is finalized, reviewed, and approved. It usually forms part of the functional baseline because the SCM plan is usually created during or before the requirements phase. So once a baseline is established for the SCM plan, all changes to the plan will have to be made in accordance with change management procedures.

6.3.3 SCM team organization

As we have seen, the SCM team size can vary from a single person to a full-fledged team depending on the many variables that can influence the project. The SCM system design team selects the members of the SCM team and allocates responsibilities to each member.

The constitution of the CCB and its workings are also finalized. The CCB usually consists of the SCM team leader and one or two key team members in addition to the project team leader, QA representative, marketing team representative, and in some cases the client representatives.

6.3.4 SCM infrastructure setup

While the SCM team is formed and responsibilities are assigned, the infrastructure facilities that will help the team function properly must also be arranged. The SCM is not a one-week or one-month affair. It is a continuous function that will be there for the entire life cycle of the project. So the SCM team needs permanent facilities, not some makeshift arrangements. But this determination will ultimately depend on the size of the project and SCM team. Ideally, the SCM team should have a separate office that is close to the project with which it is associated. This type of setup is required for manual SCM systems in fairly large projects.

Today, with most companies using SCM tools and as more SCM functions are automated, SCM tools give a lot of power and capabilities to the development team. But keep in mind that the SCM tools have become more complex and sophisticated. Their capabilities are no longer limited to change management, defect tracking, or source code control. They perform additional tasks such as automatic status journaling and status accounting, branching and interactive merging, and automatic checkout and check-in. The additional functionality and capabilities of the new-generation SCM tools have resulted in the need for highly specialized personnel (e.g., SCM administrators, database administrators, build and release managers) to operate and maintain the system. So in today's scenario, the SCM team consists of highly specialized personnel who devote their full time in managing and maintaining the SCM system.

6.3.5 SCM team training

The SCM team members may be veterans with many SCM projects under their belts or they may be fresh faces who do not have any idea about what

SCM is. The idea behind SCM team training is to familiarize the team members with the discipline of SCM and train them regarding how it is going to be practiced in a particular project.

The team members are trained on how to carry out their duties and responsibilities in the most efficient and effective manner and told what they are supposed to do and what they are not supposed to do. If SCM tools are being used in the project, then the team members are also given training on the tools. They are also briefed about their access privileges and rights. Because the configuration management process is a job that involves a lot of tact and diplomacy, in the author's opinion the training should also have a module on effective communication.

As mentioned in the previous section, the increasing popularity of SCM tools and the level of automation that is being achieved by these tools have reduced the role of the SCM team. In a manual SCM system, in which all SCM functions used to be carried out manually, full-fledged SCM teams were required, but today, with the high degree of automation and more capabilities and responsibilities being given to the development team members, the number of tasks that need to be performed by SCM team members has been reduced considerably.

6.3.6   Project team training

The success of an SCM system depends on the participation and cooperation of the project team members and on the understanding and dedication of the SCM team. So training of the project team members about the fundamentals of SCM, its concepts, advantages, and benefits, is necessary. Also, project team members should be briefed about how they are to participate in the SCM functions and carry out the SCM activities. If the project uses automated tools for change management, problem reporting and tracking, and so on, then the project team members should be trained in how to use those tools.

Both the SCM team training and the project team training are continuous activities, and provisions should be made to keep it that way. Training never ends; it is an ongoing process because new people will join both the teams and existing members will leave. So the new members need to be trained, possibly by an outgoing member or some other person designated by the project management. The training of both of these teams is based on the foundation detailed in the SCM plan. The SCM plan contains the details of how SCM is to be practiced for the particular project, and all training activities should be based on that.

6.3.7   SCM system implementation

This phase involves the installation of the SCM tools and assigning duties and responsibilities for the tool administrators and users. Once the tool and the necessary procedures are in place, the SCM team, developers, QA personnel, and other parties who will be using the system will do so under the supervision of the consultants and tool vendor's representatives. These external consultants and vendor representatives will help the employees learn how to properly use the installed SCM tool. The SCM administrator needs to set up the databases, workspaces, and libraries and should configure the tool for the organization or project. The vendor representatives will guide the administrator in this process and help him or her in understanding the intricacies of the tool. They will also give the administrator training on how to scale the different parameters as the project and team size increases. The consultants and vendor representatives will also help customize the tool to suit the organization's development processes and procedures. Once management and employees become confident about independently operating and maintaining the SCM system, the services of the consultants and the on-site presence of the vendor representatives are terminated, and the system is handed over to the employees.

6.3.8   SCM system operation and maintenance

After the external consultants and the tool vendor representatives leave, handing over the system to in-house personnel, the responsibility of managing and maintaining the system will fall on all users of the system. During this phase, the major SCM activities—configuration identification, configuration control, status accounting, and configuration audits—are performed. These four activities, or phases, form the core of the SCM activities and are discussed in detail in Chapters 7 through 10.

The SCM tool administrator will be responsible for the regular upkeep and trouble-free operation of the system, allocation of disk space, management of the controlled libraries, and other tasks. The SCM system administrator will also be in constant touch with the tool vendor, so that any new upgrades or patches that are released can be installed without delay. The SCM team members, if any, will be responsible for managing the day-to-day SCM activities such as change request processing, arranging reviews and audits, check-in and checkout, build and release management, and so on. The developers, testers, and other support personnel will follow the guidelines provided for carrying out the different operations such as initiating change requests, making changes, performing impact analysis, and conducting audits. The project managers will use the system's querying and reporting capabilities for project monitoring and tracking. During this phase, the SCM system will produce dramatic improvements in development productivity, product quality, and also on the organization's capability to react to change.

6.3.9   Records retention

Before retiring the project or software system, the documents that are records of the SCM system must be archived, retained, or destroyed. The SCM system will have accumulated a lot of documentation and records during the lifetime of the project. With the passage of time, the information contained in the documents will decline in value. These records are removed from active accessibility. Depending on the nature of the record, it is destroyed immediately upon deactivation or kept for a defined period. The documents that do not have any value once the project is retired are disposed of. The documents that have some value either for legal or contractual obligations are kept for the period specified by the law or contract. The documents that have a sustaining utility exceeding storage costs are preserved permanently in an archive.

6.3.10   SCM system retirement

The final phase in the life cycle of an SCM system is retirement. During the time of the retirement phase of the project, the SCM system for that project is also retired. Once the record retention and archival is completed, the SCM team members assigned to the project are released for other projects.

6.4   SCM tool retirement

Modern SCM systems use SCM tools to perform SCM activities. SCM tools support many projects and last several years. During this period, the tool is upgraded as and when the tool vendor releases a new version. After many years of service, a stage is reached when any further maintenance would not be cost effective. This could happen because the size, nature, and complexity of the projects have increased or because new tools that offer considerably more advantages (e.g., higher level of automation, smaller SCM teams, increased functionality) have come into the market that makes the current tool obsolete.

Another reason for retiring an SCM tool is that technological advances have made the existing tool obsolete. The hardware on which the tool runs has to be replaced by a different (more powerful and less expensive) machine with a different operating system, and it is cheaper to install a new tool rather than upgrading or modifying the existing one. In each of these instances, the existing tool is retired and a new one is installed in its place.

6.5   Why do many SCM implementations fail?

We have seen the different objectives, phases, and strategies for implementing an SCM system. Yet many SCM implementations fail miserably during the initial stages of the operational phase or fail to deliver the promised benefits. Why does this happen? Some of the most common reasons are:

  ‣ Lack of top management buy-in, commitment, and support;

  ‣ Improper planning and budgeting;

  ‣ Use of the wrong SCM tool;

> ● Lack of training;

> ● Work culture of the organization.

6.5.1   Lack of top management buy-in, commitment, and support

One of the most common reasons for a failed implementation is lack of top management support and backing. The top management must be clearly convinced about the importance of SCM, how SCM could be used as a competitive weapon, and how the company can fail if a scientific mechanism such as SCM is not available to manage and control change. If management is aware of the potential benefits of SCM and the dangers of not having an SCM system, it will give the full backing and necessary organizational resources to implement the best SCM system possible. When the employees know that the SCM implementation has full management backing, they will also want the system to succeed. There will be a lot of issues such as change of procedures, reassignment of employees, and others when the SCM system is implemented. If management can assure employees that their jobs are secure, that assurance will go a long way toward ensuring employee cooperation. The top managers should also talk to employees regarding the benefits of the SCM system and how the company can get ahead of the competition by reaping the benefits of the system.

6.5.2   Improper planning and budgeting

Before starting the SCM implementation project, detailed planning involving all of the major stakeholders is necessary for the success of the project. During this phase, decisions are made regarding procedures to be followed, tools to be bought, the budget to be allocated for implementation and maintenance, and other issues. If this planning is not done properly, factors will likely be overlooked, resulting in selecting the wrong tool, insufficient funds, inadequate team members, and other problems. All of these problems can lead to the failure of the project. In order to avoid this situation, the planning phase should be taken seriously, and meticulous research should be conducted before taking any action. Also, there should be a provision in the plan to revise and update it as the implementation progresses.

6.5.3   Use of the wrong SCM tool

We have seen that no two organizations are the same and that each organization requires an SCM tool that is best suited for its organizational environment, work culture, and development procedures. So the SCM planning team should take into account all of these factors before deciding on a tool. The team should research the available tools, match them with the organization's requirements, visit companies where the tools are installed to see them in action, and discuss end-user training, tool updates, and upgrades. Only when all team members are convinced that a specific tool is best suited for the organization, should the purchasing decision be made. Never rush the purchasing decision because the time spent on researching and analyzing before the purchase is worth the effort.

6.5.4 Lack of training

One of the main reasons the SCM fails is from the resistance of the users. The resistance is often the result of ignorance and fear—ignorance about the tool and fear of additional work or unemployment. These factors can be corrected by giving proper training. Training should be given at different levels on different aspects of the SCM implementation. The top management should address the employees' fear of losing their jobs as many tasks get automated by the tool. They should also pledge their allegiance to the SCM system and make it clear to employees that the SCM system is essential for the success of the organization in this highly competitive business environment. The SCM team members, tool vendors, and external consultants should explain the principles of configuration management, the advantages on a day-to-day basis, how it reduces rework and defects, and other benefits. Most users think of SCM as a system that creates more paperwork or documentation. Such myths about SCM should be debunked. The SCM tool vendors and external consultants, along with the in-house experts, should train users in how to efficiently use the tool and should explain to them how the SCM tools make their lives easier and help them create high-quality products without chaos and confusion. Once the users are convinced about the potential of the SCM system, the system will succeed; without user buy-in, even the best SCM system will fail.

6.5.5 Work culture of the organization

The work culture of the organization is important for the success of SCM. If the organization has a workforce that is willing to learn new things and change to new technologies, then there will be no problems for SCM implementation. But if employees resist change and see the introduction of formal methods as a means to assign accountability, they will perceive the new technology negatively. So the basic mindset of the workforce needs to be changed. This is important not only for the success of SCM, but also for the success of process improvement initiatives such as CMM, SPICE, BOOTSTRAP, and others. In changing the employee mindset, the two critical factors required are top management support and proper training.

6.6 Summary

SCM implementation needs to change the way people have been doing things, and lots of procedures are introduced for the functioning of SCM. Resistance to SCM implementation is natural, because it is human nature to resist change. Making people accept SCM and implementing it is difficult because of the myths surrounding SCM, such as SCM causing additional work and more documentation.

Most people are not aware of the potential benefits of SCM. For the SCM system to succeed and deliver those benefits, the organization has to design a good system, install procedures, and train the SCM team and project team. Once these tasks are done, there is a natural tendency to feel satisfied or complacent about what has been achieved by the implementation team. One important factor that should be kept in mind is that the postimplementation phase is critical. SCM functions are continuous and should be performed throughout the project life cycle. To reap the full benefits of the SCM system, the system should get project-wide/company-wide acceptance. To get project-wide acceptance for the SCM system, every member of the project should be made aware of the need, importance, and benefits of SCM.

Just as courtships and honeymoons are different from marriages, living with an SCM system is different from installing it. Implementing a good SCM system is not an easy job, but how the projects mesh with the SCM system determines the value that is received from it. How the SCM system is used in the project makes the difference. Even a well-designed system can be a failure if the people using it are not receptive and cooperative.

Reference

[1]   IEEE Standard for Software Configuration Management Plans (IEEE Std-828–1990), *IEEE Software Engineering Standards Collection 2003* (CD-ROM Edition), Piscataway, NJ: IEEE, 2003.

Selected bibliography

Fredrick, C. R., "Project Implementation of Software Configuration Management," *Proc. 1981 ACM Workshop/Symposium on Measurement and Evaluation of Software Quality, University of Maryland, MD,* ACM Press, NY: 1981, pp. 49–56.

Wingerd, L., and Seiwald, C., "High-level Best Practices in Software Configuration Management," Technical Report, Perforce Software (www.perforce.com/perforce/bestpractices.html).

Contents

Configuration identification

7.1 Introduction

Configuration identification is the basis for subsequent control of the software configuration. The software configuration identification activity identifies items to be controlled, establishes identification schemes for the items and their versions, and establishes the tools and techniques to be used in acquiring and managing controlled items. These activities provide the basis for the other SCM activities [1].

The configuration identification process involves the selection, designation, and description of the software configuration items. *Selection* involves grouping software into configuration items that are subject to configuration management. *Designation* is developing a numbering and/or naming scheme that correlates the software components and their associated documentation. *Description* is documenting the functional, performance, and physical characteristics for each of the software components.

IEEE [2] defines configuration identification as an element of configuration management, consisting of selecting the configuration items for a system and recording their functional and physical characteristics in technical documentation. In other words, configuration identification is the process whereby a system is separated into uniquely identifiable components for the purpose of SCM. This is the first major SCM function that has to be started in a project (the design of the SCM system and the preparation of the SCM plan are done before configuration identification begins). Effective configuration identification is a prerequisite for other SCM activities, all of which use the products of configuration identification.

The software under control is usually divided into configuration items (CIs), also known as computer software configuration items (CSCIs). A CI is an aggregation of software that is designated for configuration management and is treated as a single entity in the SCM process. In other words, CI is the term used for each of the logically related components that make up some discrete element of software. A variety of items, in addition to the code, are controlled by SCM. Software items with the potential to become CIs include plans, specifications and design documentation, testing materials, software tools, source and executable code, code libraries, data and data dictionaries, and documentation for installation, maintenance, operations, and software use. For example, if a system contains several programs, each program and its related documentation and data might be designated a CI. Determining what characteristics must be captured so that the properties and requirements of the product are correctly reflected is an important decision.

The configuration identification process should capture all characteristics of the software to be controlled: its content, the content of documents that describe it, the different versions as the contents are changed, data needed for operation of the software, and any other essential elements or characteristics that make the software what it is. A CI can contain other CIs, and these are sometimes referred to as computer software components (CSCs) and computer software units (CSUs). A CSC is a functional or logically distinct part of a computer software configuration item. CSCs may be top-level (TLCSCs) or lower-level (LLCSCs). A CSU is the smallest logical entity or the actual physical entity of the system.

The software product shall be organized as one or more CSCIs. Each CSCI is part of a system, subsystem, or prime item and shall consist of one or more TLCSCs. Each TLCSC shall consist of LLCSCs or CSUs. LLCSCs may consist of other LLCSCS or CSUs. TLCSCs and LLCSCs are logical groupings. CSUs are the smallest logical entities, and the actual physical entities implemented in code. The static structure of CSCIs, TLCSCs, LLCSCs, and CSUs shall form a hierarchical structure, as illustrated in Figure 7.1. The hierarchical structure shall uniquely identify all CSCIs, TLCSCs, LLCSCs, and CSUs.

To accomplish configuration identification, the following steps are performed:

1. Develop the criteria for selecting items to be placed under configuration control.

2. Select CIs and define the relationships between the CIs.

3. Establish a software item hierarchy (structure and elements of the complete software system) and define the interrelationships between the CIs. The structural relationships among the selected CIs, and their constituent parts, affect other SCM activities or tasks, such as software building or analyzing the impact of proposed changes. Proper tracking of these relationships is also important for supporting traceability verifications.

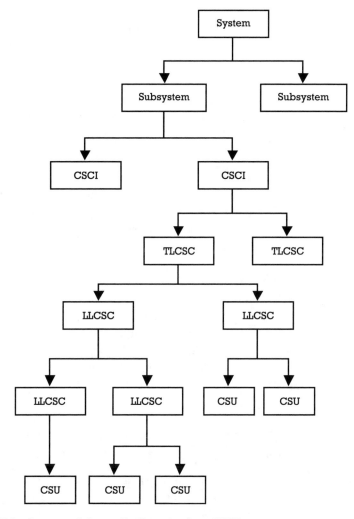

Figure 7.1 Computer Software Configuration Item (CSCI) structure.

4. Develop an identification or naming scheme for clearly and unambiguously identifying the CIs.

5. Select configuration documentation to be used to define configuration baselines for each CI.

6. Establish a release/version management system for configuration documentation.

7. Define and document interfaces to and between CIs.

8. Define and establish baselines to be used.

9. Establish the procedure for a baseline's acquisition of the items.

10. Assign identifiers to CIs and their associated configuration documentation, including version numbers where appropriate.

11. Ensure that the marking or labeling of items and documentation with their applicable identifiers enable correlation between the CI, and other associated data. The documents that capture the functional and physical characteristics of the CI and the corresponding documentation will become part of the CI. The naming of those items should be consistent with that of the CI for easy association. For example, if the name of the documentation for a program PGM_XYZ is DOC_XYZ, it will help in better correlation.

12. Ensure that applicable identifiers are embedded in the software and on its storage media. For example, the source code of the program named PGM_XYZ can contain the name PGM_XYZ. (Consider a COBOL program named PGM_XYZ; here the program name can be embedded in the source code as PROGRAM ID in the IDENTIFICATION DIVISION.)

There are no hard-and-fast rules as to the order in which these steps should be performed. It depends on the organization, project, and the SCM system designers and implementers.

EIA-649 [3] identifies configuration identification as the basis from which the configuration of products are defined and verified; products and documents are labeled; changes are managed; and accountability is maintained. The purpose and benefits of configuration identification include the following:

> Selection of products based on functionality, verifiability, supportability, complexity, risk, and management activity;

> Determination of the structure (hierarchy) of a product and the organization and relationships of its configuration documentation and other product information;

> Documentation of the performance, interface, and other attributes of a product;

> Determination of the appropriate level of identification marking of product and documentation;

> Capability to provide a unique identity to a product or to a component part of a product;

> Ability to give a unique identity to the technical documents describing a product;

> Modification of the identification of a product and documents to reflect incorporation of major changes;

> Maintaining release control of documents for baseline management;

> Enabling a user or a service person to distinguish between product versions;

- Enabling a user or a service person to correlate a product to related user or maintenance instructions;

- Facilitating management of information, including that in digital format;

- Correlating individual product units to warranties and service life obligations;

- Enabling correlation of document revision level to product version/ configuration;

- Providing a reference point for defining changes and corrective actions.

7.2   Impact of configuration item selection

Selecting CIs is an important process that must achieve a balance between providing adequate visibility for project control purposes and providing a manageable number of controlled items. Poor CI selection can adversely affect costs, and scheduling and can become an unnecessary administrative and technical burden during and after software development. The number of CIs in a system is a design decision—a decision made by the people who design the SCM system. They are the people who decide which items should be brought under configuration control.

This process should be done carefully, because the selection of CIs needs to be correct: You should not select more nor less than what is necessary. But with the introduction of SCM tools, this issue—the number of CIs—is not very important. Modern tools can efficiently and effortlessly handle any number of CIs without any problems. But the tools can only reduce the workload of managing the CIs; other problems such as reduced visibility, too much documentation, or inefficient design cannot be solved by the tools. Hence the selection of the CIs is still important. Technology can only help in automating processes, performing repetitive and monotonous tasks, and reducing the workload of managing the CIs, but when it comes to the question of what items should be made into CIs, it is still a management decision based on experience and judgment—one that can only be made by a person or group of persons who have the required knowledge about the project and relevant experience and expertise.

7.2.1   Effects of selecting too many configuration items

Selection of too many CIs may result in hampered visibility and management rather than providing improved control. Instances of such difficulties can include the following:

- *Increased administrative burden* in preparing, processing, and reporting changes, which tends to be proportional to the number of CIs;

▸ *Increased development time and cost,* as well as potential creation of an inefficient design. When there are too many CIs, the documentation and other procedures increase and take valuable time that could be devoted to design and development. So too many CIs will result in increased development time, and once the concentration is shifted from design and development to maintaining the SCM records, the chances of creating an inefficient design arise.

▸ *Potential increase in management effort,* difficulties maintaining coordination, and unnecessary generation of requirements, design, test, and system specifications for each selected CI.

7.2.2   Effects of selecting too few configuration items

Too few CIs can result in costly logistics and maintenance difficulties, such as these:

▸ *Loss of visibility down to the required level to effect maintenance or modification.* For example, if CIs are chosen only at the module level, then maintaining a function in that module will be difficult, because finding the subroutine will be difficult as there will not be any records in that name. Because the CIs are defined only at the module level, only the modules will be visible.

▸ *Difficulty in effectively managing the changes* (e.g., managing changes to individual items, which are part of a CI). If there are too few CIs, say, only at the module level, then check-in/checkout and change implementation will be difficult because checkout happens at the CI level, and a lot of unwanted items will also need to be checked out, tested, verified, and checked back in.

7.3   Baselines

As the CIs go through their development process, more components are developed until the final CIs are available for use. Generally, the life cycle process will first result in a set of requirements, then a design, then code for individual elements of the CI, and then integrated code with test cases and user manuals. The definition of SCM contains the concept of identifying the configuration of each CI at discrete points in time during the life cycle process, and then managing changes to those identified configurations.

The configuration of software at a discrete point in time is known as a *baseline.* Thus, a baseline is the documentation and software that make up a CI at a given point in its life cycle. It includes the user documentation (if any), the specifications document (or the document that contains the functional and physical characteristics), and software (if any) that make up the CI at a given point. Each baseline serves as a point of departure or reference for the next development stage. Baselines are usually established after each life cycle phase at the completion of the formal review that ends the phase. Thus we have the requirements baseline, design baseline, product baseline, and so on. We saw an overview of this topic in Chapter 2, which was summarized in Figure 2.1.

Each baseline is subject to configuration control and must be formally updated (using the change management procedures) to reflect approved changes to the CI as it goes through the next development stage. A baseline, together with all approved changes to the baseline, represents the current approved configuration. At the end of a life cycle phase, the previous baseline and all approved changes to it become the new baseline for the next development stage. The term *baseline management* is often used to describe this control process. Baseline management is the discipline of controlling a series of baselines as they evolve and are then merged into the next baseline to be defined. The SCM system provides the policies, procedures, and tools for exercising baseline management [4].

Baselines are established and placed under configuration management when it makes good management sense to start controlling subsequent changes to the CIs. When to start baselining is a management decision. Establishing a baseline does not mean that the software development is brought to a halt; it only means that subsequent changes to the CIs will be subject to formal change management procedures. Normally, the first baseline consists of an approved software requirements document and is known as the requirements baseline. The requirements baseline is the initial approved technical documentation for a CI [2]. The requirements baseline contains the details regarding what the system or software must accomplish. Through the process of establishing a baseline, the requirements and other requirements described in the requirements document become the explicit point of departure for software design. The requirements baseline is usually the first established baseline in the SCM process. When the requirements baseline is established at the conclusion of the requirements analysis phase of a project, the formal change control process commences. The requirements baseline is also the basis against which the software is authenticated.

The design baseline is the initial approved specifications governing the development of CIs that are part of a higher-level CI [5]. The design baseline represents the next logical progression from the requirements baseline and the link between the design process and the development process. The requirements baseline describes the functions that the system should have. Then the software system is designed by allocating the various functions to various components or subsystems.

Based on the RDD (part of the requirements baseline), the different functions of the software product are determined, and during the design process these various functions—user interfaces, database operations, error handling, input data validation—are allocated to the various subsystems and components. This allocation of the different functionality happens during the design phase, and at the end of the design phase, the design baseline is established where the system components would have their functionality assigned to them. So at the design baseline stage, the functionality or requirements defined in the requirements baseline is allotted to CIs in the form of design documentation (high level and low level), which is now managed within the design baseline.

The product baseline corresponds to the completed software product delivered for system integration. The product baseline represents the technical and support documentation established after successful completion of the functional configuration audit and physical configuration audit. The product baseline [6] is the initial approved technical documentation (including source code, object code, and other deliverables) defining a CI during the production, operation, maintenance, and logistic support of its life cycle. The product baseline is sometimes known as the *deliverables baseline*.

According to Ben-Menachem [4], the process of establishing baselines describes the construction of the aggregates (the software system) from the components (the CIs). So the baselines also define how the aggregates must be constructed, what tools should be used, which parts are connected and which are not, what the nature of these interconnections is, and other factors. As mentioned before, once the item is tied to a baseline, changes can be made only through the formal change management process. Thus baselines define the state of a system at a given point in time, and the proper recording of this information is critical for the success of any project.

7.4   Configuration item selection

A software system is generally split into several CIs that are independently developed and tested and then finally put together at the software system integration level. Each CI essentially becomes an independent entity as far as the SCM system is concerned, and the SCM functions are carried out on each CI. The division of the software into CIs may be contractually specified or may be done during the requirements analysis or preliminary design phase. As a general rule, a CI is established for a separable piece of the software system that can be designed, implemented, and tested independently. Some examples of items that are to be identified include project plan, requirements specifications, design documents, test plans and test data, program source codes, data, object code, executables, EPROMS, media, make files, tools, user documentation, quality manual, and SCM plan.

CI selection is not an easy process because there are no hard-and-fast rules to guide it. The selection process should involve all of the major stakeholders of the project, such as company management, the software team leader, SCM administrator or manager, QA representative, testers, maintenance and support team members (if identified), and client representatives.

7.4.1   Checklist for selection of configuration items

When a software project or system is broken down into components (the structural decomposition), we can create a sort of tree structure. The decomposition can be, say, project–modules–submodules–programs–functions–link libraries–icons and other small minor components and so on. Decomposition to this detail is neither necessary nor advisable because it creates many problems in managing the CIs and too many specifications and documentation. But if we reduce the number of CIs by limiting the system decomposition to, say, the second level (module level), it will result in poor visibility of the overall design and development requirements.

The number of CIs is determined by the system granularity desired by the SCM system's designers. The granularity decides the level of decomposition of the software system. There are no hard-and-fast rules here either. This decision varies from project to project and should be made by the SCM system development team.

We have seen that there are no hard-and-fast rules when choosing CIs, but the following questions can be used as a guide when doing so:

1. Is the item critical/high risk and/or a safety item?

2. Is the item to be used in several places?

3. Will the item be reused or designated for reuse?

4. Is the system already a CI? Is the item borrowed from some other project or system?

5. Would the item's failure or malfunction adversely affect security, human safety, or the accomplishment of a mission, or have significant financial implications?

6. Is the item individual and can it be designed, developed, tested, and maintained as a stand-alone unit?

7. Is the item newly developed? For example, a system or subsystem might be developed to add certain requested enhancements.

8. Will the item be maintained by diverse groups at multiple locations?

9. Does the item incorporate new technologies?

10. Is the item purchased off-the-shelf—commercial-off-the-shelf (COTS)?

11. Is the item supplied or developed by a subcontractor?

12. Is the item highly complex or does it have stringent performance requirements? For instance, does the item have complicated algorithms or does it need to meet a stringent performance requirement such as having a small footprint?

13. Does the item encapsulate interfaces with other software items that currently exist or are provided by other organizations?

14. Is the item installed on a different computer platform from other parts of the system?

15. Does the item interface with other CIs whose configuration is controlled by other entities (e.g., a system that interfaces with an off-the-shelf package)?

16. Is the item likely to be subject to modification or upgrading during its service life? Is the item subject to modification at a rate that is much higher than that of the other items? For example, consider an interface that reads data from some external source. Every time the external source changes (assuming that data formats will be subject to frequent changes), the item has to be modified.

17. Is there a requirement to know the exact configuration and status of changes made to an item during its service life? This refers to the criticality of the item. Some items in a system are critical or more important than others, so project management will necessarily be more interested in those types of items.

18. Is the size of the item manageable? Can it be produced by a small but efficient development team within a reasonable time? If not, should it become two items instead of one?

If most of these questions can be answered "No," the item should probably not be a CI. If most of these questions can be answered "Yes," the item should probably be a CI. But there are no hard-and-fast rules and no magic formulas to help in CI selection. The bottom line is that selection of CIs is a management decision based on experience and good judgment.

7.5   Designation: Naming of configuration items

Each software component must be uniquely identified. According to IEEE [3], the identification methods could include naming conventions and version numbers and letters. The identification system or the naming convention should facilitate the storage, retrieval, tracking, reproduction, and distribution of the CIs. A good naming system will make it possible to understand the relationship between the CIs from their names.

A good naming system uses numbers or alphabets to represent the position of the CI in the hierarchy. For example, an item labeled 1.4 is definitely created after an item with the label 1.2 and before one with the label 1.6. Note that the number is only a part of the name: the time-related part that changes when the item undergoes revisions. The other part of the name, which defines the item, is usually derived from the project or system and the type of the item and the item name. It can be a simple name such as "PGMPAY," indicating that it is the payroll calculation program named PGMPAY, or it can be a composite name such as "PRJ_MOD_PGM_SRC_PGMPAY," indicating the project, module, CI type, and name. The decision about the complexity and detail of the names will depend on the size and complexity of the project.

One important thing to remember is that the naming system should be developed so that the derived names do not produce duplicates, because this can create chaos and confusion. For large and complex projects that have thousands of CIs, the naming system is usually detailed to facilitate easy identification and tracking. As we have seen, the name part of the identification system will remain constant over time for each item, whereas the number part will undergo changes.

7.6   Configuration item description

Software components are described in specifications (i.e., software requirements specifications, software architectural design specifications, software detailed design specifications, interface control documents, and software product specifications). The description of the component becomes more detailed as the design and development proceeds through the life cycle. The description forms the basis for configuration control and configuration status accounting. The description is also the basis for the configuration audits and reviews, which ensure that the software is complete and verified. The documents or portions of documents that describe each CI must be identified and made part of the CI. The author has frequently found a document in use by several different companies (large and small) called the configuration item description (or specification). Generally, it is not much more than a listing of CIs, by configuration identifier, and an indication of the owner/ programmer, next higher CI name (parent), controlling baseline, fit into the hierarchy (CSCI, subsystem, or segment name), and perhaps some other general information. This document forms a handy reference for the CIs.

7.7   Acquisition of configuration items

The last activity of the configuration identification function is the acquisition of the CIs for configuration control. Following the acquisition of a CI, changes to the item must be formally approved as appropriate for the CI and the baseline involved, as defined in the SCM plan. This means that the CIs—both intermediate and final outputs (e.g., source code, executable, user documentation, design documents, databases, test plans, test cases, test data, project plan, SCM plan) and the elements of the environment (such as compilers, operating systems, and tools)—should be acquired and stored in a controlled environment (controlled software libraries) so they can be retrieved and reproduced when required and access can be restricted. A software library is a controlled collection of software and related documentation designed to aid in software development, use, and maintenance [4]. IEEE [6] specifies that for each such library the format, location, documentation requirements, receiving and inspection requirements, and access control procedures must be specified. Once the CIs are acquired and placed in the controlled library, as we have seen, the configuration control procedures will apply to them.

7.8 Summary

Configuration identification is the process of selecting the CIs for a system and recording their functional and physical characteristics in technical documentation. We have seen why it is important to select the CIs, how to select them, and how to establish baselines. Configuration identification is one of the important phases of SCM because it decides the level of granularity or detail to which SCM will be performed in a project.

References

[1]   Alain Abran, A., and J. W. Moore, (eds.), *SWEBOK: Guide to the Software Engineering Body of Knowledge (Trial Version)*, Los Alamitos, CA: IEEE Computer Society, 2001.

[2]   IEEE Standard Glossary of Software Engineering Terminology (IEEE Std-610–1990), *IEEE Standards Collection (Software Engineering)*, Piscataway, NJ: IEEE, 1997.

[3]   EIA, *National Consensus Standard for Configuration Management (EIA-649)*, Arlington, VA: Electronics Industries Alliance, 1998.

[4]   Marciniak, J. J. (ed.), *Encyclopedia of Software Engineering*, 2nd ed., New York: John Wiley & Sons, 2002.

[5]   Ben-Menachem, M., *Software Configuration Guidebook*, London: McGraw-Hill International, 1994.

[6]   IEEE Standard for Software Configuration Management Plans (IEEE Std-828–1998), *IEEE Standards Collection (Software Engineering)*, Piscataway, NJ: IEEE, 1998.

Selected bibliography

Berlack, H. R., *Software Configuration Management*, New York: John Wiley & Sons, 1992.

Dart, S., "Concepts in Configuration Management Systems," Technical Report, Software Engineering Institute, Carnegie-Mellon University, 1994.

Feiler, H. P., "Software Configuration Management: Advances in Software Development Environments," Technical Paper, Software Engineering Institute, Carnegie-Mellon University, 1990.

IEEE Software Engineering Standards Collection 2003 (CD-ROM Edition), Piscataway, NJ: IEEE, 2003.

Quality Management—Guidelines for Configuration Management, ISO 10007:1995(E), Geneva, Switzerland: International Standards Organization, 1995.

Magnusson, B. (ed.), *System Configuration Management: ECOOP'98 SCM-8 Symp. Proc.,* Berlin: Springer-Verlag, 1998.

CHAPTER

8

Contents

Configuration control

8.1 Introduction

IEEE [1] defines *configuration control* as an element of configuration management, consisting of the evaluation, coordination, approval or disapproval, and implementation of changes to configuration items after formal establishment of their configuration identification. So once the configuration items of a project or system have been identified, the next step is to bring in some degree of control. Restrictions have to be implemented and rules regarding who can do what to these configuration items have to be formulated. This aspect of SCM is handled by the configuration control function or the change management and control system.

Changes to all items identified in the configuration identification phase—configuration items (CIs)—should be controlled. To properly control change, procedures have to be established, guidelines have to be implemented, roles and authorities have to be defined, and all workflow processes of the change management system—change identification, change requisition, change approval/disapproval, change implementation, testing—have to be designed, documented, and implemented. How these procedures and guidelines apply to the different CIs such as source code, documents, specifications, third-party software, and subcontracted items also has to be established. These activities fall under the purview of configuration control.

Of the SCM functions, configuration control is performed most often. Configuration identification, as we saw in the previous chapter, is done only once at the beginning of the SCM implementation. Status accounting, which is the recording and reporting of the SCM activities, is done regularly. Configuration audits are performed when a configuration is complete or before a system is released. But configuration control

103

activities have to be done whenever a change request is initiated. Requests for changes will be frequent during the software development phase and after the system is released. Requests for new features, functional enhancements, and bug and defect reports can all initiate a change.

The different activities of configuration control lend themselves to automation. For example, all activities from change initiation to change disposition can be easily automated. Thus, configuration control is one SCM function that can be automated efficiently and effectively. In fact, it is imperative that one use some sort of change management tool, because except in the case of small single-person projects, change management and control is too repetitive, monotonous, and hence more prone to error and not worth the effort for manual processing. Many software tools are available, covering almost all available platforms and development environments, which can be used to automate configuration control. In fact, configuration control was one of the first functions of configuration management that was automated, which is evident from the number of change management tools available on the market.

Configuration control is not an easy task. It involves a lot of people and a lot of procedures, making it difficult to manage. The configuration control activities will increase as the project evolves, because more items will undergo change, more people will be inducted, requirements will change, new modules and subsystems will be added, different versions will have to be maintained, and so on. However, if designed intelligently, planned properly, and supported well by a good software tool, configuration control can be an easy if not exciting task.

8.2 Change

Change is one of the most fundamental characteristics in any software development process. All phases of the software development process from requirements analysis to production or maintenance are always subject to change. Making changes to software is easy. In fact, it is one of the best features of software—that it can be changed at will. But if changes are made at will, without any proper planning, chaos will result. Making changes is easy, but managing those changes—the uncontrolled changes—is not, because there is no way of knowing what was changed and hence what to manage.

Software development is a continuously evolving process. You cannot freeze one phase of software development and go to the next phase. Even though early development models such as the waterfall model were developed based on the compartmentalization of the various phases, the real-life situation is different. You cannot freeze analysis and go to design and freeze design and go to development. A great deal of overlap occurs between these phases because software development is a complex process that involves many variables, all of which can change. Changes to the requirements drive the design, and the design changes affect the code. Testing then uncovers problems that result in further changes, which might force us to return to the requirements phase. So change cannot be avoided. Managing the change process is a complex but essential task.

8.3   Proposing changes to the customer

In some instances, a change affects the customer's agreement with the developer. These changes (sometimes known as major changes) can affect the terms and conditions of a contract or purchase order related to cost, delivery schedules, or other milestone events. Other changes can affect the statement of work, specifications, or other requirement documents to which the customer has asked the developer to adhere. Thus, when these types of changes occur, a change request is prepared and submitted to the customer for approval.

Incorporation of such proposed changes cannot be implemented until the customer has given approval to do so. The procedure for processing these changes is the same as the normal change management procedures (Figure 8.1). A point to remember is that once a major change is approved, it is actually an amendment to the developer's contract. In addition, the customer normally pays for the cost of preparing the changes and incorporating them into the system and conducting the prescribed tests. Such changes may also require reidentification of the change units or modules and may, in addition, affect those of which they are a part.

8.4   Deviations and waivers

In addition to changes that may affect the functionality of the software product, developers may also run into situations where they must deviate from the prescribed specification because of a temporary inability to meet a given requirement. The constraints imposed on a software development effort or the specifications produced during the development activities might contain provisions that cannot be satisfied at the designated point in the life cycle. The customer may approve such deviations up to an agreed-on point in time or in some instances may approve a permanent deviation without requiring a major change to be submitted.

A deviation is an authorization to depart from a provision before the development of the item. A waiver is an authorization to use an item, following its development, that departs from the provision in some way. In these cases, a formal process is used to obtain approval for deviations to, or waivers of, the provisions [2].

Waivers may also be granted to cover temporary problems in meeting specifications or contract requirements. Instances include delivery of the product without having completed all of the prescribed testing or delivery of the product without certain units or modules included, because of a delaying action. A waiver, however, has a specified time factor that must be met in order to satisfy contractual or agreed-on requirements. The procedures to be followed when requesting authorized deviations and waivers are normally specified in the contract or agreement.

8.5   Change and configuration control

Change is inevitable during the software development life cycle. Changes to the software come from both external and internal sources. External changes originate from users, from evolution of operational environments, from improvements in technology, and so on. Internal changes come from improved designs and methods, from incremental development, from correction of errors, and so on. A properly implemented configuration control process is the project manager's best friend and provides potential salvation when coping with change.

Configuration control (or change management and control) is thus the process of evaluating, coordinating, and deciding on the disposition of proposed changes to the CIs, and implementing the approved changes to baselined software and associated documentation and data. The change control process ensures that changes that have been initiated are classified and evaluated, approved or denied, and that those that are approved are implemented, documented, tested, verified, and incorporated into a new baseline.

Configuration control is the set of techniques used to ensure that the components in a system achieve and maintain a definite structure (where the relationships between the components are established) throughout the system life cycle. To this end, change management and control provide the necessary procedures, documentation, and organizational structure to make sure that all items identified in the configuration identification phase, the details of the changes made to them, and other related information are available to all who need to see it (or have the necessary authority to do so) throughout the system life cycle. In other words, configuration control provides the necessary mechanism to orchestrate change, but in a controlled manner.

8.6   Problems of uncontrolled change

We have seen that uncontrolled or unmanaged change can create problems serious enough to create project failures. In their mildest forms, these changes can create confusion and chaos. Change management and control solves the four most common (and dangerous) software development/ maintenance problems: communications breakdown, shared data, multiple maintenance, and simultaneous update problems.

In any development environment, the same code (e.g., a program, function, or subroutine) is often shared by different programmers. This sharing of common items—source code or data or documentation—reduces development costs because it avoids the problem of reinventing the wheel. If a function or a program or a component library that suits one's needs is already available, then it is prudent to use it, rather than coding it again. Similarly in the case of documentation, such as RDD or SDD, the entire project uses the same document. So what is wrong with sharing data, code, or documents? As long as no one makes any changes to these shared items, there are no problems, but if changes are made to any shared item without a proper control mechanism, trouble can arise. We have already discussed these problems in detail in Chapter 3.

In the case of a properly implemented change management system, all changes made to the components of a software system are made after proper analysis and review. Because changes can be made only with proper authorization and because the authorization is given by a separate entity that is responsible for managing the changes to all of the items, the chances of effort getting duplicated or two people solving the same problem in isolation does not occur. Also, the problem of one person overwriting another person's efforts also does not occur because the changes are made to items that are stored in a controlled environment, where records of who is making change to what items are kept. So if a person is making some changes on some item, then that fact is known to all of the people in the project. In addition, the information regarding a change is reported to all concerned. Thus, a good change management system solves the aforementioned software problems and can bring discipline into the development process and improve the development productivity, because a lot of time that would otherwise be spent on debugging and reworking can be saved. The following sections describe how this goal is accomplished.

8.7   Configuration control

We have seen the dangers and problems of unmanaged and uncontrolled changes. So how do we avoid them? We should have a good change management and control system. The system should define a process and the necessary procedures to ensure that all events—from the identification of a change to its implementation and baselining—are done in a systematic, scientific, and efficient manner (i.e., following the SCM principles).

To make this happen, procedures should be established for requesting a change once the need has been identified and people have been authorized to decide whether the requested change needs to be implemented. Once the decision to implement the change has been made, a mechanism should be in place for analyzing which other resources are affected by the proposed change and then assigning the task of making the change to the resource (and if necessary to any creating resources). The necessary facilities to test, verify, and validate the changed resources also need to be in place; in other words, the changed function or program needs to be tested, verified, and approved so that it can be incorporated or promoted as the new version.

An orderly change process is necessary to ensure that only approved changes are implemented into any baselined document or software. Figure 8.1 shows a simple overview of the change management and control process. The steps mentioned here are generic and will vary from one company to another and even from one project to another.

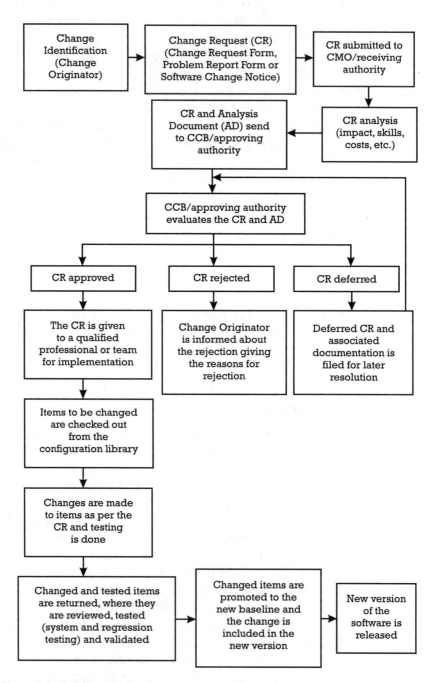

Figure 8.1 Overview of change management and control process.

The steps within the overall process can be grouped into the following categories:

1. Change initiation;

2. Change classification;

3. Change evaluation or change analysis;

4. Change disposition;

5. Change implementation;

6. Change verification;

7. Baseline change control.

These seven steps in change control are individually discussed in the following sections. We will first look at how configuration control is done manually. At a minimum, it is suggested that the following data elements always be included (as applicable) in any change control communication:

- Project name, date, requestor name, and priority (high, medium, or low);

- Name, number, and description of element(s) needing change;

- Description of change(s) required or made;

- Suggested fixes or fixes made with supporting data if needed;

- Disposition of change by a review board or person;

- Approval signatures of review board or person;

- Date of incorporation;

- Date of verification of the incorporated changes.

If one is using a change management tool or SCM tool, then most of these processes will be done automatically. For example, the change requisition, verification of the details, assignment of change request (CR) numbers, intimation of the change request evaluators, intimation of the change control board members, voting on the change request, informing the result, and so on, could be done automatically. Project managers should be careful, however, when selecting a tool that the one under consideration fits the job at hand and that the project team does not have to change form, fit, and function of the job to fit the tool. Many consultants and tool reference guides are available to help a project or firm select the type of tools that will enhance productivity and maintain good change control. More on this topic is covered in Chapter 16.

8.7.1   Change initiation

Requests for changes to software and documents come from many sources. A CR can be submitted by the developer, a member of the QA team, a reviewer, or a user. Each project should set up a CR form for documenting the proposed change and its disposition. Sometimes a change request is also called a problem report (PR) or a software change notice (SCN).

Problem reports are a special kind of change request in which the cause of the change is a defect or bug in the system. We discuss problem reports later in the chapter. But problem reports necessitate change, so the procedures for resolving the problem reports and for requesting an enhancement or a new product feature are the same. Figure 8.2 shows a sample CR form. The sample contains the basic information that should be included in a CR/PR/SCN form; however, the actual form for a particular project must correspond to the planned SCM process. Note that electronic forms, containing the same information, are being increasingly used as direct interfaces to SCM support tools.

Each project should also name an individual—the configuration management officer (CMO) or a member of the SCM team—to receive the CR form, assign it a tracking number and classification, and route it for processing. This person receives the CR and reviews it for clarity and completeness. If the CR is not complete, it is returned to the originator. Once complete, the CR is assigned a unique identifier for tracking purposes, and the information about the CR is recorded in the change request tracking database or files.

In an automated environment, the elements of the CR form are available online and simply require the originator to bring the form up and enter the necessary data. There are also many ways to make this process easier than the manual entry approach, especially when redlining the changes to be made on a source or object listing.

8.7.2   Change classification

Changes to software and associated documentation are classified according to the impact of the change and the approval authority needed. Depending on the criticality, impact, and cost involved, there will be a hierarchy of people who can approve the changes. At the top of the hierarchy is the change control board (CCB), which is discussed in more detail later in this chapter. Major changes need the approval of the CCB, whereas minor changes can be done with the approval of the project manager or development manager. This is usually done to speed up (fast-tracking) the change management process. The exact mechanism of the change classification and the approval should be defined in the SCM plan. (See Chapter 13 for more on SCM plans.)

The changes are classified into different categories with different priorities. Classification methods can be based on severity, importance, impact, cost involved, or another priority factor. For example, a change request for fixing a bug that could result in system failure will have higher priority than

```
┌─────────────────────────────────────────────────────────────────┐
│  CHANGE REQUEST                  CR No.: _____ │
│                                  Analysis Document No.: _____  │
│                                                                   │
│                                                                   │
│  System/project: _____  Item to be changed: _____  │
│                                                                   │
│  Classification: Enhancement / Bug fixing / Other: _____  │
│                                                                   │
│  Priority: Immediate / Urgent / As soon as possible / Desirable   │
│  ┌──────────────────────────────────────────────────────────────┐│
│  │ Change Description:                                           ││
│  │                                                              ││
│  │                                                              ││
│  │                                                              ││
│  └──────────────────────────────────────────────────────────────┘│
```

Status		Date	By	Remarks
Initiated				
Received				
Analyzed				
Action (A / R / D)*				
Assigned				
Check-out				
Modified and tested				
Reviewed				
Approved				
Check-in				
Baselined				

*A - Approved, R - Rejected, D - Deferred

```
┌──────────────────────────────────────────────────────────────────┐
│  Remarks:                                                          │
│                                                                    │
│                                                                    │
│                                                                    │
└──────────────────────────────────────────────────────────────────┘
```

Figure 8.2   Sample change request form.

a request for a cosmetic change. A functional enhancement request that comes from a user may not be in the same category as a change request from a member of the development team, but the classification criteria should be spelled out clearly in the SCM plan.

The individual who proposes the change may suggest a classification for that change. The CMO or the receiving authority reviews suggested classes and assigns a tentative classification. After assessment of the impact of the CR, the CCB or the approving authority will assign the final class.

8.7.3   Change evaluation/analysis

One important aspect of the configuration control process is that it provides adequate analysis of changes in terms of impact to system functionality, interfaces, utility, cost, schedule, and contractual requirements. Each change should also be analyzed for impact on software safety, reliability, maintainability, transportability, and efficiency. The project CMO routes the CR to the software engineering staff for evaluation.

In some cases, project procedures require that the CR be screened before it is analyzed. Some change requests will not have any chance of approval because of some considerations (costs or schedules) of which the change initiator may not be aware. In some cases, management may decide not to take any action in the case of changes that fall into some category or meet some predefined criteria. This information might not be or need not be communicated to all of the people involved in the project. So when such CRs—those that do not have any chance of approval—are submitted, they will get rejected in the preevaluation screening. This approach saves the cost of analysis for changes that do not have any chance of approval.

The analysis produces documentation (such as that shown in Figure 8.3), which describes the changes that will have to be made to implement the CR, the CIs and documents that will have to be changed, and the resources required to make the change. This documentation becomes part of the change package, along with the CR. After completion of the analysis, the change package is sent to the CCB.

8.7.4   Change disposition

Disposition of changes to baselined items is usually done by a CCB. The CCB evaluates the desirability of a change versus the cost of the change, as described in the documentation of the analysis. The CCB may approve, deny, or defer a change request. Sometimes the CCB may have to request more information and additional analysis.

Items for which decisions have been made are sent to the CMO for action. Rejected items are sent to the originator, along with the CCB's rationale for rejection. CRs needing further analysis are sent back to the analysis group with the CCB's questions attached. Deferred CRs are filed, to be sent back to the board at the proper time. Remember that in all cases the CCB may not be the change-approving/disapproving authority. In some cases, the project leader, the CMO, or any other designated person could make the decision. The exact mechanism of change disposition varies from one organization to another and is usually documented in the SCM plan.

The CMO sends approved items to the development team. The CMO also prepares and distributes the meeting minutes and records the current status of the CR. This information is added to the tracking database or recorded in files.

Today, with the use of change management tools, physical CCB meetings are rare. In today's development environment, e-mail or some other messaging system connects everyone in the organization. So it is possible to hold CCB meetings without the CCB members actually meeting. The change requests and the necessary information (such as evaluation reports and impact analysis reports) can be sent electronically to all CCB members,

```
┌─────────────────────────────────────────────────────────────┐
│  Change Analysis Document        No.: _____         │
│                                  CR No.: _____         │
│                                  Date: _____          │
│  System/project: _____   Item to be analyzed: _____   │
│                                                                │
│  Analyzed by: _____        │
│  ┌─────────────────────────────────────────────────────────┐  │
│  │ Implementation alternatives:                            │  │
│  │                                                         │  │
│  │                                                         │  │
│  │                                                         │  │
│  └─────────────────────────────────────────────────────────┘  │
│                                                                │
│  Items affected                                                │
│  ┌────────┬──────────────────┬─────────────┬───────────────┐  │
│  │ Item ID│ Item description  │ Version no. │Nature of change│  │
│  │        │                  │             │               │  │
│  │        │                  │             │               │  │
│  │        │                  │             │               │  │
│  └────────┴──────────────────┴─────────────┴───────────────┘  │
│                                                                │
│  Estimated effort: _____        │
│  Impact on schedule: _____        │
│  Impact on cost: _____        │
│  ┌─────────────────────────────────────────────────────────┐  │
│  │ Recommendation:                                         │  │
│  │                                                         │  │
│  │                                                         │  │
│  └─────────────────────────────────────────────────────────┘  │
└─────────────────────────────────────────────────────────────┘
```

Figure 8.3 Sample change analysis document.

and the CCB members can convey their responses in the same way. Thus, today it is possible to hold virtual CCB meetings and have online voting on change requests. The SCM tools make change disposition and management an easy task.

8.7.5 Change implementation

Approved CRs are either used directly as a change authorization form or result in a change directive being prepared by the CMO. In either case, approval results in the issuance of instructions that authorize and direct the implementation of the change in the software and associated documentation.

The development team schedules the resources to make the change. It must get official copies of the baselined component to be changed from the program library. For code changes, the design has to be developed, code has to be written, and testing has to be done and the correctness of the change verified. Moreover, the associated documentation has to be revised to reflect the change. Once the change has been made and local testing completed, the revised component and documents are returned to the control of the program library. After verification, the new version takes its place in the sequence of baselines.

8.7.6 Change verification

The implemented changes, which have been tested at the unit level, must be verified at the system level. This may require the rerun of tests that were specified in the test plan or the development of additional test plans. Regression testing will usually have to be included in the test to ensure that errors have not been introduced into existing functions by the change. Once the verification is complete, the reviewing team submits evidence of it to the program library, which will then accept the changed items for inclusion in the SCM controlled files that make up the new version of the baseline.

After the successful implementation and testing of the change described in the CR, the CMO will record the occurrence of this process into the change request tracking database or files. A change history (or patch history) is also maintained. The change history is a recording of the events that occurred to an item from the state before change to the one after. The details to be incorporated include (but are not limited to) name of the originator and receiving authority, date received, analysis done by, date of analysis, approving authority's name, date, names of the persons who effected the change, testing, review and audit, reasons for change, and a short description of change.

If an SCM or change management tool is used, then the process of recording the change implementation information, the task of changing the status of the change request, and so on do not have to be done manually. All of these activities will be taken care of by the tool. As mentioned before, the tools capture all of the information as and when the events are happening and will record them automatically. So details such as when the change was initiated, when it was evaluated, when it was reviewed, who initiated the change, who reviewed it, who approved it, when the implementation started, when it was finished, who performed the implementation, and so on will automatically be captured by the tool. So in a project where the SCM tools are used, the aforementioned activities (the activities that are performed by the CMO or SCM team members in a manual SCM system) are done automatically and without human intervention. But all of these features—the complete automation of the change control process—are available only in the more advanced and sophistated SCM tools.

8.7.7   Baseline change control

Changes to software are not complete until the code and data changes have been implemented and tested, the changes to associated documentation have been made, and all of the changes have been verified. To minimize the number of versions and the frequency of delivery of software components, changes to software are usually grouped into releases. Product release is the act of making a product available to its intended customers [3]. Each release contains software and documentation that has been tested and controlled as a total software system.

There are other reasons for product releases. One would be to satisfy a customer by customizing a software system to meet the specific needs of that customer. This is called a customer-specific release. For properly incorporating emergency fixes (a fix that was done without following any change management procedures because of the urgency of the problem or situation), a release might be made after the emergency fix has been properly incorporated. Alpha and beta releases are also used for alpha and beta testing.

Companies also do major and minor releases. Major releases are done when there is a significant increase in the product's functionality, whereas minor releases are done when the release is to correct a bug or fault in the program or system. The CCB usually decides when and how to make releases because it is the ultimate authority for making decisions about configuration control and is represented by all functions of the organization.

8.8   File-based versus change-based change management

In a file-based change management system, in order to make a change, the change initiator identifies the file he wants to change and initiates the change management process. The change request is then analyzed, the impacted files are identified during the change request evaluation phase, and the decision to approve or reject the change request is made. If the change request is approved, then the file (or files if more than one file is impacted) is checked out and the necessary changes are made to it. Then the file is tested, verified, and checked in. So if there is more than one file for the same change request, then they are not associated with one another except for what is recorded in the evaluation report.

The major drawback of the file-based system is that it fails to capture the relationships between the items that are changed as a result of a change request. In real life, a typical change is rarely limited to a single file; in most cases, more than one file needs to be changed to implement a change request. But the problem with a file-based change management system is that once the files are checked in, there is no way to determine which files were modified as a result of a particular change request. The person who has implemented the change might know or there might be some informal records somewhere, but there are no formal methods to track all of the files that were modified in response to a single change or change request. This creates a lot of problems because people often forget the details of all the files they changed and also often forget to include some of them during the system building, resulting in build failures.

To avoid the drawbacks of file-based change management, SCM practitioners started to use change-based change management. In this system, all of the files required to perform a task or to implement a change request are considered to be a single entity. Here we are tracking logical changes rather than individual file changes. But the technology of making all of the files of a change request into a single logical unit is not new. Some mainframe systems tracked changes in this manner as early as the 1970s, and companies such as IBM, Control Data Corporation, Unisys, and Tandem have used logical-change-based software tracking systems for years [4]. In 1983, SMDS (now True Software) released Aide-de-Camp as the first commercial SCM system that tracked logical changes rather than physical file changes [5].

Since then, many commercial SCM systems have added the ability to track logical changes rather than individual file changes, including Synergy/CM from Telelogic AB, AllFusion Harvest CM from Computer Associates, Dimensions from Merant, and ClearCase from Rational. SCM tools such as Merant's PVCS and StarBase's StarTeam have the ability to mark a source code change with the corresponding defect report or enhancement request.

The method of tracking software by units of logical change is a more logical and practical model because the items that are changed because of a single change request are logically linked. They are checked out together, they are tested together, they are reviewed and approved as a group, and they are checked in and promoted together. According to Weber [6], not all SCM systems use the same name for the logical unit of change. For example, ADC/Pro uses the term *change set*, AllFusion Harvest CM uses *package*, Synergy/CM and Dimensions use *task*, ClearCase uses *activity*, PCMS uses *work package*, and StarTeam uses *subproject*.

Also, not all SCM systems implement the ability to track changes in the same way. Two very different implementations have emerged: change sets and change packages. Systems that treat a logical change as the individual lines of code typically refer to the unit of change as a *change set*. Systems that treat a logical change as the set of file versions that contain the code changes are called *change packages*. A detailed discussion on change sets and change packages is not intended in this chapter, but the reader is referred to the following documents to get a comprehensive idea about change sets and change packages:

- Burrows, C., S. Dart, and G. W. George, *Ovum Evaluates: Software Configuration Management*, London: Ovum Limited, 1996.

- Cagan, M., and D. W. Weber, "Task-Based Software Configuration Management: Support for 'Change Sets' in Continuus/CM," Technical Report, Continuus Software Corporation, 1996.

▸ Weber, D. W., "Change Sets Versus Change Packages: Comparing Implementation of Change-Based SCM," *Proc. 7th Software Configuration Management Conf. (SCM7)*, Boston, MA, May 1997, pp. 25–35.

▸ Weber, D. W., "Change-based SCM Is Where We're Going," Technical Report, Continuus Software Corporation, 1997.

8.9   Escalation and notification

Escalation can be defined as the process of increasing the intensity or magnitude of an issue. In the change management process, there are times when issues need escalation. For example, consider a change request for which the evaluation report was forwarded to all CCB members for their decision. If a CCB member has not conveyed a decision within the specified time period, then the person has to be reminded about it. But if, even after the reminder, nothing happens, then the issue has to be brought to the attention of the senior member of the CCB, so that necessary corrective action can be initiated.

The escalation process is equally applicable for most of the change management processes, such as change evaluations, impact analysis, and change implementation. Also, we have seen that the change requests can be accepted, rejected, or deferred. In the case of deferred change requests, a time period can be set after which the request has to be revisited. So once the specified time is over, the change request is again reviewed. This process of keeping track of the deferred change requests and then bringing them back for review is another form of escalation.

Today's change management tools are capable of performing problem escalation and notification automatically based on predefined rules and criteria. For example, the change management tools could be programmed to escalate an issue (such as failure to convey the decision on a change request) after a specified number of days.

Multiple levels of escalation are also possible. For example, if the CCB member fails to respond to the reminders, then the issue could be escalated to her superior, and if there is still no action after a specified period, the next person in the organizational hierarchy could be informed about the issue. Here the levels of escalation, the time period before escalation, the people who are to be informed, and so on can be predefined, and the tools will do the rest. This is an important aspect that will improve the efficiency and productivity of the SCM team because they do not have to keep track of every change request; the tools will automatically perform the necessary actions when something is not happening according to the rules and schedules.

8.10   Emergency fixes

Some change requests or problem reports need immediate action and will not allow enough time to follow all change management and control procedures. For example, an emergency request from a client or a distress call from a customer cannot wait for the change evaluation, CCB meeting, change disposition, and so on. Efforts to correct these difficulties are referred to as *emergency fixes*. These are not change management processes in the conventional sense, because the sole focus of an emergency fix is to resolve the customer's difficulties right away. The most important distinction is that these emergency fixes invalidate the version of the component that they fix because these temporary measures are taken when there is not enough time or resources to process them properly. When time permits, these emergency fixes will be taken through the proper change management procedures, and the required tasks are completed.

8.11 Problem reporting and tracking

We have seen how the change management and control process works, starting with the initiation of the change request and the subsequent processing to effect the change. A change request can result from many things. It can be the result of a user needing a new feature, some enhancements of the existing functionality, or an anomaly in the software system. An anomaly is any condition that deviates from expectations based on requirements specifications, design documents, user documents, and so on, or someone's perceptions or experiences. Anomalies may be found during, but not limited to, the review, test, analysis, compilation, or use of software products or applicable documentation [7]. In common usage, the terms *error, fault, flaw, gripe, glitch, defect, problem*, and *bug* are used to express the same meaning. In this section, we deal with problem reports (PRs) or software problem reports (SPRs). The SPR or PR is a type of change request—one that is the result of an anomaly in the system.

8.12 Problem reports and change requests

An SPR will usually get more and immediate attention than a CR because it is the result of a problem, and the problem has to be fixed. It is not some cosmetic change that can wait. Also, a single SPR can create or result in more than one CR. This is because a problem or bug (e.g., navigation not working properly) can be the result of faults in two different subsystems that require different skills to fix and thus need two different persons or teams to do the job. Also, it might be better to keep the two subsystems separate if there are no direct relationships or dependencies between the two. So it is possible that a PR or SPR can initiate more than one CR.

We saw that SPRs can result in one or more CRs. In the author's opinion, the disposition of a fault or problem report should follow the same process as that of the enhancement requests once the CRs associated with the PR has been created. In other words, the processing of the problem report and the enhancement request become the same. But in the case of a prob-

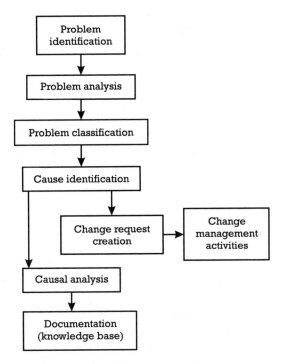

Figure 8.4 Problem reporting and tracking process.

lem report, before the creation of the CR and after the change management process is set into motion, some activities need to done. These activities are intended to prevent the same type of mistakes from recurring and also to create a knowledge base of the anomalies. Figure 8.4 shows the problem reporting and tracking process.

8.13 Problem identification

We know that a problem, bug, or defect can go undetected and can remain in the software system. It is not possible to say that a software system is 100% defect free. What we should try to do is reduce the number of defects in a system and, more important, reduce the number of critical defects. We know about the existence of a defect when something goes wrong, when the system starts misbehaving, when the performance of the system is not what it is supposed to be, or when the system stops performing.

Once the problem is identified, it should be reported and fixed, and the fixed version should be reviewed, approved, and baselined. So the first step after the detection of an anomaly or defect is to report it. Figure 8.5 shows a problem report form. Problem reports are usually handled by the SCM team, so the problem report is also received by the CMO or a representative of the SCM team. Once the problem report is received, it is checked for clarity and completeness, and if the necessary details are specified, the PR is assigned a PR number. This number serves as the identifier for the PR.

```
┌─────────────────────────────────────────────────────────────┐
│                                                               │
│  PROBLEM REPORT              PR No.: .......................  │
│                              Analysis Document No.: .........  │
│                                                               │
│  System/Project : ...........................                 │
│                                                               │
│  Place where the problem occurred  .........................  │
│                                                               │
│  Nature of the problem : ...................................  │
│  ┌─────────────────────────────────────────────────────────┐ │
│  │ Problem Description:                                     │ │
│  │                                                          │ │
│  │                                                          │ │
│  │                                                          │ │
│  │                                                          │ │
│  └─────────────────────────────────────────────────────────┘ │
│                                                               │
│   Received By :........................... Date: ............ │
│                                                               │
│   Analyzed By: ............................ Date: ........... │
│  ┌─────────────────────────────────────────────────────────┐ │
│  │ Change Management:                                       │ │
│  │ Initiation Date:  .....................................  │ │
│  │ Completion Date: ....................Status: ..........  │ │
│  └─────────────────────────────────────────────────────────┘ │
│                                                               │
│   Causal Analysis By: ...................... Date: ......... │
│                                                               │
│   Documented By: ........................... Date: ......... │
│  ┌─────────────────────────────────────────────────────────┐ │
│  │ Remarks (if any):                                        │ │
│  │                                                          │ │
│  │                                                          │ │
│  └─────────────────────────────────────────────────────────┘ │
│                                                               │
└─────────────────────────────────────────────────────────────┘
```

Figure 8.5   Sample problem report form.

Once the problem is known and the report is received, the report is given to qualified professionals (people from the project team or QA department who have the necessary technical knowledge of the system and the problem analysis methodologies) for analysis. These people will analyze the problem with the objective of determining the severity of the problem, its nature, its impact, the cause, the category, place of origin, the items affected, cost, time, and skills required to fix the problem. The analysis will also classify the defect (based on its seriousness and impact) and will create the CRs for fixing the problem. As mentioned before, a PR can result in more than one CR.

The analysis team will report its findings in the problem analysis document. Figure 8.6 shows a sample problem analysis document. This docu-

```
┌─────────────────────────────────────────────────────────────────┐
│  Problem Analysis Document          No.: _____     │
│                                     PR No.: _____        │
│                                                                   │
│                                     Date: _____       │
│  System/project: _____                       │
│  Analyzed by: _____            │
│  Severity: Critical / Fatal / Non-fatal / Cosmetic                │
│  Classification: _____        │
│  ┌─────────────────────────────────────────────────────────────┐ │
│  │ Cause of the problem:                                       │ │
│  │                                                             │ │
│  │                                                             │ │
│  │                                                             │ │
│  └─────────────────────────────────────────────────────────────┘ │
│  Items affected                                                   │
│  ┌────────┬─────────────────┬──────────────┬──────────────────┐  │
│  │ Item ID│ Item description │ Version no.  │ Nature of change │  │
│  │        │                 │              │                  │  │
│  │        │                 │              │                  │  │
│  │        │                 │              │                  │  │
│  └────────┴─────────────────┴──────────────┴──────────────────┘  │
│  Impact on cost: _____   Time: _____    │
│  Skills required in fixing the problem: _____  │
│  ┌─────────────────────────────────────────────────────────────┐ │
│  │ Implementation alternatives:                                │ │
│  │                                                             │ │
│  └─────────────────────────────────────────────────────────────┘ │
│  ┌─────────────────────────────────────────────────────────────┐ │
│  │ Recommendation:                                             │ │
│  │                                                             │ │
│  └─────────────────────────────────────────────────────────────┘ │
│  CR(s) created: _____  │
└─────────────────────────────────────────────────────────────────┘
```

Figure 8.6 Sample problem analysis report.

ment forms the basis of causal analysis, which is discussed later in this chapter. The CRs that are created as a result of the problem analysis are processed as discussed in the previous sections.

8.14 Defect classification

The classification of a defect depends on the phase in which it occurs. The following is a general classification of defects during the various phases of a project.

8.14.1   Requirements analysis

- *Incorrect requirements.* This occurs when a requirement or part of it is incorrect. This may result from a misunderstanding of the user expectations.

- *Undesirable requirements.* The requirement stated is correct but not desirable because of technical feasibility, design, or implementation cost considerations.

- *Requirements not needed.* The user does not need the stated functionality or feature. Adding this requirement does not significantly increase the utility of the project.

- *Inconsistent requirements.* The requirement contradicts some other requirement.

- *Ambiguous/incomplete requirements.* The requirement or part of it is ambiguous. It is not possible to implement the stated requirement.

- *Unreasonable requirements.* The requirement cannot be implemented because of cost, hardware, or software considerations.

- *Standards violation.* The standards set for analysis have not been followed.

8.14.2   Design phase

Design defects may relate to data definition, the user interface, the module interface, or processing logic. Each of these may be incorrect, incomplete, inconsistent, inefficient, undesirable, or violate standards.

8.14.3   Coding and testing phase

Coding and testing defects may relate to logic, boundary conditions, exception handling, performance, documentation, standards violations, and so on.

The above classifications are general and, depending on the nature of the project and degree of detail required, a defect classification system should be designed for each project.

8.15   Defect severity

Severity of a defect is a measure of the impact of the defect. During the analysis, design, and coding phases, the defects might be classified as follows:

- Major defects, which have substantial impact on several processes or subsystems. The correction activity involves changing the design of more than one process or subsystem.

> Minor defects that impact only one process or subsystem. The correction activity will be local to that process or subsystem.

> Suggestions toward improvements.

During the testing phase, the defects may be classified as follows:

> *Critical.* Errors that cause system failure.

> *Fatal.* Fatal errors that result in erroneous output.

> *Nonfatal.* Errors that are not fatal but that will affect the performance or smooth functioning of the system.

> *Cosmetic.* Minor errors such as cryptic error messages or typos in messages, screens, or user documentation.

During problem analysis, the analysis team classifies the defect and decides on its severity; these findings are recorded in the problem analysis document.

8.16   Defect prevention

The primary objective of the PR is to identify the fault and fix it. The problem analysis and CR generation and change management process achieve this goal. The secondary objective (one that is perhaps more critical in a long-term perspective) is to prevent faults from recurring. This area of problem identification and tracking is called *defect prevention*.

One of the main methods of defect prevention is causal analysis. The other method is the creation of a knowledge base that contains the classified and categorized defects, so that a programmer or designer can browse the knowledge base before he starts the analysis, design, or development, so he can be forewarned of the problems that could occur.

8.16.1   Causal analysis

The objective of causal analysis is to analyze defects and problems to determine and record the cause and initiate corrective actions so defects will not occur again. The primary document or the basis of the causal analysis is the problem analysis document, which contains the causes of the defects, where they occurred, the severity, and so on.

By studying the analysis reports, the person doing the causal analysis will be able to come up with cause patterns. For example, some of the causes for the defects are insufficient input during the analysis stage, inadequate standards, inadequate skill levels, lack of training, lack of documentation, lack of communication, oversight, and inappropriate methodology or tools. For example, in a project if the causal analysis reveals that the reason for most of the defects is lack of knowledge of a tool that is used to generate the code, team members can be given training on the tool so the problem can be prevented. Thus, causal analysis plays an important role in defect prevention.

8.16.2   Defect knowledge base and help desks

When a problem analysis document is submitted, it should result in the creation of CRs and problems being fixed. It will also form the basis of causal analysis. Its contents should also find their way into the defect knowledge base, in which defects are stored in an organized way, classified, and categorized. This knowledge base should have a search facility one can use to search for defects by category, phase of origin, cause, severity, and other similar criteria. The details about the defects, such as the project, the defect description, the cause, the solution, and how it was fixed, should be in the knowledge base.

This knowledge base will be of tremendous value because it will serve as a roadmap and guidebook for analysts, designers, programmers, and people who do the testing and maintenance. For analysts, designers, and programmers, it will serve as a guide in telling them what to do, what to avoid, and what mistakes can happen. The people who do the testing can create better test cases and test data if they know about the defects that escaped testing and how that happened. People who do the problem fixing will find similar problems and can see how they were fixed. This information will be useful for people who are managing the help desks and for the technical support team. Also, as new problems get added to the system, it will become more comprehensive and its usefulness will increase.

8.17   Change control board

We have seen that once the CIs are identified, acquired, and baselined, they come under the purview of configuration control, and formal change control procedures come into effect. This means that once the items are brought into the SCM system, the changes to it are done through a formal change management process. We have seen the exact mechanism of this process in the previous sections. Because SCM is one of the essential means of communication, changes to agreed-on baselines or points of departure should be reviewed and approved to ensure that the integrity of baselines has not been altered by a given change. In addition, such a review and approval should be made for all internal changes so communication among the development team can be maintained.

We also saw that there should be a body for deciding what changes should be made to a CI, which change requests should be rejected, and so on. This approving authority is called the change control board or configuration control board (CCB), also known as the change control authority (CCA). IEEE [1] defines the CCB as a group of people responsible for evaluating and approving or disapproving proposed changes to CIs and for ensuring implementation of approved changes. This also ensures that all proposed changes receive a technical analysis and review and that they are documented for tracking and auditing purposes. The board also has final responsibility for release management (e.g., establishing new baselines).

The basic tasks of the CCB are to declare baselines on CIs (e.g., promotions, releases), to review changes to baselined CIs, and to approve, deny, or defer their implementation. This is a short but extremely important task list. The CCB must have a strong grasp on the project. Nothing can be changed without their approval except in the case of emergency fixes. For this reason, board members must be chosen carefully.

8.17.1   CCB composition

The name *change control board* has the connotation of being a bureaucratic setup with many people, but the composition of the CCB can vary anywhere from a single person to a highly structured and formal setup with many people. For example, in small projects, the project leader alone will perform all of the functions of the CCB, but in the case of large projects such as a defense project, there will be a highly structured and formal CCB setup with well-defined procedures.

The composition, the nature of functioning (formal or informal), the number of people in the CCB, and so on depends on the complexity, size, and nature of the project. In some large projects there can be multiple levels or hierarchies of CCBs (CCBs for handling different types of problems) or multiple CCBs (each dealing with a subsystem of the project). In some cases, there can be a governing CCB to coordinate the activities of the CCBs and to act as an arbitrator to solve conflicts between CCBs of equal status and authority.

Irrespective of the size and nature of the CCBs, their function is the same: to control and manage change. In order to manage and control change in a software system, the CCB should be constituted with people who have knowledge about the system (its technical, managerial, and economic aspects) and the effects and consequences of their decisions on the system.

The CCB must be composed of representatives from all affected organizations or departments (stakeholders). It may contain a representative from the SCM group (preferably the CMO), representatives from the project team (project leader or a representative), the QA group, company management, the marketing department, project management, functional or user community, developers, test group, design group, operation personnel, interface groups, database administrators, and documentation group, among others. In some cases, the CCB must include the client's representatives. The members of the CCB should be senior people who can speak for their respective departments. Also, there should be a provision by which the CCB can summon anyone (such as the change initiator, or the person who conducted the analysis, or some outside experts) if their presence is required for better decision making. The ideal size of the CCB is around seven members, but it can be more or less depending on the organization. When all project groups are not represented, it is the members' responsibility to ensure that other groups are aware of the CCB's actions. This communication can be accomplished by the SCM recording minutes of the meeting and circulating them among all concerned parties.

Although all members of the CCB might not agree to every change, be certain that some change will affect every member of the board at some time. It should not be difficult to recall past experiences when an unwise or costly mistake could have been avoided if the right people had known about a proposed change. The chair of the CCB must be from project management—a person who can unambiguously resolve conflicts within the board and enforce the board's decisions on the project. Decisions on change implementation and CI promotion translate directly to fundamental project cost, schedule, and quality issues.

The CCB members will find that their efforts are an infuriating exercise in futility if their decisions are continually reversed or ignored by an outside entity with real decision-making authority. Do not let this happen; put that entity in charge of the board. By doing so, those who have decision authority are directly coupled to those who have expertise on the details. Decisions of the CCB should be reached by consensus whenever possible. The group dynamics must reflect the cooperative nature of a development project. The chair must nurture this cooperative vision and take unilateral action only when all other methods have been exhausted.

8.17.2 Functions of the CCB

As stated in the IEEE definition, the main function of the CCB is to evaluate and approve or deny the change requests and problem reports that have been initiated or filed. The CCB will also ensure that the approved changes are implemented correctly. The change requests and problem reports are evaluated before submitting them to the CCB. This evaluation is necessary because it will save a lot of time and effort. Also, some tasks are better accomplished by a single person than a team. So the presubmission evaluation should be done by a qualified professional, who knows the subject well. Assigning the right person to this task is the duty of the CMO. The evaluation report, along with the change request or problem report, is submitted to the CCB.

The CCB is constituted of members who are senior and have other responsibilities and whose time is valuable, so speedy resolution of the issues is a must; to attain speedy resolution and better decision making, the facts should be presented to the CCB clearly and concisely. It is a good idea to circulate the agenda of the CCB meeting and the issues and the supporting documents to the members so they can come prepared for the meeting. This task should be done by the CMO. The CCB members will evaluate the requests for their technical feasibility, economical viability, impact on marketing, and other factors. Depending on the pros and cons, the committee will decide to approve, deny, or defer the change requests.

During the presubmission evaluation, the focus of the analysis is on the impact of the program on other programs, the cost of implementation, skills required for implementing the change, the time required, and so on. During the CCB meeting, these factors, along with other issues (such as how a particular change is going to affect the system release schedule, how the change will affect the marketing strategy, and how it will affect the quality of the system), will be evaluated. In other words, the CCB members will decide on each request by looking at the overall picture. The concerns and issues the CCB discusses include the following:

- *Operational impact.* What will the effect of this change be on the final product?

- *Customer approval.* Will the change require customer approval? Is it a major change?

- *Development effort.* What is the impact of the change on interfaces and internal software elements of the final system?

- *Interface impact.* Will the change affect the established interfaces of the system?

- *Time schedule.* At what point is this change incorporated? What is the time for incorporation with minimal impact on cost and schedule?

- *Cost impact.* What is the estimated cost of implementing the change?

- *Resources impact.* What resources (e.g., infrastructure, skill, people) will be required to implement the change?

- *Schedule impact.* How will the processing and incorporation of the change affect the current schedule?

- *Quality impact.* How will the change affect the quality and reliability of the final product?

- *Feasibility.* Considering all of these factors, can this change be made economically? What is the risk of implementing the change? What is the risk of not implementing or deferring the implementation?

For example, a change request, if implemented, will delay the system release, but it is a user interface change that the marketing department feels will improve sales of the product. So the CCB has to decide whether to delay the release for better sales or to go ahead with the release and incorporate the change request into the next version. The decisions made in a CCB meeting are strategic, even though a good technical understanding is necessary to make those decisions.

8.17.3 Functioning of the CCB

The CCB should have a chairperson. Typically, the project management representative is given this post, but in some organizations, the members are assigned this post on a rotating basis. The CCB should meet at the intervals specified in the SCM plan. There should be a provision to call an emergency meeting if the need arises because certain change requests may require immediate action and cannot be delayed until the next scheduled CCB meeting.

The minimum number of people who can make a decision must also be specified. The rules for the functioning of the CCB should be formulated: How will the CCB decide on an issue? Is it by vote, and if it is by vote, what will be done in the case of a tie? These things should be specified in the SCM plan. If they are not specified in the SCM plan, these issues should be addressed at the first meeting of the CCB.

Another important point is that all transactions that happen during the CCB meetings should be recorded. The minutes of the meeting should be circulated among the CCB members. The format and the style of the meeting minutes can be formal or informal, but they should contain at least the following information:

  ▸ Members present;

  ▸ Date of the meeting;

  ▸ Agenda of the meeting;

  ▸ Action taken report (ATR) by the CMO (status of the CRs and other SCM activities since the last CCB);

  ▸ Change requests (CR number and evaluation document number) discussed at the meeting;

  ▸ Discussion details and decisions;

  ▸ Other issues discussed, if any;

  ▸ Distribution list.

The approved changes will be assigned to a qualified person or team for making the changes. If a CR is rejected, the change initiator will be notified about the decision and the reasons for rejection. The initiator can resubmit the request or file an appeal, if he or she feels that the reasons for denial are not satisfactory. The deferred change requests are filed for later decision, and the decision is conveyed to the initiator.

In the case of approved changes, the CCB will assign the task of implementing the change to someone or assign the change management process to the CMO. In such a situation, the CMO will assign the task to qualified person(s) and perform the necessary actions to complete the change management process (review, approve, promote, baseline). In the next meeting of the CCB, the CMO will present the ATR on the change requests that were approved and implemented.

As we saw earlier, with the growing popularity of SCM tools, which allow CCB meetings to be conducted electronically, the need for and importance of physical CCB meetings are slowly decreasing.

8.18 Summary

We have seen what configuration control is, why it is needed, and how it is done. We saw the reasons for change and how a change is requested, processed, and implemented. We also saw the benefits of automating the change management process.

The problem reporting and tracking process, as well as a little about defect prevention, were also discussed. Strictly speaking, defect prevention does not come under the purview of SCM, but in the author's opinion, because it is closely related to SCM, the SCM team must perform these tasks.

An integral part of any configuration control system is the change control board (CCB). We saw the composition, functions, and working of the CCB. We have seen that as change management and SCM tools become more popular, a lot of activities that were performed by the SCM team members are being automated. This automation will reduce the monotonous and repetitive nature of change management and will help make the configuration control function easier and improve development productivity, because automation will allow people to concentrate more effort on developmental activities.

References

[1]   *IEEE Standard Glossary of Software Engineering Terminology (IEEE Std-610-1990), IEEE Standards Collection (Software Engineering)*, Piscataway, NJ: IEEE, 1997.

[2]   Alain Abran, A., and Moore, J. W., (Eds.), *SWEBOK: Guide to the Software Engineering Body of Knowledge (Trial Version)*, Los Alamitos, California: IEEE Computer Society, 2001.

[3]   Bays, M. E., *Software Release Methodology*, Upper Saddle River, NJ: PrenticeHall PTR, 1999.

[4]   Cagan, M., and D. W. Weber, "Task-Based Software Configuration Management: Support for 'Change Sets' in Continuus/CM," Technical Report, Continuus Software Corporation, 1996.

[5]   Burrows, C., S. Dart, and G. W. George, *Ovum Evaluates: Software Configuration Management*, London: Ovum Limited, 1996.

[6]   Weber, D. W., "Change Sets Versus Change Packages: Comparing Implementation of Change-Based SCM," *Proc. 7th Software Configuration Management Conf. (SCM7)*, Boston, MA, May 1997, pp. 25–35.

[7]   *IEEE Standard for Software Anomalies (IEEE Std-1044–1993), IEEE Software Engi-
      neering Standards Collection 2003 (CD-ROM Edition)*, Piscataway, NJ: IEEE, 2003.

Selected bibliography

Ben-Menachem, M., *Software Configuration Management Guidebook*, New York: McGraw-Hill, 1994.

Berlack, H. R., *Software Configuration Management*, New York: John Wiley & Sons, 1992.

Davis, A. M., *201 Principles of Software Development*, New York: McGraw-Hill, 1995.

Gill, T., "Stop-Gap Configuration Management," *Crosstalk: The Journal of Defense Software Engineering*, Vol. 11, No. 2, February 1998, pp. 3–5.

Humphrey, W. S., *Managing the Software Process*, New York: Addison-Wesley, 1989.

IEEE Standard for Software Configuration Management Plans (IEEE Std-828–1998), Piscataway, NJ: IEEE, 1998.

IEEE Software Engineering Standards Collection 2003 (CD-ROM Edition), Piscataway, NJ: IEEE, 2003.

Intersolv, "Software Configuration Management for Client/Server Development Environments: An Architecture Guide," White Paper, Intersolv, 1998.

ISO, "Quality Management-Guidelines for Configuration Management," Technical Report No. ISO 10007:1995(E), Geneva, International Standards Organization, 1995.

NASA, "NASA Software Configuration Management Guidebook," Technical Report SMAP-GB-A201, Washington, DC: National Aeronautics and Space Administration, 1995.

Peters, J. F., and W. Pedrycz, *Software Engineering: An Engineering Approach*, New York: John Wiley & Sons, 2000.

Pfleeger, S. H., *Software Engineering: Theory and Practice*, 2nd ed., Pearson Education, 2001.

Pressman, R. S., *Software Engineering: A Practitioner's Approach*, New York: McGraw-Hill, 2001.

Sommerville, I., *Software Engineering*, Reading, MA: Addison-Wesley, 2001.

Weber, D. W., "Change-based SCM Is Where We're Going," Technical Report, Continuus Software Corporation, 1997.

Whitgift, D., *Methods and Tools for Software Configuration Management*, Chichester, England: John Wiley & Sons, 1991.

CHAPTER

9

Status accounting

Contents

9.1 Introduction

Configuration status accounting (CSA) is an element of configuration management that consists of the recording and reporting of information needed to effectively manage a software system and its characteristics. This information includes a listing of approved configuration identifications, the status of proposed changes to the configuration, and the implementation status of approved changes [1]. In other words, the status accounting function is the recording and reporting of information needed to manage configuration items (CIs) effectively, including, but not limited to, a record of approved configuration documentation and identification numbers, the status of proposed changes, the implementation status of approved changes, the status of pending or open change requests (CRs) and problem reports (PRs) and the build state of all units of the CIs. Status accounting is the record-keeping element of SCM, and the status accounting records are the means for SCM to report the state of the software product's development to the project management, company management, and the customer.

The aim of status accounting is to keep managers, users, developers, and other project stakeholders informed about the various configuration stages and their evolution. This implies three basic tasks: data capture, data recording, and report generation. The status accounting activity is important for maintaining the continuity of the project, avoiding duplication of effort, preventing reinventing the wheel or the same mistake happening more than once, and repeating what works.

The effectiveness of configuration management is closely linked to the flow and availability of configuration information about the product. Information is collected while performing activities associated with the configuration management (CM) processes (planning and management, identification, change management, and verification and audit). CSA correlates, stores, maintains, and provides readily available views of this organized collection of information. CSA provides access to accurate, timely information about a product and its documentation throughout the product life cycle. CSA involves the storage and maintenance of:

- Information about the configuration documentation (such as document identifiers and effective dates);

- Information about the product's configuration (such as part numbers or changes installed in a given unit);

- Information about the product's operational and maintenance documentation (such as the documents affected by each change and their update status);

- Information about the CM process (such as the status of change requests.)

The status accounting activity designs and operates a system for the capture and reporting of necessary information as the life cycle proceeds. As in any information system, the configuration status information to be managed for the evolving configurations must be identified, collected, and maintained. Various information and measurements are needed to support the SCM process and to meet the configuration status reporting needs of management, software engineering, and other related activities. A good status accounting system should be able to answer questions such as the following and many more:

- What is the status of an item?

- Has a particular CR been approved?

- What is its status of pending or open CRs and PRs?

- What items were affected by a particular CR?

- When was the CR approved and who approved it?

- Who performed the change for a particular CR and when was it completed? Who reviewed it? Who approved it?

- Which version of an item implements an approved CR?

- What CRs are assigned to whom?

- How many high-priority CRs are currently not implemented.

- What is different about a new version of a system?

- How many CRs are initiated each month and what is the approval rate?

> How many PRs are filed each month and what is the status of each of them?

> What are the major causes of the problems and defects?

The status accounting of the CIs can be compared with bank accounts, where each CI is an individual account. All transactions that happen to the CI and all activities that are performed on the CI are recorded, so individual transactions can then be tracked through each account as they occur. Some form of automated tool support is necessary to accomplish the data collection and reporting tasks. This could be a database capability, such as a relational or object-oriented database management system or a stand-alone tool or a capability of a larger, integrated tool environment.

9.2   Status accounting information gathering

Because the CSA information is a by-product of all the other CM processes, the effectiveness of CSA depends on the quality of CM implementation, supported by CM processes that ensure the information is systematically recorded, safeguarded, validated, and disseminated. Decisions on the information to be captured in the CSA system should be based on such factors as the nature of the product, the environment in which the product will be operated, the anticipated volume and complexity of change activity, and the information needs of the customer(s) [2].

The procedure of tracking the status of the CIs should be established early enough in the software development process to allow for data gathering. Also, the system should be designed so that the SCM activities will update the status accounting database rather than the person in charge of the status accounting function collecting the data regarding every change that is happening.

If control mechanisms are built into the process that make updating the status accounting database a prerequisite for further processing, then the data in the database will be current and complete. For example, when a CR is initiated, that information is recorded in the database, and if a check is made to ensure that the details of the CR have been entered in the database before it is forwarded to the CCB, then the status accounting function can be performed more effectively. For this process to happen, people should be aware of what to do and how to update the status accounting database. This is beneficial to the people who update the information because they are the same people who will be asking for information about the status of the various items at a later stage.

9.3   Status accounting database

The status accounting database is established to receive and process the data collected regarding the evolution of the various CIs of the product during the different phases of the software development life cycle. The amount of data collected and the level of detail will depend on the size, complexity, and nature of the project. The primary data of interest reflect knowledge of dates of start and completion of design and builds. Also important is accurately knowing the changes that are being made or have been made and incorporated so that the up-to-the-minute status of a CI can be known. The following list gives the necessary information for a simple status accounting report:

- CI name and identification number;
- Name of the next higher level CI;
- Design start date;
- Design approval date and revision number;
- Coding start date;
- Coding finish date;
- Testing start date;
- Testing finish date;
- Build start and finish dates and revision number;
- System merge date;
- System delivery date and revision number;
- CR date, CR number, requestor's name;
- Change disposition date;
- Change incorporation date, implementer's name, and revision number;

CRs also have IDs and descriptions. The database is the primary reference point for anything one may need to know or report about the project. The database thus should capture as much information as possible. If the database is made an integral part of the development environment, then the details necessary for effective status accounting can be captured automatically as and when it happens. This will greatly reduce the workload of the SCM team. The database should be secured and protected from tampering by authorized or unauthorized persons during the input of data, query, or generation of reports.

An important feature of the database is the ability to trace the software system upward and downward. This is the capability to track the relationship of the software requirements down through the various levels (e.g., system, program, module, unit, a process known as drill-down in knowledge management terminology) or in the opposite direction (i.e., track the relationship from the smallest element upward through module, program, system, design, to the requirements). This traceability feature is most helpful during audits and also for determining the impact of a change on all the interrelated elements.

9.4   Importance of status accounting

Status accounting refers to the information management (or data management) functions in the SCM system. For each CI designed, developed, reviewed, approved, released, and distributed, the activities that are done, how they were done, and why, where, and when they were done, who did them, and so on have to be recorded.

These details will be useful for everyone involved in the project in various ways. The information needs of a developer are different from that of a project manager, but every member of the project team and the support functions will need at least some of the information. Status accounting is the information gathering and dissemination component of SCM. It is also used by management in decision making to monitor the progress of the project and can help identify problems before they become critical so that project management can take corrective actions.

The information provided by the status accounting function helps project management identify problems, pinpoint the source of the problem, and take corrective action before the situation worsens. From the reports that are produced and by making ad hoc queries, project management can determine how the project is performing and compare the performance against the plan. One can also look at the types of changes, the rate of changes, causes for the changes, cost, and many other factors and take the necessary actions.

The status accounting reports are invaluable during the maintenance phase. To understand and identify the cause of a problem, one needs to know the history of the CI. For example, consider a program that was working until last week but is not working now. The easiest way to find out why it is not working is to identify the changes that were made to the program since last week. In situations like this one, the information provided by status accounting helps resolve the problem faster.

The information provided by the status accounting function is useful in determining the performance characteristics of the project, such as number of change requests, approval rate, number of problem reports, average time for a change resolution, average implementation time, and cost of implementing a change. This information will help when evaluating the performance of the project and when comparing different projects. Also, these details will help fine-tune the estimation and costing procedures of the organization.

So when the SCM system is designed, the information that has to be gathered by the status accounting function should be identified and selected, keeping in mind all of the uses mentioned here. A good status accounting system should provide information that is accurate, relevant, and timely.

9.5 Status accounting reports

As we saw earlier, the major functions of status accounting are to record and report information needed to effectively manage a software system and its characteristics. Reported information can be used by various organizational and project elements, including the development team, the maintenance team, project management, and QA activities. Reporting can take the form of ad hoc queries to answer specific questions or the periodic production of predesigned reports. Some information produced by the status accounting activity during the course of the life cycle might become QA records. In addition to reporting the current status of the configuration, the information obtained by status accounting can serve as a basis for various measurements of interest to management, development, and SCM. Examples include the number of change requests per CI and the average time needed to implement a change request [3]. Even though it is not possible to anticipate all possible information requests, every system must have several reports, including the change log, progress report, CI status report, and transaction log. We will look at each of these reports in some detail a little later.

The factors that should be considered while designing the reporting requirements and reports of a system include these:

- Audience for the report;
- Information contained in each report;
- Need for a routine report or need on an ad hoc basis;
- Frequency of the report;
- Distribution list.

Examples of routine reports are, as we have seen, the change log and transaction log. Some examples of ad hoc reports are as follows:

- List of all CRs that have been approved but not implemented;
- List of all CRs initiated in the last four months;
- List of how many people are working on a particular CR;
- Record of how much time was needed to implement a particular change;
- Number and details of CRs that are pending.

Ad hoc reports are generated when a user requests particular information that is not included in the routine reports. Let's look at some of the most common routine reports.

9.5.1   Change log

The change log should contain all information about the CRs in the system. The usual distribution frequency is monthly. This report should contain information such as change request number, status, originator's name, impacted items, origination date, description of change, and implementer's name.

9.5.2   Progress report

The progress report is a summary of development progress since the last report was issued and is used primarily by management to monitor the progress of the project. This report should include the reporting period (from and to dates), task ID,[1] a brief description of the work performed during the period on the task, and status of the task (complete, percentage completed).

9.5.3   CI status report

This report is prepared to summarize the status of all CIs in the system and should include information such as a list of the CIs, description, and location of the CIs (the controlled library in which they are stored). The CI description should include the name, version number, and details of dependent items.

9.5.4   Transaction log

This log contains the transactions that have happened to items, recorded in chronological order. The log should contain details such as transaction number, date, originator, nature of the entry, affected items, activity (e.g., change request, CCB approval, analysis, problem report), description, participants, impacted items, and remarks.

The objective of the transaction log is to find out what happened during a specific period, say, "What were the activities done on mm/dd/yy?" Here the idea is not to provide a detailed description on how things were done, but to give someone a snapshot of what happened during a given period.

---

1. A task is the result of a CR implementation. An approved change request can result in one or more tasks, which can be assigned to one or more persons or teams. When the task is created, the CMO creates a task ID and associates it with the CR.

9.6   Status accounting and automation

The SCM tools fully automate the status accounting function. We have seen that the SCM tools capture all SCM-related information as and when it happens and do so automatically. The SCM tools store this information in a database, so retrieval of the information is fast and efficient. Also, the information can be generated in any format the user wants. The SCM tools can be used to generate the routine reports. The SCM tools deliver their full potential when they are used to generate ad hoc reports. The user can query the system for any information she requires and get the answers immediately and in the format she wants.

If an SCM tool is not used, the SCM team will have to go through change logs, defect logs, change requests, transaction logs, and other reports to correlate and collate bits and pieces of information from different sources to create a report that satisfies the user's requirements. This is a tedious and time-consuming process that will increase the workload of the SCM team if the users start asking complex queries that involve more than one source.

An SCM tool is an ideal solution to this situation: It is quick, accurate, and customizable. In the case of an SCM tool, all SCM-related information is stored in relational databases, which makes information retrieval easy and quick. Also, in the case of a tool, the information will be up to date as the events are recorded and the information is captured as the activities occur.

Another advantage of using tools is the variety of information that can be retrieved. For example, one can obtain information about all pending CRs, all completed CRs, all CRs completed between a specific date, all CRs initiated by a particular developer, all CRs implemented by a particular person, and other criteria. The beauty of this system is that no additional cost or extra effort is required to produce these different reports. Most SCM tools will have a set of standard reports and then the facility to query the SCM database for other details. Most tools also have the facility to display the information in graphical form.

Thus, SCM tools greatly enhance the capabilities of the status accounting function because they can record and retrieve minute details with speed and accuracy to satisfy ad hoc queries. This is especially true when different users of the SCM system have different needs. The project manager's information requirements are different from that of the developer's. What the change initiator wants to know will be different from what the project leader or a QA person wants to know. With a manual system, people will have to wait while the information is compiled from records, whereas with a computerized system, retrieval is merely a matter of running a query.

Another advantage of a software tool is that the people concerned can be given read-only access so they can query the system and get the answers they need on their own. Here again, the author would like to stress the need for a computerized system. Manual systems are fine for routine reports, but an interactive system can reduce the workload of the SCM staff because the people who want the information (and have the necessary authority) can log on to the system and get the information required. Also, routine reports provide static information, but if users have access to the interactive system, they can view the reports, and if they require more information, they can drill-down and get the details they want. In this way, SCM information is more effectively used, leading to better and more well-informed decisions being made. If an SCM tool does not support flexible and customizable reporting features, then it is of limited value.

Here I would like to point out some issues regarding the SCM tools. I have mentioned that the SCM tools completely automate the status accounting process and make status accounting easier and more accurate, but this is true only in the case of high-end SCM tools. The exotic features and almost complete automation are available in top-end and sophisticated SCM tools. The level of automation possible and the capabilities of all tools are not the same. Nowadays, no one uses a completely manual SCM system. Most organizations use some sort of tools for performing SCM (at least tasks such as change management, defect tracking, and build management), and completely manual systems are rare. To take full advantage of automation (but even then all of the SCM functions could not be automated and SCM will still need humans), complex, advanced, and sophisticated tools must be used (and they cost a fortune).

We next look at some of the common report categories that are supported by most SCM tools.

9.6.1 Change/problem tracking reports

These reports contain details such as who made the change, when, who initiated it, change history, and CR status. Here the advantage, as mentioned before, is that the user can tailor the information retrieved in any format required. So one can generate reports of all unassigned CRs, all pending CRs, all CRs assigned to a particular person, CRs sorted by date, severity, priority, classification, completion date, status, and other criteria.

9.6.2 Difference reporting

It is important to keep track of the differences between versions and releases because doing so will make it easier to incorporate changes from one version to the next. Most SCM tools have the facility to generate difference reports, which will contain the differences (changes) between two versions of an item or set of items.

9.6.3 Ad hoc queries

The usefulness of having ad hoc querying capabilities can never be overstated. Ad hoc queries allow the users of an SCM system to get the information they want, when they want it, and in the form they want. The reporting tools are so advanced that many of them have graphical user interfaces that help the users write their own queries by choosing the items in which they are interested. Also, these reporting tools have drill-down features, so that a user can drill-down from a summary report to the level of detail required. This feature is particularly useful for project leaders and management.

9.6.4 Journals

The journal feature is what makes SCM tools stand apart from the manual status accounting process. A journal records all events that happen to all configuration items as they occur, thus providing users with a comprehensive picture of what happened during a particular period. This is a much advanced and more comprehensive version of the manual transaction logs.

Journals provide audit trails that can be used for a variety of purposes, including configuration audits. The advantage of having the journal details in a database is that the information contained in it can be manipulated at will. So one can re-create all of the events that happened during the transition of a configuration item from, say, version 1 to 6 or the details of activities performed by a certain developer. The advantage here is that the information can be retrieved quickly and without any extra effort.

9.7 Summary

Status accounting is the recording activity and serves as a follow-up to the results of the SCM activities of configuration identification and change control. It keeps track of the current configuration identification documents, the current configuration of the delivered software, the status of the changes being reviewed, and the status of the implementation of approved changes.

The status accounting function plays a vital role in the efficient management and control of projects by providing the necessary information to project management and the project team. SCM tools automate the status accounting function and help provide users with information that is accurate, timely, and relevant.

References

[1]   IEEE Standard Glossary of Software Engineering Terminology (IEEE Std-610–1990), *IEEE Standards Collection (Software Engineering)*, Piscataway, NJ: IEEE, 1997.

[2]   EIA, *National Consensus Standard for Configuration Management (EIA-649)*, Arlington, VA: Electronics Industries Alliance, 1998.

[3]   Alain Abran, A., and J. W. Moore (eds.), *SWEBOK: Guide to the Software Engineering Body of Knowledge (Trial Version)*, Los Alamitos, CA: IEEE Computer Society, 2001.

Selected bibliography

Babich, W. A., *Software Configuration Management: Coordination for Team Productivity*, Boston, MA: Addison-Wesley, 1986.

Ben-Menachem, M., *Software Configuration Guidebook*, London: McGraw-Hill International, 1994.

Berlack, H. R., *Software Configuration Management*, New York: John Wiley & Sons, 1992.

Bersoff, E. H., V. D. Henderson, and S. G. Siegel, *Software Configuration Management, An Investment in Product Integrity*, Englewood Cliffs, NJ: Prentice-Hall, 1980.

EIA, *National Consensus Standard for Configuration Management (EIA-649)*, Arlington, VA: Electronics Industries Alliance, 1998.

IEEE Software Engineering Standards Collection 2003 (CD-ROM Edition), Piscataway, NJ: IEEE, 2003.

Marciniak, J. J. (ed.), *Encyclopedia of Software Engineering*, 2nd ed., New York: John Wiley & Sons, 2002.

"Software Configuration Management: A Primer for Development Teams and Managers," White Paper, Intersolv, 1997.

"Software Configuration Management for Client/Server Development Environments: An Architecture Guide," White Paper, Intersolv, 1998.

Configuration verification and audits

10.1 Introduction

The objective of the configuration verification and audits is to verify that the software system matches the configuration item description in the specifications and documents and that the package being reviewed is complete. According to EIA-649 [1], configuration verification and audits establish that the performance and functional requirements defined in the configuration documentation have been achieved by the design and that the design has been accurately documented in the configuration documentation. The purpose and benefits of the process include the following:

‣ Ensure that the product design provides the agreed-on performance capabilities.

‣ Validate the integrity of the configuration documentation.

‣ Verify the consistency between a product and its configuration documentation.

‣ Determine that an adequate process is in place to provide continuing control of the configuration.

‣ Provide confidence in establishing a product baseline.

‣ Ensure a known configuration as the basis for operation and maintenance instructions, training, and spare and repair parts.

Once the software has been designed, developed, and tested, it is necessary to establish that the software product has been built in accordance with the requirements and that the software is correctly represented in the documentation that is

143

shipped along with the software. A configuration audit is a check to verify that the product package contains all of the components it is supposed to contain and performs as promised.

Configuration verification and audits enable the developer and the customer to agree that what has been designed has been built and that the testing applied to the software product configuration items (CIs) proved that the requirements of the software requirements specification (SRS) for each CI were met. The configuration audits are performed after software integration and testing. In some cases, the software is audited with the hardware—after system integration. *Reviews* are an iterative activity that start with receipt of a contract and culmination of an agreement and end with delivery of the software product and its associated documentation [2].

The configuration verification and audit process includes the following:

> ▸ Configuration verification of the initial configuration of a CI, and the incorporation of approved changes, to ensure that the CI meets its required performance and documented configuration requirements;

> ▸ Configuration audit of configuration verification records and physical product to validate that a development program has achieved its performance requirements and configuration documentation or the system/CI being audited is consistent with the product meeting the requirements.

The common objective is to establish a high level of confidence in the configuration documentation used as the basis for configuration control and support of the product throughout its life cycle. Configuration verification should be an imbedded function of the contractor's process for creating and modifying the CI or computer software configuration item (CSCI). Validation of this process by the customer or some other designated authority may be employed in lieu of physical inspection where appropriate [3]. Inputs to the configuration verification and audit activity are:

> ▸ Configuration, status, and schedule information from status accounting;

> ▸ Approved configuration documentation (which is a product of the configuration identification process);

> ▸ The results of testing and verification;

> ▸ The physical hardware CI or software CSCI and its representation;

> ▸ Build instructions and tools used to develop, produce, test, and verify the product.

Successful completion of verification and audit activities results in a verified system/CI(s) and a documentation set that may be confidently considered a product baseline. It also results in a validated process to maintain the continuing consistency of product to documentation.

Many organizations do not perform the configuration audits (FCA and PCA) and instead perform market readiness reviews or test readiness reviews, or alpha and beta testing. The market readiness review (MRR) is conducted to confirm that the distribution, service, maintenance, technical support, and field people are ready; installation, operation, and trouble-shooting manuals are ready; and product tests and trial runs were successful.

The test readiness review (TRR) is conducted to evaluate preliminary test results for one or more configuration items; to verify that the test procedures for each configuration item are complete, comply with test plans and descriptions, and satisfy test requirements; and to ensure that a project is prepared to proceed to formal testing of the configuration items. TRRs will be held for each application of a release at the completion of the software integration test and at the completion of the functional validation test. There are three levels of TRRs at the application level as defined following:

- *Development TRR.* Informal test readiness review conducted following successful completion of unit/module testing of a given application.

- *Project TRR.* Formal test readiness review conducted following successful completion of the software integration test (SIT) of a given application.

- *Enterprise TRR.* Formal test readiness review conducted following successful completion of the functional validation test (FVT) of a given application.

Alpha testing is done when the system or product has a lot of new, previously untested features. Because untested functionality exists, the development team might be uncomfortable proceeding with the final testing and release of the product until they get feedback from a limited number of users/customers. So the developers use the alpha testing primarily to evaluate the success or failure (or acceptance) of the new features incorporated into the system.

Beta testing is required when the development team decides that some level of customer evaluation is needed before the final release of the product. In the case of beta testing, developers are no longer looking for user inputs on functionality or features. The product has all of the functionality incorporated into it, so the development team will be looking for the beta testers to uncover bugs and faults in the system. Unlike alpha testing, beta testing is done on a much larger scale (i.e., the number of people who do beta testing is much higher than that for alpha testing). Companies usually distribute beta releases free of cost to people who have enrolled in the beta testing program, and in many cases, beta versions are available for download from the company's Web site. New products will have alpha testing followed by beta testing, but in the case of new versions of existing products, either alpha or beta testing is done.

As seen from the definitions of these tests and that of configuration verification and audits, it is clear that these tests and reviews are not as comprehensive and thorough and do not provide the same kind of assurance that the product is built according to the specification and is complete in all respects. Also, the configuration audits provide objective evidence of compliance of products and processes with standards, guidelines, specifications, and procedures.

10.2   Software reviews

A review is a process or meeting during which a work product, or set of work products, is presented to project personnel, managers, users, customers, or other interested parties for comment or approval [4]. Technical reviews are a series of system engineering activities by which the technical progress on a project is assessed relative to its technical or contractual requirements. The reviews are conducted at logical transition points in the development effort to identify and correct problems resulting from the work completed thus far before the problems can disrupt or delay the technical progress. Reviews are performed many times during the development process, at least at the completion of each phase and sometimes more often. So there are system requirements reviews, software requirements reviews, design reviews (preliminary design review and critical design review), code reviews, and so on. The reviews provide a method for the performing activity and tasking activity to determine that the development of a CI and its documentation has a high probability of meeting contract requirements.

On the other hand, audits are performed at the completion of the product to make sure the product is complete in all respects and the development has been performed in conformance with the development standards and guidelines.

10.3   Configuration verification

Configuration verification is an ongoing process and is common to configuration management, systems engineering, design engineering, manufacturing, and quality assurance. It is the means by which the design solution is verified. Verification that a design achieves its goals is accomplished by a systematic comparison of requirements with the results of tests, analyses, or inspections. The documentation of a product's definition must be complete and accurate enough to permit reproduction of the product without further design effort. The design of a product must be verified to ascertain that it has achieved specified requirements and desired goals; that the documentation of the design is accurate; and that the product can be produced from the documentation [1].

Conceptually, the verification occurs in sequence by first determining the acceptability of the design and then confirming that the documentation portrays that design. In practice, it may be accomplished in separate events or audits. It is often more practicable to verify these aspects incrementally during the course of the definition phase and to incorporate the verification into the design/development process flow, so that it occurs continuously.

The verification methods should be carefully planned to ensure that all requirements are addressed and the individual verification methods chosen are appropriate. Requirements analysis and test tools that flow down, account for and verify all attributes, thus facilitating the design verification process. Results are typically recorded in a matrix, indicating each discrete requirement, the method of verification, the verification procedure, and the verification results. The design output, consisting of the complete set of design information, must be accurately documented to permit reproduction of the product without further design effort. Beyond this fundamental requirement, other factors (such as the need to procure from other sources or future maintenance needs) may influence the content and formality of documentation. A product should be able to be produced from its documentation with confidence that it will meet all requirements.

A software product should also comply with published design and coding standards so that it can be maintained, modified, and upgraded. In addition, the following should be verified:

 ▸ The documentation library control system;

 ▸ Uniqueness of the product identifier;

 ▸ Validity of interfaces;

 ▸ Internal audit records of configuration management processes and procedures.

Verifying the documentation determines that it is adequate for its intended purposes and accurately reflects compliant design. The verification of design and documentation must be planned to permit its accomplishment at minimum cost. In complex physical products, the comparison of the documentation with the prototype or test article can often be accomplished incrementally, during assembly of the article, to avoid the need for later disassembly. These verifications are considered complete upon resolution of discrepancies or departures found and correction of associated documentation.

10.4   When, what, and who of auditing

Audits are the means by which an organization can ensure that software development has been performed correctly (i.e., in conformance with the development standards and guidelines). The software configuration auditing activity determines the extent to which an item satisfies the required functional and physical characteristics. Audits vary in formality, but all audits perform the same function: they provide a check on the completeness of the software system or product. Any anomalies found during an audit should not only be corrected, but the root cause of the problem should also be identified and corrected to ensure that the problem does not occur again. (Here the defect prevention methods mentioned in Chapter 8 are useful.)

Before the release of a product baseline, a functional configuration audit (FCA) and a physical configuration audit (PCA) of the CIs are usually conducted. The FCA ensures that the functions defined in the specifications are all implemented correctly. The PCA determines whether all of the items identified as being part of the CI are present in the product baseline.

A software audit is an activity performed to independently evaluate the conformance of software products and processes to applicable regulations, standards, guidelines, plans, and procedures [4]. An audit is usually done at the end of a phase in the development life cycle. Before the development proceeds to the next phase, it is a good practice to conduct an audit so that the development team has the satisfaction of knowing that they are working on something that is complete and approved. But the reality is that audits are usually performed only before a system release because the system release will go to the customer.

Conducting the audit before final release gives the company and the customer the satisfaction of knowing that what they are delivering or getting is complete in all respects and meets the requirements specified. Performing the configuration audit before the system or final release is fine in the case of the projects done in-house and when the organization is following all the development standards and guidelines and other QA procedures. Even then, however, it is a good practice to audit every major baseline or release. But items supplied by subcontractors must be subjected to a formal and rigorous auditing process.

Who should perform the configuration audits? Audits are usually performed by a representative or team of representatives from management, the QA department, or the customer/ client. In some cases, auditing is done by an external agency. It is best to have the configuration audit performed by an external auditor, because the auditing activity requires a high degree of objectivity and professionalism. The person who conducts the audit should be knowledgeable about SCM activities and functions and technically competent to understand the project's functionality. The SCM plan should describe the types of audits and reviews to be applied to a specified software project. When hardware components are also involved, special attention must be paid to what documents and data will be reviewed and audited and who will represent the hardware and software engineering functions assigned to the project.

Audits may be conducted by the organization responsible for the product development, by the customer, or by a third party designated by the customer. A representative of each party to the audit participates in audit planning and preparation. Audit plans and agendas are reviewed and agreed to before the audit. Audit of a complex product may be accomplished in a series of incremental audits.

During the conduct of an audit, audit participants record significant questions, discrepancies or anomalies, and recommended courses of action. The chairperson/head of the auditing team reviews audit findings and determine appropriate actions. Affected parties agree to action items and the plan for effecting their successful closure. Audit minutes provide a record of the audit findings, conclusions, recommendations, and action items. Follow-up occurs until all required action items are complete. The necessary resources and material to perform an audit include the following items to the extent appropriate for the type and scope of audit:

- An audit plan and agenda;
- Adequate facilities and unencumbered access;
- Assignment and availability of personnel;
- Applicable specifications, drawings, manuals, schedules, and design data, test results, inspection reports, process sheets, data sheets, safety procedures, and other documentation as deemed necessary;
- Tools and inspection equipment necessary for evaluation and verification;
- Access to the product(s) and detailed parts to be reviewed.

10.5 Functional configuration audit

The objective of the FCA is to verify that a CI's actual performance agrees with the requirements specified in the requirements definition and system design documents. IEEE [5] defines FCA as an audit conducted to verify that the development of a CI has been completed satisfactorily, that the item has achieved the performance and functional characteristics specified in the functional or allocated configuration identification, and that its operational and support documents are complete and satisfactory. A functional configuration audit will prove, right or wrong, that the software test reports correctly state that a given requirement has been met.

The FCA team reviews the test plans, the test data, and the testing methodology to verify that all functional parameters were tested and the test results were satisfactory. The audit team may ask for additional tests to be conducted if deemed necessary. Functional audits normally involve a structured and well-defined sequence of tests designed to ensure that performance of the new or modified item conforms to the requirements in the specification.

The form of the FCA will vary according to the type and extent of change involved. In most cases, the FCA represents a review of the qualification of the item, to ensure that it not only meets the specification require-ment but also that no unintended consequences are associated with the change. This process may include some or all of the following forms of test, analysis, or demonstration: environmental tests, to ensure that the new design is suitable for operation within the extremes of the operational requirements; reliability tests; user trials; interfaces with other systems; soft-ware testing; and stress testing.

As mentioned, the audit team consists of representatives from man-agement, QA, external experts, and/or client representatives. An audit team can be an ongoing part of the organization, or it can be constituted on an as-needed basis. Sometimes audit teams are from an external agency that specializes in conducting audits. The composition and struc-ture of the audit team depends on the company and the auditing stan-dards it is following.

10.6 Physical configuration audit

The objective of the PCA is to verify that a CI as built conforms to the tech-nical documentation that defines it. The PCA is usually done after successful completion of the FCA. A PCA will demonstrate that the documentation for each CI and the software system that will be delivered with the software product correctly describes the functional and physical characteristics of the product and also that the software product specification and version description documents are consistent with the software product. The audit team examines the design documentation with the source code and user documentation and any other items that will accompany the final software system. When a PCA is completed, the *product baseline* is established. In other words, the successful completion of the FCA and PCA are a prerequi-site for the establishment of the product baseline.

10.7 Auditing the SCM system

SCM system audits are carried out to ensure that implementation of SCM remains consistent with established policy and procedures. System audits are essential to ensure that defined processes are being properly applied and controlled. General aspects that may be considered part of a system audit are as follows:

- The operational change control processes, including the change con-trol board (CCB) function;

- The implementation of change requests;

- The traceability of approved changes to the original specification and requirement;

> ‣ The availability of design data and documentation in support of approved changes;

> ‣ The traceability of design decisions to the initiating requirement.

Auditing of the SCM system is done by management's representatives, QA personnel, or SCM experts. It is better to have the SCM system audits done by the people who reviewed the SCM plan, because they are familiar with the SCM system that is being practiced and thus are able to do a better job. The SCM system will be audited against the SCM plan and the standards mentioned in the SCM plan. The purpose of auditing the SCM system is to ensure that the SCM system and SCM functions and procedures are being practiced as specified in the SCM plan and to find out areas in the functioning of the SCM system that need improvement.

10.8   Role of the SCM team in configuration audits

The SCM team should schedule the audits and find qualified personnel to perform them. The SCM team also acts as the liaison between the audit team and the development and testing team and ensures that the audit team gets full support from the development and testing team to carry out the audits successfully.

Sometimes the auditors need to question the development or testing team members as part of the audit. The SCM team should act as a facilitator of such meetings and should record the points discussed in such meetings; these minutes should form part of the audit report. The SCM team should arrange for the infrastructure facilities needed, such as room(s), furniture, machine access, documents, and any other items required by the audit team.

After the FCA and PCA have been completed, the SCM team will review the auditors' comments and nonconformance reports (NCRs) and initiate the necessary corrective actions.

10.9   Configuration audits and SCM tools

SCM tools make the auditing process a lot easier than before. SCM tools capture all SCM-related information comprehensively as the activities occur. We have seen that the journal reports created by the SCM tools record all events that have happened to the CIs, thus creating an audit trail, which can be used by the auditors to perform the auditing. Also, the querying facility of the tools will help in obtaining any other information needed by the auditing team.

The automated information-gathering abilities of the SCM tools make auditing a simple process because any necessary information can be generated for verification purposes and because they can confirm whether the system or product being audited is complete and meets all requirements.

10.10 Summary

Configuration audits are carried out to ensure that the software system is functioning correctly and to ensure that the configuration has been tested to demonstrate that it meets its functional requirements and that it contains all deliverable entities.

The two types of audits are physical configuration audits and functional configuration audits. Whereas functional configuration audits authenticate that the software performs in accordance with the requirements and as stated in the documentation, physical configuration audits authenticate that the components to be delivered actually exist and that they are complete in all respects and contain all of the required items.

The SCM system should also be subjected to auditing to ensure that the implementation of SCM remains consistent with established policies and procedures. The SCM tools automate most of the auditing tasks and make auditing an easy and painless task.

References

[1]   EIA, *National Consensus Standard for Configuration Management (EIA-649)*, Arlington, VA: Electronics Industries Alliance, 1998.

[2]   Marciniak, J. J. (ed.), *Encyclopedia of Software Engineering*, 2nd ed., New York: John Wiley & Sons, 2002.

[3]   U.S. Department of Defense, *Military Handbook: Configuration Management Guidance (MIL-HDBK-61A(SE)-2001)*, U.S. Department of Defense, 2001.

[4]   IEEE Standard for Software Reviews (IEEE Std-1028-1997), *IEEE Software Engineering Standards Collection 2003 (CD-ROM Edition)*, Piscataway, NJ: IEEE, 2003.

[5]   IEEE Standard Glossary of Software Engineering Terminology (IEEE Std-610–1990), *IEEE Software Engineering Standards Collection 2003 (CD-ROM Edition)*, Piscataway, NJ: IEEE, 2003.

Selected bibliography

Alain Abran, A., and J. W. Moore (eds.), *SWEBOK: Guide to the Software Engineering Body of Knowledge (Trial Version)*, Los Alamitos, CA: IEEE Computer Society, 2001.

Arthur, J. D., et al, "Evaluating the Effectiveness of Independent Verification and Validation," *IEEE Computer*, Vol. 32, No. 10, October 1999, pp. 79–83.

Ben-Menachem, M., *Software Configuration Management Guidebook*, New York: McGraw-Hill, 1994.

EIA, *National Consensus Standard for Configuration Management (EIA-649)*, Arlington, VA: Electronics Industries Alliance, 1998.

IEEE Software Engineering Standards Collection 2003 (CD-ROM Edition), Piscataway, NJ: IEEE, 2003.

Pressman, R. S., *Software Engineering: A Practitioner's Approach*, New York: McGraw-Hill, 2001.

Sommerville, I., *Software Engineering*, Reading, MA: Addison-Wesley, 2001.

U.S. Department of Defense, *Military Handbook: Configuration Management Guidance (MIL-HDBK-61A(SE)-2001)*, U.S. Department of Defense, 2001.

Whitgift, D., *Methods and Tools for Software Configuration Management*, Chichester, England: John Wiley & Sons, 1991.

CHAPTER

11

Contents

SCM: Advanced concepts

11.1 Introduction

In this chapter, we discuss some of the advanced concepts in software configuration management. We have seen the basic concepts of SCM in Chapter 5. This chapter further builds on those topics and also deals with some important SCM functions such as interface control and subcontractor control. These topics are particularly important when writing the SCM plan, which is discussed in Chapter 14. This chapter also deals with the concept of software libraries and how important they are for performing SCM activities.

We have discussed versions, system building, and releases in Chapter 5. The foundation of SCM is based on three components: version control, system building, and release management.

11.2 Version control

A version is an initial release or re-release of a configuration item (CI). It is an instance of the system that differs in some way from the other instances. A version is usually accompanied by a version description document (VDD), which identifies a given version of a system or component. Typical contents include an inventory of system or component parts, identification of changes incorporated into this version, and installation and operation information unique to the version described [1]. A VDD is not normally required for each build and/or internal release of software or a CI. Typically, a VDD is produced only for system-level testing and for the major activities that follow the system-level test (e.g., release to client/customer/marketing, archival, re-release). The VDD may exist in hard-copy or electronic form. The VDD describes new capabilities, known problems, and platform requirements necessary for proper product operation.

Version control is simply the automated act of tracking the changes of a particular file over time. This is typically accomplished by maintaining one copy of the file in a repository and then tracking the changes to that file. The concepts of check-in and checkout make this possible. We have seen how this is done in Chapter 5. Version control has a number of benefits, including:

- Prevents unauthorized access and modification to files.

- Traces the evolution of a file from inception to the current state.

- Rolls back to a previous version of a given file in case of a problem or for debugging.

- Compares two versions of a file, highlighting differences to see what changes are made.

- Provides a mechanism for locking, forcing serialized change to any given file.

- Creates branches that allow for parallel concurrent development and the ability to combine the changes made by different people to a single file at a later stage—merging.

- Maintains an instant audit trail on every file: versions, modified date, modifier, and any additional amount of metadata your system provides for and that you choose to implement.

Thus, version control gives the ability to trace the history of all CIs in a system and to re-create any previous version of a file. This capability gives the software organization tremendous power to identify and pinpoint files that are creating problems while debugging during the maintenance and support phases. When things are not working, the files can be rolled back to previous versions and the changes made after the successfully working version can be inspected to find out what is causing the error or malfunction.

11.3   System building

IEEE defines a *build* as an operational version of a system or component that incorporates a specified subset of the capabilities the final product will provide [1]. The building activity combines the correct versions of software items, using the appropriate configuration data, into an executable program for delivery to a customer or other recipient, such as the developers, testers, and QA personnel. Build instructions ensure that the proper build steps are taken and in the correct sequence. In addition to building software for new releases, it is usually also necessary for SCM to have the capability to reproduce previous releases for recovery, testing, or additional release purposes.

During the development of a software product, the build process will be performed several times. The developers, testers, and QA personnel will perform builds during the course of the development to see whether the system that is under development performs as expected. When system development is complete and all of the items that are required for the final product are debugged, tested, reviewed, verified, validated, and audited, then the system build is performed. The system build produces the product that is given to the client or shipped to customers.

Software is built using particular versions of supporting tools, such as compilers. The two most essential characteristics that are needed for any build process are *repeatability* and *reproducibility*. In other words, you should be able to re-create the exact product that was created using a build process at a later date. For this to happen, the supporting tools and associated build scripts need to be under SCM control to ensure availability of the correct versions of the tools. The build process and products are often subject to software quality assurance (SQA) verification. Outputs of the build process might be needed for future reference and may become QA records.

Tools are useful for selecting the correct versions of software items for a given target environment and for automating the process of building the software from the selected versions and appropriate configuration data. For large projects with parallel development or distributed development environments, this tool capability is a must. Most software development environments provide this capability. These tools vary in complexity and features; some use scripting languages whereas others employ graphical user interface (GUI)-oriented approaches that hide much of the complexity of the build facility.

11.4   Release management

The term *release* is used in this context to refer to the distribution of a software configuration item outside the development activity. The primary purpose of a release is to make the application available to its end users. Thus, a release can be to internal users as well as to customers.

Release management is closely tied to build management in that a specific release is essentially a production build of your application. In addition to putting the runtime software in its final form, release management includes the deployment process as well as the update of related metadata that goes into tracking a given version of a software application. When different versions of a software item are available for delivery, such as variants for different platforms or versions with varying capabilities, it is frequently necessary to re-create specific versions and package the correct materials for delivery of the version. The software library is a key element in accomplishing release and delivery tasks. We will see more about software libraries later in this chapter.

Software release management encompasses the identification, packaging, and delivery of the elements of a product such as the executable, documentation, release notes, and configuration data. The software product will be continuously subjected to changes and enhancements. Hence, one of the main considerations for release management is determining when to issue a release. The severity of the problems addressed by the release and measurements of the fault densities of prior releases affect this decision [2]. Pressure from competitors, entry of new products and technology, and other environmental factors also affect the decision of when to release.

The packaging task must identify which product items are to be delivered and select the correct variants of those items, given the intended application of the product. The set of information documenting the physical contents of a release is known as a VDD, which was discussed earlier. The package to be released also contains loading or upgrading instructions. The latter can be complicated by the fact that some current users might have versions that are several releases old. SCM tools are needed to support these release management functions.

Software released to customers must comprise items that have been approved as fit for their intended use. Usually this requires that the items are fully approved by the CCB, although beta test or prototype releases may be less than fully approved. It also requires that the correct variant of the system be issued to clients. Variants differ only in the platform or language supported but have the same functionality. So a client who wants a Windows version of the product will not be happy if he receives a UNIX version.

11.5   Interface control

In today's environment, interface design has become an important segment of the software engineering process. One is not only faced with the normal system-to-system interfaces, but other functions such as local area networks to wide area networks or workstations to files servers to mainframes. Those interfaces that affect the software are identified and documented by the systems analyst and, in turn, are placed under configuration control.

An *interface* is the functional and physical characteristics required for a common boundary to exist between two or more software products and computer systems that are provided by different organizations or sources. *Interface control* is the process of identifying, documenting, and controlling all performance, functional, and physical attributes relevant to the interfacing of two or more products provided by one or more organizations. *Interface documentation* consists of interface control drawings or other documentation that depicts physical, functional, and test interfaces of related or co-functioning products [3]. An interface control document defines the interfaces that may affect the operation of co-functioning CIs and is used for control as well as delineating the interface criteria and technical detail necessary to effect an economical and viable interface [4].

For product interfaces external to the enterprise, the SCM system must establish an interface agreement and a mutually agreed-on documentation of common attributes. Product attributes include defined interfaces with products that are developed, produced, and supplied by organizations outside of the enterprise. External interfaces are documented in a product's configuration documentation. To document and control the interface, there must be a relationship between the interfacing organizations.

If the relationship is a buyer-seller relationship, the interface definition is included as part of the purchase agreement (e.g., by reference to a defined catalog item or by use of a control drawing). If there is no direct relationship, an interface agreement is established between the developing enterprises. It delineates procedures for defining and maintaining the common interface. The procedures (for defining complex interfaces and coordinating proposed changes to them) may employ a joint interface control working group. A mutually agreed-on interface definition (including performance, functional, and physical attributes) is typically detailed in an interface document or drawing.

NASA-DID-M200 provides for an interface control plan and states in simple terms that the purpose of the plan is to define the process by which the developer defines and manages all external interfaces between the software and all users—both human and software. It may be appropriate to roll out this plan when there are major coordination concerns and risks between the developer and the organizations responsible for the interfacing units [5].

MIL-STD-483B states that interface control is the coordinated activity required to ensure that the functional and physical characteristics of systems and equipments are compatible [6]. The interface control activity is responsible for ensuring that the configuration identification conforms to the functional interfaces established by system engineering and that the affected CIs are logically compatible and can be operated and supported as needed. The interface activity is also responsible for the control of documentation, including an assessment of the impact of changes to control documentation or changes emanating from other document changes that could affect the interfaces.

Most of the software specifications and documents define or explain the interfaces between the CI being identified and another CI or computer system. All of these interfaces must be mapped so that everyone on the project will understand what has been defined and will be able to carry out their specified tasks. SCM treats the interface design documents and drawings in the same manner as other documentation, except that SCM also provides for assessment of impacts to interfacing entities.

The days of one organization developing all of the components of a system are long gone. This is the era of distributed development, where development teams from around the world and from different organizations work jointly to produce a software system. In such cases, an interface control working group (ICWG) comprising the representatives of the participant companies or teams is established. This group may be necessary because the large number of developers and organizations that may be participating in the design effort make it imperative to ensure compatibility of all interfacing entities and to establish better communication.

In most cases, an ICWG is formed at the start of the project. It is composed of the interfacing developers and users and the prime developer's SCM activity. The SCM activity will identify all of the interface specifications and documents authorized by the ICWG, and when released by the ICWG, place them under SCM control. The change process for an interface document is the same as that of any other CI; the only exception is that the CCB is replaced by the ICWG [7]. The SCM activity will also maintain the status accounting of the documentation and changes and provide periodic reports to the various participating organizations represented on the ICWG. Status accounting will also provide the mechanism for requirements traceability to enable communication of the impact created by such changes as they occur. Tools are now in use that will map the entire software system, including interfaces, and delineate the changes that have occurred by some form of reference marking, such as version number or version letter. Such information can be acquired online (if SCM tools that capture this information are used) by the SCM activity and the project for immediate information.

11.6   Subcontractor control

A subcontractor is any supplier, distributor, vendor, or firm that furnishes supplies or services to or for a prime contractor. Subcontractor control is another SCM activity provided for in the software project's SCM plan. It is most important that the developing organization select qualified developers who, in turn, can demonstrate an adequate understanding of performing the SCM process and can meet the requirements that have been flowed down to them by the prime developer.

Configuration management requirements appropriate to the product being acquired are passed down to the subcontractor(s), typically via a purchase order or other subcontractor agreement instrument. Tailoring of requirements for subcontractors is a major SCM planning activity. The performing activity takes on the role of customer (buyer) to the supplier. Suppliers are monitored via data reviews, configuration change management, design reviews, product test results, configuration audits, and SCM surveillance reviews, as appropriate.

Data reviews typically include assessment of supplier plans, procedures, and configuration documentation. *Configuration change management* typically includes review of proposed changes to buyer-approved or imposed configuration documentation. *Design reviews* assess the supplier's progress and provide a level of confidence that the product, when developed, will meet its specified attributes. *Product test results* are positive or negative indicators that required attributes will or will not be satisfied. *Configuration audits* verify that the required attributes have been achieved and the product design has been accurately documented. *SCM surveillance reviews* verify continuing application of supplier SCM processes.

There can be several categories of development subcontracts, including (1) full authority is given to design, develop, build, test, and deliver a specified CI or multiple CIs; (2) limited design authority is given, such as when modifying existing software or performing coding and unit testing only; and (3) no design responsibility is given, and the software to be delivered is termed as a nondevelopmental item (NDI) or commercial off-the-shelf (COTS) software.

The level of configuration change management exercised by the buyer (prime contractor) ranges from none to total, depending on the nature of the product and the conditions of purchase. For a COTS product or NDI, the buyer generally has no control over the product attributes, but can choose not to buy the product.

In the case of a product purchased using a buyer-prepared control drawing, the buyer typically exercises configuration control authority over the specified form, fit, and function attributes. For a product developed to the buyer's specifications, the buyer normally exercises configuration control authority over the product's requirement attributes. The buyer may also exercise control over the product design if more rigorous SCM has been flowed down to the supplier.

11.7   Software library

The software library is the heart of SCM. It contains everything that is important to a software project: source code, user and system documentation, test data, support software, specifications, project plans, and derived items [8]. The software library must be secure. It must only be accessed in ways that are consistent with sound SCM. Both read access and write access must be controlled, the former to prevent unauthorized disclosure and the latter to prevent unauthorized or accidental change or deletion.

The software library is an important asset to the performance of the SCM process, especially in carrying out change control, release management, and status accounting activities. A software library is defined as a controlled collection of software and related documentation designed to aid in software development, use, or maintenance [1]. Types include development library, controlled library, and master library.

The *development library* (sometimes called *dynamic library*) holds newly created or modified software entities, data units, or documentation. The dynamic library is the working library for the development of the source code and is usually managed by developers. This can be a collection of many independent libraries, each owned by different developers. The items in the dynamic library are not under configuration control.

The *controlled library* (sometimes called *production library*) is used to manage current baselines and control changes made to them. It maintains CI units promoted for integration. The controlled library is the entity for retention of approved or released CIs as well as the retention of approved and released software documentation that will be delivered to the customer or distributed to the marketplace.

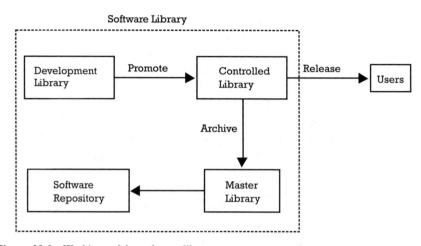

Figure 11.1 Workings of the software library.

The *master library* (also known as *static library*) maintains archives of various baselines released for general use. This library contains master copies and authorized copies of software and documentation released for operational use. The items in the master library should not be changed under any circumstances. The master library usually consists of many different physical repositories or storage media. The *software repository* is the entity that archives software and related documentation at the close of the project. All released documentation and software in the master library should be backed up. The working interfaces of the various software libraries are shown in Figure 11.1.

The status accounting activity will account for all of the software documentation and code in the various library segments and report their status at any given time, including the changes underway, approved, or incorporated.

11.8 Summary

The principles of SCM revolve around three key components: version control, system building, and release management. Version control is simply the automated act of tracking the changes of a particular file over time. Version control gives the ability to trace the history of all CIs in a system and to re-create any previous version of a file. The system build produces the product that is given to clients or shipped to customers. Software release management encompasses the identification, packaging, and delivery of the elements of a product such as the executable, documentation, release notes, and configuration data.

Two other important aspects of SCM are interface control and subcontractor control. Interface control is the process of identifying, documenting, and controlling all performance, functional, and physical attributes relevant to the interfacing of two or more products provided by one or more organizations. Subcontractor control is an activity in which the procedures for ensuring the quality and completeness of products and components of the system that are being developed by a subcontractor or bought directly from the market are established. Both interface control and subcontractor control procedures should be described in the SCM plan. We also saw the different types of software libraries and the role they play in the practice of SCM.

References

[1] IEEE Standard Glossary of Software Engineering Terminology (IEEE Std-610–1990), *IEEE Software Engineering Standards Collection 2003 (CD-ROM Edition)*, Piscataway, NJ: IEEE, 2003.

[2] Sommerville, I., *Software Engineering*, Reading, MA: Addison-Wesley, 2001.

[3] EIA, *National Consensus Standard for Configuration Management (EIA 649)*, Arlington, VA: Electronic Industries Alliance, 1998.

[4] U.S. Department of Defense, *Configuration Management Data Interface (MIL-STD-2549)*, 1997.

[5] NASA, *NASA Software Documentation Standard (NASA-STD-2100-91)*, Washington, DC: National Aeronautics and Space Administration, 1991.

[6] U.S. Department of Defense, *Configuration Management Practices for Systems, Equipment, Munitions and Computer Programs (MIL-STD-483B)*, 1985.

[7] Berlack, H. R., *Software Configuration Management*, New York: John Wiley & Sons, 1992.

[8] Whitgift, D., *Methods and Tools for Software Configuration Management*, Chichester, England: John Wiley & Sons, 1991.

Selected bibliography

Alain Abran, A., and J. W. Moore (eds.), *SWEBOK: Guide to the Software Engineering Body of Knowledge (Trial Version)*, Los Alamitos, CA: IEEE Computer Society, 2001.

Ben-Menachem, M., *Software Configuration Management Guidebook*, New York: McGraw-Hill, 1994.

Berlack, H. R., *Software Configuration Management*, New York: John Wiley & Sons, 1992.

EIA, *National Consensus Standard for Configuration Management (EIA 649)*, Arlington, VA: Electronic Industries Alliance, 1998.

IEEE Software Engineering Standards Collection 2003 (CD-ROM Edition), Piscataway, NJ: IEEE, 2003.

Marciniak, J. J. (ed.), *Encyclopedia of Software Engineering*, 2nd ed., New York: John Wiley & Sons, 2002.

Pressman, R. S., *Software Engineering: A Practitioner's Approach*, New York: McGraw-Hill, 2001.

Sommerville, I., *Software Engineering*, Reading, MA: Addison-Wesley, 2001.

U.S. Department of Defense, *Military Handbook: Configuration Management Guidance (MIL-HDBK-61A (SE))*, 2001.

Whitgift, D., *Methods and Tools for Software Configuration Management*, Chichester, England: John Wiley & Sons, 1991.

SCM standards

12.1 Introduction

Configuration management (CM) got its start in the U.S. defense industry as a technique to resolve problems of poor quality, wrong parts ordered, and parts not fitting, which were leading to inordinate cost overruns. In 1962, the U.S. Air Force published the first standard on configuration management—AFSCM 375-1. The AFSCM 375-1 identified CM as the key element in the design, development, test, and operation of the item to be delivered, because CM procedures facilitated better communication and prevented uncontrolled change. In 1964, the National Aeronautics and Space Administration (NASA) developed a CM standard (NPC 500-1), which was based on AFSCM 375-1, for the design and development of the Saturn V spacecraft. This standard played an instrumental role in the Saturn V and Apollo space programs. During the same time, the U.S. Army came out with its version of a CM standard (AMCR 11-26), and in 1965 the U.S. Navy also followed suit with its standard, NAVMATINST 4130.1 (Configuration Management Policy and Guidance Manual). In 1968 four major standards related to CM were published. They were:

1. Department of Defense Directive (DOD D) 5010.19—Configuration Management

2. MIL-STD-480—Configuration Control Engineering Changes, Deviations and Waivers

3. MIL-STD-482—Configuration Status Accounting Data Elements & Related Features

4. MIL-STD-490—Specification Practices

These standards gave a new thrust to the practice of CM and were integrated into the defense contracts, so that not only the military used these standards internally, but also the defense industry (the government contractors and commercial corporations that supplied materials and equipment to the military) started subscribing and implementing these standards

In 1971, the U.S. Air Force issued MIL-STD-483—Configuration Management Practices for Systems, Equipment, Munitions, & Computer Programs. This was the first standard that recognized CM of both hardware and software. Even though the industry, through the various associations, such as the Electronics Industries Alliance (EIA), Aerospace Industries Association (AIA), National Security Industrial Association (NSIA), and American Electronics Association (AEA), was reviewing the military standards, commercial standards did not appear until 1988. In 1988, the assistant secretary of defense for acquisition, Dr. Costello, wrote a memo indicating that the government should get out of the standards-writing business and entrust the job of developing standards to the organizations that were developing standards on various topics. He also stated that the military would use the standards written by organizations such as the EIA, Institute of Electrical and Electronics Engineers (IEEE), Society of Automotive Engineers (SAE), American National Standards Institute (ANSI), and International Organization for Standardization (ISO) for procuring materials from the commercial market. These organizations had a good track record at developing standards. For example, the EIA had written many standards on electronics, electrical, and communications protocols. The SAE had developed standards on automotive development and related topics. IEEE was one of the pioneers in the development of software standards. Thus, commercial standards on CM from these organizations began to appear.

Now hundreds of CM standards are available, which cover every aspect of CM. A search by the author at the site of one of the largest vendors of technical standards for CM standards, brought up 206 standards. The following list gives some of the popular military and commercial standards:

Note: Some of the standards (mainly MIL and DOD standards) in the following list are cancelled and are no longer active. These cancelled standards cannot be used or referred to in any formal agreement or contracts. These standards are mentioned here because they contain valuable information (which could be used as reference material), and most of them are available on the Internet free of cost.

1. DOD-STD-2167A—Defense System Software Development (cancelled for SCM)

2. DOD-STD-2168—Defense System Software Quality Program

3. MIL-STD-973—Configuration Management, 1990 (cancelled)

4. MIL-HDBK-61A (SE)—Military Handbook for Configuration Management Guidance, 2001

5. MIL-STD-2549—Configuration Management Data Interface, 1997

6. MIL-STD-480B—Configuration Control Engineering Changes, Deviations and Waivers, 1988 (cancelled)

7. MIL-STD-481B—Configuration Control Engineering Changes (Short Form), Deviations and Waivers, 1988 (cancelled)

8. MIL-STD-482—Configuration Status Accounting Data Elements & Related Features, 1974 (cancelled)

9. MIL-STD-483B—Configuration Management Practices for Systems, Equipment, Munitions and Computer Programs, 1985 (cancelled)

10. MIL-STD-490A—Specification Practices, 1985

11. MIL-STD-1521B—Technical Reviews and Audits for Systems, Equipment and Computer Programs, 1985 (cancelled)

12. RCTA DO/178B-92—Software Considerations in Airborne Systems and Equipment Certification

13. NATO STANAG 4159—Configuration Management, 1992

14. STANAG 4427—Introduction of Allied Configuration Management Publications (ACMPs), 1997

15. ACMP-1—NATO Requirements for the Preparation of Configuration Management Plans, 1997

16. ACMP-2—NATO Requirements for Configuration Identification, 1997

17. ACMP-3—NATO Requirements for Configuration Control—Engineering Changes, Deviations and Waivers, 1998

18. ACMP-4—NATO Requirements for Configuration Status Accounting, 1998

19. ACMP-5—NATO Requirements for Configuration Audits, 1998

20. ACMP-6—NATO Configuration Management Terms and Definitions, 1998

21. ACMP-7—NATO Configuration Management Guidance on the Application of ACMPs 1 to 6, 1998

22. NATO NAT-PRC-2—Software Project Configuration Management Procedures

23. UK MOD DEF-STAN 05-57/2—Configuration Management Policy and Procedures for Defense Material

24. NASA Sfw-DID-04—Software Configuration Management Plan Data Item Description, NASA, 1986

25. NASA D-GL-11—Software Configuration Management for Project Managers, NASA, 1987

26. IEEE Std-610.12-1990—IEEE Standard Glossary of Software Engineering Terminology, 1990

27. IEEE Std-828-1998—IEEE Standard for Software Configuration Management Plans, 1998

28. ANSI/IEEE Std-1042-1987—IEEE Guide to Software Configuration Management, 1987

29. ANSI/IEEE Std-730-2002—IEEE Standard for Software Quality Assurance Plans, 1998

30. ANSI/IEEE Std-730.1-1995—IEEE Guide for Software Quality Assurance Planning, 1995

31. ANSI/IEEE Std-1028-1988—Standard for Software Reviews and Audits, 1988

32. IEEE/EIA 12207.0-1996—Industry Implementation of International Standard ISO/IEC 12207: 1995, Standard for Information Technology—Software Life Cycle Processes, 1996

33. IEEE/EIA 12207.1-1997—Industry Implementation of International Standard ISO/IEC 12207: 1995, Standard for Information Technology—Software Life Cycle Processes—Life Cycle Data, 1997

34. IEEE/EIA 12207.2-1997—Industry Implementation of International Standard ISO/IEC 12207: 1995, Standard for Information Technology—Software Life Cycle Processes—Implementation Considerations, 1997

35. ISO 9001:1994—Quality Systems—Model for Quality Assurance in Design, Development, Production, Installation and Servicing, 1994

36. ISO 9001: 2000—Quality Management Systems—Requirements, 2000

37. ISO 9000-3—Guidelines for the Application of ISO 9001 to the Development and Maintenance of Software, 1997

38. ISO 10007—Quality Management—Guidelines for Configuration Management, 2003

39. ISO/IEC TR 15846:1998—Information Technology—Software life-cycle processes –Configuration Management, 1998

40. EIA 649—National Consensus Standard for Configuration Management, 1998

41. EIA 836—Configuration Management Data Exchange and Interoperability, 2002

42. EIA CMB4-1A-84—Configuration Management Definitions for Digital Computer Programs, 1984

43. EIA CMB4-2-81—Configuration Identification for Digital Computer Programs, 1981

44. EIA CMB4-3-81—Computer Software Libraries, 1981

45. EIA CMB4-4-82—Configuration Change Control for Digital Computer Programs, 1982

46. EIA CMB5-A-86—Configuration Management Requirements for Subcontractors/Vendors, 1986

47. EIA CMB6-1C-94—Configuration and Data Management References, 1994

48. EIA CMB6-2-88—Configuration and Data Management In-house Training Plan, 1988

49. EIA CMB6-3-91—Configuration Identification, 1991

50. EIA CMB6-4-91—Configuration Control, 1988

51. EIA CMB6-5-88—Textbook for Configuration Status Accounting, 1988.

52. EIA CMB6-6-96—Textbook for Reviews and Configuration Audits, 1996

53. EIA CMB6-8-88—Data Management In-house Training Course, 1988.

54. EIA CMB6-9-90—Configuration and Data Management Training Course, 1990

55. EIA CMB7-1-91—Electronic Interchange of Configuration Management Data, 1991

56. EIA CMB7-2-91—Guidelines for Transitioning Configuration Management to an Automated Environment, 1991

57. ESA PPS-05-09—Guide to Configuration Management, Issue 1, November 1992

58. FAA-STD-021—Software Configuration Management

59. FEI-4—Software Configuration Management

60. NIST S.P. 500-161—Software Configuration Management—An Overview

61. BS 6488-84—Code of Practice for Configuration Management of Computer-based Systems

62. JPL D-4011—Software Configuration Management Planning, December 1988

The following sections provide an overview of a few representative standards from the list, both military and commercial.

12.2 Military standards

The standards published by the U.S. Department of Defense (DOD) are used by all North Atlantic Treaty Organization (NATO) countries and by countries that use military equipment manufactured in the United States. The next few sections discuss the following CM-related military standards:

1. DOD-STD-2167A—Defense System Software Development (cancelled for SCM)

2. DOD-STD-2168—Defense System Software Quality Program

3. MIL-STD-973—Configuration Management (cancelled)

4. MIL-HDBK-61A (SE)—Military Handbook for Configuration Management Guidance

5. MIL-STD-2549—Configuration Management Data Interface

6. MIL-STD-480B—Configuration Control Engineering Changes, Deviations and Waivers (cancelled)

7. MIL-STD-481B—Configuration Control Engineering Changes (Short Form), Deviations and Waivers (cancelled)

8. MIL-STD-482—Configuration Status Accounting Data Elements & Related Features (cancelled)

9. MIL-STD-483A—Configuration Management Practices for Systems, Equipment, Munitions and Computer Programs (cancelled)

10. MIL-STD-490A—Specification Practices

11. MIL-STD-1521B—Technical Reviews and Audits for Systems, Equipment and Computer Programs (cancelled)

12.2.1 DOD-STD-2167A

This standard supersedes the DOD-STD-2167—Defense System Software Development, 1985. The purpose of this standard is to establish requirements to be applied during the acquisition, development, or support of software systems. The requirements of this standard apply to the development of computer software configuration items (CSCIs). Even though this standard was developed for the DOD environment, it can be tailored to handle rapidly evolving software technology and to accommodate a wide variety of state-of-the-art software engineering techniques. The standard allows the user to incorporate the SCM plan into the software development plan (SDP) or to treat it as a separate document. The benefit of handling the SCM plan as part of the SDP is that, for the projects where SCM is either tightly tied to development life cycle or where the SCM function is relatively small, it allows the SCM plan to be placed in the SDP, where it is more appropriate.

12.2.2 DOD-STD-2168

This standard contains requirements for the development, documentation, and implementation of a software quality program. This program includes planning for and conducting evaluations of the quality of software, associated documentation, and related activities, and planning for and conducting the follow-up activities necessary to ensure timely and effective resolution of problems. This standard, together with other military specifications and standards governing software development, configuration management, specification practices, project reviews and audits, and subcontractor management, provide a means for achieving, determining, and maintaining quality in software and associated documentation.

12.2.3 MIL-STD-973

This standard defines CM requirements, which are to be selectively applied, as required, throughout the life cycle of any configuration item:

 ▸ Developed wholly or partially with government funds, including nondevelopmental items when the development of technical data is required to support off-the-shelf equipment or software, or

 ▸ Designated for configuration management for reason of integration, logistics support, or interface control.

This standard applies to DOD activities and contractors who are tasked with the application of CM.

12.2.4 MIL-HDBK-61A (SE)

This military handbook provides guidance and information to DOD acquisition managers, logistics managers, and other individuals assigned responsibility for CM. Its purpose is to assist them in planning for and implementing effective DOD CM activities and practices during all life cycle phases of defense systems and configuration items. It supports acquisition based on performance specifications and the use of industry standards and methods to the greatest practicable extent. Revision B of this document is currently in draft form and is being reviewed (as of 2004).

This military handbook's content is structured to provide a comprehensive guide (roadmap). After the initial three sections—Scope, Applicable Documents, and Definitions—the handbook is divided into the following major sections:

> *CM Life Cycle Management and Planning* (Section 4). Because management and planning are the keys to effective implementation of CM, Section 4 provides the focus for the entire handbook. It contains an overview of the CM process, a discussion of CM's relationships to other processes, and a synopsis of government/contractor CM during the entire program life cycle. It addresses global CM activities applicable to all phases, such as planning, process implementation, and performance measurement.

> *Major CM Functions* (Sections 5 through 9). In support of Section 4, Sections 5 through 9 contain detailed information in the form of activity descriptions, activity models, principles and concepts, and activity guides (e.g., diagrams, checklists, tables) for the following topics: configuration identification, configuration control, configuration status accounting, configuration verification and audit, and data management.

Appendix F of this handbook contains a comparison of the CM standards such as ISO 10007, IEEE Std-828, and MIL-STD-973 against EIA-649. This matrix is useful because it gives the relative strengths and weaknesses of the four CM standards.

12.2.5 MIL-STD-2549

This document establishes a standard interface for the delivery of, or access to, electronic CM data. This interface prescribes the data elements, the data element definitions, and the data element relationships that define the conceptual schema for CM data. These interface requirements have been subdivided into data information packets to support various CM needs. This standard applies to all activities responsible for procuring, recording, maintaining, and disseminating CM information.

12.2.6 MIL-STD-480B

This standard establishes the requirements, formats, and procedures to be utilized in the preparation of configuration control documentation. Included are requirements for:

1. Maintaining configuration control of configuration items (CIs), both hardware and software;

2. Preparing and submitting Engineering Changes Proposals (ECPs), Requests for Deviations/Waivers (RFDs/RFWs), Notices of Revision (NORs), and Specification Change Notices (SCNs);

3. Evaluating, coordinating, and approving or disapproving ECPs, and RFDs/RFWs applicable to the DOD, commercial, or nondevelopmental items (NDIs).

The purpose of this standard is to establish configuration control requirements and procedures applicable to the acquisition and modification of items procured by the DOD. This standard is to be used by contractors and government activities to:

1. Establish and maintain effective configuration control of the approved configuration identification.

2. Propose engineering changes to configuration items, both hardware and software, which are designed, developed, or modified for DOD activities.

3. Request deviations or waivers pertaining to such items.

4. Prepare NORs and SCNs.

5. Control the form, fit, and function of privately developed items used in configuration items, including NDI items.

12.2.7 MIL-STD-481B

This standard establishes requirements, formats, and procedures for the preparation, submission, and approval or denial of abbreviated ECPs. Where complete descriptions of ECPs are required, MIL-STD-480 should be specified in contracts. The purpose of this standard is to establish configuration control requirements and procedures applicable to the acquisition and modification of items procured by the DOD. It is intended that this standard be applied to contracts or orders for procurement of the following:

1. Multiapplication or standard items, which were not developed as subdivisions of a specific system;

2. Items fabricated in accordance with a mandatory detail design, which was not developed by the fabricator;

3. Privately developed items (e.g., COTS items), when the procuring activity has determined that the application of change control to such items is necessary and that the short-form ECP is applicable.

12.2.8 MIL-STD-482

To ensure the use of uniform, clearly defined status accounting management information throughout the DOD and the DOD–defense industry interface, this standard prescribes status accounting standard data elements, interim (nonstandard) data elements, and their related data items, codes, use identifiers, and data chains (referred to as "related features"). The data elements and related features are to be used as the content of those configuration status accounting records prepared by or for the department or agencies of the DOD in accordance with the provisions of DOD Directive 5010.19 and DOD Instruction 5010.21.

12.2.9 MIL-STD-483A

This military standard sets forth CM practices, which are to be tailored to specific programs and implemented by the contract work statement. The standard also establishes CM requirements, which are not covered in MIL-STD-480, MIL-STD-481, MIL-STD-482, and MIL-STD-490.

12.2.10 MIL-STD-490A

This military standard sets forth practices for the preparation, interpretation, change, and revision of program-peculiar specifications prepared by or for the departments and agencies of the DOD. This military standard was prepared to establish uniform specification practices in response to the need for a document comparable to DOD-STD-100 (which has been cancelled), covering engineering drawing practices and in recognition of the configuration identification concepts of the DOD configuration management program established by DOD Directive 5010.19 and DOD Instruction 5010.21.

12.2.11 MIL-STD-1521B

This standard supersedes MIL-STD-1521 (Technical Reviews & Audits for Systems, Equipment, & Computer Software). This standard prescribes the requirements for the conduct of technical reviews and audits on systems, equipment, and computer software. The program manager shall select the following technical reviews and audits at the appropriate phase of program development:

- System Requirements Review (SRR);
- System Design Review (SDR);
- Software Specification Review (SSR);
- Preliminary Design Review (PDR);
- Critical Design Review (CDR);
- Test Readiness Review (TRR);
- Functional Configuration Audit (FCA);
- Physical Configuration Audit (PCA);
- Formal Qualification Review (FQR);
- Production Readiness Review (PRR).

Technical reviews and audits defined in this standard are to be conducted in accordance with this standard to the extent specified in the contract clauses, statement of work (SOW), and the contract data requirements list.

12.3   International/commercial standards

A host of standards have been developed by many organizations such as the EIA, Electric Power Research Institute (EPRI), European Computer Manufacturers Institute (ECMI), Federal Aviation Authority (FAA), Institute of Nuclear Power Operations (INPO), European Space Agency (ESA), Nuclear Information & Records Management Association (NIRMA), NASA, and NATO, but usage of these standards is limited to the members of those organizations. The most popular international standards on CM are those by ANSI/IEEE and the ISO. In the next paragraphs, we discuss the following popular international/commercial standards:

1. EIA-649—National Consensus Standard for Configuration Management

2. IEEE Std-828-1998—IEEE Standard for Software Configuration Management Plans

3. ANSI/IEEE Std-1042-1987—IEEE Guide to Software Configuration Management

4. ANSI/IEEE Std-730-2002—IEEE Standard for Software Quality Assurance Plans

5. ANSI/IEEE Std-1028-1988—Standard for Software Reviews and Audits

6. IEEE/EIA 12207.0-1996—Industry Implementation of International Standard ISO/IEC 12207: 1995, Standard for Information Technology—Software Life Cycle Processes

7. IEEE/EIA 12207.1-1997—Industry Implementation of International Standard ISO/IEC 12207: 1995, Standard for Information Technology—Software Life Cycle Processes—Life Cycle Data

8. IEEE/EIA 12207.2-1997—Industry Implementation of International Standard ISO/IEC 12207: 1995, Standard for Information Technology—Software Life Cycle Processes—Implementation Considerations

9. ISO 9001:1994—Quality Systems—Model for Quality Assurance in Design, Development, Production, Installation and Servicing

10. ISO 9001: 2000—Quality Management Systems—Requirements

11. ISO 9000-3: 1997—Guidelines for the Application of ISO 9001 to the Development and Maintenance of Software

12. ISO 10007: 2003—Quality Management—Guidelines for Configuration Management

Note: IEEE/EIA 12207 is described as follows as an international standard. In the United States, this standard has been modified for those companies that do not do business on an international scale. The modified standard is identified as US-12207 and carries the same parts as its international parent.

12.3.1   EIA-649-1998

This standard provides an understanding of the technical/program management principles fundamental to CM and the best practices used to implement them. This is one of the most user-friendly standards on CM available. This standard presents CM from the viewpoint that CM practices are employed because they make good business sense rather than because requirements are imposed by an external customer. The standard discusses CM principles and practices from an enterprise view; it does not prescribe which CM activities individual organizations or teams within the enterprise should perform. Each enterprise assigns responsibilities in accordance with its own management policy. The standard explains the major CM functions rather than mandates them. The explanation includes purpose, benefits, and best practices. Within each topic, the basic principles of CM are addressed. According to EIA 649, the CM process addresses the composition of a product, configuration documentation defining the product, and other data and products that support it. It provides tailored methods and procedures for effectively planning, recording, controlling, and validating product requirements and data that contain the requirements. Appendix A of EIA 649 is a useful and informative list of 50 CM principles discussed in the standard.

12.3.2   IEEE Std-828-1998

This standard is concerned with the activity of planning for software configuration management. SCM activities, whether planned or not, are performed on all software development projects; planning makes these activities more effective. Good planning results in a document that captures the planning information, makes the information the property of the project, communicates to all who are affected, and provides a basis for ongoing planning. This standard establishes the minimum required contents of an SCM plan. It is supplemented by IEEE Std-1042-1987, which provides approaches to good software CM planning. The primary users of this standard are assumed to be those planning SCM activities or performing SCM audits.

12.3.3   ANSI/IEEE Std-1042-1987

This is the most comprehensive international standard available on SCM. This standard describes the application of CM disciplines to the management of software engineering projects. SCM consists of two major aspects—planning and implementation. For those planning SCM activities, this standard provides insights into the various factors that must be considered. Users implementing SCM disciplines will find suggestions and detailed examples of SCM plans in this standard. This standard introduces the essential concepts of SCM, particularly those of special significance (e.g., libraries and tools) to software engineering. It then presents planning for SCM in terms of documenting a plan following the outline of ANSI/IEEE Std-828, so that a user who is unfamiliar with the discipline of SCM can gain valuable insights into the issues. For those preparing SCM plans, the second part of the guide provides sample plans for consideration.

12.3.4   ANSI/IEEE Std-730-2002

The purpose of this standard is to provide uniform, minimum acceptable requirements for preparation and content of software quality assurance plans (SQAPs). This standard applies to the development and maintenance of critical software. For noncritical software, or for software that has already been developed, a subset of the requirements of this standard may be applied. Although this document does not require the use of IEEE/EIA Std 12207.0-1996 and IEEE/EIA Std12207.1-1997, it is consistent with those two standards. An SQAP meeting the requirements of this standard will be in document compliance with the SQAP information item of IEEE/EIA 12207.1-1997.

12.3.5   ANSI/IEEE Std-1028-1988

The purpose of this standard is to provide definitions and uniform requirements for the review and audit processes. It does not establish the need to conduct specific reviews or audits; that need is defined by local policy. Where specific reviews and audits are required, standard procedures for their execution must be defined. This standard provides such definition for review and audit purposes that are applicable to products and processes throughout the software life cycle. Each organization should specify where and when this standard applies and any intended deviations from this standard.

12.3.6   IEEE/EIA 12207.0-1996

This international standard establishes a common framework for software life cycle processes, with well-defined terminology, which can be referenced by the software industry. It contains processes, activities, and tasks that are to be applied during the acquisition of a system that contains software, a stand-alone software product, and software service and during the supply, development, operation, and maintenance of software products. Software includes the software portion of firmware. This international standard also provides a process that can be employed for defining, controlling, and improving software life cycle processes.

CM process is mentioned under the supporting process (Section 6.2). The standard defines configuration management as a process of applying administrative and technical procedures throughout the software life cycle to identify, define, and baseline software items in a system; control modifications and releases of the items; record and report the status of the items and modification requests; ensure the completeness, consistency, and correctness of the items; and control storage, handling, and delivery of the items.

According to the standard, the CM process consists of the following activities: process implementation, configuration identification, configuration control, configuration status accounting, configuration evaluation, and release management and delivery.

12.3.7   IEEE/EIA 12207.1-1997

This guide defines the life cycle data of IEEE/EIA 12207.0 by relating the tasks and activities defined in IEEE/EIA 12207.0 with the following kinds of documentation: description, plan, procedure, record, report, request, and specification. This standard provides a mapping of the various life cycle data (input and output) produced as required by IEEE/EIA 12207.0 with the kind of documentation to be produced as described in Clause 5 of IEEE/EIA 12207.1, the clause containing specific content guidelines, and available standards, guides, and technical reports published by IEEE, ISO/IEC JTC1/SC7, and other organizations. This table is called the Information Item Matrix (IIM).

You can use IEEE/EIA 12207.1 as a guide or as a standard. When used as a standard, there are two ways to claim compliance with IEEE/EIA 12207.1. One may claim that an individual document or group of documents complies with the requirements of IEEE/EIA 12207.1. To be compliant, the document or group of documents shall satisfy the characteristics summarized in the IIM. You can also claim that your organization's processes comply with the requirements of IEEE/EIA 12207.1. An organization may claim that one or more organizational processes comply with IEEE/EIA 12207.1 by documenting that those processes would produce documents or document groups complying with the corresponding rows of the IIM. The standard provides the content guidelines for SCM plans and SCM records.

12.3.8   IEEE/EIA 12207.2-1997

This guide provides implementation consideration guidance for the normative clauses of IEEE/EIA 12207.0. The guidance is based on software industry experience with the life cycle processes presented in IEEE/EIA 12207.0. According to the standard, use of the CM process should achieve the following objectives:

- Identify, define, and control all relevant items of the project.

- Control modifications of the items.

- Record and report the status of items and modification requests.

- Ensure the completeness of the items.

- Control storage, handling, release, and delivery of the items.

12.3.9   ISO 9001:1994

ISO 9001:1994 is a model for QA when conformance to specified requirements is to be assured by the supplier during design, development, production, installation, and servicing. This standard specifies quality system requirements for use where a supplier's capability to design and supply conforming product needs to be demonstrated. The requirements specified are aimed primarily at achieving customer satisfaction by preventing nonconformity at all stages from design through servicing. ISO 9000 is not a standard that is specific to software development. It is a general standard that can be tailored to any industry. This standard does not mention the term *configuration management* anywhere in it but contains most CM concepts. A few examples are given as follows:

- All design changes and modifications shall be identified, documented, reviewed and approved by authorized personnel before their implementation. (Section 4.4.9, Design changes)

- The documents and data shall be reviewed and approved for adequacy by authorized personnel prior to issue. A master list or equivalent document control procedure identifying the current revision status of documents shall be established and be readily available to preclude the use of invalid and/or obsolete documents. (Section 4.5.2, Document and data approval and issue)

- Where and to the extent that traceability is a specified requirement, the supplier shall establish and maintain documented procedures for unique identification of individual product or batches. This identification shall be recorded. (Section 4.8, Product identification and traceability)

- Nonconforming product shall be reviewed in accordance with documented procedures. It may be reworked to meet the specified requirements, accepted with or without repair by concession, regarded for alternative applications, or rejected or scrapped. (Section 4.13.2, Review and disposition of nonconforming product)

- The supplier shall implement and record any changes to the documented procedures resulting from corrective and preventive action. (Section 4.14.1, Corrective and preventive action: General)

12.3.10   ISO 9001: 2000

ISO 9001: 1994 is now replaced by ISO 9001: 2000. The standard also does not extensively use the term *configuration management* (although the term is mentioned once in a note), but the concepts are very much present. Some examples are given as follows:

- There should be a mechanism to control quality system documents. This mechanism should approve documents before they are distributed, provide the correct version of documents at points of use, review and re-approve documents whenever they are updated, specify the current revision status of the documents, monitor documents that come from external sources, prevent the accidental use of obsolete documents and preserve the usability of your quality documents. (Section 4.2.3)

- The organization should maintain quality system records and should be able to prove that requirements have been met using the records. A procedure to control the records should be developed and it must be ensured that all the records are useable. (Section 4.2.4)

- You should manage design and development changes by identifying, recording, reviewing, verifying, validating and approving the changes in product design and development. (Section 7.3.7)

- You should identify and track your products by establishing, maintaining and recording the identity of the products. (Section 7.5.3)

- The organization should control nonconforming products by developing a procedure to control nonconforming products, identifying and controlling the nonconforming products, re-verifying the nonconforming products that were corrected, controlling nonconforming products after delivery or use and maintaining records of nonconforming products. (Section 7.5.3)

- You must correct actual nonconformities by reviewing the nonconformities, finding out what causes your nonconformities, evaluating whether you need to take corrective action, developing corrective actions to prevent recurrence, recording the results that your corrective actions achieve and examining the effectiveness of your corrective actions. (Section 8.5.2)

12.3.11   ISO 9000-3: 1997

The ISO 9000 series of standards were not primarily designed for software but for manufacturing processes. ISO 9001 is the model for QA in design/development, production, installation, and servicing (in other words, manufacturing processes that have design aspects). The standard ISO 9000-3 contains guidelines for the application of ISO 9001 to the development, supply, and maintenance of software. This standard mentions identification of CM procedures as a part of quality planning, mentions the need to develop an SCM plan, and stresses the importance of bringing the various artifacts under configuration control before use. For CM functions and procedures, this standard refers to ISO 10007.

12.3.12 ISO 10007: 2003

This international standard gives guidance on the use of CM in industry and its interface with other management systems and procedures. It first provides a management overview and then describes the process, organization, and detailed procedures.

ISO 10007 defines *configuration management* as a management discipline that applies technical and administrative direction to the development, production, and support life cycle of a configuration item. The main objective of CM is to document and provide full visibility of the product's present configuration and on the status of achievement of its physical and functional requirements. Another objective is that everyone working on the project at any time in its life cycle uses correct and accurate documentation.

This standard is applicable to the support of projects from concept through design, development, procurement, production, installation, operation, and maintenance and to the disposal of products. The application of CM may be tailored to suit individual projects, taking into account the size, complexity, and nature of the work.

The standard offers definitions of CM terms, and Annex A provides an excellent template for creating the CM plan. Annex C provides a correlation between the different project life cycle phases and the various CM activities.

12.4 Summary

The ANSI/IEEE standards are the most widely used SCM standards, and the coverage of SCM and its functions is elaborate, comprehensive, and thorough. ISO 9000-3 and ISO 10007 provide another set of good CM standards. EIA-649 is perhaps the most readable SCM standard available. The DOD and MIL standards are mainly used in defense industry projects, and even though they could be tailored for any project, their use is generally limited to the defense industry and military organizations within and outside the United States.

The SCM standards (most preferably EIA-649) are the starting point for the practice of CM and related functions in any project or organization. They are the first place one should look for guidance when starting a CM program. If your organization does not deal with the defense industry, it would be better to base your SCM system on one of the commercial standards, such as EIA, ANSI/IEEE, or ISO. This is because these standards are written for the entire industry (whereas the DOD standards were written for their specific segments of industry), and hence they are more flexible and can be customized more easily to suit your needs. Also, these standards have greater potential for timely updates than the DOD standards; because this standard is used by the general industry, it must maintain relevance to the current software engineering principles and practices or face obsolescence. The CM standards have played a crucial role in shaping the way in which CM is practiced today.

Table 12.1 compares the coverage of the CM principles, procedures, and functionality by four standards: EIA-649, IEEE Std-828, ISO 10007, and MIL-STD-973.

Table 12.1 Comparison of CM Standards

CM Principles	649	828	10007	973
CM Planning and Management	5.1	4	4.2.2 6.2 7.2.1 7.7	4.2
Identifying Context and Environment	5.1.1	1.1	6.1 6.2 7.7	4.2
Configuration Management Plan	5.1.2	4	4.2.3 7.7	4.2 5.2.1
CM Plan Template	—	4*	Annex A	Appendix A
CM Plan Maintenance	—	4.6	—	—
Implementation Procedures	5.1.3	4.4	4.2.3 7.2, 7.4, 7.5, 7.6	4.2 5.2.1
Training	5.1.4	4.5	6.2	—
Performance Measurement	5.1.5	—	4.2.4 8	5.5.7
Supplier Configuration Management	5.1.6	4.3.6	6.2	5.6.1.1
Configuration Identification	5.2	4.3.1	5.2	4.4 5.3.1 5.2.5
Product Information	5.2.1	4.3.1.1	7.2.2	5.3.1 5.3.4.1 5.3.4.2
Product Structure	5.2.2	4.3.1.1	5.2.1 7.2.1	5.3.1 5.3.2
Product Identifiers	5.2.3	4.3.1.2	7.2.3	5.3.6 5.3.6.1 5.3.6.2 5.3.6.4 5.3.6.5 5.3.6.7

Table 12.1 Comparison of CM Standards *(continued)*

CM Principles	649	828	10007	973
Identifying Individual Units of a Product	5.2.3.1	—	A.3	5.3.6.6
Identifying Groups of Units of a Product	5.2.3.2	—	—	5.3.6.6
Document Identification	5.2.4	4.3.1.1 4.3.1.2	5.2.3 7.2.3	5.3.6.3
Baselines	5.2.5	4.3.1.1	5.2.4 7.2.4	5.3.3 5.3.4
Establishing Baselines	5.2.5.1	4.3.1.1	5.2.4 7.2.4	5.3.3 5.3.4 5.3.5
Types of Baselines	5.2.5.2	—	5.2.4 7.2.4	5.3.3 5.3.4
Release System	5.2.5 5.2.5.1 5.2.5.2 5.3.3	—	5.3	5.3.5
Product Identification Recovery	5.2.6	—	—	—
Interface Control	5.2.7	4.3.5	—	5.3.7
Configuration Change Management	5.3	4.3.2	5.3	4.5 5.4 5.4.1 5.4.2.1
Change Identification	5.3.1	4.3.2	5.2.3 7.2.3 7.4.1	5.4.2
Requesting Changes	5.3.1.1	4.3.2.1	7.4.1	5.4.2
Classifying Changes	5.3.1.2	4.3.2.1	5.3 7.4.1	5.4.2.2.1 5.4.2.4
Documenting Request for Changes	5.3.1.3	4.3.2.1	5.3 7.4.1	5.4.2.2.3 5.4.2.3.5 5.4.2.4.1
Change Evaluation and Coordination	5.3.2	4.3.2.2	5.3 6.2 7.4.2 7.4.3	5.4.2.1
Change Impact Assessment	5.3.2.1	4.3.2.2	5.3 7.3 7.4.2	5.4.2.1
Change Effectivity Determination	5.3.2.2	4.3.2.2	—	D.5.1.21 D.5.1.23

Table 12.1   Comparison of CM Standards *(continued)*

CM Principles	649	828	10007	973
Change Cost/Price Determination	5.3.2.3	4.3.2.2	—	D.5.4.2
				5.4.2.2.3.3
Change Approval Authority	5.3.2.4	4.3.2.3	5.3	5.4.2.3.1
			7.3	5.4.2.4.3
			7.4.3	5.4.2.4.4
				5.4.2.4.5
Change Implementation and Verification	5.3.3	4.3.2.4	5.3	5.4.2.1
			7.4.4	
Change Management Process applied to Variances	5.3.4	—	5.3	4.5
			7.3	5.4.3
				5.4.4
Configuration Status Accounting (CSA)	5.4	4.3.3	5.4	4.6
			7.5.1	5.5.1
CSA Information	5.4.1	4.3.3	5.4	4.6
			7.5.2	4.5.2
			7.5.3	5.5.4
				5.5.5
				5.5.8
CSA System	5.4.2	4.3.3	5.4	5.5.3
			7.5.2	
			7.5.3	
Configuration Verification and Audit	5.5	4.3.4	5.5	4.7
				5.6.1
				5.6.2
				5.6.3
Design and Document Verification	5.5.1	4.3.4	5.5	5.6.2
			7.4.4	5.6.3
			7.6	
Configuration Audit	5.5.2	4.3.4	7.6	5.6.1
				5.6.2
				5.6.3
Continuing Performance Audits and Surveillance	5.5.3	4.3.4	7.6	4.7
Configuration Management of Digital Data	5.6	—	7.2.3	4.3
Digital Data Identification	5.6.1	—	7.2.3	4.3.2
Data Status Level Management	5.6.2	—	5.3	4.3.2
Maintenance of Data and Product Configuration	5.6.3	—	7.2.3	4.3.2
Data Version Control and Management of Review, Comment, Annotation, and Disposition	5.6.4	—	7.2.3	4.3.2

Table 12.1 Comparison of CM Standards *(continued)*

CM Principles	649	828	10007	973
Digital Data Transmittal	5.6.5	—	—	4.3.1
				4.3.2
				4.3.3
Data Access Control	5.6.6.	—	—	4.3.1
				4.3.2
				4.3.3
Subcontractor Control	—	4.3.6	—	5.6.1.3
				A.4.2.14
				A.5.1.14
Resources	5.1	4.5	—	4.2
				5.6.1.2

* The format provided in IEEE Std-828 is converted to template form and explained with examples in IEEE Std-1042 (IEEE Guide to Software Configuration Management).

Selected bibliography

Alain Abran, A., and J. W. Moore (eds.), *SWEBOK: Guide to the Software Engineering Body of Knowledge (Trial Version)*, Los Alamitos, CA: IEEE Computer Society, 2001.

Ben-Menachem, M., *Software Configuration Management Guidebook*, New York: McGraw-Hill, 1994.

Berlack, R. H., *Software Configuration Management*, New York: John Wiley & Sons, 1992.

IEEE Software Engineering Standards Collection 2003 (CD-ROM Edition), Piscataway, NJ: IEEE, 2003.

Ince, D., *ISO 9001 and Software Quality Assurance*, London: McGraw-Hill, 1994.

Marciniak, J. J. (ed.), *Encyclopedia of Software Engineering*, 2nd ed., New York: John Wiley & Sons, 2002.

Peach, R. W. (ed.), *The ISO 9000 Handbook*, New York: McGraw-Hill. 1997.

Pressman, R. S., *Software Engineering: A Practitioner's Approach*, New York: McGraw-Hill, 2001.

Sommerville, I., *Software Engineering*, Reading, MA: Addison-Wesley, 2001.

Whitgift, D., *Methods and Tools for Software Configuration Management*, Chichester, England: John Wiley & Sons, 1991.

13

Software process improvement models and SCM

13.1 Introduction

A process is a series of interrelated activities that bring about a result or that are directed toward a particular aim. Process improvement is the analysis and redesign of processes to eliminate organizational problems and inefficiencies in small increments, over time, by improving one or two processes at a time. Process improvement is done on an operational level (as opposed to radical reengineering, which is done on a strategic level) and is carried out primarily by the people who are most involved in the process. The incremental process improvement approach builds in small successes that motivate teams to continue. Failure, if it occurs, has less potential to do serious damage because the scope is limited to one or two processes at a time.

Process improvement models define the various processes and activities that will help an organization to move from a stage of total confusion, lack of discipline, and ad hoc processes to a stage where the organization has well-defined and mature processes that help the organization not only to deliver high-quality products and services repeatedly but also to continuously improve the quality of the products and services and efficiency of the organization.

The software process improvement models assess the current state of an organization and determine where it belongs in the process maturity scale. Then these models give specific guidelines to move from the current state to a process maturity level, where the organizations have the necessary processes to continuously improve their products and services.

This section describes some of the most common process assessment and improvement models and standards. These include CMM, CMMI, ISO/IEC 15504 (formerly SPICE),

BOOTSTRAP, and Trillium. We will see what the role of configuration management is in process improvement and how the aforementioned process improvement and assessment models relate configuration management and process improvement.

13.2 Capability Maturity Model

The Capability Maturity Model[SM] (CMM) for software describes the principles and practices underlying software process maturity and is intended to help software organizations improve the maturity of their software processes in terms of an evolutionary path from ad hoc, chaotic processes to mature, disciplined software processes. The CMM is organized into five maturity levels: initial, repeatable, defined, managed, and optimizing. A maturity level is a well-defined evolutionary plateau toward achieving a mature software process. Each maturity level provides a layer in the foundation for continuous process improvement.

Except for level 1, each maturity level is broken down into several key process areas that indicate the areas an organization should focus on to improve its software process. Key process areas identify the issues that must be addressed to achieve a maturity level. Each key process area identifies a cluster of related activities that, when performed collectively, achieve a set of goals considered important for enhancing process capability. *Configuration management* is a key process area for level 2. So for any organization that wants to achieve CMM level 2 or above, configuration management practices have to be performed in accordance with the guidance provided by the CMM document.

According to the CMM documents, the configuration management practice should achieve the following four goals:

1. Software configuration management activities are planned.

2. Selected software work products are identified, controlled, and available.

3. Changes to identified software work products are controlled.

4. Affected groups and individuals are informed of the status and content of software baselines.

To achieve these goals, the CMM requires certain commitments from the organization—*Commitment to Perform*. The organizations should also have the necessary resources (e.g., funding, tools, training capabilities) to achieve these goals—*Ability to Perform*. The CMM also specifies several activities to be performed to achieve the goals—*Activities Performed*. The model also provides for mechanisms for measuring and reviewing data—*Measurement and Analysis*, and for analyzing, determing status, and auditing—*Verifying Implementation*.

13.3 Capability Maturity Model Integration

The CMMI^{SM} project was formed to to address the need that computer system development environments were concerned with more than just software. The CMMI product team's mission was to combine three source models:

1. The Capability Maturity Model for Software (SW-CMM) v2.0 draft C

2. The Systems Engineering Capability Model (SECM)

3. The Integrated Product Development Capability Maturity Model (IPD-CMM) v 0.98

The combination of these models into a single improvement framework is intended for use by organizations in their pursuit of enterprise-wide process improvement.

There are two types of CMMI model representations: staged and continuous. The staged representation is the approach used in the SW-CMM. This approach uses predefined sets of process areas to define an improvement path for an organization. This improvement path is described by a model component called a maturity level. A maturity level is a well-defined evolutionary plateau toward achieving improved organizational processes for a project (i.e., the project moves through the maturity levels).

The continuous representation allows an organization to select a specific process area and improve relative to it. The continuous representation uses capability levels to characterize improvement relative to an individual process area. A capability level is a well-defined evolutionary plateau toward achieving improved organizational processes for a particular organization (i.e., an organization (functional group, e.g., SCM) moves through the capability levels).

Configuration management comes under the Support process area of CMMI. CMMI defines *configuration management* as a discipline whose purpose is to establish and maintain the integrity of work products using configuration identification, configuration control, configuration status accounting, and configuration audits.

The Configuration Management process area supports all process areas by establishing and maintaining the integrity of work products using configuration identification, configuration control, configuration status accounting, and configuration audits. The work products placed under configuration management include the products that are delivered to the customer, designated internal work products, acquired products, tools, and other items that are used in creating and describing these work products. Examples of work products that may be placed under configuration management include plans, process descriptions, requirements, design data, drawings, product specifications, code, compilers, product data files, and product technical publications.

The specific goals for configuration management as defined in CMMI are:

1. *Establish baselines.* Baselines of identified work products are established.

2. *Track and control changes.* Changes to the work products under configuration management are tracked and controlled.

3. *Establish integrity.* Integrity of baselines is established and maintained.

The specific goals are achieved by following several specific practices. The practices for each specific goal of configuration management are:

▸ Establish baselines (SG 1)

1. Identify configuration items (SP 1.1-1)

2. Establish a configuration management system (SP 1.2-1)

3. Create or release baselines (SP 1.3-1)

▸ Track and control changes (SG 2)

1. Track change requests (SP 2.1-1)

2. Control configuration items (SP 2.2-1)

▸ Establish integrity (SG 3)

1. Establish configuration management records (SP 3.1-1)

2. Perform configuration audits (SP 3.2-1)

13.4 ISO/IEC 15504

ISO/IEC 15504 is a process improvement and assessment standard. This standard was developed jointly by the Joint Technical Committee 1/Sub Committee (JTC1/SC7) of the International Organization for Standardization (ISO) and International Electrotechnical Commission (IEC). The work was assigned to a group called WG10, which established a special project called SPICE (*S*oftware *P*rocess *I*mprovement and *C*apability d*E*termination). The SPICE project, which was established in 1993, developed a set of draft standards that finally (after countless reviews and revisions) evolved into the ISO/IEC 15504 standard.

ISO/IEC 15504 process model is divided into five categories: organizational process (ORG), management process (MNA), customer-supplier process (CUS), engineering process (ENG), and support process (SUP). Each of these processes is divided into several process areas. *Configuration management* comes under the support process—SUP.2.

The purpose of SUP.2 is to establish and maintain the integrity of all work products of a process or project. The successful implementation of the process should lead to the following outcomes:

- Identifying, defining, and baselining all relevant items generated by the process or project;
- Controlling modifications and releases;
- Recording and reporting the status of the items and modification requests;
- Ensuring the completeness and consistency of the items;
- Controlling storage, handling, and delivery of the items.

The standard defines nine best practices that will lead to the successful implementation of a configuration management (CM) system. These include developing a CM strategy, establishing a CM system, identifying the configuration item, maintaining the configuration item description, establishing formal change management procedures, managing product releases, maintaining the configuration item history, reporting configuration status, and managing the release and delivery of configuration items.

This model has six levels (0 to 5) of process capability: incomplete, performed, planned and tracked, established, predictable, and optimizing. Because this model is continuous, CM must be performed at the different levels. To obtain level 1, CM must be performed so that the expected outcomes are achieved. Level 2 requires placing the work products under configuration control and developing a CM plan. To obtain level 3, the CM procedures should be documented, and the resources required for performing CM must be made available. Level 4 requires establishing metrics for measuring the performance of CM and controlling performance based on the measurements. At level 5, CM metrics are used to improve CM performance and again used to measure this improved performance.

13.5 BOOTSTRAP

BOOTSTRAP is a method to evaluate and improve the quality of the software development and management processes of an organization. BOOTSTRAP is based on the assumption that the capabilities of an organization increase one step after the other. The concepts behind this approach were published by Watts Humphrey while he was working for the Software Engineering Institute (SEI) at Carnegie-Mellon University. The Capability Maturity Model^{SM} (CMM) distinguishes five levels of process quality, while the Capability Maturity Model Integration (CMMI) has six levels. This model is now the software process standard in the United States. BOOTSTRAP uses the same basic principles. The reference model has been extended to cover the requirements imposed by ISO 9000. BOOTSTRAP delivers not only the maturity level, but also a detailed capability profile of the organization and the projects investigated.

BOOTSTRAP adopts a process model that addresses the processes and practices for the organization and the project. The process areas are categorized into organization, methodology, and technology. The process categories comprise process areas, which contains activities and best practices. The methodology process is again divided into three process areas: process engineering, product engineering, and engineering support functions. Each of these process areas contains various activities. Configuration and change management is an activity under engineering support functions. The BOOTSTRAP process model contains many best practices for the configuration and change management activity that are similar to those of ISO/IEC 15504.

BOOTSTRAP has five maturity levels: initial, repeatable, defined, managed, and optimizing. The process areas are not confined to a single level but cover several levels.

13.6   Trillium Model

The goal of the Trillium Model is to provide a means to initiate and guide a continuous improvement program. The model is used in a variety of ways:

- ▸ To benchmark an organization's product development and support process capability against best practices in the industry;

- ▸ In self-assessment mode, to help identify opportunities for improvement within a product development organization;

- ▸ In precontractual negotiations, to assist in selecting a supplier.

This model and its accompanying tools are not in themselves a product development process or life cycle model. Rather, the Trillium Model provides key industry practices, which can be used to improve an existing process or life cycle. The practices in the Trillium Model are derived from a benchmarking exercise that focused on all practices that would contribute to an organization's product development and support capability. Trillium has a telecommunications orientation, provides a customer focus, provides a product perspective, covers CMM, ISO 9001, ISO 9000-3, Bellcore's TR-NWT-000179 and TA-NWT-001315, Malcom Baldrige National Quality Award criteria, and IEEE and IEC standards, includes technological maturity, includes additional Trillium-specific practices, and provides a roadmap approach that sequences improvements by maturity.

The Trillium Model has been developed from a customer perspective, as perceived in a competitive, commercial environment. In this context, *capability* is defined as the ability of a development organization to consistently deliver a product or an enhancement to an existing product that meets customer expectations with minimal defects for the lowest life cycle cost and in the shortest time. A telecommunications product typically includes hardware, software, documentation, training, and support services.

The Trillium scale spans levels 1 through 5. The levels can be characterized in the following way:

1. *Unstructured.* The development process is ad hoc. Projects frequently cannot meet quality or schedule targets. Success, while possible, is based on individuals rather than on organizational infrastructure. (Risk: High)

2. *Repeatable and project-oriented.* Individual project success is achieved through strong project management planning and control, with emphasis on requirements management, estimation techniques, and configuration management. (Risk: Medium)

3. *Defined and process-oriented.* Processes are defined and utilized at the organizational level, although project customization is still permitted. Processes are controlled and improved. ISO 9001 requirements, such as training and internal process auditing, are incorporated. (Risk: Low)

4. *Managed and integrated.* Process instrumentation and analysis is used as a key mechanism for process improvement. Process change management and defect-prevention programs are integrated into processes. Computer-aided software engineering (CASE) tools are integrated into processes. (Risk: Lower)

5. *Fully integrated.* Formal methodologies are extensively used. Organizational repositories for development history and process are utilized and effective. (Risk: Lowest)

Each level (except level 1) contains several capability areas, which in turn contain roadmaps, which consist of activities. This approach is similar to the CMM. Each capability area spans multiple levels. For example, the development practices capability area spans levels 2, 3, and 5. The development practices capability area contains the *configuration management roadmap*, among six other roadmaps. This is shown in Table 13.1.

13.7 Summary

Configuration management is a vital discipline for all of the process improvement efforts and models that exist today. Process improvement models such as CMM, CMMI, SPICE, BOOTSTRAP, and Trillium require configuration management. To achieve certification, the existence of formal configuration management and procedures is a must.

Table 13.1   Configuration Management in Trillium Model

Level	Criteria	Description
2	Scope	Source code is under configuration management (CM) control.
		All project and product (internal and external) documents are under CM control.
	Function	A board having the authority to manage the project's product baselines (i.e., a product configuration control board) exists or is established.
		A function is responsible for coordinating and implementing CM for the project.
	Funding	Adequate resources and funding are provided to perform the CM activities.
	Planning	A CM plan is prepared for each project according to a documented procedure.
		A documented and approved CM plan is used as the basis for performing the CM activities.
	Repository	A CM system is established as a repository for product baselines.
		The product repository ensures secure storage of configuration items (e.g., code units, design documents) and the secure and controlled retrieval of current and previous versions of configuration items.
		The product repository ensures the secure and controlled retrieval of current and previous baselines.
		The status of configuration items/units is recorded according to a documented procedure.
		The product repository maintains records of the status and change history of all configuration items and baselines.
	Traceability	There is traceability between design specifications and source code and also between design specifications and integration test cases.
	Change Control	Change requests and problem reports for all configuration items/units are initiated, recorded, reviewed, approved, and tracked according to a documented procedure.
		Configuration items and baselines are changed formally according to a documented procedure.
	Baselines	Baseline(s) are created and released formally.
		Product baseline audits are conducted according to a documented procedure.
	Reporting	Standard reports documenting the CM activities and the contents of the product baselines are developed and made available to affected groups and individuals.
3	Scope	Plans, descriptions, product test procedures, requirements specifications, design specifications, review results, and test cases (e.g., integration, system, operation) are under CM control.
		All development tools are under CM control.
	Traceability	There is full forward and backward traceability between all configuration items (e.g., design specification forward to code units, design specification backward to requirement specification).
5	Scope	The complete development history (e.g., design decisions, design rationale) is captured and maintained under CM control.

Selected bibliography

Bell Canada, *Trillium: Model for Telecom Product Development & Support Process Capability* (Release 3), Bell Canada, 1994.

Chrissis, B. M., M. Konrad, S. and Shrum, *Introduction to CMMI*, Reading, MA: Addison-Wesley, 2003.

Caputo, K., *CMM Implementation Guide*, Reading, MA: Addison-Wesley, 1998.

CMMI Product Team, Capability Maturity Model® Integration (CMMI[SM]), Version 1.1: CMMI[SM] for Systems Engineering and Software Engineering (CMMI-SE/SW, V1.1), Continuous Representation, Technical Report (CMU/SEI-2002-TR-001), Software Engineering Institute, Carnegie-Mellon University, 2001.

CMMI Product Team, Capability Maturity Model® Integration (CMMI[SM]), Version 1.1: CMMI[SM] for Systems Engineering and Software Engineering (CMMI-SE/SW, V1.1), Staged Representation, Technical Report (CMU/SEI-2002-TR-002), Software Engineering Institute, Carnegie-Mellon University, 2001.

CMMI Product Team, Capability Maturity Model® Integration (CMMI[SM]), Version 1.1: CMMI[SM] for Systems Engineering, Software Engineering, and Integrated Product and Process Development (CMMI-SE/SW/IPPD, V1.1), Continuous Representation, Technical Report (CMU/SEI-2002-TR-003), Software Engineering Institute, Carnegie-Mellon University, 2001.

CMMI Product Team, Capability Maturity Model® Integration (CMMI[SM]), Version 1.1: CMMI[SM] for Systems Engineering, Software Engineering, and Integrated Product and Process Development (CMMI-SE/SW/IPPD, V1.1), Staged Representation, Technical Report (CMU/SEI-2002-TR-004), Software Engineering Institute, Carnegie-Mellon University, 2001.

CMMI Product Team, Capability Maturity Model® Integration (CMMI[SM]), Version 1.1: CMMI[SM] for Systems Engineering, Software Engineering, Integrated Product and Process Development, and Supplier Sourcing (CMMI-SE/SW/IPPD/SS, V1.1), Continuous Representation, Technical Report (CMU/SEI-2002-TR-011), Software Engineering Institute, Carnegie-Mellon University, 2002.

CMMI Product Team, Capability Maturity Model® Integration (CMMI[SM]), Version 1.1: CMMI[SM] for Systems Engineering, Software Engineering, Integrated Product and Process Development, and Supplier Sourcing (CMMI-SE/SW/IPPD/SS, V1.1), Staged Representation, Technical Report (CMU/SEI-2002-TR-012), Software Engineering Institute, Carnegie-Mellon University, 2002.

CMMI Product Team, Capability Maturity Model® Integration (CMMI[SM]), Version 1.1: CMMI[SM] for Software Engineering (CMMI-SW, V1.1), Continuous Representation, Technical Report (CMU/SEI-2002-TR-028), Software Engineering Institute, Carnegie-Mellon University, 2002.

CMMI Product Team, Capability Maturity Model® Integration (CMMI[SM]), Version 1.1: CMMI[SM] for Software Engineering (CMMI-SW, V1.1), Staged Representation, Technical Report (CMU/SEI-2002-TR-029), Software Engineering Institute, Carnegie-Mellon University, 2002.

Garcia, S. M., *Evolving Improvement Paradigms: Capability Maturity Models & ISO/IEC 15504* (PDTR), Software Engineering Institute, Carnegie-Mellon University, 1996.

Marciniak, J. J. (ed.), *Encyclopedia of Software Engineering*, 2nd ed., New York: John Wiley & Sons, 2002.

Paulk, M. C., *A Comparison of ISO 9001 and the Capability Maturity Model for Software, Technical Report* (CMU/SEI-94-TR-12), Software Engineering Institute, Carnegie-Mellon University, 1994.

Paulk, M. C., et al, Capability Maturity Model[SM] for Software, Version 1.1, Technical Report (CMU/SEI-93-TR-024), Software Engineering Institute, Carnegie-Mellon University, 1993.

Paulk, M. C., et al, Key Practices of the Capability Maturity Model[SM], Version 1.1, Technical Report (CMU/SEI-93-TR-025), Software Engineering Institute, Carnegie-Mellon University, 1993.

Pressman, R. S., *Software Engineering: A Practitioner's Approach*, New York: McGraw-Hill, 2001.

SEI, *ISO/IEC 15504: Frequently Asked Questions*, Software Engineering Institute, Carnegie-Mellon University, 1998.

Sommerville, I., *Software Engineering*, Reading, MA: Addison-Wesley, 2001.

Trillium Model Home Page (*www2.umassd.edu/swpi/BellCanada/trillium-html/trillium.html*).

Weber, C. V., et al, *Key Practices of the Capability Maturity Model*, Technical Report (CMU/SEI-91-TR-25), Software Engineering Institute, Carnegie-Mellon University, 1991.

Zahran, S., *Software Process Improvement: Practical Guidelines for Business Success*, Harlow, England: Addison-Wesley, 1998.

14

Contents

SCM plans

14.1 Introduction

We have seen that once the SCM system is designed, it should be documented so that the working of the SCM system, the procedures, and the functions, duties, and responsibilities of each member are transparent and known to all members of the SCM team, the project team, the subcontractor's team (if any), and others. This document is called the software configuration management plan (SCM plan) or simply the plan.

An initial draft of the SCM plan should be created and circulated among the various groups involved in the project during the initial phases (i.e., during the analysis or design phase). Once feedback from the various groups—project team, QA team, management, and others—is obtained, it can be incorporated, and the approved SCM plan can be made available so that everyone is clear about the various SCM procedures and their duties and responsibilities.

According to Bounds and Dart [1], the CM plan is one of the three keys to the success of attaining a CM solution (the other two are the CM system and the CM adoption strategy). It is generally the case that an SCM solution is part of a corporate-wide process improvement plan and, as such, the solution is coordinated with that effort. This means that the SCM plan needs to be in agreement with any other plans related to the corporate improvement effort.

An SCM plan clearly describes how SCM is accomplished and how consistency between a system's configuration and the configuration records is achieved and maintained. The SCM plan is a central source of information for the SCM program. The major benefits of creating an SCM plan include an assurance that the appropriate SCM processes are applied, the responsibilities for the various SCM activities are assigned, detailed descriptions of these responsibilities are documented, accurate knowledge concerning required resources are available, and a foundation for continued improvement is put in place.

The objective of the SCM plan is to create and document a system that will describe and specify, as accurately as possible, all tasks that are to be performed by the agency responsible for the configuration of the system or product. Thus, the main function of the SCM plan is to create an awareness among the various groups involved in a software project about the SCM functions and how they are to be performed in that project.

SCM is not a well-known subject, and in most cases, people—even people who have been in the software profession for many years—are not aware of SCM and how an SCM system works. So in order to create awareness among the project team members, SCM team members, and other people who are in some way related to the project (such as QA personnel), a document that describes how SCM will be practiced for the project is needed. Thus, the SCM plan forms the basis of training the personnel who are part of the project team and SCM team. It will be used as a reference manual for the SCM functions and in the resolution of conflicts regarding the practice or implementation of SCM functions in the project.

The SCM plan can be created either for the organization or for each project. If the plan is created for the entire organization, its suitability should still be assessed for each project and necessary modifications should be made. In the case of organizations in which the projects that are carried out differ in nature, complexity, and size, it is desirable to create separate plans for each project tailored to suit the needs and characteristics of the project.

14.2   SCM plan and the incremental approach

Some companies adopt what is called the incremental approach to SCM implementation. In the incremental approach, SCM functions are implemented in stages. The system starts with just some of the components, say, a change/problem tracking system or a source code control and revision management system. Then slowly, as time progresses, the other components are introduced until the full spectrum of SCM functionality is achieved.

The natural question when considering the incremental approach is that of how an SCM plan can be developed when the full SCM system is not being implemented. Another question is that of why an SCM plan is needed, because many of the components will not be part of the plan during the first phase of implementation.

In the author's opinion, irrespective of whether the company chooses the big-bang approach (in which full SCM functionality is implemented in one shot) or the incremental approach, it is always better to have an SCM plan. This is because, even for the incremental approach, the broad outline of what the final system will be like must be decided at the outset. There is no need to go into the finer details of the portions that are not being implemented in the first phase, but a high-level outline of how these missing components will fit into the final system and the chosen implementation strategy (the when and how of implementing those functions) should be documented. This is important because, if the different functions of the SCM system are implemented without considering the overall picture (i.e., the effect of each subsystem on the overall SCM system), then integration of the different subsystems will not be seamless.

So, even when the incremental approach is used, the full SCM system should be designed and the SCM plan prepared based on a full implementation. Otherwise, as components are added and full SCM functionality is finally reached, the SCM tools will not be well integrated.

14.3   SCM plan and SCM tools

Another question that is often asked about SCM plans by companies using SCM tools is that of whether the SCM plan is really necessary. Here also, the answer is "yes." The SCM plan records how the different SCM functions will be performed. Only after analyzing and deciding how the SCM system should function, what its functions will be and which functions will be automated, and the peculiarities of each organization/project can the decision about which tool to use be reached.

The SCM plan has a section on SCM resources in which details are given about the software tools, techniques, equipment, personnel, and training necessary for the implementation of the specified SCM activities. The SCM plan, as we have seen earlier, is the basis for SCM training and auditing of the SCM system. So it is still important to have an SCM plan. In fact, the author strongly advocates training employees in the fundamentals and concepts of SCM and on how the SCM functions are carried out before training them on the tools. This approach will give users a better understanding of what they are doing and how their actions will affect others in the project. In practice, if one is using a tool, he can perform the SCM functions without knowing the SCM concepts, so the tool's user manual is enough. But if the user wants to know why he is performing a function, he will need to be aware of the SCM concepts.

So even though it is possible to use SCM tools without knowing much about SCM concepts and functions, it is the author's opinion and experience that a person who knows the SCM concepts is a better user of the SCM tool than a person who has been told just to perform certain activities. There is always a difference between doing something just because someone is told to do it that way and doing something after knowing why a task has to be performed and what will be the effect of that action.

14.4   SCM plans and standards

Almost all configuration management standards advocate some sort of a document or plan. Except for some minor differences, the format specified by most of the standards for the SCM plan is similar. According to a study conducted by Bounds and Dart [1], in which they compared three standards (by IEEE, NASA, and DOD) based on six criteria (i.e., ease of use, completeness, tailorability, consistency, correctness, and life cycle connection), the IEEE standard had the best rating.

As mentioned before, many standards exist for SCM plans. We will examine four of them, which is a representative sample of the lot. They are:

1. ANSI/IEEE Std-828–1998, IEEE Standard for Software Configuration Management Plans, and ANSI/IEEE Std-1042–1987, IEEE Guide to Software Configuration Management;

2. MIL-HDBK-61A(SE)-2001, Military Handbook: Configuration Management Guidance;

3. EIA-649-1998, National Consensus Standard for Configuration Management;

4. ISO 10007: 2003, Quality Management—Guidelines for Configuration Management.

14.4.1 ANSI/IEEE Std-828–1998 and ANSI/IEEE Std-1042–1987

ANSI/IEEE Std-828–1998 is the standard for configuration management plans. Complementing this standard is a guide: *IEEE Guide to Software Configuration Management* (ANSI/IEEE Std-1042–1987), which contains an explanation of the standard and sample SCM plans for different kinds of projects. In the author's opinion, these two standards together form the most comprehensive standards available on SCM and SCM plans.

The IEEE standard is a comprehensive standard on SCM that is tailorable (i.e., it can be customized easily to suit one's needs). This standard intentionally addresses all levels of expertise, the entire life cycle, other organizations, and the relationships to hardware and other activities on a project.

The ANSI/IEEE Std-828–1998 provides a format for creating the SCM plan. According to the standard, the SCM plan should consist of six sections, as shown in Table 14.1.

ANSI/IEEE Std-1042–1987, the guide to SCM plans, explains how Std-828 should be implemented. This guide has several appendixes for different types of SCM plans (e.g., real-time, critical projects, maintenance projects) that can be easily customized to suit individual needs and requirements.

14.4.2 MIL-HDBK-61A(SE)-2001

The purpose of MIL-HDBK-61A (SE) is to assist configuration managers in planning for and implementing effective U.S. Department of Defense (DOD) configuration management activities and practices during all life cycle phases of defense systems and configuration items. It supports acquisi-

Table 14.1   Format of SCM Plan per ANSI/IEEE Std-828–1998

No.	Section Name	Description
1	Introduction	Purpose of the plan, scope, definition of key terms, and references.
2	SCM Management	Describes the allocation of responsibilities and authorities for SCM activities to organizations and individuals within the project structure.
3	SCM Activities	Identifies all functions and tasks required for managing the configuration of the software system as specified in the scope of the SCM plan. Both technical and managerial SCM activities must be identified.
4	SCM Schedules	Establishes the sequence and coordination for the identified SCM activities and for all events affecting the SCM plan's implementation.
5	SCM Resources	Identifies the software tools, techniques, equipment, personnel, and training necessary for the implementation of the specified SCM activities.
6	SCM Plan Maintenance	Identifies the activities and responsibilities necessary to ensure continued SCM planning during the life cycle of the project.

tion based on performance specifications and the use of industry standards and methods to the greatest practicable extent.

According to MIL-HDBK-61A (SE), CM planning is a vital part of the preparation for the next phases of a program life cycle. The CM plan documents the results of that planning to enable it to be communicated and used as a basis in managing the program configuration management activities.

Appendix A of this handbook provides guidance in the content, use, and maintenance of government CM plans. It also provides guidance in evaluating contractor CM plans. The appendix also provide two activity guides, which give the contents and guidance for writing a government CM plan (GCMP) and a contractor CM plan (CCMP).

The primary objective of the GCMP is to document the planning for the government CM activity to take place during the upcoming phase and to schedule specific actions necessary to implement those activities. The second purpose is to communicate and coordinate the Government's intentions with the contractor or contractors involved in the program so that efficient and effective interfacing processes and working relationships may be established. The GCMP communicates to the contractor the government's CM objectives for a given phase and the associated risks if those objectives are not met. It describes the expected deployment and use of the system/configuration item (CI) and indicates the CM process, systems, and methodologies the government plans to use and the interfaces the contractor will be expected to establish. According to the handbook, the content of the GCMP should include the following six sections: (1) introduction, (2) reference documents, (3) government CM concept of operations and acquisition strategy, (4) CM organization, (5) data management, and (6) government configuration management process.

The CCMP describes the contractor's CM objectives, the value-adding CM activities that will be employed to achieve them, and the means of measuring and ensuring that they are effectively accomplished. The content of the CCMP should have the following sections: (1) introduction, (2) reference documents, (3) CM organization, (4) configuration management phasing and milestones, (5) data management, (6) configuration identification, (7) interface management, (8) configuration control, (9) configuration status accounting, (10) configuration audits, and (11) subordinate performing activity/vendor control. The handbook gives a detailed description and phase-by-phase guidance for each section.

14.4.3 EIA-649-1998

According to EIA-649, the purpose and benefits of CM planning and management include:

- Assurance that the appropriate CM processes and activities are applied;
- Establishes organizational responsibilities for CM activities;
- Necessary resources and facilities are identified and made available;
- Forms a basis for continuous improvement;
- Enhanced maturity of the enterprise's process.

EIA-649 discusses in detail the requirements of the plan and considerations that should be taken into account in its development. A CM plan should not be a one-size-fits-all document. Rather, it must be tailored to meet the needs of the agency responsible for CM. In particular, EIA-649 points out that a well-developed plan will aid in the training of personnel in CM and will help explain the process to outside personnel, such as upper-level management and auditors. A comprehensive CM plan that reflects efficient application of CM principles and practices to the identified context and environment would normally include the following topics:

- General product definition and scope;
- Description of CM activities and procedures for each major CM function: configuration planning and management, configuration identification, configuration change management, configuration status accounting, configuration verification and audit, and configuration management of digital data;
- CM management
- Organization, roles, responsibilities, and resources;
- Definitions of terms;

> • Programmatic and organizational interfaces;

> • Deliverables, milestones, and schedules;

> • Subcontract flow-down clauses;

> • Definitions of terms.

If these topics are covered in detail in the plan, the CM program will have a sound blueprint to guide its effective implementation.

14.4.4   ISO 10007: 2003

This international standard gives guidance on the use of CM in industry and its interface with other management systems and procedures. This standard defines a CM plan as a document that sets out the organization and procedures for the CM of a specific product or project. The standard states that the CM plan provides the CM procedures that are to be used for each project, and states who will undertake these procedures and when. The standard also states that the plan should be subjected to document control procedures.

This standard specifies a format for the CM plan (Annex A: Recommended Structure and Content of a Configuration Management Plan). According to ISO 10007, a CM plan should have the six chapters listed in Table 14.2.

The standard also specifies that whenever an existing procedure or standard is used, reference be made to it rather than giving the details so that duplication can be avoided and simplicity can be maintained. In the

Table 14.2   Format of SCM Plan per ISO 10007

No.	Chapter Name	Description
1	Introduction	Description of the system or CIs to which the plan applies, a schedule of the CM activities, the purpose and scope of the plan, list of related documents, and so on.
2	Policies and Procedures	CM policies, CM organization and structure of the CCB and the other committees, selection criteria for the CIs, frequency, distribution, and control of reports, and agreed-on terminology.
3	Configuration Identification	Family tree of the CIs, numbering conventions, baselines to be established, and so on.
4	Configuration Control	Organization and composition of the CCB, change management procedures, and so on.
5	Configuration Status Accounting	Procedures for collecting, recording, processing, and maintaining the data for status accounting reports, definition of all CM reports, and so on.
6	Configuration Audit	List of audits to be conducted, the audit procedures, the authorities and disciplines involved, format of the audit reports, and so on.

author's opinion, this is a good practice to follow irrespective of which standard you are using, because it will make the SCM plan simple, short, and free of redundancy. For example, according to the preceding standard, the audit procedures that will be followed have to be mentioned in Chapter 6, Configuration Audit. If the audit is conducted as per the ISO guidelines for auditing quality systems, instead of defining and describing the auditing process, the plan can just say that SCM auditing will be done in accordance with ISO 10011–1:1990, ISO 10011–2:1990, and ISO 10011–3:1990 (ISO guidelines for auditing quality systems, Parts 1, 2, and 3).

In a study conducted by Bounds and Dart [1], users of CM plans were asked whether CM procedures should be part of the CM plan or separate. The overwhelming response was that the procedures should be kept separate from the plan, but that the plan should reference the procedures. Although many reasons were cited for this preference, the most common reasons were that separating the procedures allows users to focus only on what applies to them and makes maintenance of the procedures and plan much easier. Respondents also stated that procedures should focus on how to do something, whereas a plan should focus on what is to be done.

The same study recommended the use of IEEE standards as the best standards to use in developing SCM plans for these reasons:

▸ The IEEE standard was written explicitly for use by anyone within the industry, whereas the NASA and DOD standards were written for their specific segments of industry.

▸ The IEEE standard is, by far, more complete than the other two standards, and is the only standard that can be treated as a stand-alone document.

▸ The IEEE standard has greater potential for timely updates than the other standards because it is used by the general industry.

14.5 Audit of the SCM plan

An SCM plan is a controlled document as well as a CI. So all document control procedures that are applicable to a controlled document and all change management procedures that are applicable to a CI are also applicable to the SCM plan. This means that distribution of the SCM plan should be controlled. A distribution list should contain the names of persons having a copy of the plan. Also, access to the plan should be controlled: the level of control is decided based on the nature of the project. If the plan is hosted on the company intranet or bulletin board, then access to that forum should be controlled.

Another aspect is that changes to the plan should be made in accordance with the change management procedures mentioned in the plan. When a change is implemented, the new versions should be made available to all who are in the distribution list. If the plan is hosted on the intranet, then it should be updated.

The SCM plan should be subject to auditing. Like any other CI, the plan should undergo the functional and physical configuration audits. The purpose of the auditing is to ensure that the plan is complete and correct and satisfies the requirements as described in the standard or standards on which it is based.

14.6   How to write a good SCM plan

Writing the SCM plan is not an easy task. It takes time; good knowledge of SCM functions, the peculiarities of the project, and the organization; and knowledge of other procedures, such as auditing and testing, to write a good SCM plan. It is also not a task that should be taken lightly, because the practice of the SCM function in a project or organization is based on the procedures and tasks specified in the SCM plan. It is not too strong a statement to say that the SCM plan can make or break a project. A bad and improperly designed SCM plan will create unnecessary and cumbersome procedures, and instead of assisting the development process and improving productivity, it will result in creating confusion and increasing the workload of the project team as well as the SCM team. In the following paragraphs, we look at some practices and tips that will help in the creation of good SCM plans.

The most important decision that affects the quality of an SCM plan is the capability and knowledge of the person or the team that writes the plan. Ideally, the plan should be written by the people who have designed the SCM system for the project or organization. Here we are talking about experienced people who have a good understanding of the project or organization and the SCM system. Once they have written the plan, the technical documentation team can copyedit it so that typos and grammatical mistakes are eliminated. This is a good practice to follow, because the writing skills of the technical people may not be on par with their technical skills. The copyeditors should be given clear instructions not to touch the structure of the plan, just to check for grammatical and spelling errors. Perhaps it would be a good idea to have the editor sit with the technical team during the writing process, so if any issues arise, they can be resolved immediately.

The second most important decision is selecting the standard on which the SCM plan is going to be based. As mentioned earlier, the IEEE standards emerge as the best and most popular choice, but it is good practice to see what other standards have to offer, and it may not be a bad idea to borrow good ideas from them. There is nothing wrong with formulating an SCM plan based on more than one standard, because all standards will have some weak areas, and adapting that area from another standard is not a bad idea. Some of the standards that could be referenced include the following:

1. ANSI/IEEE Std-828–1998, IEEE Standard for Software Configuration Management Plans, IEEE, 1998

2. ANSI/IEEE Std-1042–1987, IEEE Guide to Software Configuration Management, IEEE, 1987

3. ISO 10007, Quality Management: Guidelines for Configuration Management, ISO, 1995

4. DOD MIL-STD-973, Military Standard for Configuration Management, Department of Defense, 1995

5. MIL-HDBK-61A (SE)—Military Handbook: Configuration Management Guidance, 2001

One can get a feel for how to write the SCM plan by studying some sample plans and also reading books on software configuration management. Today, getting sample SCM plans is not a difficult task. IEEE Std-1042–1987 has four appendixes consisting of sample SCM plans for different types of projects. Also, hundreds of SCM plans—of all types and sizes—are available on the Web. A simple query for configuration management plans on the Web by the author in 2004 produced more than 2,000 results.

The next step in writing the SCM plan is to identify the procedures that should be followed in the practice of SCM. If the SCM system is using procedures that are from standards or are part of other standards, then it is sufficient to simply reference those standards. These standards can be industry standards or the organization's internal standards or even the project's own standards. But before referencing a standard, it is a good idea to ensure that all mentioned standards are available and, if possible, to bring them under document control, so they are readily available for reference.

We have researched the standards and literature, discussed the sample plans, and identified the procedures that will be followed and the documents that define these procedures. The next step is to write the plan using any of the existing templates that are available. Many SCM plan templates are available on the Web; the IEEE standard provides a customizable template; and the ISO has a reasonably good template. The choice of template is a matter of taste and convenience. The contents of both the IEEE and ISO templates are almost the same, but the IEEE template is more comprehensive. But if the company is using ISO standards, then the ISO 10007 template can be used. You should choose a template that is suited to your purpose (and similar to your project or organization) and customize it to your specific needs. Once the template or the table of contents is ready, the next step is to fill in the blanks or put the procedures and other details in place to complete the plan. The resulting document is considered the initial draft of the SCM plan. Copies of this document—the initial draft—should be circulated to all groups who will be involved in implementing the SCM system and performing the various SCM functions. This process, involving everyone who matters in plan development, is important. SCM is a team effort. So in order to implement and manage an SCM system successfully, the SCM team will need cooperation from all quarters. One way to ensure that cooperation is to get others involved by sending copies of the initial draft and asking for feedback.

Once feedback from the various groups is received, the SCM plan's authors can review the plan, accept valid comments, and incorporate them into the plan. Once the final draft is ready, it is a good idea to get it reviewed by an external agency—a person or team of experts. This review can throw light on issues that the plan might have failed to address or bring up inadequacies or even detect errors that the internal reviews have missed. The external audit also provides a stamp of approval from a body that is supposed to be an expert in this area, which will help increase the credibility and acceptance of the plan. Once the SCM plan is reviewed and approved, it can be baselined.

14.7   Contents of a typical SCM plan

The SCM plan can be written in any format as long as it contains all necessary information. The standards offer considerable latitude and freedom to the person who writes the SCM plan. All standards require you to address certain topics, such as scope, purpose, definitions, SCM organization, SCM functions, responsibilities, and resources, but how this material should be presented is decided by the author of the plan. The degree of detail, the amount of additional information, and so on that you include in the SCM plan depends on the nature of the project.

A sample outline for an SCM plan is given next. All items, sections, and subsections need not be present in all projects. Some will have additional information. This structure relies heavily on the IEEE standards. The explanation of each section and subsection is given at the end.

    i. Cover Page
    ii. Copyright Page
    iii. Distribution List
    iv. About the Document
    1.0 INTRODUCTION
        1.1 Purpose
        1.2 Scope
        1.3 Definitions
        1.4 References
    2.0 SCM MANAGEMENT
        2.1 SCM Organization
        2.2 SCM Responsibilities
        2.3 Relationship of SCM to Software Process Life Cycle
        2.4 Interfaces to Other Organizations on the Project
        2.5 SCM Responsibilities of the Organizations
    3.0 SCM ACTIVITIES
        3.1 Configuration Identification

3.1.1 Identification of Configuration Items
3.1.2 Naming Configuration Items
3.1.3 Acquiring Configuration Items
3.2 Configuration Control
3.2.1 Change Initiation
3.2.2 Change Evaluation
3.2.3 Change Management—Approval Process
3.2.4 Change Implementation
3.2.5 Change Control Boards (CCBs)
3.3 Configuration Status Accounting
3.3.1 Identifications of Information Needs
3.3.2 Information-Gathering Mechanisms
3.3.3 Reports, Their Contents, and Frequency
3.3.4 Access to Status Accounting Data
3.3.5 Status Accounting Information Dissemination Methods
3.3.6 Release Details
3.4 Configuration Auditing
3.4.1 Audits to Be Performed
3.4.2 CIs under Audit
3.4.3 Audit Procedures
3.4.4 Audit Follow-Up Activities
3.5 Interface Control
3.6 Subcontractor/Vendor Control
4.0 SCM SCHEDULES
5.0 SCM RESOURCES
6.0 SCM PLAN MAINTENANCE

i. Cover Page: This page should have the title Software Configuration Management Plan and the details regarding the project, the organization, the authorities, the version number, release date, and so on.

ii. Copyright Page: Copyright information of the SCM plan.

iii. Distribution List: Name and number of copies distributed. Also, a description of how the documentation control activities will apply to this document.

iv. About the Document: A short description about the document and its sections.

1.0 INTRODUCTION: This section provides an overview of the plan, the SCM activities, the audience for the plan, and how to use the plan, so that the user will have a clearer understanding of the plan. The introduction should contain at least the following four topics: purpose, scope, definitions, and references.

1.1 Purpose: This section addresses the need for the plan and the intended audience.

1.2 Scope: The scope covers the plan's applicability, limitations, and assumptions. This section provides an overview of the software development process in the project or organization and how the SCM functions and activities fit into the project.

1.3 Definitions: This section defines the key terms used in the document.

1.4 References: This section identifies all documents, standards, procedures—both internal and external—to be used in the plan. This section also identifies where the documents can be found so readers of the plan can retrieve them.

2.0 SCM MANAGEMENT: This section gives information about the organization of the SCM team, allocation of responsibilities to teams and individuals, and so on.

2.1 SCM Organization: This section describes the organizational structure of the SCM team and how it fits into the organizational structure with respect to other groups, such as the project team, the QA team, and top management. Also included in the structure are clients/customers and vendors/subcontractors, if any are involved in the SCM activities. An organization chart depicting the structure is useful in this section. This section also describes the composition of the CCB and other auditing and review teams that will be part of the SCM activities.

2.2 SCM Responsibilities: This section describes the duties and responsibilities of all those involved in carrying out the SCM activities. This section identifies the responsibilities of the CCB and other committees and boards necessary for configuration management, the structure of which has been defined in the previous section.

2.3 Relationship of SCM to the Software Process Life Cycle: This section relates the SCM activities to the different phases of the software development life cycle. It spells out what SCM activities need to be performed during each phase of the life cycle.

2.4 Interfaces to Other Organizations on the Project: Describes how the SCM team will interact with other organizations in the project, such as QA, Test, Project Management, and Requirements, and is to include vendors and subcontractors.

2.5 SCM Responsibilities of the Organizations: This section describes the responsibilities of the vendors, subcontractors, and other organizations in relation to carrying out SCM functions. In other words, this section describes what is expected from them.

3.0 SCM ACTIVITIES: This section identifies the tasks and functions that are required to manage the configuration of the system as specified in the scope of the plan. This section deals with the core SCM activities and how they are performed in the project.

3.1 Configuration Identification: This section describes how to identify, name, and document the functional and physical characteristics of the configuration items. Once the items are identified, they are acquired and moved into the controlled environment.

3.1.1 Identification of Configuration Items: Identifies the items to be selected as configuration items that will be controlled by the SCM activities. This section gives a list of configuration items in the project. Inclusion of a tree structure showing the various configuration items and their interdependencies is ideal.

3.1.2 Naming Configuration Items: This section of the plan specifies the identification system, naming conventions, version numbers, and letters used to identify the configuration items.

3.1.3 Acquiring Configuration Items: This section describes how the configuration items are to be stored, how access to them will be controlled, the details of the configuration libraries, the procedures for check-in and checkout of configuration items from the library, and so on.

3.2 Configuration Control: This section describes the change management processes, such as change initiation, change disposition, change implementation, reviews, approval, and baselining.

3.2.1 Change Initiation: Describes how to initiate a change. A change can be the result of a fault or problem or the result of an enhancement or new feature. This section describes the procedures to be followed to initiate a change request or problem report so that the change management activities are started.

3.2.2 Change Evaluation: This section describes how the evaluation of a change request is carried out. This section also details how to handle the problem analysis, problem classification, and so on. The section gives details on how to classify the changes/problems, how to perform an impact analysis, and so on. The section also specifies the qualifications of the people who will be doing the change/problem evaluation.

3.2.3 Change Management: This section describes how a change request is processed. It spells out clearly the procedure for receiving change requests, assigning change requests for evaluation, the CCB meetings, how to disposition the change requests carried out, and so on.

3.2.4 Change Implementation: Once the change request is approved, it has to be implemented. How to select the change implementation team or person, how to conduct the verification and validation processes, and how to promote the item to the new baseline are described in this section.

3.2.5 Change Control Boards (CCBs): This is the apex body that decides the fate of the change requests. This section describes the functioning of the CCB. If multiple CCBs are present, the authority of each CCB must be specified, and if more than one CCB of the same authority is present in the project, then conflict resolution mechanisms should also be documented.

3.3 Configuration Status Accounting: This section deals with the details of recording the status of the configuration items and reporting them to people who need to know about them.

3.3.1 Identification of Information Needs: This section describes the information requirements of the project: what kind of information is required, who requires it, the nature of the requirement (e.g., routine, ad hoc), the frequency of the reports, and so on.

3.3.2 Information-Gathering Mechanisms: This section describes how the status accounting information is gathered. Ideally, the information should be entered into the configuration management database by the initiators of the SCM activities rather than by the SCM person chasing the activities and updating the status accounting data. For example, when a change request is initiated, if the person who initiates the change request creates a record of that in the database, then the job of information gathering is easy. But in order to accomplish this task, the necessary forms and access privileges should be given to the different users of the system. This section describes the exact mechanism of how the information is captured for status reporting.

3.3.3 Reports, Their Contents, and Frequency: Describes the various reports that will be created, their contents, and the frequency of each report.

3.3.4 Access to Status Accounting Data: The status accounting function cannot anticipate all of the information requirements of users and produce reports to meet all these requirements. Also, in many cases, information requests will be for ad hoc reports, which may be generated only once. If the status accounting system is computerized, then an interactive query facility can be made available to the users to get this information. If such a facility is available, this section will describe the procedures for using that facility. In the case of manual processing, this section will describe how the manual records can be accessed for ad hoc information needs.

3.3.5 Status Accounting Information Dissemination Methods: This section describes how and to whom the status accounting information will be disseminated.

3.3.6 Release Details: Detailed information, such as what is contained in a release, to whom the release is being provided and when, the media the release is on, known problems with the release, known fixes in the release, installation instructions, and so on.

3.4 Configuration Auditing: This section describes what types of audits are to be performed, the audit procedure, frequency, and the auditing authority, and so on.

3.4.1 Audits to Be Performed: This section describes the different types of audits that will be performed and when they will be performed. The typical audits include functional configuration audits (FCAs), physical configuration audits (PCAs), subcontractor audits, and external audits.

3.4.2 CIs under Audit: This section specifies the list of CIs that are to be audited.

3.4.3 Audit Procedures: Describes the procedure to be followed for each audit: the auditing authority, the documents required, how the audit should be conducted, the format of the audit report, and so on.

3.4.4 Audit Follow-Up Activities: This section describes the activities that should be carried out after the audit, such as resolution of nonconfirmation reports (NCRs) and so on.

3.5 Interface Control: This section describes the coordination of the changes to the CIs with the changes to the interfacing items outside the scope of the plan, such as the hardware system, off-the-shelf packages, support software, and so on. The plan must identify each of these external items and should define the nature of the interface, the affected groups, how the interface items will be controlled, and how the interface items will be approved to be included as part of a baseline.

3.6 Subcontractor/Vendor Control: This section describes the activities necessary to incorporate the items developed outside of the project environment into the project environment, in particular, items that are the responsibility of subcontractors and vendors. This section should describe the SCM functions and activities that should be followed by the vendor/subcontractor, mechanisms to ensure that they are followed, procedures to audit the items that are submitted by the vendor/subcontractor, and the items that must be supplied by the vendor/subcontractor. This section also describes how the items will be received, tested, and placed under SCM, how change requests to these items will be processed and implemented, and so on.

4.0 SCM SCHEDULES: This section describes the sequence of the SCM activities, their interdependencies and relationship to the project life cycle, and project milestones. The schedule will identify the life cycle phases or project milestones where the different baselines (e.g., functional baseline, allocated baseline, product baseline) will be established. This section also establishes the schedule for the different configuration audits. Graphical representation using PERT charts or Gantt charts helps enhance the usefulness of this section.

5.0 SCM RESOURCES: This section identifies the software tools, techniques, equipment, personnel, budget, and training necessary for the implementation of the specified SCM activities.

6.0 SCM PLAN MAINTENANCE: This section describes the activities that are required to keep the plan current during the life cycle of the project. The plan should be monitored and synchronized with the activities of the project. This section describes the mechanism for the synchronization and identifies the person or team responsible for those activities.

14.8   Sample SCM plans

We have just looked at a generic structure for SCM plans, which can be tailored to suit the needs of the individual projects. We have also discussed tips for writing good SCM plans. As mentioned before, it is a good idea to go through a few sample SCM plans of similar projects before you start writing the SCM plan.

The sample SCM plans can be obtained from a host of sources, but two of the easiest sources are as follows:

1. *Internet.* Thousands of SCM plans covering a spectrum of projects (e.g., military, government, research, commercial) of various sizes and complexity are hosted on the Internet. You can use a search engine to locate them. By spending a few hours on the Internet, you can browse through the different types of SCM plans.

2. *ANSI/IEEE Std-1042–1987.* This is the *IEEE Guide to Software Configuration Management.* There are four appendixes for this document, which are sample SCM plans for different types of projects.

Also, in the author's opinion, anyone who is writing an SCM plan will benefit tremendously from the document "CM Plans: The Beginning to Your CM Solution" by Nadine M. Bounds and Susan Dart of the Software Engineering Institute, Carnegie-Mellon University. This is an excellent primer for SCM plans.

14.9   Summary

The SCM plan defines the SCM system and how SCM is to be practiced in a project. The SCM plan documents what SCM activities are to be done, how they are to be done, who is responsible for doing specific activities, when they are to happen, and what resources are required.

The SCM plan should be prepared irrespective of whether the organization is using an incremental approach or using SCM tools. Preparing a good SCM plan requires knowledge of the SCM concepts and functions, SCM tools, SCM standards, software engineering and quality assurance procedures, and standards and knowledge of the organization or project for which the standard is being written. The SCM plan can be based on a single standard or on more than one standard.

The SCM plan is a configuration item and should be updated and reviewed whenever required. The SCM plan should be prepared with the cooperation of all those who will be involved in the functioning of the SCM system and should be audited by external SCM experts. It is a good idea to go through some SCM plans before starting to write the plan. Hundreds of sample plans are available on the Internet. Anyone who is writing an SCM plan will benefit tremendously from the document by Bounds and Dart [1].

Reference

[1] Bounds, N. M., and S. Dart, "CM Plans: The Beginning to Your CM Solution," Technical Report, Software Engineering Institute, Carnegie-Mellon University, 1998.

Selected bibliography

Alain Abran, A., and J. W. Moore (eds.), *SWEBOK: Guide to the Software Engineering Body of Knowledge (Trial Version)*, Los Alamitos, CA: IEEE Computer Society, 2001.

Arthur, J. D., et al, "Evaluating the Effectiveness of Independent Verification and Validation," *IEEE Computer*, Vol. 32, No. 10, October 1999, pp. 79–83.

Babich, W. A., *Software Configuration Management: Coordination for Team Productivity*, Boston, MA: Addison-Wesley, 1986.

Ben-Menachem, M., *Software Configuration Management Guidebook*, New York: McGraw-Hill, 1994.

Berlack, H. R., *Software Configuration Management*, New York: John Wiley & Sons, 1992.

Bersoff, E. H., V. D. Henderson, and S. G. Siegel, *Software Configuration Management, An Investment in Product Integrity*, Englewood Cliffs, NJ: Prentice-Hall, 1980.

IEEE Software Engineering Standards Collection 2003 (CD-ROM Edition), Piscataway, NJ: IEEE, 2003.

Pressman, R. S., *Software Engineering: A Practitioner's Approach*, New York: McGraw-Hill, 2001.

Sommerville, I., *Software Engineering*, Reading, MA: Addison-Wesley, 2001.

Whitgift, D., *Methods and Tools for Software Configuration Management*, Chichester, England: John Wiley & Sons, 1991.

Contents

SCM organization

15.1 Introduction

Configuration management—like any other management function—needs people to perform the various activities and to produce results. Configuration management is a discipline that applies technical and administrative direction and surveillance to (1) identify and document the functional and physical characteristics of a configuration item, (2) control changes to those characteristics, (3) record and report change processing and implementation status, and (4) verify compliance with specified requirements [1]. As you can see, this definition states a lot of tasks—configuration identification, change management, change disposition, change implementation, configuration control, status accounting, and configuration audits, to name a few—that have to be performed in order for the SCM system to function properly.

To perform all of these functions effectively and efficiently, one needs procedures and resources. We looked at the various SCM procedures in the last few chapters, and we saw that the most important resource is people. So for any SCM system to function properly, there should be enough qualified people to conduct the various functions.

The number of people on an SCM team will vary depending on the nature, size, and complexity of the project. In the case of large and complex projects with hundreds of programmers and thousands of programs, the SCM team will be big with lots of full-time members, whereas in the case of small projects, the project leader might do all of the SCM functions. Also, there are people whose services will be required on an as-needed basis. For example, for a change request evaluation, an outside expert might be called, and once the evaluation is over and the report is submitted, that person will leave. There might also be permanent personnel on the SCM team who are in charge of receiving the various change and problem reports, ensuring the completeness of these forms, assigning them to the right people for evaluation, coordinating the change control board (CCB) activities, and so on. In this chapter, we review the structure of a typical SCM team based on the different functions.

15.2   SCM and the organization

We know that SCM is a support function, so let's look at where and how SCM fits into the organizational structure. Different organizational structures will require the SCM team to be structured or positioned differently. In many cases, a central SCM team will take care of all the SCM activities of the different projects in the company. This type of SCM team will act as a support function and will use project team members to get SCM activities done.

The main responsibilities of the SCM team in such an arrangement are to complete the SCM activities of the different projects, such as receive the change requests, assign the implementation, and convene the CCB meetings. The advantage of this kind of setup is that the central SCM team can have standardized procedures and policies enforced for all projects and can prioritize the SCM needs of the different projects based on the overall company objectives. This type of arrangement is shown in Figure 15.1.

Some companies have a central SCM team along with individual teams for each project. The central team creates the guidelines and policies and the general organization-wide SCM plan and is responsible for the proper functioning of the SCM system in the company as a whole. The individual teams associated with each project customize the plans and procedures to suit the needs of the particular project and are responsible for the SCM activities in the project. These SCM teams in the different projects usually have a dual reporting arrangement, in which they report to the central SCM team leader and also to the project leader of the project with which they are associated. This type of arrangement is shown in Figure 15.2.

In a third situation, there may be no central SCM team, but each project will have its own SCM team. This is usually applicable to large projects, where the size and complexity of the project warrants a full-fledged SCM team of its own. This type of arrangement is shown in Figure 15.3.

The SCM team needs strong support from management, because it does not have the necessary muscle power to enforce its decisions like the line functions do. But if proper awareness is created about the importance of SCM and its benefits, and if the SCM system is designed so that SCM approval is a prerequisite for moving from one phase to another, the SCM team can get the necessary cooperation from the project team and other support functions to carry out its tasks.

Another important aspect that should be remembered is that the SCM team will have to enlist the help of other professionals in the organization. The SCM team will require help from the management team, the QA team,

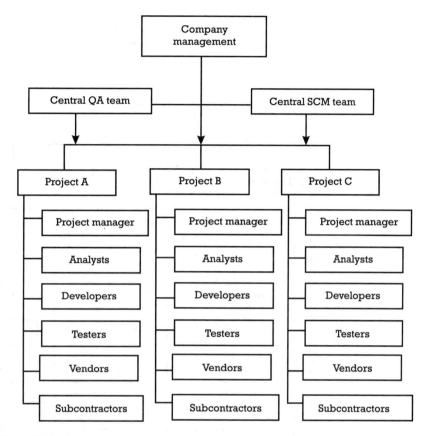

Figure 15.1   Organizational structure in which a central SCM team deals with the different projects.

the project team, and others to carry out the various functions. For example, the CCB's permanent members include management, QA, marketing, and project team representatives. Also, for conducting change request evaluations or causal analysis, outside help might be required. So a mechanism should be in place for determining how these human resources will be made available to the SCM team. Ideally, the SCM team should make a request to the concerned group and the group should cooperate, but if cooperation is not forthcoming, the SCM team might need management support to get the required personnel.

15.3   SCM organization

The configuration management officer (CMO) is the head of the SCM team. This person is usually part of the SCM system design team and has most probably written the SCM plan. This person is responsible for all SCM activities in the project and reports to the CCB. The main responsibilities of the CMO include setting up the SCM system, training the SCM team, assigning duties and responsibilities, constituting the CCB(s) as the case may be, coordinating between the project team and the CCB, managing the change con-

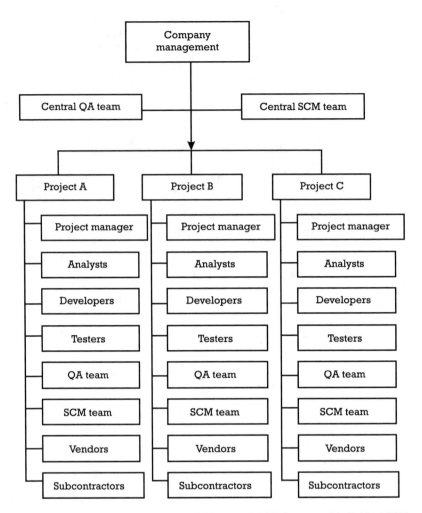

Figure 15.2 Organizational structure in which a central SCM team and individual SCM teams are used.

trol activities, setting up the SCM libraries and other control mechanisms, and coordinating between the audit team and the project team. The CMO will be part of the CCB and will ensure that the CCB meetings are convened according to the schedule or whenever the need arises (emergency meetings).

Other members of the SCM team have the responsibility of assisting the CMO in performing SCM tasks. These include both technical people and administrative personnel. The technical people will be concerned with tasks such as configuration identification, library management, change management, version control, release management, configuration audits, causal analysis, and updating the configuration knowledge base. The administrative staff will ensure that meeting information is sent on time, the minutes of the meetings are sent to the people on the distribution list, the decisions made in the meetings are conveyed to the appropriate people, the status

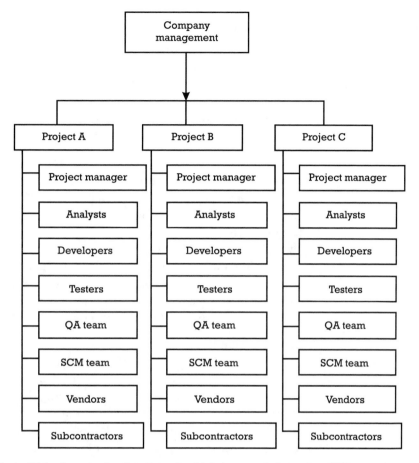

Figure 15.3 Organizational structure in which there are independent SCM teams for each project.

accounting reports are delivered, the skill inventory database is updated regularly, and other tasks are completed as necessary.

Other people will work with the SCM team on an ad hoc basis. These people include those who conduct the change request evaluation, problem analysis, causal analysis, and configuration audits and who serve as subject experts in the CCB meetings.

So in a typical SCM setup, different people will carry out the various SCM functions. Some of the people in an SCM environment are listed as follows, and a brief description is given about what they do.

- *Developers.* Developers are the project team members who develop the software system or product. They do the analysis, design, and coding.

- *Testers.* Testers conduct the testing of the programs developed by the developers. In most cases, the developers do the unit testing and hand over their programs to the testers. The testers do the module testing, integration testing, and system testing. These people are responsible for coordinating the alpha and beta testing phases. The testers originate the defect or problem reports, make enhancement suggestions, and collect and collate feedback from the alpha and beta testing programs. Then they initiate the problem-tracking and change management process for each of the defects or enhancements found. The role of the testers varies slightly from project to project (e.g., in some projects, there are separate teams for alpha and beta testing), but their main responsibility is to find the bugs and report them.

▶ *Quality assurance representatives.* The goal of a good QA program is to prevent defects from occurring or recurring. So the main responsibility of QA personnel is to develop standards and guidelines for the different activities in the project, such as design, coding, and testing. They must also make sure that these policies and standards are followed by everyone on the team. To ensure this is the case, they conduct quality audits. QA personnel also form part of the CCB and play a vital role in the change disposition. In many organizations, QA team members perform the change request evaluation, problem analysis, casual analysis, and the knowledge base and help desk maintenance.

▶ *Assigners.* An assigner is the SCM team member responsible for scheduling tasks that are to be performed, based on their severity and impact, and assigning these tasks to other people in the team. Assigning the change requests for evaluation, giving the problem reports for analysis, giving the task of implementing a change to someone, and ensuring that all activities are performed on schedule is the assigner's responsibility. The assigner's function may also be performed by a Pre-CCB Screening Committee (sometimes called the Software Review Board, SRB). The SRB may also be given some measure of authority, by the CCB, to act on minor change requests and problem reports, such as approval, rejection, and request for additional information.

▶ *Build manager.* This person handles the various builds and releases. This person is responsible for ensuring that the configuration items are given the correct version numbers, proper baselines are established, build files are accurately kept, branching and merging of the file or files is done properly, and so on. The primary goal of this person is to take all of the necessary steps to ensure that the SCM system is capable of configuring and building the system or its components completely and accurately at any time.

▶ *Administrator.* This person performs database administration of the various SCM databases and repositories, assigns access privileges to the different team members, makes backups, and completes other administrative tasks as necessary. This person works closely with the build manager to ensure that the build process proceeds without any problem.

We have already seen that many other people are involved in the SCM team. The roles just mentioned are generally full-time jobs and are usually present in every project that has SCM. The other personnel in the SCM team, possibly with the exception of the CMO and a few administrative people, are called in as needed. For example, the CCB members are called only when a change request has been submitted that needs to be resolved or a decision has to be made about the release of a product.

15.4 Automation and SCM team size

With tools automating every possible aspect of configuration management, the number of people required to manage SCM functions is decreasing, but some areas—analysis, evaluation, audits—still require human intervention. Also, not all projects will use totally automated SCM tools; some projects will use tools that automate certain areas, such as change management, version control, build management or system building, and status accounting. So depending on the nature of the project and level of automation, the organization of the SCM team will vary.

Another factor that should be considered is the additional capabilities, features, and functionality offered by the new generation of SCM tools. These tools are highly complex and sophisticated and hence require highly trained specialists, such as system administrators, database administrators, and release and build managers, to manage them effectively and efficiently. So even though SCM tools automate the repetitive and monotonous activities, with the added capabilities, the number of people required to manage the SCM system has not decreased considerably. The advantages of automation are that people do not have to perform the repetitive and tedious tasks, the chances of errors being made are less, and accurate and up-to-date information is available.

15.5 Skill inventory database

The SCM team relies heavily on professionals from other groups in the organization to carry out its various functions. So the SCM team should know whether the people (with the necessary qualifications) whom they want are available, and if available, where they are located and so on. The author has worked on many projects in which one of the main problems faced by the SCM team was tracking down the right people to do particular functions, such as impact analysis, problem evaluation, and causal analysis.

In one particular project for which the author was the CMO, this problem—the task of finding the right people—was acute. The company had more than 1,500 employees in five or six different offices. The skills and availability of people was difficult information to obtain. So the idea of a skill inventory database was used, and it was successful. The idea was borrowed from industrial engineering.

This technique of creating a skill inventory of the shop floor workers has been used to implement modern production systems such as the Toyota production system and in small group manufacturing, where finding the people with the right skills fast is a necessity. So that technique was used in the SCM system, and it worked so well that the author has since used it in many projects with equal success. It is a good idea for the SCM team to have a skill inventory database of the company's personnel. The database can store the details of every professional whose services will be required by the SCM team. This includes top management, QA team members, project team members, SCM team members, vendor/subcontractor team members, members of the hardware group, and other support functions. A sample of such a database is shown in Table 15.1.

A skill inventory database will come in handy in large organizations where the SCM manager or team requires the details of the people who can conduct impact analysis, people who have the necessary qualifications to be part of the CCB, people who can conduct the reviews, FCAs, PCAs, and so on. In big organizations, the SCM team may not know all of the employees and the skills set each person has. Employee turnover adds to this lack of information. CCB members who have left the organization have to be replaced, and orphan configuration items (CIs whose authors/owners have left the company or have been promoted and have more responsibilities than doing an impact analysis) have to be reassigned. So it is helpful for the SCM team to have a skill inventory database, so they can find the right people for different tasks.

The skill inventory database captures the skills of every person in the company. The SCM team should decide which skills need to be captured. For example, knowledge of SCM procedures; experience in conducting quality audits, causal analysis, and change evaluation; and knowledge of programming languages and database management systems are all skills that could be captured in the database.

The numbers in the columns in Table 15.1 represent the experience in years for each skill. The number of years of experience in a particular field is

Table 15.1 Sample Skill Inventory Database

Name	Thomas	Barbara	Ishtar	Bob
Location/project	L1/P1	L2/P2	L2/P2	L1/P2
SCM activities	7	2	0	0
Quality audits	4	0	3	0
Causal analysis	3	4	3	0
COBOL	10	0	5	2
DB2	7	0	3	2
CICS	7	0	3	2
Oracle	0	4	0	0
Visual Basic	0	5	0	0

not always a good guide to a person's knowledge level and expertise in that field, but this is the most easily available yardstick. Other criteria can be used, such as a merit rating or point rating system. If the company has a good personnel evaluation system, then those ratings could be used instead of the number of years of experience.

Although it is perfectly fine to store this information in an electronic spreadsheet, it would be ideal if it were stored in a relational database, because this makes identifying the right people an easier task. For example, if you need a person to do an evaluation of a change request that involves a program developed in the COBOL-DB2-CICS environment, then you need a person who is familiar with the SCM activities and who has good knowledge of COBOL, DB2, and CICS. If you were using a spreadsheet or a manual log, it would be a time-consuming job to locate the people you want, but if the data is stored in a relational database, you can get an answer by simply querying the database as follows:

```
SELECT name, Location
FROM skill_inventory_table
WHERE SCM >=2 AND COBOL >=2 AND DB2 >=2 AND CICS >=2;
```

This query will bring up the names of all people who have two or more years of experience in SCM, COBOL, DB2, and CICS. Then you merely choose someone from the resulting list.

Some overhead is required in maintaining the skill inventory database. The skill inventory database is usually managed by the HR department. They need the list of skills possessed by every employee of the company. This information is required in order to identify the training needs of employees, to forecast skill requirements, and to formulate the recruitment strategy. So the HR department usually asks employees to complete the skill inventory database records and update them regularly—as and when new skills are learned. The SCM team can ask the HR department to include the list of skills they want in the database. Because the HR department is constantly in touch with employees and knows which employees have left and which have joined the organization, the responsibility of managing the skill inventory database is ideally given to them. The SCM team can access the database whenever they want to get the necessary information about the people they require to perform various SCM functions. The skill inventory database is of little use if it is not kept current and up-to-date. As mentioned before, people leave the company, new people join, and people learn new skills, all of which should be reflected in the database.

15.6   CCB organization

The change control board (CCB) is the apex body that decides whether to carry out a change. Depending on the size, complexity, and nature of the project, there will be a single CCB, multiple CCBs, or even multilevel CCBs.

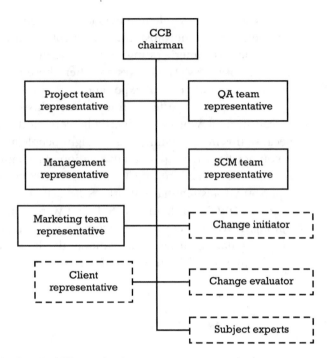

Figure 15.4   Sample CCB organization.

In most projects, there will be only one CCB. For small projects, there may not even be a CCB, in which case, the project leader will decide whether to accept or reject a change request. For projects having a CCB, the CCB will have both permanent and ad hoc members. The permanent members include representatives of the management, project team, QA team, marketing team, SCM team, and in many cases client representatives. The ad hoc members are people who are called (and whose expertise is required) in to resolve issues that the CCB is not able to resolve or needs expert advice to resolve. Sometimes the CCB may summon the change initiator or evaluator for clarification. A sample structure for the CCB is shown in Figure 15.4.

In some large and complex projects, more than one CCB is required, with each handling different modules of the project. This situation arises when the project is large and may be distributed geographically, so that a single CCB will not be able to handle disposition of all the change requests

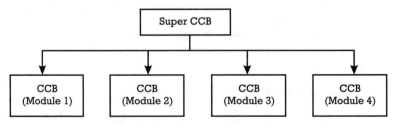

Figure 15.5   Multiple CCBs.

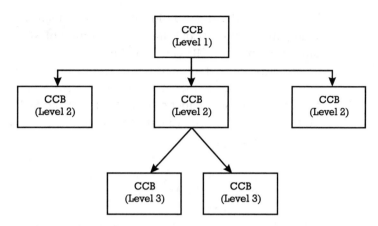

Figure 15.6 Multilevel CCBs.

and problem reports. In cases where multiple CCBs are present, there should be a "super CCB" (SCCB) or Project CCB (PCCB) to oversee the functioning of the CCBs and to resolve conflicts, if any, among the CCBs. This type of setup is shown in Figure 15.5.

In some cases, multilevel CCBs will be required, as shown in Figure 15.6. The difference is that each level of CCB will handle a particular kind of change request or problem report. For example, a level 3 CCB will handle problems with low severity. The CCBs are classified based on the types of change requests they handle, whereas in the case of multiple CCBs, they are classified based on the module or subsystem they handle.

So in the case of a multiple CCB environment, all change requests from a particular module will be handled by the same CCB, but in a multilevel CCB, all change requests with the same severity level will be handled by a single CCB. Multiple CCBs are useful when the project is large and has many modules and development takes place in different locations. Multilevel CCBs are applicable to large projects that are complex in nature but for which the development takes place in one location. The multiple levels help resolve simple problems faster because the lower-level CCB would be constituted by the module leader and an SCM representative, who can make decisions faster, rather than waiting for the full CCB meeting to happen. Thus, the load on higher-level CCBs is reduced, and they can focus their attention on critical and severe problems, which will have huge impacts on costs and project schedules.

15.7 Summary

The place of the SCM team in the organizational structure depends largely on the organization and varies from one organization to another. We have seen the different organizational structures, but irrespective of the position in the organizational hierarchy, the SCM team performs the same functions.

We also saw the organization of the SCM team and the different people who play significant roles in the functioning of SCM activities. We saw the different types of CCBs and how they function.

Because SCM tools are automating more tasks, the role of the SCM team and the tasks they have to perform are being reduced. So, in the future, we can see reductions in the size of the SCM team, except in some areas such as analysis, evaluation, and audits, where human intervention is still required.

Reference

[1]   IEEE Standard Glossary of Software Engineering Terminology (IEEE Std-610–1990), *IEEE Software Engineering Standards Collection 2003 (CD-ROM Edition)*, Piscataway, NJ: IEEE, 2003.

Selected bibliography

Alain Abran, A., and J. W. Moore (eds.), *SWEBOK: Guide to the Software Engineering Body of Knowledge (Trial Version)*, Los Alamitos, CA: IEEE Computer Society, 2001.

Ben-Menachem, M., *Software Configuration Management Guidebook*, New York: McGraw-Hill, 1994.

IEEE Software Engineering Standards Collection 2003 (CD-ROM Edition), Piscataway, NJ: IEEE, 2003.

Marciniak, J. J. (ed.), *Encyclopedia of Software Engineering*, 2nd ed., New York: John Wiley & Sons, 2002.

Pressman, R. S., *Software Engineering: A Practitioner's Approach*, New York: McGraw-Hill, 2001.

Sommerville, I., *Software Engineering*, Reading, MA: Addison-Wesley, 2001.

Whitgift, D., *Methods and Tools for Software Configuration Management*, Chichester, England: John Wiley & Sons, 1991.

SCM tools

16.1 Introduction

Software configuration management tools are becoming more important in today's complex software development environments. Today a typical software development project consists of multidisciplinary teams, spread across different parts of the globe, and working in networked environments and in different time zones. To avoid chaos and to bring in discipline and improve development productivity, the role played by SCM tools is becoming increasingly more important.

SCM tools are nothing new. They have existed in the mainframe and UNIX environments for many years, and now they are available for every platform and every kind of development environment. In fact, hundreds of SCM tools are available in the marketplace, but it is important to remember that no SCM tool is a panacea for all SCM problems. The purchase of a sophisticated tool is just one step toward effective SCM. Using the wrong tool, or using the right tool ineptly or insensitively, makes SCM problems worse, not better [1]. In this chapter, we look at exactly what SCM tools are and what they can do to automate the SCM process and improve development productivity. We also discuss how to select an SCM tool that is best for your project or organization and look at the question of whether to make or buy your organization's SCM tools.

16.2 Evolution of SCM tools

Initially, SCM was just a means of controlling changes to the source code. Tools such as Source Code Control System (SCCS) and Revision Control System (RCS) under UNIX were created for that purpose, but their function was limited. Eventually, the abilities to manage revisions, compress deltas, handle binary file types, and increase security levels were added, and source code control turned into version control.

SCM evolved into a more comprehensive process as developers realized the need to track more than just changes to the source code. Today, SCM tools include such diverse features as build management, defect and enhancement tracking, requirement tracking, release management, software production control, software packaging and distribution control (licensing and generation of serial numbers, CD keys, codes), and site management. The ability to identify components, re-create deliverables, monitor problems and change requirements, and deliver a product of consistently high quality is the current goal of SCM. Thus, it involves monitoring every phase of a software product's life cycle.

SCM tools have come a long way from just managing the source code. They are now one of the critical functions of software engineering that help keep projects on track and manage them effectively. Today's SCM tools are getting bigger, better, and bolder. They are bigger because they no longer manage just code; they can manage the development of any object in the system's life cycle. They are better because they support parallel as well as incremental development. They are bolder because they have expanded their functionality beyond the control and management of objects and into the control and management of processes [2].

16.3   Reasons for the increasing popularity of SCM tools

The market for SCM tools is clearly very hot. Industry analysts are forecasting steady growth rates for the SCM tools market. Why have so many companies replaced their manual or semi-automated SCM systems with SCM tools? Why are so many companies, which were using old SCM tools such as SCCS or RCS, changing to more sophisticated tools? Here are some reasons:

- *Development time reduction.* SCM tools reduce development time by improving development productivity and reducing mistakes.

- *Increased business agility.* Improved productivity and reduced development time mean less time is needed to get a product to market. This coupled with the SCM tool's ability to manage and track problems, fix them, rebuild the systems easily, accurately, and quickly, and release them faster results in improved customer satisfaction. So the company can be more agile and more responsive to customers' needs without compromising product quality.

- *Error reduction.* SCM tools automate most of the monotonous and repetitive tasks that were previously done by people. Thus, SCM tools have greatly reduced the opportunity for human error.

> *Information integration.* One of the major functions of SCM is to provide sufficient, relevant, and accurate information about the software system to the different people in the project—programmers, managers, analysts, auditors, and so on—allowing the software development and maintenance processes to proceed smoothly. Earlier, people had to rely on reports provided by the status accounting function. These reports were not capable of answering ad hoc queries. But today's SCM tools have all the information the user needs and can deliver it to the user in any format desired almost instantly. This information integration capability and flexibility is one of the most important advantages of SCM tools.

> *Automation.* SCM tools automate many processes, such as configuration control, defect tracking, status reporting, version control, and build management. These tasks were considered the necessary evils of manual SCM systems. By automating these tasks, SCM tools have improved development productivity and given people more time for the system development process.

These are some of the reasons for the increasing popularity of the SCM tools market. As more companies join the race, the competition is getting hotter, and SCM tool vendors are gearing up to meet the competition by offering more features and better capabilities for their products. So the future will see a fierce battle for market share and mergers and acquisitions aimed at gaining strategic and competitive advantage. The ultimate winner in this race will be the customer, who will get better products and better services at affordable prices.

16.4 Advantages of SCM tools

Installing an SCM tool has many advantages, both indirect and direct. The indirect advantages include a better corporate image, improved customer goodwill, and customer satisfaction. The direct advantages include improved development efficiency (people will have more time to work on developmental activities), information integration for better decision making, faster response time to customer queries, and so on. Some more of the direct benefits are:

> Information integration;

> Flexibility;

> Better analysis and planning capabilities;

> Use of latest technology.

16.4.1   Information integration

The first and most important advantage lies in the promotion of integration. SCM tools are called integrated because they have the ability to automatically update data between related SCM components. For example, you need only update the status of a change request at one place, say, in the change management system; all of the other components will automatically get updated. So when a developer checks in a component after making changes, the status of a change request automatically changes from "Assigned" to "Complete." The new file or files that are checked in are automatically assigned new version numbers. The dependency details are updated to reflect the new change. The new versions are designated as the latest versions of the items. The next time you create a status report, all of these modifications will be reflected in that report.

The beauty of this system is that information updating happens instantaneously. So you get up-to-the-minute information at your fingertips. This information integration leads to better decision making and resolution of problems.

Another advantage of this integration is that the people who are involved in a project are also connected to each other. This integration has tremendous potential for improving productivity. For example, one can have virtual CCB meetings, online polls, and automatic notification.

16.4.2   Flexibility

The second advantage of SCM tools is their flexibility. Diverse multinational environments are covered in one system, and functions that comprehensively manage multiple locations and distributed and parallel development can be easily implemented. To cope with globalization, distributed development, and sophisticated development projects (development of large, complex, and mission-critical systems), this flexibility is essential, and one could say that it has major advantages, not simply for development and maintenance, but also in terms of management.

16.4.3   Better analysis and planning capabilities

Another advantage provided by SCM tools is the boost to the planning functions. By enabling the comprehensive and unified management of related SCM functions (such as configuration control, status accounting, configuration audits) and their data, it becomes possible to fully utilize many types of decision support systems and simulation functions, what-if analysis, and so on. For example, we could simulate the impact on the project cost and schedule of using more than one person on a change implementation. Furthermore, it becomes possible to carry out flexibly and in real time the filing and analysis of data from a variety of dimensions. The decision makers can get the information they want, thus enabling them to make better and more informed decisions.

16.4.4 Use of latest technology

The fourth advantage is the utilization of the latest developments in information technology (IT). SCM tool vendors realized that in order to grow and to sustain that growth, they would have to embrace the latest developments in the field of information technology. So they quickly adapted their systems to take advantage of the latest technologies, such as open systems, client/server technology, and the Internet or intranets. This quick adaptation to the latest changes in IT makes flexible adaptation to changes in future development environments possible. This flexibility makes the incorporation of the latest technology possible during system design, development, and maintenance phases.

16.5 Why do many SCM tool implementations fail?

In Chapter 6 we saw the reasons for the failure of SCM system implementations. In this section we explore why many SCM tool implementations fail. SCM tools—if chosen correctly, implemented judiciously, and used efficiently—will raise productivity, shorten development times, improve responsiveness, and result in better customer satisfaction. To use the tool efficiently, it has to be the right tool (right in the sense that it integrates well with the organization's business processes) and the people who use the tool have to be properly trained. But many projects or organizations fail in this regard because they use the wrong product, conduct an incompetent and haphazard implementation, and suffer inefficient or ineffective usage.

SCM is first an attitude; second, a process; and only third, a set of tools [3]. Attitude refers to the feeling or mood of the people in the organization toward SCM. So the users of the SCM system have to be convinced about the real benefits of using SCM. This can be done by educating people about its benefits and exposing the misconceptions about SCM. This is important because, if people believe SCM is unnecessary, they will try to bypass it. And unless a consistent SCM process is integrated into the development methodology, no one will know when to apply the SCM tools, or even what those tools are.

To work successfully, SCM solutions need a lot of factors to click. There should be good people who know the SCM concepts and the project or organizational details, the vendor should be good, and the vendor's package should be the one best suited for the company's needs. The implementation should be planned well and executed perfectly, and end-user training should be done so that people understand the system and the effect of their efforts on the overall success of the program.

SCM can be implemented in a variety of ways. It can be implemented in a phased manner (the incremental approach) or it can be implemented in one shot (the big-bang approach). Irrespective of the implementation methodology chosen, the development process has to be mature and the development environment and the organizational culture must be conducive to the implementation of SCM and its tools. If the implementation is done in an environment where the people are not ready for SCM and the work culture is not suited to it, then the implementation will fail. So the first step in the SCM implementation process is to make the organizational environment suitable for SCM.

Organizations exist at different levels of process maturity. The ease and correctness with which they can execute a process depends on their maturity. As such, it is generally not fruitful to impose a sophisticated process on an organization whose maturity is low. The maturity of an organization depends not only on the skill sets of the individuals but also on the chemistry of the team. This makes improvement an incremental process. The lessons, habits, and practices learned doing simple tasks provide the foundation to take the organization toward more sophisticated tasks [4]. So the maturity level of the organization is critical to the success of an SCM implementation.

Also, many SCM tool implementations fail because they try to implement SCM in the "tool" way rather than in the "process" way. As we saw earlier, SCM is first an attitude, then a process, and only third a set of tools. One can implement sophisticated, all-encompassing SCM tools, loaded with features, but if the people who are using them do not know why they are doing a particular task or what happens when they do something or the effect of their actions (or lack of it) on others, then the chances of such an implementation succeeding are slim.

Thus, for an SCM tool implementation to succeed, the implementation has to be planned well, the people must be ready for SCM, the development process must be in place, the selected tool should be well integrated with the process, and everyone involved in the project should understand the importance of SCM and the role each person has to play to make implementation a success.

16.6   SCM tools and SCM functions

The days when a single programmer developed an application along are a thing of the past. Today's software development is a team effort. When more than one person is involved in the development of a software system, it can lead to communications breakdowns, shared data problems, simultaneous update problems, and other issues. We have seen how an SCM system could help solve these problems. Manual SCM is a tedious, monotonous, and time-consuming process. Many tasks such as change management, record keeping, and status reporting are repetitive in nature, so we need to automate these tasks. A good SCM tool should automate the project coordination and management tasks, support repeatable processes, manage changes and issues, and automate the system builds.

In a manual SCM scenario, a developer or programmer spends more time on nondevelopmental activities such as documentation, modification, revision of the requirements and design documents, and bug fixing. Another portion of the nonprogramming time is spent on handling change requests, tracking user requirements, doing causal analysis, and creating status reports. Even though all of these tasks are necessary for the smooth functioning of the project, spending the precious time of programmers and developers on these mundane tasks, which could easily be automated, is a cardinal offense—and this is where automated SCM tools can be invaluable.

SCM tools automate the manual tasks and hence set the development teams free to actually develop. Also, today's software systems are more sophisticated, highly complex, support multiple platforms (sometimes they are cross-platform), use complex technologies, and are developed in distributed environments by diverse (different cultural, social, educational, and ethnic backgrounds) development teams. Managing a project of this kind manually is almost impossible. So today SCM tools are no longer a luxury, but a necessity. Not having an SCM tool can become a strategic disadvantage and can lead to the catastrophic consequences of failed projects, cost and time overruns, customer dissatisfaction, and more.

We have seen that SCM tools automate most of the SCM functions. We now look at the features of SCM tools that help automate the SCM functions, reducing human intervention and improving productivity.

16.6.1   Version management

Version management is a critical function of SCM and is the basis on which other functions are built. Version management is the storage of multiple images of the development files or set of related files in an application. With a good version management system, one can get an image—a snapshot in time of the development process—and re-create the file or files as they were at that discrete point in time.

Any good SCM tool will support version management activities such as creating, working, and changing versions. A version consists of a file or a set of files, each with a particular version label (i.e., unique identification/name). SCM tools have the capability to define what file or files make up a version. Once a version is defined, the user is able to check out the files that make up a version. The SCM tool is able to identify the changes to the components of a version and then create or define a new version. In this area—identifying the changes and creating new versions—and in the system building (or build management) area, the version management system works in conjunction with the change management system and build management system so that the correct versions are incorporated into the system builds.

16.6.2   Change management

Most SCM tools completely automate the change control procedures. They manage the repositories. When a change request is made, the information about it goes to all concerned personnel (e.g., management, project leads, CCB members) so they can send their approval or denial immediately by e-mail or some other messaging system. This eliminates the time lag between change initiation and disposition. Virtual CCB meetings and online polls are now standard with almost any good SCM tool. The change management system can be configured (a rule-based system) to automatically receive the change requests, process them based on a set of rules, get the responses from the appropriate sources regarding the disposition, and allocate the implementation work to qualified professionals and notify them regarding the work allocated to them. All of these things can be done without human intervention. This kind of workflow automation helps improve productivity and shorten the change process. Also, when a developer checks out the file(s),[1] the change management systems will begin tracking the activities that affect those file(s).

The change management system is also notified when the task of implementing a change is allotted to someone. So only authorized personnel can check out or make changes to the specific files. The change management system keeps track of the modifications made to the change set and its components, and when the change is completed and the items are checked in, the system can compare the before and after images and create the change history, the delta, and store the items in the most efficient manner. In addition, the details of the change process, such as who initiated the change, which people were involved in the decision making, who implemented the changes, how much time was taken to implement the change, how the change was implemented, and a host of other details, are captured automatically. This information is relevant to the status accounting function and helps in managing the project more effectively.

We have seen that the configuration identification function is an element of configuration management, consisting of selecting the configuration items for a system and recording their functional and physical characteristics in technical documentation. In an automated environment, this type of information can be captured and updated automatically. The parsing tools can determine the interdependencies of the various configuration items so that when shared components get modified, the system can alert users about the other impacted items. This automatic capturing of the component interdependencies saves a lot of time that would otherwise be spent on impact analysis when a change request is initiated. With this information already in the system, users just have to query the system repository to determine the impacted items.

Most change management systems support team development, parallel development, and distributed development. Many of the modern tools allow more than one person to work on the same file or set of files. In parallel development, two or more users may need to work on the same file, just as they would do in concurrent development. In the case of concurrent development, the branches are eventually merged into a single item, whereas in the case of parallel development, the branches will go ahead

---

1. A person can check out more than one file because a change request implementation is rarely confined to a single file, and even if it is confined to a single file, the associated analysis and design documentation, user manuals, and so on also have to be updated.

without merging. Parallel development is necessary when the development teams are producing versions of the same component for different hardware platforms or operating systems (also called variants).

Multiple development paths are usually supported with branches. Branching allows users to store more than one path for the same file. In the case of concurrent development, once the changes are made and the different people check in their files, the system will compare the changes and automatically merge them. There is also the facility to do interactive merging, where the system will highlight the changes made by different people with respect to the ancestor object. The systems can be configured to perform automatic merging or interactive merging depending on the user's preference.

The change management systems keep a chronological record (or journal) of all activities that are applied to the system components so that at any point any object or component in the system can be brought back to any of the previous states. This is helpful in cases where you need to unwind the impact of an emergency fix that was done in the middle of the night, so that it can be thoroughly checked, tested, and re-promoted.

Another important and useful feature of SCM tools is their graphical interface. The tools use different colors, icons, and other features to help users absorb information quickly and determine patterns and exceptions easily.

16.6.3   Problem tracking

Problem reporting and tracking takes a lot of time and effort. The problem has to be reported, analyzed, and fixed, and the defect prevention methods have to be carried out. The existing problem records (the knowledge base) can be scanned for similar incidents that may have been solved already. This searching is best done by a computer, especially in large knowledge bases. The computer can easily find the records that match the search criteria, in a fraction of the time taken by a manual process.

The problem tracking components of the SCM tools track the problem from its origin to completion and capture the details of the problem, such as originator, date of problem identification, cause of the problem, how and when it was fixed, how much time was taken, and what kind of skills were needed. These details are captured automatically as the activities happen. Modern problem tracking tools are sophisticated and have advanced features such as automatic receiving of the problem reports, automatic categorization of the reports, rule-based actions, automatic notifying, and alerting mechanisms.

Many tools are capable of automatically notifying concerned personnel by e-mail or pager messages about the arrival of a problem report, depending on predefined criteria chosen, such as severity and/or impact. These tools are also capable of creating alerts (automatic notification and problem escalation) based on the promotion of the problem through stages of resolution.

16.6.4 Promotion management

As the software system is being developed, it goes through the software development life cycle process. Depending on the life cycle model chosen, the phases will differ, but all software components have to go through the various phases of analysis, design, development, testing, release, and maintenance. The promotion management tools automatically record the phases through which the configuration items in the system proceed and the various details such as when each phase started and when it was finished. These tools capture information and create trails, which is useful when one needs to know exactly what happened or needs to re-create an event or an item before or after a particular event. For example, if we know exactly what was done just after alpha testing, we can re-create an item so that it is in the state it was in before the test, when it did not have any problems.

Obtaining this information and these facilities is also possible in manual systems, but with an SCM tool the degree of detail that can be captured is almost infinite.

16.6.5 System building

When the components of a software system are ready to be tested or shipped, we do what is called system building. We combine all files and may compile them, link edit them, and create an application. This build can be done for a subsystem, a module, or an entire system, in support of integration testing, alpha or beta testing, and/or system release. At this stage, capturing the details of every build and the building process is of paramount importance—which components were used in the build, what versions of the components were used, which operating system was used, which version of the operating system, what compiler and linker options were in effect, and more. This information is important because each build should be reproducible and repeatable, and that reproduction has to be reliable and accurate. SCM must be able to re-create, for example, the alpha test version of the system perhaps one year after the actual testing was done. In order to do this, one needs the information mentionedpreviously.

The SCM build management tools capture this information (in most cases automatically) and help provide reliable, repeatable builds. The automatic source code scanning, the dependency analysis capabilities, and the creation of build audit trails (footprinting) are just some of the features of SCM tools that save time, shorten build cycles, and eliminate build errors by providing repeatable, automated builds of software projects. SCM tools make the cross-platform builds that span multiple platforms, operating systems, and development environments easier, faster, and more accurate.

Many of these systems also maintain the history of the previous builds and releases in their repositories. This helps when monitoring conflicts between the new releases and any of the previous releases that are still in use.

16.6.6 Status accounting (querying and reporting)

Status accounting consists of recording and reporting information needed to manage a configuration efficiently. With manual systems, one has to record all events that will be needed later. This record keeping is a tedious and monotonous job that requires effort by the many people who perform the different SCM functions. There is also a limit to what details can be captured. In addition, the manual reporting function basically relies on routine reports to satisfy the information needs of the various participants in the software development process. Ad hoc queries are always time consuming and difficult to accommodate.

When one uses an SCM tool, however, information integration happens. There is no need for active record keeping; the system monitors all activities and keeps a record of them to the level of detail specified by the user. Once the information is in the SCM tool's database, it can be managed at will. The powerful querying tools allow users to get accurate answers to their numerous and varied information needs, when they need them. The reports can be generated in any format specified by the user. Graphical interfaces and templates or wizards are available to create a query and get the answers. This accurate and immediate access to information is one of the most often developer-requested features of SCM automation.

16.6.7 Configuration audits

Auditing means validating the completeness of a product and maintaining consistency among the components by ensuring that the product is a well-defined collection of components. For auditing requirements, one needs a history of all changes, traceability between all related components in the product and their evolution, and a log containing all details about work completed [5]. The reporting features of SCM tools provide this information.

The reporting feature of SCM tools identifies the differences between the versions and releases. The ad hoc query facility of the tool helps answer any specific questions the auditor has. The SCM tools automatically record all activities happening to the configuration items, and thus provide a comprehensive audit trail of the activities performed on an item and the events that have happened. These reports and logs help a great deal in automating the auditing process and make the configuration audits a lot easier than the manual process.

16.6.8 Access and security

The information contained in the SCM tool is sensitive and should not be available to all. Also, the items in the repository should be accessible only to those who have the necessary authorization. In the case of manual systems, the configuration managers will have to take action to prevent unauthorized access to files or information, but the SCM tools have features that aid in managing access to the system.

The system can be configured so that only people with the necessary authorization will get to see the information or will have access to the files. These access privileges and security mechanisms can be enforced using the user ID and login password of the users, so that the exact mechanism is transparent to them.

A user can log in to the system and access all information he is authorized to see, and what he is authorized to see can be set based on the user ID (or designation, title, role). With distributed development scenarios, where developers access the SCM information and files using the Internet, encryption methods are used to ensure secure transmission of data and information across the Internet.

16.6.9 Customization

The era when you had to buy a tool and implement it as it came out of the box is over. SCM tool vendors are now offering the ability to customize their tools. The extent of the customizations varies from tool to tool. SCM tools are being enhanced with customization facilities so that customers can easily modify certain features of the tools (such as screen layout, colors, and state names and transitions). More complex customizations (such as changing the associated semantics, roles, access rights, and transition conditions of the states) typically require source code changes or additional scripts using triggers and event mechanisms. Vendors are moving toward creating parameters for these more complex customizations [6].

These customization capabilities will help customers obtain tools that perfectly match their requirements. Thus, instead of developing a process around the tool, now customers can choose a tool that will integrate seamlessly with their development process.

16.6.10 Web enabling

As with every other software market, SCM tool vendors are being forced to move from a client/server to browser/server architecture to web-enable their tools. The popularity of distributed development makes web enabling a must-have feature in SCM tools. Today's developers need to access the corporate databases and repositories when they are on the move and when they are working away from the office. Also, the different people working on the same project need to share central databases and repositories for performing the various SCM activities. The most cost-effective way to do this is to use the Web. The availability of high-speed Internet access and technologies such as virtual private networks (VPNs) and better encryption methods makes using the Internet a cost-effective and secure medium to do distributed development.

In the previous section, we discussed the general characteristics of the modern SCM tools and their advantages. There are more than 50 SCM tool vendors in the marketplace, and new players are entering the market. A list of the major SCM tools is given in Appendix A: SCM Resources on the Internet.

As we saw earlier, SCM tool selection is one of the critical factors for the success of SCM implementation. The success of a company lies in selecting an SCM tool that suits its needs and matches its profile. In the next section of this chapter, we look at how to select the right SCM tool for your organization or project.

16.7   SCM tool selection

SCM tools have gained in popularity, and their usefulness has increased to a point where software development without an SCM tool is almost nonexistent. Also, a manual SCM system is not acceptable, except for small, single-person projects. All other projects benefit from the use of automated SCM tools.

SCM tools are now available in all sizes and shapes for all platforms and development environments. Evaluating the SCM tools available in the marketplace and then selecting one for your organization or project are critical parts of the process. This decision can make or break an organization.

Of the more than 50 SCM tools available, the features they offer vary, as do the technologies they support, the technologies they use, the architecture on which they are built, and the available platforms. Each tool has its own strengths and weaknesses. For example, some are better at change management, whereas others have excellent build management and versioning capabilities. Some SCM tools cover the entire spectrum of SCM functionality, and others just do source control.

Deciding which tool is suited to your organization is a difficult task. Each piece of marketing literature from the tool vendors claims that their product is the best among the lot and has all of the features you will ever need. So if you go by what is written in the product brochure or what the salespeople say, you will find it difficult to make a decision and might end up with the wrong choice. According to Dart [6], "such literature [the marketing literature of the tool vendors] is valuable for giving the reader an overview of functionality and a glimpse at the differentiator for that vendor's offering. But, if you compare the literature or listen to a vendor's presentation, it would be very difficult to evaluate which package is the best or which would be most suitable for your organization." So tool selection should be done systematically and scientifically. In this section, we examine how to select an SCM tool that will suit your needs.

The most important factor to keep in mind when analyzing the different packages is that none of them is perfect, and this needs to be understood by everyone on the decision-making team. The objective of the selection process is not to identify a package that covers every requirement (a perfect fit). The objective is to find a package that is flexible enough to meet the company's needs. In other words, to find a tool that can be customized to obtain a good fit.

Because there are so many tools, analyzing all SCM packages before reaching a decision is not a viable solution. It is also a time-consuming process. So it is better to limit the number of packages that is evaluated to less than five. It is always better to do a thorough and detailed evaluation of a smaller number of packages than to do a superficial analysis of dozens of packages. So the company should do a preevaluation screening to limit the number of packages that is to be evaluated by the committee. The preevaluation process should eliminate those packages that are not at all suitable for the company's business processes. One can zero in on the few best packages by looking at the product literature of the vendors, getting help from external consultants, and most important, finding out what package is used by similar companies. It is a good idea to look around to find out how the different packages are performing in environments similar to yours. Once you select a few packages after the screening, you can call the respective vendors to request presentations or demos.

Dart [6] classifies the SCM tools into three categories: version control tools, developer-oriented tools, and process-oriented tools. The SCM tool evaluation process can be narrowed down to a few tools if the company knows which category of tools they need. The tools vary in features, complexity, and functionality, with the process-oriented tools being the most sophisticated and having more functionality than the other two types.

A version control tool would typically suit a small company or a research and development group that has a small number of releases and possibly no variant releases. A developer-oriented tool would typically suit a medium- or large-sized company that does not have a lot of formal processes defined and is not focused on standards certification. The company might have many variant releases and would need strong support for parallel development and build management, as well as more reliability from the configuration management repository. A process-oriented tool would typically suit a large corporation with formal processes that need to be automated, that is focused on process improvement in general, and that has sophisticated build management and change management needs [6]. The categorization of the SCM tools can be used to narrow the list of candidates in the preevaluation screening process.

After the decision to buy an SCM tool has been made, the company needs to develop selection criteria that will permit the evaluation of all chosen packages on the same scale. To choose the best system, the company should identify the system that meets the business needs, that matches the development process, and that identifies with the development practices of the company. It will be impossible to get a system that performs its development and maintenance functions in exactly the same way as the company does, but the goal is to get the system that has the least number of differences.

16.7.1 Selection process

The selection process is one of the most important phases of SCM implementation, because the tool that you select will determine the success or failure of the project. Because SCM tools involve a huge investment, once a package is purchased, it is not an easy task to switch to another one. So it is a "do it right the first time" proposition. There is little to no room for error.

16.7.2   Selection committee

It is a good idea to form a selection or evaluation committee to conduct the evaluation process. The selection committee should be entrusted with the task of choosing a package for the company. The package experts or the consultants can act as mediators or play the role of explaining the pros and cons of each package.

The evaluation committee should be made up of various representatives of the user community [7]. It can include developers, testers, QA people, technical leaders, build managers, and project managers. All of these users provide perspectives and ensure that their needs are addressed, while providing their own experiences, skill set, and processes to address the three important areas apart from functionality requirements: usability, performance, and scalability requirements.

16.8   Working with vendors

Once you decide to buy an SCM tool, the marketing executives of the different vendors will swamp you. Each will have colorful and superbly produced brochures and presentations claiming that their product is the best one for you. They will try eagerly to convince you of that fact. So you should have a strategy in place for working with these vendors.

As mentioned, you should conduct a detailed evaluation of not more than five packages that meet your preselection criteria. When the vendors arrive for their presentations, you should be thoroughly prepared; otherwise, they may overwhelm you with their presentations and you will not have time to ask questions. This point is being stressed repeatedly because most vendors are able to make presentations that leave potential users dazzled, and without proper consideration of all aspects, the selection may end up being based on a set of factors that is insufficient for arriving at a well-informed and judicious decision.

So instead of just listening to presentations, you should be prepared to ask questions. The questions should be prepared beforehand and should address all of your concerns. The responses that you get to your questions will help you either eliminate a vendor or strengthen its case. The questions, if properly prepared and asked, will expose the weak or problem areas, if any, that exist in the vendors' products. Also when you are asking questions, it means that you are not taking anything for granted. It is a good idea to prepare minutes of the meeting and ask the vendors to sign off on them. This will prevent the vendors from making false claims, and you can make them accountable if they fail to deliver what they have promised.

The vendors should be asked to show testimonials and practical demonstrations of the system. The vendor should provide references for organizations in which the system has been implemented successfully. But all vendors will also have customers for whom the tools have failed. In the author's opinion, getting those names and reasons for the failure is more important than the success stories. Also, it is the author's experience that while vendor representatives are well prepared for the success stories, the question about failed implementations usually reveals points and issues that the vendor is trying to downplay. So it is important to ask about failed implementations. The vendor will often send two representatives to visit you, a marketing agent and a technical expert. Most of your questions should be directed to the technical expert. The marketing agent should be asked about warranties, licenses, cost, support, and training, whereas the technical expert should be asked about the functionality and capabilities of the system they are offering.

16.9   Role of technology

The existing technology will play an important role in the SCM tool selection process. Each organization has its own technological environment—how the development process works, what kind of hardware and software are used, and a particular database management system that is preferred. These factors can greatly influence the selection process in the sense that they can limit the number of packages available for evaluation. So management must decide whether the SCM tool will be selected taking the existing infrastructure into consideration or whether the existing systems will not be considered (in which case some of them will have to be scrapped). This is a difficult decision, and it is always better to find a package that is compatible with the hardware, software, and technology the company already has in place. Also, if the organization has the necessary infrastructure, then it can think of buying the required components from the vendors and integrating them with the existing system.

For example, if an organization is using the operating system's library management system and is satisfied with it, then it can go in for a change management and problem-tracking tool and not the complete offering from the vendor. Later, if the organization wants to switch from the operating system's library management, it can then purchase the remaining modules of the package. So it is not imperative that all of the components offered by the vendor be bought. The evaluation committee, in association with the vendor, can select the required components and then integrate them with the existing infrastructure. But do not forget to get the vendor's assurance (in writing) that the existing system will integrate smoothly and seamlessly with the purchased components.

16.10   Selection criteria

SCM tools come in all sizes and shapes, with all of the frills, bells and whistles, gizmos and gadgets that you can imagine. So it is a good practice to specify selection criteria for evaluating the packages that survive the pre-evaluation screening. The criteria can be in the form of a questionnaire, and a point system can be implemented. This will help make the selection process more objective.

The questions should address the organization's needs and concerns, and each issue or question should be given a weight according to how critical that function is for the company. For example, if the company is doing distributed development and has development centers in different countries, then the ability to handle distributed development and Web features becomes an important criterion. Likewise, the selection criteria should be divided into categories—vital, essential, and desirable—and points should be given to each criterion. This point rating system simplifies the evaluation process, but remember that the importance of human intuition (gut feeling) and judgment should never be underestimated.

The best method for preparing the selection criteria is to conduct a requirements analysis—find out what the company needs. The requirements must reflect those factors that the company considers indispensable for the successful running of the business according to the company's work culture and practices. A set of questions that could form part of the selection criteria can be found in the following documents:

> ▸ Mosley, V., et al., "Software Configuration Management Tools: Getting Bigger, Better, and Bolder," *Crosstalk: The Journal of Defense Software Engineering*, Vol. 9, No. 1, Jan. 1996, pp. 6–10.

> ▸ Firth, R., et al., "A Guide to the Classification and Assessment of Software Engineering Tools," Technical Report CMU/SEI-87-TR-10, Software Engineering Institute, Carnegie Mellon University, 1987.

> ▸ Berlack, R. H., *Evaluation and Selection of Automated Configuration Management Tools*, Amherst, NH: Configuration Management International, 1995.

Here are some examples of selection criteria:

> ▸ The package should have distributed development support.

> ▸ The package should support parallel development of variants.

> ▸ The package should have both automatic and interactive merging facilities.

> ▸ The package should have a customizable report-generation facility and the facility to export the reports to other systems.

- The tool should support a footprinting feature for build management.

- The change management and problem-tracking system should have the facility to conduct virtual CCB meetings, online polls, and automatic notification.

- The system should have a graphical user interface.

- The performance of the system should be within specified limits.

- The vendor should have been in the business for at least "x" years.

- The package should have at least "x" number of installations, out of which at least "y" should be in organizations similar to your organization.

- The cost of the package with all of the necessary modules should be less than "x" dollars.

- The package should support incremental module addition. For example, the company should be able to buy the core modules initially and then purchase additional modules as and when desired.

- The vendor should provide implementation and postimplementation support.

- The vendor should train company employees on the package.

- The package must be customizable, and the customization process should be easy (something that could be done in-house).

- The package should be scalable or should be capable of growing with the organization.

- The vendor's policy and practices regarding updates, versions, and so on should be acceptable.

In this way, the issues, concerns, and expectations that the company has regarding the package can be consolidated and made into a list. Then the items in the list should be divided into the vital, essential, and desirable categories. Then using this list, each package should be evaluated. Many items in the list will have descriptive answers. The committee should analyze these issues and assign points to these items.

One important thing to keep in mind is that whenever a decision is made, the committee should discuss it and a consensus must be reached. In doing so, the chances of conflict between different functions (such as the development team, QA team, and other support teams) are reduced. Remember that the SCM tool belongs to all functions, so it is better for decisions to be arrived at via a consensus. This will create the feeling that the tool belongs to everyone, and it furthers the idea that a commitment from everyone is needed to make it happen. Most important, because both the SCM experts (people who know the tools well) and project team members (people who know the project and work culture well) are involved, they can point out areas and issues that should be given more importance and the aspects that should be scrutinized more thoroughly.

Another source from which the evaluation committee can get information about the tools is independent research agencies and companies. These sources supply information, comprehensive analyses, and comparison reports about the leading tools. But these reports, although excellent sources of information and a single-point reference about the leading SCM tools, are not totally unbiased, completely accurate, and totally objective and therefore should not be taken as gospel truth. But these reports can provide valuable information about the tools, so at least a few reports by these research groups should be studied along with the vendor's literature to get a complete picture of the SCM tool marketplace. These reports analyze and compare the tools and their features, predict market trends, forecast the position of the different players in the coming years, and so on. Several companies and consultants do this kind of analysis. Prominent among them are Ovum Limited (*www.ovum.com*), the International Data Corporation (*www.idc.com*), and the Butler Group (*www.butlergroup.com*). Sometimes the trade magazines, such as *Communications of ACM, IEEE Software, IEEE Computer,* and *Application Development Trends,* publish articles about SCM and its current state. This information is also worth looking into because it is independent and unbiased.

Once the committee has evaluated all of the tools that have cleared the preevaluation stage, listened to the vendor presentations and demos, and cleared pending issues, a decision is reached on which tool to buy. Once the committee has reached a decision on a tool, it is a good idea to visit a few companies that have installed the particular package to see it in action. But many people will not admit when they have made a mistake, so anything the existing owners say about a package should be taken with a grain of salt. Visiting four or five installations should give the committee members a good idea about the package. If the committee members feel that their decision is right and what they thought is what they have seen, then the company can proceed with the purchase and implementation of the chosen tool.

If anyone is uneasy about some aspect of the decision or does not feel that the product meets the expected standards, then the committee members should revisit the question of which tool to choose and be prepared to conduct the analysis once again. The package that received the maximum score in the point rating system might not be the one that is best suited for the company. So the extra time spent on analysis and evaluation is not a waste; in fact, it could save the company from a potential disaster.

16.11   Tool implementation

Once the right tool has been selected, then the next step is implementation. Making a major change in a company, such as changing over to a new automated configuration management tool, is both a significant opportunity and a major responsibility [8]. It is an opportunity because it enables a company to address its configuration management problems and improve processes to result in better management of its data and its development and maintenance activities. But changing over is a major responsibility because of the ramifications and the resources required to make the change. Many tricky technical, political, organizational, cultural, process-oriented, risk-related, and personnel issues need to be addressed in making the change, and people need to be committed to the change.

So in order to adopt an SCM tool successfully or to make the changeover from one tool to another, careful planning is a must. All possible aspects of the implementation should be addressed satisfactorily before starting the implementation or changeover. This includes the implementation of new procedures, the changing responsibilities of users (with SCM tools, users get more freedom than with a manual system, such as the ability to check out and check in files and interactively merge the changes), the changing responsibilities of the SCM team (because most of the processes become automated, a significant reduction is seen in the size of the team), and the role of the CCB members, QA members, and the audit team (they will have to be trained in the new technologies, which enable them to conduct virtual CCB meetings, online polls, and audits).

Many people will need to be trained or retrained on the new tool. Many will have to be trained on the concepts of SCM and its functions. In the author's experience, it makes a tremendous difference if the people are first trained regarding the concepts of SCM and then trained on the tool. In this way, they can correlate what they are doing with the tool with the actual SCM concepts and functions. If employees are just trained to use the tool without understanding the underlying SCM concepts, then they will be doing their tasks without knowing how their actions affect others. It is possible to implement an SCM tool and use it without actually knowing anything about SCM concepts, but in the long run it is better to do it the right way—that is, provide training on the tools along with training on the SCM concepts and how the concepts are implemented in the tool.

The following issues need to be addressed before the SCM implementation or changeover begins: process, culture, roles, risk management, environment, application, requirements, management, and planning [8]. The organization should address the current process and new SCM process and how the new tool will be different. The work environment and work culture of the organization and whether they have to be changed or adapted to meet the needs of the new tools need to be analyzed. This is important because a new tool will bring about changes in the roles of the users and give them more power, freedom, and responsibility. The people and the organization should be geared to handle this change.

The new roles of the staff need to be clearly defined. Because most processes are automated by the introduction of the SCM tool, many existing jobs will no longer be needed, and many job profiles will change. The implementation team should make the staff aware of the postimplementation scenario and what exactly will happen to their jobs after the tool is implemented. This is important to secure the cooperation of users, which is a critical success factor for the tool.

The organization should also identify and assess the potential risk factors in making the transition to the new tool and try to reduce or resolve them. The tool implementation team should also consider which projects are going to use the tool and which project will be the pilot project. If the tool is implemented for a single project and not for the entire organization, then the team should identify which subsystems of the project are to be under control of the tool, whether the work given to the subcontractors will be put under the control of the tool, and which module is going to be chosen for the pilot implementation.

The organization should also have realistic knowledge of what it can expect from the tool and what the limitations are. This information should also be given to users of the tool, because unrealistic expectations about a tool can turn into dissatisfaction, misuse, lack of use, or noncooperation when the tool fails to deliver what the user expects it to deliver. So users should be educated about the capabilities and limitations of the tool. During and after the implementation, management support is essential for the success of the tool. So management must take an active interest in the tool and should designate one of the top executives who has the necessary authority and firepower as the leader of the tool implementation team. As Dart [8] says, many brave decisions need to be taken and resources have to be used, schedules have to be altered, and so on, and for this one needs a senior person at the helm of the implementation team. Finally, all of these issues should be documented and plans, cost estimates, budgets, time schedules, and so on should be prepared before the implementation begins.

Once the planning stage is over, the implementation team in association with the vendor's representative can start the implementation. The tool can be first implemented on the pilot project. Selecting the pilot project is another critical factor, because failure in the pilot project can end the implementation process. So the pilot project must be carefully chosen, considering the project members, the project environment, and other variables. The users in the pilot project have to be given thorough training on the tool and the SCM concepts, how it is going to affect the work environment, and how the processes are going to be automated.

Choosing a high-profile project for the implementation is advantageous and at the same time dangerous: advantageous in the sense that if the pilot project is an unqualified success, then winning over company-wide acceptance is easy; dangerous because if it fails, then everyone will know about it. So if the implementation team is sure about making the pilot implementation a success, then in the author's opinion, it is better to choose a high-profile project. If the tools have been chosen correctly, if the implementation is well planned, if the project team is well prepared and well trained, then there is no reason why the project should fail. Also, with constant monitoring during the initial phases, any signs of a disaster can be easily detected and corrected. The pilot project will also give information about the organization and its peculiarities that will be useful when the company-wide implementation is done.

Any organization that is going to implement an SCM tool or change over to a new SCM tool will benefit greatly from reading the technical paper "Adopting an Automated Configuration Management Solution" by Susan A. Dart [8] and Chapter 5 ("Configuration Management Tool Selection and Deployment") of her book *Configuration Management: The Missing Link in Web Engineering* [9].

Finally, a caveat: The most critical factor that decides the success of any SCM tool implementation is the support of the people who use the system. Even the best tools will fail if there is no user support. So the decision of the committee should be a consensus. If some people's views are overridden by a majority vote, then management should make every effort to make them understand the reasons for the decisions and should spare no effort to win them over. Disagreements are common in any group discussion, but the success of the group lies in the fact that the decisions made by the group are owned by all members of the group, everyone emerges as a winner, and the choice was made by the group as a whole. This feeling is important, because the company will need everyone's goodwill and support to achieve success during implementation and after implementation.

16.12   SCM tools: Make or buy?

So far we have seen three possible scenarios for implementing an SCM system:

1.   The manual system;

2.   The semi-automated system, in which some components such as the change management system or build management system are automated;

3.   The integrated system, in which the configuration management tools are integrated into the development process.

Except for the first case, the other implementation scenarios use some sort of an SCM tool. The question is whether to make the SCM tools in-house or to buy them.

Why can't companies develop their own SCM tools? Developing an SCM tool is a complex and time-consuming process that requires a lot of skilled labor and other resources. Many companies have personnel on their payrolls who can absorb the necessary knowledge and who have experience in developing sophisticated systems. The problem is that SCM tool development is not the main business of these companies. They should be directing all of their available resources into improving their own products or services so they can remain competitive, better serve their customers, and continue to grow.

SCM tool vendors are people who have invested huge amounts of time and effort in research and development to create packaged solutions. SCM tool vendors spend billions of dollars in research and come up with innovations that make the packages more efficient, flexible, and easy to implement and use. Also, with the evolution of new technologies, the vendors will be able to constantly upgrade their products to take advantage of the best and latest advancements in technology because their main focus is on improving the capabilities of their tools.

Because designing and implementing SCM tools is not the business of most companies, or a focus of their executives, the systems an in-house team comes up with will never be equal in quality, scope, functionality, or technology with those created by software firms whose business is SCM tools. These software firms (SCM tool vendors) can produce sophisticated packages and provide their clients with products that allow them to maintain a focus on their own chief activities, thus improving revenues, profits, and shareholder returns.Until the 1990s, not many vendors were producing SCM tools; hence, the company needing a specialized SCM tool was often left to its own devices and ingenuity to develop something that would suit its needs. In today's marketplace, many SCM tool vendors are actively pursuing all of the niches and circumstances in which SCM tools can solve problems for development organizations.

But situations do exist in which a company will have to develop or make its own SCM tools. The main reasons are still unavailability of tools suited for the company or the peculiar nature of the company or the project. For example, an organization the author worked with had more than 2,500 professionals spread around the globe in 54 offices in 15 countries. The main development was carried out in the headquarters, with dedicated lines connecting the client sites on different continents. The professionals were constantly moving from one project to another, from one country to another. The company had a central SCM team and individual teams within each project. The company personnel were connected via e-mail. The main problem the SCM team of the company faced was finding the appropriate people to deal with a change request evaluation, problem evaluation, or auditing. Because the people were always on the move, a person who was on a project today could be on another continent the next day. So the configuration team was finding it difficult to allocate the tasks to the right people. The solution was to create a skill inventory database of all employees (as described in Chapter 14) that was always kept current and up to date. The information was stored in a relational database. The company had something called a Manpower Allocation Task Committee (MATC), which assigned the various professionals to different locations and projects. The MATC records were always current and updated because MATC did the allocation and coordinated the travel plans. So these details (the availability details) were imported from the MATC database to the configuration management database.

The company also had a good performance evaluation system, which included asking the employees to update their skill inventory (i.e., how many years of experience they had in each of their skills). The skills included programming languages, database management systems, graphical user interface design, testing, and auditing, to name a few. For each skill, for which the employee had more than six months of experience, he or she was asked to take an online test. The test scores were multiplied by the experience in months to arrive at a point rating system. So the configuration database had the employee availability, the skill set, the competency level, and other details of the employee such as work phone number, e-mail ID, and so on. The configuration team could query this database and obtain details about people who were currently available for a task. Because the contact information was also available in the database, the concerned person could be contacted immediately and the task assigned. This was a requirement that no tool supported, and the company had to make the tool in-house. The company already had tools for most of the other SCM functions such as change management and system building. This employee-tracking tool integrated seamlessly with the other tools and proved effective in eliminating the delays in change request processing, problem report evaluation, and auditing.

In another company, the problem was quite different. The company had a workflow automation system based on Lotus Notes. All of the users in the company were familiar with the Lotus Notes environment. Bringing in an SCM tool was discussed but discarded, because it would not integrate well with the existing infrastructure. The author was in charge of the SCM implementation. The SCM implementation team discussed the various options and found that the most cost-effective solution was to build a tool in-house. Lotus Notes' inherent strengths in workflow automation, security administration, and Web features made it easier to design and develop the SCM tool. The SCM tool that was finally developed integrated seamlessly with the existing environment and was a huge success. Also, there was no need for extensive training; the project members needed training only on the concepts of SCM and how it was implemented in the system. Because all of them were comfortable with the environment, the transition was almost painless.

To conclude, it is always better to buy SCM tools. Many tools are available free of cost, but the main problem with them is lack of technical support. Also, these tools will not be updated to take advantage of the latest technological developments. But the commercial tools are getting better, bigger, and have more features. Also, they have been developed by people who specialize in developing those types of tools. Most of the tools could be customized to suit your needs. So unless, and until, your project or organization has a need that cannot be fulfilled by the available tools, it is better to buy the tools rather than make them.

16.13   Summary

This chapter discussed SCM tools and their selection. Except for small, single-person projects, SCM tools can dramatically improve development productivity. This chapter also discussed how to choose a tool that is right for an organization and how to deploy the tool in that organization. We also looked at making a decision about whether to make or buy SCM tools.

References

[1]   Whiftgift, D., *Methods and Tools for Software Configuration Management*, Chichester: England, John Wiley & Sons, 1991.

[2]   Mosley, V., et al., "Software Configuration Management Tools: Getting Bigger, Better, and Bolder," *Crosstalk: The Journal of Defense Software Engineering*, Vol. 9, No. l, Jan. 1996, pp. 6–10.

[3]   Weatherall, B., "A Day in the Life of a PVCS Road Warrior: Want to Get PVCS Organized Quickly in a Mixed-Platform Environment?" Technical Paper, Synergex International Corporation, 1997.

[4]   Jasthi, S., "SCM Without Tears, "http://pw2.netcom.com/-siasthi/index.htm], 1997.

[5]   Dart, S., "Concepts in Configuration Management Systems," Technical Report, Software Engineering Institute, Carnegie-Mellon University, 1994.

[6]   Dart, S., "Not All Tools are Created Equal," *Application Development Trends*, Vol. 3, No. 9, 1996, pp. 45–48.

[7]   Dart S., "Achieving the Best Possible Configuration Management Solution," *Crosstalk: The Journal of Defense Software Engineering*, September 1996, pp. 9–13.

[8]   Dart S., "Adopting An Automated Configuration Management Solution," Technical Paper, STC'94 (Software Technology Center), Utah, April 12, 1994.

[9]   Dart, S., *Configuration Management: The Missing Link in Web Engineering*, Norwood, MA: Artech House, 2000.

Selected bibliography

Alain Abran, A., and J. W. Moore (eds.), *SWEBOK: Guide to the Software Engineering Body of Knowledge (Trial Version)*, Los Alamitos, CA: IEEE Computer Society, 2001.

Alder, P. S., and A. Shenhar, "Adapting Your Technological Base: The Organizational Challenge," *Sloan Management Review*, Fall 1990, pp. 25–37.

Berlack, R. H., *Software Configuration Management*, New York: John Wiley & Sons, 1992.

Bochenski, B., "Managing It All: Good Management Boosts C/S Success," *Software Magazine* Client/Server Computing Special Edition, November 1993, p. 98.

Bones, M., "Technology Audit: True Software Suite," White Paper, Butler Direct Limited, 1998.

Bouldin, B. M., *Agents of Change: Managing the Introduction of Automated Tools*, Englewood Cliffs, NJ: Yourdon Press, 1989.

Cagan, M., and D. W. Weber, "Task-Based Software Configuration Management: Support for 'Change Sets' in Continuus/CM," Technical Report, Continuus Software Corporation, 1996.

"Change Management for Software Development," Continuus Software Corporation, 1998.

Chris, A. "Why Can't I Buy an SCM Tool?" *Proc. ICSE SCM-4 and SCM-5 Workshops (Selected Papers)*, Berlin, Springer-Verlag, 1995, pp. 278–281.

"Cost Justifying Software Configuration Management," PVCS Series for Configuration Management White Paper, Intersolv, 1998.

Dart, S., *Configuration Management: The Missing Link in Web Engineering*, Norwood, MA: Artech House, 2000.

Dart, S., "Past, Present and Future of CM Systems," Technical Report, Software Engineering Institute, Carnegie-Mellon University, 1992.

Dart, S., "Spectrum of Functionality in Configuration Management Systems," Technical Report, Software Engineering Institute, Carnegie-Mellon University, 1990.

Dart, S., "To Change or Not to Change," *Application Development Trends*, Vol. 4, No. 6, 1997, pp. 55–57.

Dart, S., and J. Krasnov, "Experiences in Risk Mitigation for Configuration Management," *Proc. 4th SEI Conference on Risk*, Monterey, CA, November 1995.

Feiler, P. H., "Configuration Management Models in Commercial Environments," Technical Report, Software Engineering Institute, Carnegie-Mellon University, 1991.

Fichman, R. G., and C. Kemerer, "Adoption of Software Engineering Innovations: The Case of Object Orientation," *Sloan Management Review*, Winter 1993, pp. 7–22.

Hall, E. M., *Managing Risk: Methods for Software Systems Development*, Reading, MA: Addison-Wesley, 1998.

Hurwitz, J., and A. Palmer, "Application Change Management-True Software, Inc.," White Paper, Hurwitz Group, 1997.

Kolvik, S. "Introducing Configuration Management in an Organization," *Proc. ICSE '96 SCM-6 Workshops (Selected Papers)*, Berlin, Springer-Verlag, 1996, pp. 220–230.

Mason, R. P., "Enterprise Application Management in the Age of Distributed Computing: The True Software Approach," White Paper, International Data Corporation, 1998.

Marciniak, J. J. (ed.), *Encyclopedia of Software Engineering*, 2nd ed., New York: John Wiley & Sons, 2002.

Parker, K., "Customization of Commercial CM System to Provide Better Management Mechanisms," *Proc. ICSE SCM-4 and SCM-S Workshops (Selected Papers)*, Berlin, Springer-Verlag, 1995, pp. 289–292.

Pressman, R. S., *Software Engineering: A Practitioner's Approach*, New York: McGraw-Hill, 2001.

"Software Configuration Management: A Primer for Development Teams and Managers," White Paper, Intersolv, 1997.

"Software Configuration Management for Client/Server Development Environments: An Architecture Guide," White Paper, Intersolv, 1998.

Sommerville, I., *Software Engineering*, Reading, MA: Addison-Wesley, 2001.

Weber, D. W., "Change Sets Versus Change Packages: Comparing Implementation of Change-Based SCM," *Proc. 7th Software Configuration Management Conf. (SCM7)*, Boston, Massachusetts, May 1997, pp. 25–35.

Contents

Documentation management and control and product data management

17.1 Introduction

Software development produces a lot of documents. According to Visconti and Cook [1], low-quality, poor, obsolete, or missing documentation is a major contributor to low product quality and high development and maintenance costs. Documentation is the written record of what the software is supposed to do, what it does, how it does it, and how to use it.

Virtually everyone agrees that good documentation is important to the analysis, development, and maintenance phases of the software process and is an important software product. It can be said that to develop high-quality software products, high-quality documentation is a must. Most information and documentation these days are in digital form, and their format is completely different from that of conventional documents. State-of-the-art tools are available to share and convey information as efficiently as possible. All software projects involve the production and control of documentation.

According to Wallace [2], mainly four types of documents are produced by a software development project:

- *External deliverable (permanent).* Permanent documentation such as a deliverable from the project (e.g., "Help" information, user manuals, training materials).

- *External deliverable (temporary).* Temporary documentation that is an external deliverable from the project but has no value once the project has been completed (e.g., discussion papers, draft documents, interim progress reports).

255

- *Used by project team (permanent).* Permanent documentation to support the maintenance and enhancement of the system (e.g., design specifications, database definitions, source code, process diagrams).

- *Used by project team (temporary).* Temporary documentation that is only for internal communication (e.g., ideas, issues, control, working papers).

These factors—permanency and target audience—affect the requirements for quality, review, and update of documentation. For example, external deliverables need to be of high quality, whereas internal documents may be informal and incomplete; permanent documentation will need to be updated as circumstances change, but temporary documentation will usually be left unchanged or disposed of after use.

Many types of documents have varying purposes, natures, and life cycles. Some documents, such as standards and guidelines that are used in the project, are produced even before the start of the project, and many of these documents (such as standards) are created by other organizations. After the development project has been completed, documents will still be produced during the operation and maintenance phases. Many documents get updated and modified during the course of the project. This will make the older versions obsolete, and their continued usage can create a lot of problems. The large amount of documents makes it more difficult to locate the information required. Thus, it is essential that all project stakeholders— from clients to end users—should use the correct version of the documents. This is an enormous and difficult task, one that requires the institution of systematic and scientific procedures and methods to manage the creation, classification, modification, change, distribution, and archiving or deletion of documents. The process that ensures everyone in a project uses the current and correct versions of the documents, changes made to the documents are effected in all copies of the document, and unauthorized changes are not made to the documents is called documentation management and control (DMC). DMC is an integral part of configuration management.

The primary purpose of DMC is to provide the right users with the right information at the right time. It should provide an efficient way of sharing knowledge, information, and thinking among the project's participants. All participants should find it easy to consult the project's documentation repository to find all content that is relevant to their interests. It should be equally easy for them to lodge in the repository any documented information that they feel is of value to the team, and all of these activities should be conducted in a systematic and controlled manner.

17.2   Document life cycle

Like software products, documents also have a life cycle. They also start as an idea or concept, and once their use is over, they are either archived or destroyed. The DMC activities focus on enabling documents to service their users during the life cycle. The documentation process records information produced by a life cycle process or activity. The process contains the set of activities, which plan, design, develop, produce, edit, distribute, and maintain those documents needed by all concerned parties, such as managers, engineers, and users of the system or software product.

The different phases of the document life cycle are creation, storage, publishing, viewing, modification, review, approval, retention, archiving, and disposal. The document life cycle phases are shown in Figure 17.1. These phases are not linear, because many phases occur more than once during the life cycle. For example, once the document is created, published, and viewed, modifications or changes are made. Once the modifications are made, the document is reviewed by a competent authority. Once the reviewer approves the changes, the documents are again published and viewed. This modification, review, and approval process happens many times during the life cycle of a document. Unauthorized modification and publishing without proper review and approval can cause problems for users of the document. Preventing this from happening is the job of a good

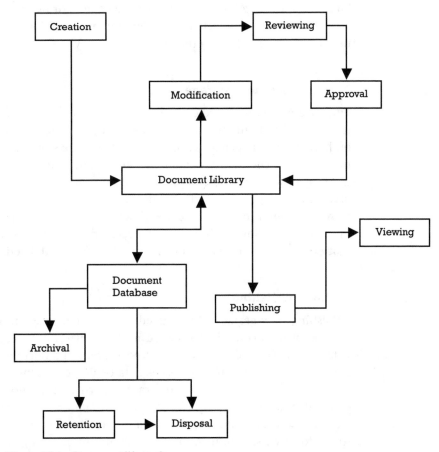

Figure 17.1   Document life cycle.

DMC system. We will see the different phases of the document life cycle in a little detail in the next sections.

17.2.1   Document creation

Documents can be created in several ways and from several sources. The documents can be written by people in your organization, external consultants, or partner organizations, or can be bought from external sources. Standards, statutory regulations, and guidelines are usually developed by external organizations. Documents developed by consultants include implementation guidelines and programming standards, for which the consultant has more expertise than the company employees. If your organization works with other organizations or develops products for other organizations, documents such as design specifications and interface control documents might come from those organizations. Other documents are created by your own organization, such as project plans, SCM plans, requirements specifications, design documents, test plans, and user manuals. The documents can come in a variety of formats and on a variety of media using a variety of tools. The documents can be text, images, sound, video, or a combination of these. All documents that are created or procured from external sources should be subjected to review and approval by authorized personnel before placing them in the document library.

17.2.2   Document storage

The documents are stored depending on the format. Paper documents need to be stored in filing cabinets, whereas digital documents need to be stored on hard disks. The place where the documents are stored is called the document library. The library contains all active documents that are needed by the project. With the advances in technology and the reduction in the cost of digital storage and retrieval mechanisms, today most documents are stored in digital form on a server that the project participants can access. The document library should have necessary control and safety measures that prevent unauthorized viewing, modification, and deletion.

17.2.3   Publishing

Publishing includes activities related to document presentation. The same content or data could be presented in different formats (e.g., text, graphs, video clips). The ability to separate the content of a document from its format is increasing. So the same sales data could be presented as a text document, a spreadsheet, or a set of graphs. Each presentation format has its own advantages. Keeping the content and format independent of one another gives the publisher the flexibility to choose the format that is best suited for each situation. Another function of publishing is to combine the different documents or different document elements (e.g., text, pictures, sound) in a single document and make them accessible to users. Even though the different document elements exist in the document library separately, the process of combining them should be transparent to users.

17.2.4 Viewing

The documents are created and stored so that end users can view the documents. In most cases, users will be using the same tools to view documents that were used to create the documents. This could create problems if the user does not have the tool with which the document was created. To avoid this problem, document management uses standard formats such as XML, HTML, PDF, and others. In other words, more tool independence is achieved. In this way, presentation tools such as Web browsers and PDF readers are not part of the DMC system. This approach has dramatically improved the accessibility of documentation and information sharing.

17.2.5 Modification/change, review, and approval

Once the documents are created and published, and as people start using them, the need for modification or making changes arises. The modification could be needed because of errors in the documentation, changes in the environment for which the document was created, change in technology, or change in the organization's priorities. All changes to documentation should be in writing and processed in a manner that ensures prompt action. All changes will be documented by a formal change procedure and approved by the technical authority responsible for originating and revising the document. Once the need for changing the document has been identified, the document is checked out from the document library and the changes are made. Any other documents that are affected by the changes in the current document are also changed. The modified documents are reviewed and approved by authorized personnel and then returned (checked in) to the document library and given a new version number. This is similar to the change control process described in Chapter 8.

17.2.6 Records retention

With time, the value of many documents will diminish, and maintaining these documents is a waste of space and effort. The documents fall into three categories: (1) documents that do not have any value after the completion of the project, (2) documents that have value as reference material for future projects, and (3) documents that should be retained to satisfy some statutory requirement or contract regulations.

The documents and records that fall in the last category come under the purview of records retention. The records retention policy will usually be specified in the SCM plan—documents that are to be retained, for how long they are to be retained, and so on. So the records and documents that are to be retained are not destroyed for the specified period.

17.2.7   Document disposal

The documents that are not needed after completion of the project, such as status reports, internal memos, and draft versions, are permanently deleted to free up storage space. The document disposal need not be at the end of the project. It can be a periodic activity. Deleting unwanted and obsolete documents from the document library will reduce clutter and improve the efficiency of the document retrieval systems. A word of caution: Before any documents are removed or deleted from the project, the organization's records retention policy should be reviewed and complied with to avoid deleting documents that are required to be kept.

17.2.8   Archiving

Records and documents that have a sustaining utility exceeding storage costs are preserved permanently in an archive for long-term storage. The difference between records retention and archival is that retention is performed to carry out some legal or contractual obligation and has a time dimension attached to it, whereas archival is done because of the value of the document as a reference material, and there is no time limit for how long the archived documents will be kept. The documents are usually archived to magnetic media or some other backup mechanism.

17.3   Documentation and SDLC phases

We have seen that various documents used during the software development life cycle (SDLC), such as standards and guidelines, are available much before the requirements analysis or conceptualization phase. Many documents are created during the development phase; many more documents are created during the operation and maintenance phases. Most documents undergo revisions and modifications during the course of development of the product. Table 17.1 lists some typical documents used during the development, operation, and maintenance of a software system.

17.4   Documentation management and control

DMC is the discipline of creating and managing the documents used in a project. The primary objective of this discipline is to ensure that documents are created, stored, changed, used, and disposed of systematically and scientifically. This system ensures that the right information is available to the right personnel at the right time. It also makes sure that unauthorized access, modification, and corruption of documents does not happen and that any change made to a document is made after formal approval. Once the changes are made, the documents are reviewed and approved before they are reissued for use. The use of the DMC process should achieve the following objectives:

- Identify all documents to be produced by the process or project.

- Specify the content and purpose of all documents and plan and schedule their production.

- Identify the standards to be applied for development of documents.

- Develop and publish all documents in accordance with identified standards and in accordance with nominated plans.

- Maintain all documents in accordance with specified criteria.

Table 17.1   Documentation and SDLC Phases

Document Name	Conceptualization	Requirements Definition	Systems Analysis & Design	Coding & Unit Testing	Integration Testing	Implementation	Operation & Maintenance	Retirement
Standards & Guidelines	X	X	X	X	x	X	X	X
Project Plan (PP)		X	X	X	x	X	X	X
Software Configuration Management Plan (SCMP)		X	X	X	x	X	X	X
Requirements Definition Document (RDD)		X	X	X	x	X	X	X
System Analysis Document (SAD)			X	X	x	X	X	X
System Design Document (SDD)			X	X	x	X	X	X
Change Requests (CR)		X	X	X	x	X	X	
Problem Reports		X	X	X	x	X	X	
Impact Analysis Report		X	X	X	x	X	X	
SCM Documentation		X	X	X	x	X	X	X
Configuration Status Accounting Reports		X	X	X	x	X	X	
System Test Specification (STS)			X	X	x	X	X	X
System Test Plan (STP)			X	X	x	X	X	X
Unit Test Specification (UTS)				X	x	X	X	X
Unit Test Plans (UTP)				X	x	X	X	X
Audit and Review Reports		X	X	X	x	X	X	X
Test Results				X	x	X	X	X
User Documentation				X	X	X	X	X
Enhancements Requests						X	X	X

ISO 9001 [3] specifies that organizations must establish and maintain documented procedures to control all documents and data, including, to the extent applicable, documents of external origin such as standards. Documents and data can be in the form of any type of media, such as hard copy or electronic media.

The documents and data must be reviewed and approved for adequacy by authorized personnel before issue. A master list or equivalent document control procedure identifying the current revision status of documents should be established and readily available to preclude the use of invalid and/or obsolete documents.

Changes to documents and data should be reviewed and approved by the same functions or organizations that performed the original review and approval, unless specifically designated otherwise. The designated functions or organizations should have access to pertinent background information on which to base their review and approval. Where practicable, the nature of the change should be identified in the document or the appropriate attachments. The documentation should be traceable, handled, stored, responsive to change requests, and consistent with the SCM plan.

The organization must establish and maintain procedures for controlling all documents to ensure the following [4]:

- They can be located.

- The relevant copies of appropriate documents are available at all locations where operations essential to the effective functioning of the quality system are performed.

- They are periodically reviewed, revised as necessary, and approved for adequacy by authorized personnel.

- The current versions of relevant documents are available at all locations where operations essential to the effective functioning of the environmental management system are performed.

- Obsolete documents are promptly removed from all points of issue and points of use, or otherwise assured against unintended use.

- Any obsolete documents retained for legal and/or knowledge preservation purposes are suitably identified.

Documentation must be legible, dated (with dates of revision) and readily identifiable, maintained in an orderly manner, and retained for a specified period. Procedures and responsibilities should be established and maintained concerning the creation and modification of the various types of document.

According to IEEE/EIA 12207.0 [5], every document should have the following parts:

- Title or name;

- Scope and purpose;

- Intended audience;

- Procedures and responsibilities for inputs, development, review, modification, approval, production, storage, distribution, maintenance, and configuration management;

- Schedule for intermediate and final versions.

In addition to this information, the documents should have the following:

- Date of creation;

- Copyright information;

- Identification: An identification scheme should be developed that is descriptive and gives an indication of the date of creation, revision, and name of the document;

- Created by (name of the organization, department, and person);

- Distribution list: List of people to whom copies of the documents are distributed;

- Change history: List of changes (additions, deletions, modifications) with date of change and signature of the persons who authorized, reviewed, and approved the change;

- Security classification: Security classification indicating whether the document is for the general public or classified and restricted for certain users;

- In the case of revised documents, suitable identification marks (line or symbols) indicating the places where changes have been made;

- Table of contents;

- Glossary of terms used in the document;

- Errata (if any).

According to ISO 10007 [6], in order to protect the integrity of the configuration and to provide a basis for the control of change, it is essential that configuration items, their constituent parts, and their documentation be held in an environment that:

- Is commensurate with the environmental conditions required (e.g., for computer hardware, software, data, documents, drawings);

- Protects them from unauthorized change or corruption;

- Provides means for disaster recovery;

▸ In the case of software, data, documentation, and drawings, permits the controlled retrieval of a copy of the controlled master;

▸ Supports the achievement of consistency between the as-built/produced state of a configuration and the as-designed state.

Operation of the DMC system during the project should be made as easy and efficient as possible, but without losing the degree of control and audit that is required. The task of DMC is usually performed by the SCM function. Individual participants should be able to access, request changes and enhancements to, and point out errors in the documents. There should be well-defined procedures, authorities, and controls for approving the change requests, checking–out files, making changes, reviewing, approving, checking–in files, and promoting the documents.

The DMC system should also track changes to the documents that come from external sources such as standards and new versions or updates of the standards, and other external documents should be incorporated whenever necessary. For example, consider a situation where a revised version of a standard that is used in the project has been released. This standard was used to create some other documents (say, a quality assurance manual) used by the project. In such cases, the new standard should be brought under document control, all of the documents affected by the revision to the standard should be identified, and the necessary modifications should be made.

The documentation manager should know the status of each document and should have a reporting mechanism (similar to the configuration status accounting) to know which documents are under creation, their estimated date of completion, how many documents are under review, how many people are using a particular document, and whether the obsolete versions are deleted or archived.

At the end of a phase of the project, all planned deliverables should have been completed, finalized, approved, and distributed. Internal documents should also have been completed, subjected to the defined reviews, and finalized. Quality audits should be conducted to ensure that all planned items were produced in accordance with the defined controls and procedures. At the end of the project, permanent items will be retained for future use (e.g., for the maintenance and support phase), and external deliverables will be distributed to customers or end users and master copies will be maintained.

17.5 PDM and DMC

Management of product data is an activity that exists in the manufacturing industry. The product data—text and drawings—were previously archived on paper. But advancements in technology and proliferation of computers have greatly reduced the need for paper documents, and today product data is stored in digital format. The business environment is becoming highly competitive as companies have to compete globally. In order to compete in today's highly competitive marketplace, manufacturers must find new ways to reduce costs, improve quality, improve developmental productivity, and reduce the time-to-market. Product data management (PDM) allows organizations to become more competitive by better managing and controlling their product data.

Software is becoming more important, and almost all systems from toy planes to fighter planes are controlled by software systems. Both software professionals and hardware engineers have to collaborate to create the products that are required today. This collaboration necessitates that professionals from both disciplines should learn about how the other side is performing activities. So today's software professionals should learn the fundamentals of product data management to become more competitive and help their counterparts who are engaged in the design and production of hardware in a better and more efficient manner.

Many of the functions performed by PDM are closely related to DMC. In both PDM and DMC, the activities performed to manage the product or project data are the same or similar. While PDM keeps track of the data and documents related to the hardware artifacts, DMC does the same for the software artifacts, so it is beneficial and necessary to be aware of the close relationship that these two disciplines share.

17.6 Overview of PDM

PDM is the discipline of controlling the evolution of a product and providing other procedures and tools with accurate product information at the right time in the right format during the entire product life cycle [7]. So PDM involves supporting departments such as manufacturing, marketing, sales, and purchasing. It also involves supporting the organization's vendors, subcontractors, and business partners. PDM is also known as collaborative PDM (cPDM), product information management (PIM), and electronic PDM (ePDM). PDM performs the following functions to achieve its objectives:

> ▸ *Data vault management.* Every PDM system has a centralized data vault in which all master copies of all documents, drawings, and other data are stored. The data vaults can be filing cabinets, secured directories in a computer system, or even databases. The data stored in these data vaults can come from various applications, such as data from computer-aided design (CAD), computer-aided engineering (CAE), computer integrated manufacturing (CIM), operating instructions, service manuals, drawings, technical specifications, and reports. In addition to this data, the PDM system stores information about the various documents (called *metadata*), such as title, date of creation,

names of the persons who created, reviewed, and approved the document, and history of changes made. The metadata is used to search the database for a particular document or information.

- *Workflow management.* During the development of a product, many thousands of parts may need to be designed. For each part, files need to be created, modified, viewed, checked, and approved by many different people, perhaps several times over. In addition, each part will call for different development techniques and different types of data—solid models for some, circuit diagrams for others, finite element analysis (FEA) data for others. As if this is not confusing enough, work on any of these master files will have a potential impact on other related files. So there needs to be continuous cross-checking, modification, resubmission, and rechecking. With all of these overlapping changes, it is all too easy for an engineer in one discipline to be investing considerable time and effort in pursuing a design that has already been invalidated by the work someone else has done on another part of the project. Bringing order to this highly complex workflow is what PDM systems do best. In particular, they keep track of the thousands of individual decisions that determine who does what next.

- *Product structure management.* Every product is made up of thousands of component parts. A product can have many subassemblies, each of which can be made of many more subassemblies. A product structure is a division of parts into a hierarchy of assemblies and components until it reaches the lowest level—the component level. The product structure comprises components and the properties of the components and the relationship between them. The major activities performed by product structure management are identifying and controlling product configurations, linking product data to the structure, and transferring the product structure and other data between PDM and material resource planning (MRP) and enterprise resource planning (ERP) systems.

- *Classification management.* This function deals with the uniform classification of standard components. The main objective of classification is to promote reuse of components. The components are classified and information (attributes) about them is stored in the PDM database, in such a way that promotes reuse. The designers can search the PDM database for components that are suited for their purpose, and only if such a component does not exist do they need to think of a new component. By improving reusability, the number of components in a product can be reduced, which can result in shorter design times, fewer parts to purchase, and reduced time-to-market.

- *Communication and notification.* The workflow management supports automatic notification and communication. The system can be programmed to automatically send notification when specified events occur (such as an item has been checked in to the database or a change has been approved). Users can be given the authority to subscribe to the notification that is of interest to them. This automatic notification process improves the overall awareness of project team members about what is happening in the project.

‣ *Query management.* As you can imagine, you need to be able to access the components and assembly data by a variety of routes. You could move up and down a classification tree; pick your way through a product structure; simply call up the data you want by searching for it by name or part number, or search for groups of data by specifying an attribute or combination of attributes. The query management function allows you to do this using querying languages such as SQL or graphical interfaces.

In today's brutally competitive business environment, the challenge is to maximize the time-to-market benefits of concurrent engineering while maintaining control of your data and distributing it automatically to the people who need it, when they need it. PDM systems cope with this challenge by holding the master data in a centralized secure vault, where its integrity can be assured and all changes to it monitored, controlled, and recorded.

17.7   Data management

Manufacturing companies are usually good at systematically recording component and assembly drawings, but they often do not keep comprehensive records of attributes such as size, weight, where the component is used, and other information. As a result, engineers often have problems accessing the information they need. This leaves an unfortunate gap in their ability to manage their product data effectively. PDM systems should be able to manage attribute and documentary product data, as well as relationships among them, through a relational database system. In the world of information explosion, where sometimes too much data is being generated, a technique to classify this information easily and quickly needs to be established.

Classification is a fundamental capability of a PDM system. Information of similar types should be capable of being grouped together in named classes. More detailed classification would be possible by using attributes to describe the essential characteristics of each component in a given class.

17.8   Process management

Data management that includes organizing data so that it is easy to access, refer to, and cross-reference deals with passive procedures. Process management, on the other hand, is about controlling the way people create and modify data, which are active procedures. Process management systems normally have three broad functions:

1.   They manage what happens to the data when someone works on it.

2.   They manage the flow of data between people.

3.   They keep track of all the events and movements that happen in functions 1 and 2 during the history of a project.

Engineers create and change data for a living. The act of designing something is exactly that. A solid model, for example, may go through hundreds of design changes during the course of development, each involving far-reaching modifications to the underlying engineering data. Often the engineer will wish simply to explore a particular approach, later abandoning it in favor of a previous version. A PDM system offers a solution by acting as the engineer's working environment, meticulously capturing all new and changed data as it is generated, maintaining a record of which version it is, recalling it on demand, and effectively keeping track of the engineer's every move. Thus, when an engineer is asked to carry out a design modification, all of the information needed will be available in the PDM system. Because the PDM system stores the documents and drawings in a central database to which access is controlled, the chances of two people working on the same component are eliminated. Also, once the modifications are complete and the item is checked in, the automatic notification feature will inform all concerned parties about the change, thus preventing the production or purchase of obsolete and unwanted items.

PDM systems should not just keep comprehensive database records of the current state of the project; they should also record the states the project has been through. This means that they are a potentially valuable source of audit trial data. The ability to perform regular process audits is a fundamental requirement for conformance to international quality management standards such as ISO 9000, EN 29000, and BS 5750. But project history management is also important to allow you to back-track to specific points in a project's development when a problem arose or from which you may wish to now start a new line of development. The PDM system captures the changes and modifications to the components and the system. This creates a work history for the product development. This level of historical tracking, as well as providing comprehensive auditing, also permits active monitoring of individual performance.

17.9   Benefits of PDM

Some of the benefits of PDM systems are reduced time-to-market; improved design productivity, creativity, and accuracy; better control of the project; and better engineering change management. Properly managed data will help productivity significantly, even when a single work group is using it.

However, PDM achieves its real potential in an enterprise-wide environment, supporting and coordinating the activities of many teams. The benefits result from managing data throughout product life, sharing data and
information among users, supporting concurrent processes, and reducing
product cost through increased reusability, development productivity, and
accuracy. We will see the benefits of PDM in the following sections.

17.9.1   Reduced time-to-market

This is the major benefit of a PDM system. Three factors limit the speed at
which you can bring a product to market: (1) the time it takes to perform
tasks, such as engineering design and tooling; (2) the time wasted between
tasks, such as when a released design sits in a production engineer's in-box
waiting its turn to be dealt with; and (3) the time lost in rework. A PDM
system can significantly reduce all of these time limitations by doing the following:

- Speeds up tasks by making data instantly available as it is needed;
- Supports concurrent task management;
- Allows authorized team members access to all relevant data, all the
  time, with the assurance that it is always the latest version.

17.9.2   Improved design productivity

With a PDM system providing the engineers with the correct tools to access
this data efficiently, the design process can be dramatically shortened. By
reducing the time the engineers need to spend in search of the right information and tools and allowing them to concentrate on designing, an efficient PDM system gives engineers more time to design.

17.9.3   Improved design and manufacturing accuracy

An important benefit of PDM systems is that everyone involved in a project
is operating on the same set of data, which is always up to date. This eliminates overlapping or inconsistent designs, even when people are operating
concurrently. Naturally, this leads to far fewer instances of design problems
that only emerge at manufacturing.

17.9.4   Better use of creative team skills

Designers are often conservative in their approach to problem solving for no
other reason than because the time penalties for exploring alternative solutions are so high. The risks of spending excessive time on a radically new
design approach that may not work would be unacceptable. PDM opens up
the creative process in three important ways: (1) it keeps track of all the
documents and test results relating to a given product change, minimizing

design rework and potential design mistakes; (2) it reduces the risk of failure by sharing the risk with others and by making the data available to the right people fast; and (3) it encourages team problem solving by allowing individuals to bounce ideas off each other using the packet-transfer facility, knowing that all of them are looking at the same problem.

17.9.5 Data integrity safeguarded

The single central vault concept ensures that, while data is immediately accessible to those who need it, all master documents and records of historical change remain absolutely accurate and secure.

17.9.6 Better control of projects

PDM systems enable you to retain control of the project by ensuring that the data on which it is based is firmly controlled. Product structure, change management, configuration control, and traceability are key benefits. Control can also be enhanced by automatic data release and electronic sign-off procedures. As a result, it is impossible for a scheduled task to be ignored, buried, or forgotten.

17.9.7 A major step toward total quality management

By introducing a coherent set of audited processes to the product development cycle, a PDM system should go a long way toward establishing an environment for ISO9000 compliance and total quality management (TQM). Many of the fundamental principals of TQM, such as empowerment of the individual to identify and solve problems, are inherent in the PDM structure. The formal controls, checks, change management processes, and defined responsibilities should also ensure that the PDM system you select contributes to your conformance with international quality standards.

17.10 PDM and SCM integration

PDM is a class of enterprise software that manages product data and relationships, facilitating innovation and increasing engineering productivity. It allows you to manage, control, and access data surrounding new product design, engineering, and manufacturing processes. By providing controlled and secure global data access, PDM empowers the organization to deliver higher-quality products to market faster and more efficiently. This process impacts the entire life cycle of a product, because employees at each phase in the product development process can access the right information at the right time.

SCM, as we have seen, is the discipline of identifying the configuration of a system at discrete points in time to systematically control changes to this configuration and maintain the integrity and traceability of this configuration throughout the system life cycle. SCM is a collection of techniques that coordinate and control the construction of a software system. Today's software systems consist of a myriad of component parts, each of which evolves as it is developed and maintained. SCM ensures that this evolution is efficient and controlled, so that the individual components fit together to form a coherent whole.

So we can say that while PDM ensures that product development goes on smoothly, SCM makes sure that software development is done efficiently. Today most products—both hardware and software—are becoming more complex. Another fact is that in today's environment, neither software nor hardware can exist in isolation. Software is the integral part and the driving force in almost all machines and systems, from mission-critical applications such as controlling the operations of satellites and intercontinental ballistic missiles, directing air traffic control systems, managing the functions of banks and hospitals, and handling airline and railway reservation systems to performing mundane tasks such as operating a door-locking system.

In the past, the SCM and PDM disciplines have existed and evolved with little interaction. The SCM and PDM disciplines can help an organization to achieve greater efficiencies in its product development, marketing, and customer support efforts, but the days of SCM and PDM working in isolation are gone. To survive, thrive, and successfully compete in today's highly competitive business environment, organizations must conceive, build, test, and market high-quality products in the most efficient and effective manner. Customer support, bug fixes, product enhancements, and product evolution must be done quickly (at Internet speed) and with minimum wasted effort. In order to achieve these goals, the SCM and PDM disciplines must be integrated.

Only when the hardware and software development teams fully understand what is happening in the other's domain, only when the hardware-software boundaries disappear, and only when seamless information integration occurs between the hardware and software development environments will organizations be able to realize their full potential and become market leaders. If this is to happen, organizations must integrate their SCM and PDM efforts.

17.11 PDM resources

There are many sources for learning more about PDM, but software professionals need to be familiar with PDM and how it relates to SCM. The best book, in the author's opinion, to serve that purpose is the following: Crnkovic, I., U. Asklund, and A. P. Dahlqvist, *Implementing and Integrating Product Data Management and Software Configuration Management*, Norwood, MA: Artech House, 2003.

The following list gives some resources that will provide comprehensive information about PDM:

- Antti Saaksvuori, A., and A. Immonen, *Product Lifecycle Management*, Berlin: Springer-Verlag, 2003.

- Belliveau, P., *The PDMA Tool Book for New Product Development*, New York: John Wiley & Sons, 2002.

- Burden, R., *PDM: Product Data Management*, Eau Claire, WI: Resource Publishing, 2003.

- PDM Information Center, *www.pdmic.com*

- Rosenau, M. D., et al, *The PDMA Handbook of New Product Development*, New York: John Wiley & Sons, 1996.

- Workflow Management Coalition, *www.wfmc.org*

17.12   Summary

This chapter discussed documentation management and control. We saw that low-quality, poor, obsolete, or missing documentation is a major contributor to low product quality and high development and maintenance costs. The DMC function helps in producing high-quality software by managing and controlling—in a scientific and systematic manner and using well-defined procedures and controls—the documents throughout all phases of a project's life cycle. We have seen the requirements specified by the various standards for the proper functioning of the DMC process.

PDM is the discipline of controlling the evolution of a product and providing other procedures and tools with accurate product information at the right time in the right format during the entire product life cycle. We saw that both PDM and DMC are closely related and perform similar functions to achieve their goals. SCM is a collection of techniques that coordinate and control the construction of a software system. Because today's products rely on tightly integrated hardware and software components, system and software engineers and project and product managers need to have an understanding of both PDM and SCM.

References

[1]   Visconti, M., and C. Cook, "Software System Documentation Process Maturity Model," *Proc. 1993 ACM Conf. Computer Science*, 1993, pp. 352–357.

[2]   Wallace, S., The ePMBook, *www.epmbook.com*, 2004.

[3]   ISO, *Quality Systems—Model for Quality Assurance in Design, Development, Production, Installation and Servicing (ISO-9001: 2000)*, Geneva, Switzerland: International Organization for Standards, 2000.

[4]   ISO, *Environmental Management Systems—Specification with Guidance for Use (ISO-14001: 1996)*, Geneva, Switzerland: International Organization for Standards, 1996.

[5]   IEEE, *Industry Implementation of International Standard ISO/IEC 12207: 1995 (ISO/IEC 12207), Standard for Information Technology—Software Life Cycle Processes (IEEE/EIA 12207.0-1996)*, New York: Institute of Electrical and Electronic Engineers, 1998.

[6]   ISO, *Quality Management—Guidelines for Configuration Management (ISO-10007: 1995 (E))*, Geneva, Switzerland: International Organization for Standards, 1995.

[7]   Crnkovic, I., U. Asklund, and A. P. Dahlqvist, *Implementing and Integrating Product Data Management and Software Configuration Management*, Norwood, MA: Artech House, 2003.

Selected bibliography

IEEE, *IEEE Standard for Software User Documentation (IEEE Std-1063-2001)*, New York: Institute of Electrical and Electronic Engineers, 2001.

Wallace, S., The ePMBook, *www.epmbook.com*, 2004.

Watts, F.B., *Engineering Documentation Control Handbook*, 2nd ed., Norwich, NY: Noyes Publications / William Andrew Publishing LLC, 2000.

18

Contents

SCM implementation

18.1 Introduction

Implementing an SCM system in an organization is not an easy task because the implementation needs support from a lot of departments, from top management to the developers or programmers. It probably involves changing the way the organization is doing software development and maintenance. The SCM system will introduce new procedures and controls, and people will have to follow those procedures to get something done.

In a non-SCM scenario, changes could be made at will, but once SCM is implemented, change management procedures have to be followed. SCM also brings accountability because all events are recorded, and these records could be used to trace the person who made a particular change or modified a program's source code. Thus, resistance to SCM may be a factor that can create problems during an SCM implementation.

As with any project, SCM implementation also cannot succeed without the complete cooperation of all people involved, whether it is the top managers who will use the status accounting reports to monitor the project or the developers who have to follow the SCM procedures. In this chapter, we look at some of the techniques that will help overcome resistance to SCM and any other problems during an SCM implementation.

18.2 Managing the implementation

The nature of the SCM implementation is such that it is best handled within a project management context. The implementation involves a series of activities that do not fit naturally into the normal business cycle of events. These activities are of finite duration. They have an end point, after which any further work should become absorbed into the normal business activity. SCM implementation also requires allocated resources and the development of specific skills. It is multidisciplinary and team-oriented. The complexity is compounded by the need to involve an increasing number of people over time, distracting them from their normal activities. Thus, the way of working tends to contrast with the software development process businesses.

For project management to be effective, it needs to have the right environment. One of the main reasons for a failed project can be the wrong environment. This can take the form of a counterproductive organizational culture, inadequate corporate commitment or sponsorship, or any number of other things.

18.3 SCM implementation plan

Before implementing an SCM system in an organization or project, it is crucial that the implementation process be planned. Implementation planning includes developing the implementation strategy and implementation schedule and organizing the implementation team.

The implementation plan documents the who, what, why, where, when, and how of the project. It is the outcome of discussions with affected people and involves negotiations over resources, time scales, and costs and their agreement. The plan should be realistic; otherwise, if time scales are too short, potential disruption will be built into the plan and, if time scales are too long, the momentum can be lost. The plan provides a guide to the project and is used to monitor progress. It enables people to carry out a set of interconnected tasks in a coordinated manner. Setbacks are highlighted and remedial action is established. If necessary, dates are rescheduled. Importantly, the plan is communicated to all who need to know about the project, making them aware of progress and changes.

The implementation plan should address all concerns, such as the existing procedures, the effect of the SCM implementation on the procedures, how it will affect employees, the work environment of the organization, the SCM awareness of employees, and creation of SCM user manuals.

The most basic plan will identify all of the activities, those doing them, and the time frame. A project plan can be handwritten or produced using some computer application. A spreadsheet offers simplicity and is readily available. Furthermore, it can be easily distributed to others because a spreadsheet tends to be a standard tool on many PCs. Alternately, specialized packages such as Microsoft Project are available. These capture a lot of detail about the project, enable different views of the project, such as time scale or critical path, and facilitate reporting of many different issues (e.g., costs, resource usage, and overdue activities). The key concern is the amount of complexity to be organized, manipulated, and updated—a function of the amount of detail required. So it is necessary to ask what detail is going to be useful. Another consideration is distribution of the plan. With a specialized package, not all intended recipients may have the required software, raising the dilemma of what to distribute and how.

A project plan should include the major tasks, the estimated duration (usually specified in months), resources required, and people who will be doing the tasks. The high-level plan will give an overview of the project and can be used by top management to monitor the project. But this high-level plan cannot be used by the person who is responsible for day-to-day activities of the project—the project manager. The project manager will develop a detailed project plan, where the high-level plan is broken down into a lot more detail, with the time scales being weeks or days rather than months. Additional columns may be used to identify start dates, end dates, amount of work (hours), estimation of percentage completion, lateness, costs, and any other issues deemed relevant. Some tasks will depend on the completion of others (interdependencies), whereas other tasks can run in parallel (concurrent engineering).

Time scales should be realistic. If they are overly optimistic, then the project will soon fall behind and is unlikely to catch up. This will have the effect of demoralizing the team. Likewise, if the time scales are too long, then the momentum may never build up and delays may result from inertia. Having produced a plan, it is important to maintain that plan against progress, revising it as necessary. When problems arise, so does the potential for delays. It can be argued that it is better to push out dates rather than not get it right, because a sloppy solution may reemerge at a later date with a magnified impact.

18.4   Risk assessment

Even the most detailed project plans can go astray for events that could have been anticipated and prevented. It is prudent to carry out a risk assessment. The aim is to anticipate possible problems, assess their likelihood of occurrence and their intensity of impact, and establish how they can be prevented or best handled if prevention is not possible (e.g., causal analysis).

There are various approaches to risk assessment. For many, the prerequisite for understanding what is involved in a risk assessment is denied by the virtue of never having been there before. To keep it simple, a basic approach is adopted. The starting point is to recognize that the project has the potential to fail. The first question that should spring to mind is: Why?

The first task is to understand what is involved. Risk assessment should be done at the first possible opportunity by an individual or team of experienced professionals. An appreciation of what is involved will enable the potential risks to be determined. An insight into potential issues can be gained by reviewing the main problems experienced by others. Many risks tend to be people-related. Technology and methodological issues tend to be of lesser prominence. The result may be an unwieldy, long list. In this case, it may be desirable to establish which risks are the most important and focus on those. Each risk is assessed for how severely it can impact the project and the business and for the likelihood that it will occur. This process is subjective and can be aided by the views of others. If a risk has a high severity and a high likelihood of occurrence, then this requires immediate attention. Likewise, risks rated with low severity and high likelihood of occurrence will require attention if they are not to be disruptive. Cases for which there is a low likelihood of occurrence can be put to one side. Note that they are not discarded. This process prioritizes those issues that need attention. The result should be a reduction in the likelihood that things will go wrong. However, while it is proposed that this assessment be carried out at the outset of the project, it should be regularly revisited. Process developments and changes in project conditions may raise the profile of risks that were previously viewed as insignificant.

18.5 Implementation strategy

One of the key decisions is the scope of the implementation. One option is to undergo a complete switchover from any old systems to the new system—the big-bang approach. Another option is to introduce the software in stages—core functionality first and then rolling out additional functionality in successive stages. In both situations there is the option of whether to have both the old and new systems run in parallel. Consideration should be given to the following factors:

- Speed or urgency of the implementation;
- Availability of people for carrying out the implementation tasks;
- Availability of time for training all users;
- Cost;
- Confidence in the new system;
- Disruption to operations;
- Total time scale.

Whichever option is decided, it must be remembered that for those involved in the implementation, a lot of time will be spent on development work, which would otherwise be spent on normal duties. The question arises about how these normal duties are to be fulfilled. One option is to recruit temporary staff to carry out the normal tasks, but this assumes that the required skills can be acquired. An additional option may be available for those programs or organizations that are running multiple projects: a pilot project. The organization would select one project, which could be representative of the others, ideally a project that is not too large, and implement SCM for that project, running the SCM pilot as a project unto itself.

The implementation plan should identify the implementation strategy—that is, whether the incremental approach or the big-bang approach will be used and whether SCM will be implemented in all projects simultaneously or introduced in a pilot project. When the incremental approach is used, full SCM functionality is not implemented in one step. The different functions are introduced one by one. For example, the organization might choose to implement the change management system first and then the other functions at a later date. The advantage of the incremental approach is that the company can get feedback on the implementation and how it is received and possibly fine-tune the implementation strategy based on the feedback. Another advantage is that the company can spread the investment over a period of time.

The advantage of the big-bang approach is that the company can start reaping the full benefits of SCM soon after implementation. The big-bang approach is effective if the organization is mature and conducive to SCM and the people are ready for SCM. Here there is no room for error; it is a "do it right the first time" proposition. Implementing SCM in a pilot project is a good idea because it will give the implementation team a feel for the issues in an actual implementation, the peculiarities of the organization, and the work environment. A successful pilot project can be used as an effective tool to convince staff, alleviate any doubts, and eliminate fears about SCM. But the pilot project must be selected carefully: it should be a project for which the team members are willing to face the challenge of doing something new, have an open mind, and can adapt to new systems. There is nothing like a successful pilot project implementation to convince others why they should also implement SCM in their projects.

18.6 Budget

With the costs identified (during the planning stage), a budget can be established. It should also be anticipated that problems and unforeseen issues are likely to result in additional expenditure. Whether an allowance is made for this situation is a policy decision by the finance management. Actual expenditure is monitored against budget for the duration of the project. Variances to be aware of include high consultancy costs, particularly in the early stages of the project, and low training costs. Details of consultancy costs should be identified during the selection process and monitored to avoid overspending. Unless the project specification has changed between then and the implementation, this estimate should roughly reflect what is incurred. If a significant variance exists, then the reason for the discrepancy should be determined. The other major cost to monitor is training. When there is an indication that budgets are going to be overspent, the training budget tends to suffer. However, training is one area that is often reported as being inadequate.

18.7   Cost

It is unlikely that a financial director would support the idea of unlimited funding for the SCM implementation project. Instead, from a control stance, a budget needs to be established. This will be based on an estimate of the likely costs. In identifying where the costs are likely to arise, consideration should be given to the following items:

- Hardware;

- Operating system;

- Database license fee;

- Core software license fee;

- Additional module license fee;

- Additional seat license fee;

- Third-party software license fee;

- Integration of third-party software;

- Software customization;

- Project management;

- Consultancy;

- Training;

- Living and travel expenses (also travel time);

- Software maintenance or warranty renewal;

- Upgrades.

Much of this cost information will be provided by the vendor. Although the vendor will probably provide a specific figure for each item, this may only be an estimate. And although the costs of the software can be precisely stated, where there is uncertainty about what is involved, the cost will only be an estimate. This is likely to be the case for such items as consultancy, which history suggests is an area for potential overspending. In this case, an upper and lower value and the expected value should be sought to give a more complete reflection of the potential cost exposure.

Some of these costs (e.g., hardware, training, and consultancy) will be one-off items, whereas others will be ongoing (e.g., maintenance). To get a better picture of the cost exposure, a long-term perspective should be taken. A meaningful time horizon is five years. By the time five years have passed, it is possible that the application has been reviewed and a new budget established for additional work, such as an upgrade or additional functionality.

Not to be overlooked are the indirect costs, which are mainly internal costs. These can include:

▸ Time and consequent cost of employees involved in the project;

▸ Costs of temporary personnel to replace those involved in the project;

▸ Costs incurred from other activities not being carried out;

▸ Costs related to off-site travel and sustenance (e.g., off-site training);

▸ Costs related to the internal resources, such as the implementation team or work team, who administer and maintain the system and provide internal technical support.

You may be surprised at how a significant proportion of the total budget is the annual maintenance fee. Is it worth asking what is provided for this fee? Each situation will be different depending on a host of variables, including the complexity of the processes affected, the number of users, the amount of customization, and dependency on consultants. It should be possible to pin down most of the costs, especially the main costs, to a lower and upper value and a most likely cost. However, unexpected isues can disturb this picture. Some costs will not be readily apparent and can be overlooked. Alternately, they can be underestimated. It is not uncommon for the yearly cost to be in the neighborhood of 10% of the initial cost outlay.

The danger arises when a budget is set, but costs during the project continue to escalate. This is particularly true with regard to consultancy and training costs. Overspending on consultancy is often compensated for by a cutback in training. This is not helped by the fact that training costs tend to be underestimated in the first place. The dilemma faced is that having started the project, so much has been invested in it that it must be finished. But at what cost? This raises the need for cost control throughout the project. Project planning software may have the facility to attach costs to resources used in activities planned. This can provide a means to determine indirect costs. Upon completion of the tasks, the plan is updated to reflect the actual resources used and the time taken. This gives an indication of the actual cost incurred and is particularly useful for gauging the costs of internal personnel.

From a practical point of view, the one area for which costs are most likely to get out of control is the use of consultants. On-site attendance of vendor personnel can boost costs if uncontrolled or the unexpected occurs. Thus, it may be desirable to contrast the estimated costs of personnel on a time and materials basis with a fixed-cost implementation. Although the latter option may be more expensive at quotation stage, the reality may be the opposite. Typically, SCM tool consultants (whether independent or the vendor's representative) will cost in excess of $1,000 per day.

18.7.1   Cost-benefit analysis

Once the need has been defined and the costs identified, it is useful to determine what the benefits are and whether they justify the cost. This justification can strengthen the argument about the need. However, the dilemma arises as to how to carry out this justification. The SCM implementation is by its nature a complex activity. It involves many people who need to act over a long period in a coordinated manner in order to produce a coordinated way of working using a technology that may not function precisely as desired.

A similar case can be made for the determination of the benefits. While the tangible benefits of reduced defects may be readily quantified, the increased revenue resulting from more efficient operations will prove difficult. Furthermore, the quantification of any intangible benefits will prove difficult. However, from a practical viewpoint, this exercise is not required to be—and cannot be—an exact science. The aim is to get a useful picture of the situation in terms of what to expect. Through the application of models, such as Six Sigma, the company should see a considerable drop in software defects as a result of implementing SCM activities.

The identified costs are assessed within the context of what is understood about the future and the benefits likely to be gained. With a time horizon likely to be five years, much can happen in that time. Thus, the approach should be simple, with assumptions clearly defined. This analysis can also be used to establish reference points or benchmarks, which can be used to assess progress and whether the anticipated benefits are achieved. Furthermore, it is prudent to be cautious about potential gains. History suggests that costs will overrun and benefits will fail to materialize. This is aside from the skill required of the project manager in controlling both the costs and realization of the benefits.

Finally, consideration must be given to the context within which the justification is being used. Who is producing the justification? How will others use these benchmarks—now and in the future? If the situation changes in the future, then the relevance of a specific benchmark may change. All too often, forecast numbers are cast into stone, yet when the conditions change that make these numbers nonsense, this is ignored.

18.8   Performance measurement

The notion of performance is associated with the concepts of control and targets. We have already seen three performance-related measures—costs, time, and benefits. However, an SCM implementation has a notorious reputation for being overspent, late, and with benefits failing to be realized. Furthermore, with the time scale long, it is not practical to wait until the operation phase to find out if everything is functioning as intended.

The project plan identifies what tasks need to be done. The aim is then to carry out the tasks. It is desirable to have some indication that tasks are taking place as required and that they have accomplished what was intended of them. The assumption is that when a task is completed, it achieves an objective(s). Thus, the training of a user should result in a user being able to perform a set of tasks better or gain a better understanding of SCM concepts.

For each step or series of steps of the implementation, objectives can be defined that, if achieved, represent progress. By achieving these deliverables, there is less likelihood of problems arising at a later date as a result of an earlier event. Conversely, failure to achieve these deliverables and the subsequent progression to the next stage will increase the likelihood of potentially significant problems arising at a later stage. Furthermore, progress can be monitored methodically. Each task or set of tasks is evaluated regarding its successful completion (e.g., has training been effective, are documents complete, are processes fit for the purpose)?

Together, the four measurables (i.e., cost, time, benefits, and deliverables) present different dimensions for measuring the performance of an implementation. Often, only the cost and time dimensions are monitored. Understandably, these have a visible effect on the finances and operations of the business, but rarely are the benefits assessed. It can be argued that monitoring benefits is carried out after the event, so what is the value of this activity? However, by assessing whether benefits have been achieved or not (and the reasons), an opportunity is created to learn from what has happened. These lessons can then be applied to further phases in the implementation.

The use of deliverables provides the opportunity to assess the effectiveness of what is being done. However, potential conflict arises. To ensure that a task is properly completed may involve an unanticipated increase in the amount of work and lead to it being late. Although the deliverable has been met, it is at the expense of two other measurables—time and cost. So when it comes to determining whether the project has been a success, consider which measurable is being used. This dilemma is magnified when targets are misused as a tool to blame someone or to score points over others. It is important to remember that measurables provide a means to assess progress and attainment, but they do not determine success. They merely provide reference points for further action. They are not a substitute for managing people so that they give their best and more.

18.9   SCM implementation team

The SCM implementation project is a joint effort of many groups of people: the in-house implementation team, the package vendor's team, outside consultants, end users, and company management. In this section, we discuss how to organize the internal resources of the company for an SCM implementation.

The most frequently asked question is: "Who within the company should participate in the project?" The natural response is everyone who is involved in the SCM process: developers, the QA team, project leaders, support personnel, the marketing team, and top management. Because the SCM system is an integrated package, almost everyone in the company must participate in one way or another. The functionality of today's sophisticated SCM systems will extend to practically every sector of the company.

The usual organization of the implementation team takes the following format: The person who manages the implementation is the project manager. The project manager reports to an executive committee, which reviews progress and resolves any territorial, resource, or policy disputes. The CEO or managing director leads the executive committee and sponsors the project.

Working for the project manager are the members of the project management team, who carry out the various tasks to implement the system. They are the people who set up the infrastructure, produce documentation, and train the employees. The tool vendor will appoint one or more of its consultants to provide support to the project manager, manage the client account, and coordinate other vendor resources. Vendor consultants advise about best working practices, software functionality, and technical issues. Training is provided in the first instance by the vendor to the project management team through either the consultants or specialist trainers. Once the project team have developed and proven the new way of doing things, they produce the procedural documentation and train other employees.

But just because everyone in the company should be involved in the project does not mean that everyone should stop their jobs and join in the SCM implementation effort, thus virtually stopping the company's day-to-day functioning. The company will need an owner or sponsor for the project—someone to lead the implementation. This should be a senior person who has knowledge of the SCM system and the organization and the necessary authority to make decisions and implement them. Then the company will need at least one professional from each major department to carry out a specific project function. Roles will vary in complexity and time involved, but all are equally important for the success of the implementation.

It is important for all business functions having some relation to the SCM system to be represented adequately in the project team—from the top level to the lowest level of operation. These are the key people who will make the SCM system acceptable to everyone in their own departments. So if the implementation team consists of people from all departments, from all levels, they can convey what they have learned about the SCM system and thus help overcome the initial resistance the system is bound to face.

Implementation of the SCM system demands that the managers and operational staff understand how the new information environment is going to work. They should be given a clear picture about what is to be changed in the current setup and what additional facilities the new technology will give the end users. This is important because the new technology and the additional responsibilities that arise when the new system is in place can overwhelm many people. So it is important to give everyone involved an idea of what to expect before the project starts.

For the right level of participation to occur, a group of representatives selected from various departments of the company will need to involve themselves at several levels. Some members of the project team will work on the project full time—in tandem with the in-house experts, external consultants, and the vendor's team. Others will help coordinate the tasks of the different sections and make available all of the resources required to the implementation team. Management's representatives will monitor the progress of the project and make decisions and corrective actions to keep the project on schedule and within budget. Other members will participate part time during workshops and training.

One important thing to keep in mind is that effective participation of in-house personnel is not possible without full commitment of top management. It is the responsibility of top management to ensure that the people who are designated to the implementation team on a full-time basis are not interrupted in any other way or with any other work.

18.9.1   Composition of the implementation team

Who should be assigned to the implementation team? This is an important question because the success of the implementation and the continued functioning of the system depend on these people and their ability to grasp the new tasks and technologies.

Once the SCM system is implemented, the current processes and procedures will be replaced by new ones. The job descriptions and responsibilities will undergo some changes. The information integration will happen, and many processes will be automated. An action taken by an employee can trigger a lot of procedures and affect a lot of other functions—almost instantaneously. The technology will bring with it a series of new concepts and resources that must be mastered and correctly used to get the best out of the SCM system. The format, the speed, and the content of the management information systems will change. The decision-making process will change because the decision makers will be able to get accurate information, in the form they want, when they want it. The SCM packages will institute new development models and practices.

So the company should appoint its best and most efficient employees to the implementation team. The company should invest in these people and should create opportunities for them to excel within the company so they can grow with it. But these people are actually running the business; these people do not have time for anything else; these are the people everyone will turn to in a crisis. Yet these people should be assigned to the implementation team.

SCM implementation is a complex and sophisticated project, involving technological as well as cultural changes. It is not the place for people without any initiative, dedication, and enthusiasm, people who do not have any team skills or who have communication problems, or people whom the boss does not want. In fact, assigning some people just because they are the only ones available is one of the most crucial mistakes management can make. They can jeopardize the entire project by taking such an action. The SCM implementation project needs people who can grasp new ideas quickly, who have an open mind to new technologies and concepts, and who love challenges. These people should have a never-say-die attitude and should be capable of working as a team.

These people will have a lot of demands placed on them. They will need to develop a detailed understanding of how the software works, pick up new skills (e.g., process mapping), carry out totally unfamiliar tasks (e.g., prototyping and training), and deal with problems that they normally would never encounter (e.g., establishing which process path is more acceptable). These men and women will be pioneers as they take their organizations through untested environments and uncharted waters, so their ability to think quickly, improvise effortlessly, innovate fast, and act without hesitation is critical to the success of the project.

So when faced with the decision of assigning members to the implementation team, management should be willing to send their best staff members. Invariably, these people are those whose work cannot be interrupted and responsibilities cannot be delegated, but the company has to find a way. If the company decides—early enough—who they are going to send, and if those people are informed, they might be able to train replacements to do their work until they return. No matter what it takes, sending the best people is worth the effort.

Those selected—the pioneers—will have greater demands made on their time. They are likely to work long hours for many months, including weekends, to cover their normal duties and also their project tasks. During this time, it may be necessary to restrict when they take their vacations, because this may coincide with a critical stage in the implementation. The continual intrusion into free time may affect family life and needs to be accommodated. Therefore, it would not be unreasonable to review remuneration or vacation entitlement for the team members. It should be acknowledged that people have their own learning styles and different rates of working, particularly when dealing with the unfamiliar. As time passes, the team members need to be watched for loss of interest, resentment, or burnout and handled with care. If team members leave the company, bringing replacements up to speed will cause delays.

18.9.2 Organization of the implementation team

Figure 18.1 shows the organizational chart for a typical implementation team for medium to large companies. For a small company, there is not much difference in the organization except that the team size will be smaller, and the executive committee and the project management committee might be merged. At the top of the chart is the executive committee, headed by someone from top management. Then there is the project management team, followed by the technical and administrative support personnel. Then we have the work team. Let's look at the functions of each team in some detail.

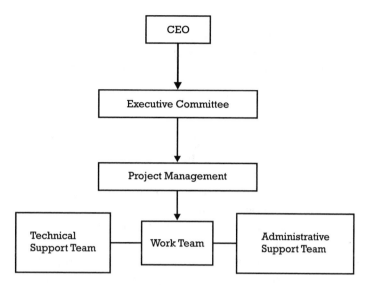

Figure 18.1   Organization of the SCM implementation project.

18.9.2.1   Chief executive officer

The most senior role is that of the CEO. This person has two key responsibilities. The first is to promote the vision of what can be achieved using the implementation as the opportunistic catalyst for change. How radical this vision is depends on the individual and also senior colleagues, because these colleagues should share and make their own contribution toward this vision. The vision of what needs to be achieved must reflect what the organization is capable of accomplishing. Irrespective of whether the organization has the capability to move mountains or only molehills, the focus is on progress. However, the greater the ambition, the more commitment is required. This is particularly true of the senior and middle management, who, in a changing environment, are traditionally the most resistant. It is the CEO's role to assess this capability and lead accordingly.

The other responsibility is sponsorship of the project. This means that support is given to the project in such a way that promotes its importance, supports the position of the project manager, and brings into line dissenting middle and senior managers; the CEO also acts as arbitrator and carries out any other activities necessary to ensure that the project does not flag, including replacing the project manager if necessary. The CEO needs to ensure that the gap is bridged between talk and action if cynicism is to be avoided.

18.9.2.2   Executive committee

The executive committee is a group of senior managers who represent the interests of the company management and is headed by the person who is in charge of the SCM project implementation (sponsor)—a person in whom the company places its highest confidence, someone who is considered a leader and who has the necessary authority and carries enough clout within the company to make things happen. Usually the CEO or a senior manager will be the sponsor for the SCM implementation. In the case of large corporations, the CEO or top management may not be members of the executive committee because they will be busy with strategic planning and decision making. In such companies, the responsibility of SCM sponsorship will be entrusted to someone in the top or middle management, usually someone who reports to the chief technology officer or the chief information officer.

Irrespective of the title of the sponsor and the executive committee members, their primary function is to make sure everyone knows that SCM has strong management backing and support. These people should also have enough authority (or direct access to people who have authority) to make and implement decisions that are required for the smooth progress of the implementation. The committee should also include the external consultant's representative and a consultant from the package vendor.

The executive committee defines the objectives, monitors progress, and quickly resolves issues that are brought to their attention. They ensure that the conditions are right for the implementation. This means that they eliminate any possible conflicts of interest that the project team members may experience. This also means that the project manager is able to escalate concerns to the executive committee and the concerns will be acted on, and that the extra time and effort of those involved is recognized. The executive committee also ensures that corners are not cut for the sake of convenience, and they are committed to removing any barriers that may hinder both progress and the realization of benefits. The committee should be aware of, and adjust for, possible discord between the discipline of project management and its own management style, particularly if project management is not a familiar practice within the organization.

The executive committee is responsible for monitoring and evaluating the project and its progress. The committee approves budgets and initiates corrective actions when things are not going according to plan, so the committee should establish a reporting and monitoring mechanism by which it will be kept abreast of progress. The monitoring mechanism should have facilities to alert the committee about impending disasters and delays well in advance so that corrective and preventive measures can be taken. The committee should meet at least once a week with a provision for emergency meetings. The project manager reports to the executive committee at the weekly business review meetings to enable the required discussions to take place.

18.9.2.3 External consultants

The role of external consultants in the implementation is to advise the project manager and the implementation team in all areas for which there are no in-house experts. The cost of using external consultants is a huge drain on the implementation budget, and hence should be kept to a minimum. If the company is already using an SCM system or has previous experience in implementing SCM systems or employees who have the necessary expertise, then the number of external consultants could be kept to the minimum. But in the case of companies that are doing SCM implementation for the first time and whose employees do not have much experience, it is absolutely a must to get professional help because otherwise the result can be failed implementations or a poorly designed and implemented SCM system. The basic principle should be to use external experts when the company does not have in-house expertise, but to otherwise use the in-house experts.

18.9.2.4 Project manager

The pivotal role in an SCM implementation project is that of the project manager. The project manager is the catalyst—the person who makes things happen. A project manager profile has the following characteristics: can-do attitude, communicator, knowledgeable about the business, credible within the company, diplomat and facilitator, impervious to criticism, and resilient. The project manager is also an administrator, keeping records about project progress, maintaining the project plan, handling correspondence, and checking invoices.

The project manager can become ineffective if support is not demonstrated from the top. The project manager may require people over whom he has no authority to do things. If the person is well liked, then this may sway people to cooperate. Problems will arise, as in the case where members of the project team split their time between their normal duties and those of the project. Operational demands will prevail when it comes to deciding which takes priority. Likewise, decisions about tasks may lead to the desire to shift work from one department to another. Although it may make sense to make this change, there may be objections from the departmental head. The department may already be overstretched, and the question arises about head count. The role of the sponsor is to deal with these and other predicaments. Thus, the roles of project manager and sponsor are complementary and essential for success. There are cases of projects that have progressed well and then stumbled when the sponsor departed. Tasks that should take days take months because the project manager does not have the status that the sponsor has to progress tasks.

18.9.2.5 Project management team

The project management team is headed by the project manager and comprises the technical leader (leader of the external consultant team), the vendor's project manager, and the implementation project manager. The project manager will report the project's progress, problems, and other issues to the executive committee.

The project management team is responsible for conducting the scheduled work, administering the project, and communicating with the in-house team and consultants. The team members should monitor the implementation team's progress and assess the amount and quality of the contribution of team members—both in-house and consultants—and resolve the issues that exist. Because the project management team has the project manager, the consultant team's head, and the vendor team's head, most problems could be resolved at this level. If any problems cannot be resolved at this level, then the project manager will escalate them to the executive committee for resolution.

The project management team should also ensure that company personnel and consultants are working together as a team and that full cooperation exists between the two groups. They are also responsible for ensuring that consultants are transferring their knowledge to the in-house team and that all documentation is done properly. The project management team should make sure that even after the external consultants and vendor representatives leave, the system will run smoothly.

18.9.2.6 Work team

The work team is composed of people who will actually perform the tasks set forth in the project plan. These tasks range from migrating the project information to the new system to training users to monitoring the start-up of the new system. The people on this team should be the best in the company and should dedicate their full time and attention to the SCM implementation project.

The team's job requires knowledge of the company's work culture and environment, awareness of company policies and regulations, good analysis skills, team spirit, a cooperative attitude, good communication skills, patience, persistence, self-confidence, and sound common sense.

The work team normally includes hired consultants and the in-house team. These consultants should have a good understanding of the software that is being implemented. That is why they are hired in the first place. These consultants most certainly must have participated in the implementation of similar projects before.

The company's in-house team is the people with the knowledge of how the company works. They are the people who are going to use and run the system in the future. They and the consultants together decide on how the system should work. The in-house team members will be the first people to receive training on how to operate the software. They must know how the system works in order to evaluate the impact of the software on the company's current business processes. They will also discuss with the consultants and the package vendor the level of customization the product will require in order to function properly in the company. The work team will do the system testing once the system is installed. The work team will also participate in training end users of the system. The in-house team will contain people from the company's various functions or departments. The work team will also have hardware engineers who will manage the technical requirements of hardware, network, and software.

The work team manager should hold regular meetings that bring the team members together so they are all aware of what is happening. This is an opportunity for progress to be reviewed, issues to be highlighted, and problems to be shared.

Consideration should be given to the team's work environment. The ideal setup is a dedicated room where people can work undisturbed. This room should have plenty of wall space so that charts can be hung on the walls. It should be equipped with networked PCs, tables, shelving for documentation, and flip charts. Laptop links should be available so consultants can link their equipment into the network. This room will serve as the nerve center for the project. As well as being a work environment, it will hold project meetings and serve as a training venue. This room need not be abandoned after the implementation is over, because it can serve as an operations room for continuous improvement teams and also as a training venue for new recruits, those wishing to upgrade their skills, or those wishing to test out refinements to processes.

18.9.2.7   Technical support team

The function of the technical support team is to create an environment that is suitable for implementation of the software. The size of the technical support team is directly proportional to the size of the work team; usually the team size is three to four people. This team works closely with the work team and takes care of issues such as data migration, data backup and recovery, hardware infrastructure, and performance tuning of the databases.

In short, the technical support staff is responsible for ensuring that the machines will be up and running, the network is functional, and the hardware infrastructure is in good shape for the work team to implement the software package. These people will be doing these activities once the implementation is over and the system is live, so they should interact with the consultants and the package vendor to assess any special arrangements, hardware, maintenance, or backup and recovery procedures that may be required for the system.

18.9.2.8   Administrative support team

The job of the administrative support team is to make the life of all others on the implementation team easier, so they can concentrate on their tasks and be more productive and efficient. Here also, the team size will be three to four people. The support team's responsibilities include making available the workspace, tables, conference rooms, telephones, stationery, filing cabinets, refreshments (of course!), and any other resource required by the project team. Other duties include arranging the meetings and conferences, making photocopies of documents, circulating documents to the right people, and any other administrative tasks that could make the life of the work team easier.

We have seen the organization of the SCM implementation project team. Each implementation project is different and will have its own characteristics. So there will be some changes in the exact constitution of the teams, but these components should be there for the proper functioning of the implementation project.

18.9.3 How the implementation team works

So far, we have seen how the project implementation team is organized. At the top is the executive committee, and one of its main responsibilities is monitoring and evaluating the progress of the project. It was also specified that the executive committee should develop a management and reporting mechanism so it knows what is happening to the project on a regular basis. In this section, we look at how this is done. How can the company establish an information base to determine whether the work is progressing according to plan? How will the company decide that the present course is the correct one and will lead to the successful completion of the project?

One of the main roles of the members of the executive committee is to check and verify that the work that is being done is satisfactory and that the momentum, morale, and enthusiasm of the work team who are performing the tasks are maintained. During executive committee meetings, the members should receive reports and other information from the project managers as to how the work is progressing and whether everything is going according to schedule. The executive committee should receive data that induces them to maintain confidence in the implementation process.

Before the implementation starts, the external consultants and company representatives prepare a work plan. This plan details every activity that needs to be carried out and when they should be carried out. The consultants should lead the process of work plan preparation, because they have experience implementing the same package in similar conditions. The in-house team should point out company-specific issues and help the consultants create a realistic work plan.

The work plan or the project plan forms the basis for project tracking and monitoring. The project plan contains numerous activities, the person-hours required to complete them, and the resources needed to perform the tasks. The project plan is often built using a project management package (such as MS Project) that permits one to focus on planned activities from various perspectives—the chronological sequence or time table, specific activities and who is responsible for them, the prerequisites for carrying out a specific task, or a PERT chart of the activities. Preparing the project plan using such a tool helps improve the quality of the plan and makes it easier to make changes and adjustments.

Once the project is under way, the plan can be updated regularly and planned versus actual reports can be produced in varying detail and in varying formats including graphical. The project management software can generate comparisons between the actual and planned completion dates, expenses, and so on. These software tools allow responsibilities to be assigned to different persons, so it is easy to find out who is lagging behind and who is excelling.

Keep in mind, however, that irrespective of whether the plan is created manually or by using a software package, all of the parties involved—the executive committee, the vendor, the consultants, and the in-house team—should agree with the contents of the plan.

How often should the executive committee monitor the project? The answer is "It depends." If the company has really assigned its best personnel to the job, then natural monitoring of the project's daily activities will occur. The company professional assigned to serve as the project owner or sponsor is in an ideal position to evaluate how things are going. Because company-wide SCM implementation projects last for several weeks or months, it is adequate for the executive committee to meet once a week or once in two weeks (with a provision to hold emergency meetings when necessary).

Another choice is to set up milestones in the project plan and have a meeting when the milestone's planned completion date is over, but there are no hard-and-fast rules regarding how frequent the executive committee should meet. During the final stages of the project, when the system is being tested, the committee might need to meet more frequently to discuss the various issues that could arise.

The project management team should report to the executive committee and present the facts and figures. Because these meetings are managerial in nature, the project management team should prepare a presentation that describes the situation at a level of detail appropriate to the audience. Highly technical topics should be condensed, and excessive use of jargon should be avoided. It is a good idea for the material used in the presentation to serve also as documentation of the status of the project to that date. This is important because, in order to track the progress at future meetings, it may become necessary to recall the issues presented in a previous meeting, so as to explain why the evolution of the work has taken a particular route.

Another objective of the executive committee meetings is to address the issues that involve decisions by top management. Such decisions will not be made at every meeting, but when they have to be made, they need careful preparation. The project management team should circulate details about the issues well in advance so committee members can do their homework and come prepared for the discussions. It is the project management team's duty to analyze alternative solutions and their advantages, disadvantages, and consequences and circulate them to committee members well in advance of the meeting.

So in an SCM implementation project, the work plan or the project plan is of paramount importance. Adherence to the plan, along with constant monitoring and taking appropriate corrective actions before the project gets out of control, will ensure the success of the project. The key players in project tracking and monitoring are the project management team and the executive committee.

To guarantee that a complex and sophisticated project that requires technological and cultural changes in the company will reach its conclusion successfully, it is not enough to sell it or approve it. The project team needs to resell it constantly, by demonstrating that it is evolving in an appropriate manner toward the stage at which benefits will be generated as initially anticipated.

18.10 Problem resolution

During the implementation, many issues will be raised that will require resolution. The danger is that some of these issues, having been identified, are forgotten, only to surface at a later date, perhaps after the system is live. Thus, it is desirable that an agreed-on procedure is established for recording issues and their resolution. Whether this is by use of a flip chart or a more sophisticated process, it should be accepted practice that when an issue is raised, it is recorded. When the issue has been resolved, it can then be marked as closed. By adopting a simple approach, unresolved issues are highlighted. This may reveal that some issues have simply been ignored for the time being. Alternately, it may reveal issues that need additional support, perhaps an executive decision or vendor support. By keeping track of problems, they can be systematically dealt with in turn. The likelihood of something unpleasant manifesting at a later date is reduced.

18.11 SCM tool vendors and vendor management

Nowadays most SCM systems use some sort of tool (in other words, manual SCM systems are vrare), so the implementation team should include vendor representatives. Vendors are the people who have developed the SCM tools. They are the people who have invested huge amounts of time and effort in research and development to create packaged solutions. Because the vendors know the tool best, they definitely have a role to play in the implementation. The vendor should supply the product and its documentation as soon as the contract is signed.

Once the contract has been exchanged, the vendor will guide the company, in particular the project manager and the project team, through a series of events culminating in the use of the tool. The project manager, as with all other resources, will need to manage the vendor so that everything progresses as intended. One cautionary word concerns the power of the vendor. The vendor potentially has the upper hand in the client-vendor relationship. The client, having signed the contract and perhaps having given a preliminary payment, will be reluctant to terminate the relationship if the vendor fails to meet expectations. Consultants may not be available because of split commitments. Software bugs may not be fixed when required. Software links may simply not work. These problems all contribute to delays. It is the project manager's task to manage this situation.

The vendor will most likely appoint a single point of contact, the vendor's project manager. The role of this person will be to provide support to the project manager, advise on and agree to the project plan, manage the client account, and coordinate vendor-provided resources. A procedure should be agreed on between the two managers about how work done by the vendor is to be authorized by the client. The vendor's project manager will be the first point of contact for resolution of problems, whether they are technical, best practice related, or related to vendor invoices. Within the contract, a clause should define how problems are to be handled and the time scale allowed. If problems are not resolved, then an escalation path should be defined, identifying the people to be contacted. Communication should be backed up in writing. This reduces the likelihood of misunderstandings developing later.

Only after the software is delivered can the company develop the training and testing environment for the implementation team. The vendor is responsible for fixing any problems in the software that the implementation team encounters, so the vendor should have a liaison officer who constantly interacts with the implementation team. Another role the vendor has to play is that of the trainer—to provide the initial training for the company's key users, people who will play lead roles in the implementation of the system. These key users are the ones who will define, together with the consultants (external experts), how the software is to serve the company. These in-house experts will decide how the functionalities are to be implemented, as well as how to use or adapt the product to suit the company's unique requirements. So it is critical that these key users be given thorough training on the features of the package. Vendor training should show the key users how the package works, what the major components are, how the data and information flow across the system, what is flexible and what is not, what can be configured and what cannot, what can be customized and what should not, the limitations, the strengths and weaknesses, and so on.

The objective of vendor training is to show how the system works, not how it should be implemented. This means that the vendor demonstrates the product as it exists and highlights the available options. The company's employees who are participating in the vendor training should try to understand the characteristics of the package and the impact of the system on the company's business processes. The trainees should use these training sessions to question the vendor on all aspects of the system.

The external consultants (or the package/SCM experts) also have a role to play during this vendor training. They should participate in the training sessions to evaluate how the users react to the reality that is starting to take shape from the detailed presentations and demos. Consultants should also ask questions that the vendors are trying to avoid and of which the users are unaware. This is the best way to present the real picture to the users and will also prevent the vendors from making false claims.

The role of the package vendor does not end with training. The vendor also plays an important project support function and must exercise quality control with respect to how the product is implemented. The vendor understands the finer details and subtleties of the product and can make valuable suggestions to improve performance of the system. It is also in the best interests of the vendor for this type of participation to continue, because if the implementation fails, most of the blame will fall on the vendor. Also, a successful implementation means another satisfied client, improved good-will, and good referrals, so the vendor will continue to participate in all phases of the implementation, mostly in an advisory capacity, addressing specific technical questions about the product and technology.

The project manager should monitor and control the costs incurred by the vendor. By monitoring the time that the vendor's personnel are on-site, it is possible to monitor consultancy costs, a potential area for overspending. Mistakes do happen, and it is advisable that the vendor's invoices be checked. Queries should be brought to the vendor's attention for resolution, for which there should be a provision within the contract regarding with-holding payment. Finally, the project manager should ensure that the ven-dor is paid on time.

18.12   Training

Training is perhaps the most misjudged activity of the implementation life cycle. A major complaint is that not enough training is done. Although training is a project-managed activity, it appears to be widely neglected or is inconsistent in application. Furthermore, because most training takes place toward the end of the implementation cycle, when it looks like overall costs will exceed budget, training is the first activity to be curtailed.

This section provides an overview of the main issues to be considered when embarking on the training activity. Although it may be convenient to take an informal approach to training, whereby people pick up knowledge and skills as they go along, this method is unpredictable in terms of a suc-cessful learning outcome. A more formal approach to training tends to involve the following stages:

- *Define learning objectives.* What will the learner be able to do as a result of the training?

- *Determine content.* What skills and knowledge are to be developed?

- *Plan.* When and how will the training be delivered? What resources, materials, and facilities are required? How will the content be struc-tured?

- *Deliver.* Was the training delivered as specified in the plan? Were the trainees able to understand and learn the topics and tasks they were supposed to learn? How successful was the training in imparting the specified skills and knowledge to the trainees?

- *Assess the learner.* Has the learner met the objectives?

- *Review effectiveness of the training session.* What went wrong? What can be done better?

Those at the receiving end of the training are initially the project team members and the system administrators, and then later in the project the developers, QA team, testers, and the project leaders and managers. Each group of learners will have different requirements. Thus, the nature of the training is likely to be different for each different audience.

A training strategy can be developed, defining the training policy and outlining the training program. Each stream will be identified and outlined in terms of these stages. The strategy will provide an overview of the training objectives, identifying the people involved, the different streams, and the content of each stream, organized into courses and sessions. A plan will provide an overview of where, when, and how the training will be delivered. Preliminary consideration will be given to the assessment of the learners. How can their knowledge and skill competencies be assessed? Furthermore, consideration is given to the effectiveness of the training and how this is assessed. Finally, the projected cost will be calculated. These costs can then be used to set a budget. The resultant strategy provides a framework within which to conduct the training activity.

If the strategy is accepted by the company, it can be implemented. If the strategy is not accepted, then it needs to be reviewed. A core issue is the company's commitment to training. The right balance needs to be struck between getting the training right and being cost effective. The training strategy has two objectives: (1) the transfer of knowledge from the vendor's personnel and external consultants to the organization's key personnel and (2) the dissemination of this knowledge throughout the organization. More precisely, the learning objectives establish what the learner should be able to do as a result of the training. Knowledge may be sought, particularly if related to operational best practices. One then has to ask how this knowledge can be used within the company. However, it is likely that the main thrust of training is on the development of skill competencies in the use of software functionality.

The executive committee members need to have sufficient understanding of what is involved in an implementation project so they appreciate the potential problems and are able to give the commitment and support that is required. This is particularly true for the project sponsor. His lack of appreciation of the issues may result in him viewing the implementation as just another project and lead to his distancing himself from it. He may have a poor understanding of the roles and responsibilities of all the participants, and when problems arise, he may fail to appreciate that his involvement is required.

The project team members need to develop such knowledge and skills that will enable them to establish how to best use the functionality for the operation and maintenance phase. Because the project team members will become the trainers of other employees, they need to develop the skill to be able to formulate and deliver a training course. The users need to have the skill in using the functionality relevant to their roles. They should understand the basic concepts of SCM and also how to perform the day-to-day activities in the SCM system. Others who require training include managers, who should have at least an appreciation of what the system does. Ideally, the project manager should have a good understanding of all aspects of the system so she can be effective in dealing with any issues raised.

A select number of people will require more specific technical training so they can design databases, write scripts, manage users, generate reports, and query the database for specific ad hoc requirements. The system administrators need to be able to set up the system and then maintain it. They will require knowledge about how to handle system security and deal with technical problems. They will need to develop a level of understanding of the system's functionality so that, at some stage after implementation when the project team is disbanded, they are able to manage the system smoothly.

Additionally, over time it can be expected that the SCM tool will evolve, to some degree, along with the company and projects it serves. It may be necessary to conduct additional training sessions periodically to keep everyone abreast of the changes that have been implemented.

18.13   Employees and employee resistance

Implementing an SCM system is a change, and it is human nature to resist change, so any SCM implementation will face some amount of resistance. Users will be skeptical about the new system, but for an SCM implementation to succeed, the cooperation of everyone involved is an absolute necessity. As we saw earlier, SCM is first an attitude. So if employees are not convinced about the importance of SCM, the benefits of using an SCM tool or system, they will not be fully cooperative, which can result in the failure of the system. It is therefore important that users be won over before implementing the system. Forcing the system on unwilling people will only harden their resolve to revolt.

One main reason for resistance is ignorance. People always have a lot of misconceptions about SCM: that it will increase workload, hinder creative work, and so on. But if the SCM implementation team, backed by management, spends a little time and effort educating users about SCM and how it will help the company and users, then user resistance can be reduced if not fully eliminated.

Another method of reducing resistance is by creating champions. According to Mosely [1], one of the most efficient ways to transition to new technology is to find a well-respected potential user of the technology. Train the user on the process and the technology, have this user evaluate the technology, and encourage this user to champion the merits of the technology to coworkers and management. The champion becomes the expert user, facilitator, and trainer of the tool, so all members of the implementation team and the pilot project team are potential champions. There will always be people who adapt to change slowly and maybe even begrudgingly, but do not look to them to be your champion. Instead, look for the people who are the first to embrace change, to adopt new technology, and to find a way to do things better—those are the people you want for champions.

18.14   Pilot project

We have seen that implementing the SCM system in a pilot project is a good idea because it minimizes the risk of failure. This is because the entire implementation team can concentrate on the pilot project. The SCM system can be tested before going for company-wide deployment. Any issues that were not anticipated during the planning stage that are encountered during the pilot implementation can be considered, and the implementation plan can be refined and fine-tuned. During the pilot implementation, the existing data of the pilot project is migrated to the SCM system; team members are given training on the SCM concepts and how to use the SCM system (and tools, if tools are used). The implementation team monitors the various implementation issues, such as how people find the system, their feedback, tricky issues in the implementation, the learning period, how long it takes for the users to get comfortable with the system, and whether the user manuals and other implementation documentation are satisfactory or need revisions and modifications.

Based on the experiences of the pilot project implementation, the implementation plan and the implementation guide will be revised and modified. The pilot project will warn the implementation team about what could go wrong, how the potential pitfalls could be avoided, and provide other valuable insights. Also, a successful pilot project is a morale booster for the implementation team and a good marketing tool.

18.15   Company-wide implementation

Once the pilot project has been successfully implemented and the implementation strategy and other items such as user manuals and technical guides have been revised and modified, the implementation team can proceed to company-wide implementation, in which the SCM system is implemented in all projects in the company. This involves (1) training users in SCM and SCM tools and procedures, (2) migrating data to the tool repositories, (3) assigning roles and responsibilities to the project team members wherever necessary, and (4) monitoring the SCM system until it reaches a stable state.

As SCM is implemented in more projects, and as people learn of the benefits of an SCM system, the job of the implementation team will become easier. Project team members should be given adequate training, and there should be enough documentation (i.e., user manuals, FAQs, how-to guides) so that new people joining the project will not have difficulty getting the necessary training and information regarding the SCM tool and SCM concepts.

18.16 SCM implementation: The hidden costs

SCM implementation promises great benefits, but what costs are involved? Exactly how much will a company have to pay to have an SCM system? In most cases, the SCM implementation costs exceed the budget. Why is this? Even a well-planned and well-thought-out budget is often exceeded. In this section, we examine the areas that most planners miss accounting for in their budgets—in other words, we discuss the hidden costs of SCM implementation.

Although different companies find different hurdles and traps in the budgeting process, those who have implemented SCM systems agree that some costs are more commonly overlooked or underestimated than others. Armed with insights from across various industries, SCM implementation veterans agree that one or all of the following four areas are most likely to result in budget overruns: (1) training, (2) integration and testing, (3) data conversion/migration, and (4) external consultants. Each is discussed in turn next.

18.16.1 Training

Training is the unanimous choice of experienced SCM implementers as the most elusive budget item. It is not so much that this cost is completely overlooked as it is consistently underestimated. Training expenses are high because workers almost invariably have to learn a new set of processes, not just a new software interface. Training is the first item that gets cut when budgets have to be squeezed, and this is a major mistake, according to most SCM implementers. A successful training experience will account for a minimum of 10% to 15% of the total project budget. Unwise companies that scrimp on training expenses pay the price later. Training costs cannot be avoided, but there are a few ways to keep the price tag under control. One way is to train an initial batch of employees who can then train their colleagues in turn. This approach solves two problems: (1) the huge training bills of consultants are reduced; and (2) because the training is done by their own colleagues, other employees' resistance to change is reduced, and people will be more ready to accept the new system. In fact, it is a good idea to identify these would-be trainers early in the implementation phase and make them part of the implementation group, so they will have hands-on experience and will understand the big picture.

18.16.2 Integration and testing

Today's SCM systems are complex. Interfacing with those systems is not an easy task. Testing the links between SCM tools and other corporate software—links that have to be built on a case-by-case basis—is another essential cost that is easily missed. Most companies will have some development environments that will not integrate with the SCM tool and will have to be separately interfaced. In most cases, these integrations are costly.

18.16.3   Data conversion/migration

It costs money to move existing project information to the new system. Most data in most legacy systems is rubbish, but most companies seem to deny that their data is dirty until they actually have to move it to the new client/server setups. As a result, those companies are more likely to underestimate the cost of data migration. But even clean data may demand some overhaul to match the process modification necessitated or inspired by SCM tool implementation.

18.16.4   External consultants

The extravagant cost of external consultants is a well-known fact. Like training expenses, this cost is hard to circumvent. Choosing a lesser-known SCM tool to avoid premium-priced consultants does not necessarily help. When users fail to plan for disengagement from the existing system, consulting fees will overshoot the budget. To avoid this scenario, companies should identify objectives for which its consulting partners must aim when training internal staff. It is a good practice to include performance metrics and time schedules for the consultants. For example, a specific number of the company's staff should be trained to a certain specified level of expertise within a certain time frame.

18.17   Summary

We have seen how to implement the SCM system in an organization. We have seen how to monitor the implementation project and why it is important to do this monitoring. We saw that one of the most critical factors in the success of an SCM implementation is participation and cooperation of the users.

This chapter also reviewed the different methods of making the implementation a success, including vendor participation, user education, and having in-house champions. We discussed the factors that result in cost overruns and how to tackle them. We also saw the permanent nature of the SCM systems and how the organizations should gear up to live with the SCM systems and reap the full benefits from them.

The key message is that an SCM implementation is characterized by its complexity. Lots of issues need to be recognized and handled. Many can be identified during the planning stage, but some issues will come up during the implementation, so the organization should have a plan to deal with these uncertainties.

Every situation is unique. The complexity of the SCM implementation is such that one cannot anticipate the unexpected, particularly when people are involved. So the project management team should monitor what is happening and pay close attention to the details, no matter how trivial they might appear.

The SCM implementation cannot succeed without cooperation of the employees. The employees should be involved in every phase to ensure that they use the system properly and willingly. Most technical issues can be fixed, but people problems are more difficult to fix, if they can be fixed at all. The evidence of people problems are employee turnover, disputes, and low levels of motivation. So the implementation should give the first priority to employees and their problems.

Reference

[1]   Mosley, V., et al., "Software Configuration Management Tools: Getting Bigger, Better, and Bolder," *Crosstalk: The Journal of Defense Software Engineering*, Vol. 9 No. 1, January 1996, pp. 6–10.

Selected bibliography

Buckley, F. J., "Implementing a Software Configuration Management Environment," *IEEE Computer*, July 1994, pp. 56–61.

CM Crossroads, The Configuration Management Community, *www.cmcrossroads.com*

Dart, S., "Achieving the Best Possible Configuration Management Solution," *Crosstalk: The Journal of Defense Software Engineering*, September 1996.

Dart, S., "To Change or Not to Change," *Application Development Trends*, Vol. 4, No. 6, 1997, pp. 55–57.

Dart, S., *Configuration Management: The Missing Link in Web Engineering*, Boston, MA: Artech House, 2000.

Estublier, J., "Software Configuration Management: A Roadmap," *Proc. Conf. on the Future of Software Engineering*, Limerick, Ireland, 2000, pp. 279–289.

Feiler, P. H., "Software Configuration Management: Advances in Software Development Environments," Technical Report, Software Engineering Institute, Carnegie-Mellon University, 1990.

Irish, D. E., "Putting the Horse Before the Cart: Preparing Your Staff for Project Management Software," *Proc. ACM SIGUCCS 2001*, Association of Computing Machinery, 2001, pp. 59–62.

Kolvik, S., "Introducing Configuration Management in an Organization," *Proc. ICSE '96 SCM-6 Workshops (Selected Papers)*, Berlin, Springer-Verlag, 1996, pp. 220–230.

Moor, S. R., J. Gunne-Braden, and K. J. Gleen, "Enterprise Configuration Management— Controlling Integration Complexity," *BT Technology Journal*, Vol. 15, No. 3, July 1997, pp. 61–72.

Telliolu, H., and I. Wagner, "Negotiating Boundaries: Configuration Management in Software Development Teams," *Computer Supported Cooperative Work (CSCW): The Journal of Collaborative Computing*, Vol. 6, No. 4, 1997, pp. 251–274.

Thompson, S. M., "Configuration Management—Keeping It All Together," *BT Technology Journal*, Vol. 15, No. 3, July 1997, pp. 48–60.

CHAPTER

19

Contents

SCM operation and maintenance

19.1 Introduction

Most companies treat SCM implementation as projects, with the assumption that someday the project will end. And they are right; the implementation project will end, but the SCM system cannot end with the implementation. In fact, once the implementation phase ends and staff have started using the SCM system, the real benefits of the SCM will be seen. An SCM system is not a project; it is a way of life. No organization can say "we're finished," and few ever will. There will always be new modules, features, and versions to install, new persons to be trained, new technologies to be embraced, refresher courses to be conducted, and more. Even if an organization could declare final victory on implementation of SCM, more time will be needed to gain real business value from the SCM system. So SCM implementation requires a lifelong commitment by company management and users of the system.

Ideally, when the SCM system goes live, people switch from their old practices to those required by the new system. If everyone is properly trained, then each person will know what he or she has to do when the new system is in place—operation and maintenance (O&M) phase. If the processes have been properly tested, then operations will progress smoothly. If the data migration has been properly handled, then the data will make sense to those using it. The success of this phase is measured by the lack of problems, but the implementation is not finished. Work then begins on realizing the benefits of the new system. If problems are experienced during the O&M phase, mechanisms need to be in place to deal with them.

When problems arise, there should be a problem response mechanism that deals with them and of which everyone is aware. This mechanism should be simple and provide a means for tracking progress in resolving the problem. When a problem is identified, it should be reported to the person assigned with responsibility for coordinating problem resolution. This will usually be the project manager. Initial investigation will reveal whether the problem is readily resolved, requires further investigation, or needs to be transferred to the vendor to deal with. Details about the problem are required. This will include a description of what was being done at the time the problem arose. The problem coordinator will establish who is going to deal with the problem and keep track of progress in resolving the problem. Readily resolved problems can be closed off quickly. The rest need to be monitored to ensure that they are being addressed. If this sounds a lot like the issues that were covered earlier, concerning software problems, you are correct. To go a step further, a company often uses its existing software problem reporting mechanism to deal with SCM system problems and issues. The benefit here is that nothing new has to be developed to deal with SCM-specific problems and issues. This is another benefit of the SCM system.

The permanent nature of the SCM system has numerous implications. The following sections discuss some of them. SCM implementation is just the beginning. For any organization to succeed and reap the benefits of the SCM system, it has to take actions while keeping in mind the permanent nature of the SCM system.

19.2   Employee relocation and retraining

One problem the SCM implementation can present is what to do with the existing SCM teams. This is applicable only in cases where an organization had large SCM teams and decided to introduce an SCM tool. The SCM tool will automate most of the SCM functions, and many jobs in the SCM team will become redundant. So the company should have a plan to relocate these people whose jobs are taken over by the SCM tool, but the tools will also create new job openings as they eliminate old ones. The complexity of today's SCM tools makes it necessary to have specialists to manage and maintain these tools. Today's tools need database administrators, system administrators, operations personnel, build and release managers, and others. So some of the team members who have lost their jobs by the introduction of the SCM tool can be given training and allotted to these jobs.

The development of new processes will result in the emergence of new job descriptions. Automation of manual tasks and the creation of new tasks make this inevitable. However, people tend to resist change. Thus, human resource personnel need to be involved at an early stage in the implementation. The implications relating to changes in job descriptions need to be handled in an agreeable and friendly manner. Throughout, the benefits of what is being pursued should be promoted, as well as the well-being of those affected. In organizations in which change is a pervasive feature of life, this should not be a problem, but in organizations in which change is unknown, this has the potential to become a big issue. If the change is handled carefully, everyone should emerge smiling.

19.3   Organizational structure

Most organizations create implementation project offices and appoint project managers with the assumption that the project will end and life will go back to normal, but it will not. So what the organizations need is not a project office, but a new organizational structure that reflects the ongoing need for SCM-related activity. Sponsorship is one example of the need. Many companies appoint senior executive sponsors for implementation projects. Their expectations are probably that these executives could go back to their responsibilities once the installation is over, but many companies do SCM implementation incrementally. That is, they install the core modules first and then the additional modules until full SCM functionality is achieved. Who is going to oversee those changes and ensure that they fit with the rest of the business? If the executive sponsor is temporary, who will ensure that the system and the business evolve hand in hand? The company should assign a person who is willing to take ownership of the SCM system on a long-term basis.

19.4   Roles and skills

The post-SCM organization will need a different set of roles and skills than an organization with less integrated systems. At a minimum, everyone who uses these systems needs to be trained on how they work, how they relate to the business process, and how a transaction ripples through the entire company whenever they press a key. The training will never end; it is an ongoing process. New people will always be coming in, and new functionality will always be entering the organization.

Many companies use consultants to help with the implementation process. This is not a bad idea, but the problem is how most companies use consultants in SCM implementations. They do not transfer knowledge from consultants to internal employees. Because these systems are going to be around for some time, it is important for company employees to have good knowledge (as good as the consultants) about how these systems work and how they can be configured to fit the organization. The person in charge of the implementation must make sure that the consultants allow the employees to work side by side with them on the implementation project, and before they leave, tap the most knowledgeable consultants on long-term system evolution issues.

In every business function and department that is affected by SCM, you will need one or more people who know the system and its relationship to the departmental processes. These people have to save the system in the early days after you install the system. These people also have to guide, motivate, and help their colleagues by working with them. They will answer questions, find needed work-arounds, and let you know what is working and what isn't. These people will be the SCM team representatives—the champions—in each department. These people should have a dual reporting relationship with their managers and to the SCM manager. It is also useful to convene meetings of these people periodically so they can share knowledge and compare notes.

19.5 Knowledge management

It is imperative that the knowledge and experience that is gained during SCM implementation and after are captured on an ongoing basis and made available to all. So when someone encounters a problem, she can look up the knowledge base to determine if such a problem has occurred before. When new problems are identified and solved, they should be added to the knowledge base. Thus, over a period of time, your knowledge base will provide answers to most of the problems. In this way, even if a key employee leaves, the knowledge will remain with the company. Many companies have successfully implemented this strategy through a frequently asked questions (FAQ) interactive database.

19.6 SCM tools and technology

Once the SCM tools are introduced, the way in which the companies conduct SCM will change. With the SCM tools will come automation and new technologies. The company should make it a point to familiarize users with these technologies and find ways to motivate them to use these technologies. For example, most SCM tools have the facilities to send notifications to the change control board (CCB) members regarding a change request that was submitted. The CCB member has the facility to see the details of the change request and then query the SCM database to analyze its implications. So the CCB members can send their replies almost immediately, but for this to happen, the CCB members need to use these technologies. One member abstaining from this process can delay the change request disposition. So the company should have a plan to train and then motivate its employees to get the most out of the new features and facilities that are available to them.

Most systems can be configured to have an escalation mechanism—one that can escalate the issue to a higher authority if something does not happen within a specified period. For example, the system could be configured to send a mail notification to the supervisor of a CCB member if that member has not replied within a specified period. In such cases, senior managers should find out why the person is not using the technology and take the necessary steps to get him involved. Many people are dazzled by the technology or are afraid to use it. These fears should be alleviated for the proper functioning of the SCM system and to get the maximum benefit from the system.

The success of an SCM system is not primarily dependent on the sophistication or features of the tools that are installed. It is the attitude and cooperation of the people—the users—that make the SCM systems capable of delivering the quality and productivity improvements of which they are capable.

19.7   Review

Once the implementation is complete and the organization has started to use the system and has reached a stable state, a review of the system must be performed. The review provides an opportunity to learn from the implementation by asking the following questions:

- Does the software do what is expected of it?

- What are the outstanding or emergent issues?

- What can be learned from the implementation?

- What could have been done better? How can this information be used in the future?

- What time scale/budget is required to deal with the remaining issues?

- Has the project been a success? This is particularly invaluable if there are successive phases involving the introduction of additional functionality.

The review should include eliciting feedback from users and managers. This feedback may reveal issues that can be readily addressed, such as provision of extra training or modification of existing procedures.

19.8   Operation of the SCM system

We have seen the postimplementation scenario of the SCM system. During the O&M phase, the SCM system delivers the full benefits of which it is capable, but this will not happen automatically. Just because you have an excellent SCM system, a good tool, and completed the implementation successfully, you cannot assume that everything will go on nicely and without any problems.

It should be noted that the O&M phase of the SCM system is different from that of the software system(s). In the case of software, the operational phase commences when the system is turned over to the customer; hence, the system is operational. The maintenance phase is implemented at the same time if the customer is paying the developing organization to maintain the system after delivery (i.e., for bug fixes, enhancements, modifications).

Otherwise, the system is considered turnkey, and all activity ceases when the system is delivered (i.e., the customer or buyer is on its own). In the case of the SCM system, the O&M phase starts once the system is implemented and the software development starts.

The O&M phase has to be carefully planned. During the O&M phase, the SCM sponsor should monitor the progress of the SCM system with the assistance of the project manager. The SCM sponsor or senior SCM manager is the most logical person to become the head of the SCM team—*the configuration management officer (CMO)*. This person has the experience, knowledge, contacts with tool vendors and external consultants, and a close relationship with the SCM champions in the organization. So appointing this person as the CMO team is a good idea because things will be easier for him or her to accomplish than for anyone else.

The main objectives of the O&M phase are to ensure that the SCM system achieves its projected benefits, users are satisfied, and there are no conflicts. The organization of the SCM system and SCM team will depend on the nature of the organization. As discussed in Chapter 15, there can be a central SCM team or independent SCM teams for each project. In either case, the SCM team members report directly or indirectly to the CMO. The CMO maintains close relationships with the other support departments, such as development, QA, testing, marketing, and technical support, so the CMO can coordinate SCM-related activities. For example, the marketing department has the major say in deciding the release date of a product, but other factors could contribute to the decision, such as unfinished enhancements, unfinished changes, and so on, which only the development team knows. By coordinating and discussing with the representatives of all the various departments that have a role in the SCM activities, the CMO can eliminate interdepartmental conflicts and can make sure that all departments are working toward a common goal.

The main activities of the CMO are ensuring that SCM activities are performed correctly, coordinating SCM issues with the various departments, assessing the deficiencies in the system and correcting them, assessing the training needs of the existing and new users and giving them training, meeting with the top management, giving the progress reports, and getting the resources.

19.8.1 Interdepartmental coordination

As mentioned earlier, for the SCM system to function smoothly, the cooperation of all departments is necessary. These departments might have conflicting interests. The marketing department might want the maximum number of features and release of the system at the earliest possible date. The development team may not be able to incorporate all of the enhancement requests and features and complete the development according to the time schedule of the marketing team. The financial department might not want to give additional resources to a project in case of cost overruns. Managing these conflicting requirements is a difficult task. The CMO can act as a liaison among these departments and between these departments and company management and arrive at solutions that are satisfactory to all. For example, if the marketing team wants an early release of the product, then some features could be assigned to the next release.

19.8.2   SWOT analysis

The CMO and the SCM team can assess the strengths, weaknesses, opportunities, and threats (SWOT) of the SCM system. The strengths should be reinforced, so they become ingrained into the organizational culture. The weaknesses should be rectified through appropriate corrective actions, so the organization can be competitive. The opportunities and threats are identified at the strategic level by management, but these should be converted into operational-level tasks and be performed by the various departments in the organization. For example, the technical service department of the organization is finding it difficult to provide timely and quality service to customers. This is a threat to the organization because customers will become dissatisfied and will move to another vendor. If the SCM team can create a help desk of all the problems that have occurred in the past and how they were fixed, then the technical support team will be able to answer the customer queries quickly, if the help desk has a record of a previous instance of such a problem. If the help desk is kept up-to-date by adding the new problems and their fixes, the efficiency of the technical support team will increase dramatically over a period of time. Similarly, many threats that affect the organization at the business level could be solved using SCM activities because SCM keeps tracks of all the activities, changes, problems, and their solutions.

19.8.3   Documentation

During the implementation phase, the SCM plan is prepared and the SCM system is designed. During the course of the implementation, the plan will be revised and updated to reflect the changes that occurred during implementation. The SCM plan is the fundamental document for performing SCM activities. It is the CMO's job to ensure that all SCM team members and members of the organization have access to the latest copy of the SCM plan.

During the training phase, vendors and external consultants will prepare user manuals, procedures, and best practices documents for training and reference. These documents—their latest versions—should also be accessible to all users of the system. These documents could be hosted on the company intranet or on the Internet (in the case of distributed teams). Access to these documents could be restricted or controlled using usernames and passwords.

Procedures and work instructions describe how tasks are carried out, the latter in more detail. The procedures and work instructions include process descriptions, roles and responsibilities, process flow, and other details.

Production of these documents is not a task for one person, but for all those who define the processes. The process of producing this documentation commences during the SCM system design stage and develops through the implementation phase, at the end of which it is finalized. The procedures can be either in hard-copy form or electronic form and can be posted on the company intranet or the company Web site. These procedures are actually part of the documentation control and should be revised following the appropriate change management procedures. Only the latest copy should be available for viewing.

19.8.4   Training

Training is a never-ending activity. One of the main tasks of the CMO or the SCM team is training new employees on the SCM concepts, tool usages, procedures, and best working practices. For this task, the SCM team can conduct an induction program at regular intervals and ask project managers to send their new team members for training at the earliest possible occasion. Once new employees are given SCM training and told how SCM is practiced in the organization, they will do things according to the system from the beginning.

19.8.5   Audits and reviews

The SCM tools allow most activities, such as check-in, checkout, and change request initiation, to be performed by the developer. The SCM team should conduct periodic audits to ensure that these activities are performed correctly (e.g., check to ensure that people are not attempting to check in things back to the library without first going through the authorized review procedures). The SCM plan and the SCM system should also be reviewed and audited periodically.

The CMO should find qualified auditors and reviewers so that the configuration items (CIs) can be reviewed during the development stage, and the functional and physical configuration audits can be conducted before the system is handed over to the customer. The procedures and checklists for these reviews and audits should be developed and made available to the reviewers and auditors. The SCM database should be updated with the information regarding these reviews and audits.

19.8.6   CCB formation

Another task of the CMO is the formation of CCBs. The number of CCBs in a company will vary depending on the size and complexity of the projects. Whether it is a single CCB or multiple CCBs, it is the CMO's job to find qualified personnel for the CCB. The CCB is usually chaired by the CMO or a senior member of the SCM team. Once the change request is initiated, change management activities should be performed without any delay, so the problem is resolved as soon as possible.

19.8.7   SCM database management

The CMO or the SCM team should also ensure that the SCM database is up-to-date and not corrupted so the status accounting function can be performed accurately. If the integrity of the data in the SCM database is not accurate, the information produced will be outdated, incorrect, and useless. The status accounting function is the eyes and ears of the project and company management for tracking the progress of the project. So the SCM team should make it a priority to ensure that the right information is provided to the right person at the right time. This will improve the quality of decisions and make the organization more effective and efficient.

19.8.8   Software upgrades, enhancements, and modifications

The real value of a good SCM system is realized during the O&M phase. The SCM system has all of the information about which files were changed, what the change was, why it was changed, what other files were changed along with it, when it was changed, what files went into a particular version of the system, what tools were used, and a lot of other similar details. In other words, the SCM system contains a recoding of all the significant activities that happened during the development and evolution of the product or system. We have seen in Chapter 8, the change/problem management process and the creation of help desks. The SCM database, together with the help desks, provide an environment in which software could be upgraded, bugs could be identified and fixed, and enhancements could be incorporated. All of these tasks could be performed quickly and without any wasted effort because everyone knows exactly where to look for items and which items need modification.

Most software companies support more than one version of their software. For example, when the latest version of a product is 8.0, many users may still be using older versions, even version 1.0. So if some user from Timbuktu, who is using version 1.0 encounters a problem and calls technical support, the support team might have to re-create version 1.0 to find out the source of the problem. This is possible, thanks to SCM; one just has to run the build script that created version 1.0 (with the appropriate software and compiler versions). Because the build scripts are under configuration control, they will be readily available in the SCM library. Thus, the bug can be fixed and the bug-fixed version could be delivered to the customer, and the organization has a satisfied customer in Timbuktu.

The capability to deliver bug-fixed versions faster to customers is important in this age where the presence of bugs in the software spreads fast (through the Internet). So if a flaw is identified, the time it takes the company to release a bug-fixed version to the customer is crucial. If the flaw is a security problem, which leaves the software vulnerable to attacks from hackers or viruses, then the gravity of the situation increases exponentially. If SCM practices were not around to help organizations in these areas, then many companies that releases patches on an almost daily basis would have filed for Chapter 11 bankruptcy protection by now!

19.8.9   Help desks

Help desks are repositories of the organizational knowledge that can be used by the maintenance and support team. The help desk contains correct operating practices, problems with the software, how to solve them, details of change and problem reports, and resolution. When encountered with problem reports from customers, the maintenance team and support personnel can query the help desk to see if a similar or the same problem has occurred in the past. If so, problem resolution will be quick. In order to get the maximum benefit out of help desks, they should be designed properly. They should contain all of the details arranged and stored so information can be retrieved easily and intuitively. Many companies post FAQs and their answers on their support Web sites and encourage users to first check the FAQs before calling technical support. A well-organized and categorized FAQ list can substantially reduce the workload of technical support personnel. As new problems and their solutions get added to the help desk, they will simultaneously get updated on the Web site too.

19.8.10   Change/problem requests from customers and in-field emergency fixes

Change and problem requests can come not only from the QA and testing team but also from users once the system is released for general use. These requests (both internal and external) are handled in the way described in Chapter 8, by following formal change management and control procedures. Emergency fixes are required when a problem occurs and there is not enough time to resolve it using formal change management and control procedures. Here the priority is to find and fix the bug and resolve the issue as soon as possible so the customer can continue using the product. Emergency fixes are not left unattended after the emergency. Once the emergency is over, when the organization has enough resources, the change evaluation, impact analysis, CCB meetings, and other steps are conducted. The proper documentation is created, and the SCM database is updated with these details. This process is used to ensure that the integrity of the data is maintained. If the emergency fix is left once the fix is delivered to the customer, then there will not be any record of that in the SCM database, which can result in various serious problems that the SCM is trying to prevent.

19.8.11   Reusability improvement

Every project will have reusable items. Reusable items are CIs that could be used in more than one place. When the number of reused CIs increases, the number of items to be developed decreases. If the same item can be used by different subsystems of the system, then there is no point in the two groups developing two different versions of a program or function that performs the same thing. With increased reuse, the reinventing the wheel phenomenon can be avoided. Thus, increased reusability will have a direct impact on productivity because it saves design, development, and testing time. It will also reduce the number of CIs that must be managed, thereby reducing the SCM workload.

To promote reusability, the designers and developers of the project should know that a CI exists that performs the same function as the one they are designing or developing. So the SCM team should identify such CIs that have the potential to be reused and place them in a separate controlled library, usually known as the reusability library. The items in the reusability library are also under SCM control, but they are placed in a separate library to promote reusability. An index of the CIs and a small description of the function(s) performed by each CI can help the programmers and developers in searching for and identifying the components they could use, before they start to develop the components once again.

Taking this process one step further, the central SCM team can maintain a reusability library for the entire organization in which the reusable items from the different projects are placed and managed. This will improve reusability at the organizational level. In many cases, many items developed, tested, reviewed, and approved for one project could be used in another project. Date manipulation functions, string manipulation functions, and programs for displaying error messages are some of the items that have uses in almost all projects.

19.8.12   Metrics

You have implemented and are operating the SCM system, but how will you know that the SCM system is delivering the promised improvements? More important, how will you know that the SCM system is helping in improving your software development process? You should measure the various parameters of the system. If you do not measure your current performance and use the data to improve your future work estimates, those estimates will just be guesses. Because today's current data becomes tomorrow's historical data, it is never too late to start recording key information about your project. You cannot track project status meaningfully unless you know the actual effort and time spent on each task compared to your plans. You cannot sensibly decide whether your product is stable enough to ship unless you are tracking the rates at which your team is finding and fixing defects. You cannot quantify how well your new development processes are working without some measure of your current performance and a baseline to compare against. Metrics help you better control your software projects and learn more about the way your SCM system and organization work.

As time goes on and people become more comfortable with the system, performance should improve. You will be able to find this out only if you have measured the various parameters from the beginning. If the metrics reveal that performance is not improving, then management should investigate the reasons and take the necessary corrective actions. The following are some of the SCM-related parameters you can measure:

- Average time taken for the resolution of a change request;

- Average time taken to resolve a technical support query;

- Number of change requests and problem reports;

- Percentage of approved change requests and problem reports;

- Percentage of time spent on development;

- Percentage of time spent on testing, QA, debugging, etc.;

- Number of defects found after each release;

- Number and type of changes (e.g., bugs, enhancements, emergency fixes);

- Number and severity of defects found during development;

- Number and severity of defects found during testing;

- Average time taken to identify the source of a defect (defect identification);

- Average time taken to resolve a defect;

- Amount of reused code;

- Number of unfixed bugs in each release;

- Number of enhancements in each release;

- Average number of CIs impacted by a change request or problem report;

- Product development cycle time;

- Difference between the estimated and actual values for each activity.

This list is by no means exhaustive. It is just a representative list of what can be measured. You should decide what more should be measured depending on the nature of your organization and projects.

19.9   SCM maintenance phase

To function properly, the SCM system needs regular maintenance. The SCM plan needs revision and updating in accordance with the changing situations in the organization. We have already seen that the SCM system should be reviewed regularly. The review comments and suggestions should be incorporated into the system. Also, the SCM system needs fine-tuning as employees become familiar with it. Once the SCM system has reached a stable state, necessary actions should be taken to improve performance. The SCM metrics identified in the previous section could indicate whether the SCM system is functioning properly or not.

The SCM tools that are implemented are another area that needs maintenance. The CMO should be in regular contact with the vendors to see whether any upgrades or updates are available. All patches and upgrades should be installed to ensure that the tools are working at their maximum efficiency. Employees should be given refresher courses on the new functionality that gets added with each new upgrade. The training documentation should also be updated so it is in sync with the procedures and processes.

19.10 Summary

We have seen how to operate and maintain the SCM system after it has been successfully implemented. Proper maintenance needs careful planning on the part of the SCM team and adherence to best practices by users of the system. We also saw how to maintain and keep the SCM system in top shape. For the successful O&M of the SCM system, the support and sponsorship of top management is absolutely essential.

Selected bibliography

Buckley, F. J., "Implementing a Software Configuration Management Environment," *IEEE Computer*, July 1994, pp. 56–61.

CM Crossroads: The Configuration Management Community, *www.cmcrossroads.com*.

Dart, S., "Achieving the Best Possible Configuration Management Solution," *Crosstalk: The Journal of Defense Software Engineering*, September 1996.

Dart, S., "To Change or Not to Change," *Application Development Trends*, Vol. 4, No. 6, 1997, pp. 55–57.

Dart, S., *Configuration Management: The Missing Link in Web Engineering*, Boston, MA: Artech House, 2000.

Estublier, J., "Software Configuration Management: A Roadmap," *Proc. Conf. on the Future of Software Engineering*, Limerick, Ireland, 2000, pp. 279–289.

Feiler, P. H., "Software Configuration Management: Advances in Software Development Environments," Technical Report, Software Engineering Institute, Carnegie-Mellon University, 1990.

Irish, D. E., "Putting the Horse Before the Cart: Preparing Your Staff for Project Management Software," *Proc. ACM SIGUCCS 2001*, Association of Computing Machinery, 2001, pp. 59–62.

Kolvik, S., "Introducing Configuration Management in an Organization," *Proc. ICSE '96 SCM-6 Workshops (Selected Papers)*, Berlin, Springer-Verlag, 1996, pp. 220–230.

Moor, S. R., J. Gunne-Braden, and K.J. Gleen, "Enterprise Configuration Management—Controlling Integration Complexity," *BT Technology Journal*, Vol. 15, No. 3, July 1997, pp. 61–72.

Telliolu, H., and I. Wagner, "Negotiating Boundaries: Configuration Management in Software Development Teams," *Computer Supported Cooperative Work (CSCW): The Journal of Collaborative Computing*, Vol. 6, No. 4, 1997, pp. 251–274.

Thompson, S. M., "Configuration Management—Keeping it all Together," *BT Technology Journal*, Vol. 15, No. 3, July 1997, pp. 48–60.

SCM in special circumstances

20.1 Introduction

SCM can be practiced in a variety of situations. Projects for which SCM is practiced can vary from small, single-person projects to large, complex projects involving hundreds of people. Even though the SCM concepts are the same irrespective of the size of the project, the way in which SCM is practiced, the procedures followed, the degree of control and presence of formal procedures, the use of SCM tools, and the level of automation are not the same. They will vary from project to project.

Also, the development environments are changing. Now we have integrated development environments (IDEs) and computer-aided software engineering (CASE) environments. These are quite different from earlier project environments. Today, a software system can be cross-platform (the software system can span more than one hardware or software platform) and can involve more than one development environment. The use of CASE tools for application development is now commonplace. We now have distributed development environments, with development happening in different parts of the world. In this section, we present a brief overview of how configuration management is practiced in these situations.

20.2 SCM and project size

The size and number of people involved in a project can definitely affect how SCM is practiced in a project. There can be single-person projects, a single person managing more than one project, projects involving more than one person, and projects involving thousands of people. In the case of a single person doing a project, SCM is not an absolute must, because

317

issues such as communications breakdowns, shared data problems, and simultaneous update problems are not encountered. But even in this kind of project, practicing SCM is useful because human characteristics such as carelessness, oversight, and forgetfulness can result in the work that is already done being overwritten, the same problem being solved more than once, and other issues.

Also, the person who is doing the project will not be around forever. So when a new person takes charge of the project, she has to have the information available to her. If no documentation and records are kept, and the only record of what happened to the project is in the other person's head, it will be difficult for the new person to manage the project. Questions such as why a change was made, what items were changed, and which items will be affected if this module is changed will not have answers. To get those answers, the new person will have to go through all of the programs and hope to find the answers.

So even in the case of small projects on which only one person is involved, practicing SCM is a good idea. Here there is no need to use an SCM tool and formal change management procedures with CCB meetings. An informal SCM system, in which every change, the reasons for change, the item dependencies, information about versions and releases, and so on are documented, would be more than enough. If the organization has an SCM tool and if all developers have been trained on the tool, then even small projects can benefit from using an SCM tool.

In the case of larger projects involving many people, SCM must be practiced. In the earlier chapters, we saw why practicing SCM is important. It is always advantageous to automate the various SCM functions using SCM tools because it will improve development productivity and reduce errors. In today's brutally competitive world, where everyone is fighting for survival and market share, SCM can be used as a strategic weapon that will give the organization an edge over the others who are not using SCM or using it less effectively.

20.3   SCM in large projects

The SCM system and management of the SCM system is different in the case of large projects. By large software projects I mean a project that has more than 100 team members at a time, a project that requires the effort of more than 1,000 human years, a project in which a lot of work is subcontracted and a large number of subcontractors are used, a project that involves development of an application for many platforms, a project that is cross-platform, a project that is developed by more than one geographically distributed team, or a project that is a combination of any of these criteria. These are some indicative figures and criteria, and to qualify as a large project, the project has to involve a lot of people and must have millions of lines of code.

Here the emphasis is not on the complexity or the criticality of the project, but on the size of the project and project team and the number of groups involved. The SCM principles used in these projects are the same as those used in small projects or in mission-critical projects, but what makes these projects different is the sheer size and the management and organizational challenges that such a size poses. Some examples of such systems include database management systems (such as Oracle or DB2), ERP systems (such as SAP R/3 or the BaaN ERP system), and operating systems (such as Windows, UNIX, MVS), to name a few. Typically, these projects will have many modules or subsystems, each of which can function in a semi-autonomous fashion. These independent subsystems could be developed by different teams from different companies in different geographic locations.

Management of such complex systems is impossible without a good SCM system because in projects of such large size, the chances of all of the classic problems—communications breakdown, shared data, simultaneous update, and multiple maintenance—occurring are high. Configuration management in these projects is formal with numerous controls and procedures. It is practically impossible to do configuration management of these projects manually, so these projects ideally should use a high-end SCM tool.

20.3.1   Performance of SCM tools

The SCM tool used in a large project should be capable of supporting hundreds of developers and testers with tens of millions of lines of code. The system should do this without degradation of performance, so the tool selection process must take these performance factors into account. Questions such as how many people will be using the system concurrently, how much data will have to be handled, whether the system has to be available around the clock (to support people in different time zones), and so on should be considered during selection, and the implication of these factors on the performance of the tool must be analyzed. Only a tool that can take the load without compromising performance should be selected.

20.3.2   Implementation strategy

We saw in the chapter on SCM tools that large projects use SCM tools that fall into a category called process-oriented tools. According to Dart [1], these tools include version control capabilities and at least some of the developer-oriented capabilities. These tools have the ability to automate the software flow life cycles, roles, and their responsibilities and to customize the out-of-the-box process model. These tools provide an integrated approach to change management in which problem tracking is associated with the code.

So in a large project where formal procedures are to be implemented and automated, and tools have to carry out more than just version control, these types of tools will be used. Here the key phrases are process dependency and information automation and integration. A large project by its nature requires formalized and automated procedures, so a tool that is capable of taking care of these things is an absolute necessity.

During implementation of the tool, it is better to start with a pilot project. In this case, the pilot project will be a module or subsystem of the project. Because these kinds of projects use a lot of automated tools, such as CASE tools, code generators, test data generators, automatic testing tools, and code analyzers, how the SCM tool will integrate and interact with these tools must be analyzed and studied. If possible, it is better to automate the information flow from the other tools used in the project to the SCM tool's repository, so that no effort is wasted. Suitable interfaces have to be built or bought. But in some cases, it might be wise to enter the information manually from the tools used in the project into the SCM tool's repository, because making or buying an interfacing system could be costly. So here project management will have to do a cost-benefit analysis and decide which strategy to adopt.

During pilot project implementation, all of these issues should be addressed and solutions should be identified. It is better to choose a module or subsystem that is representative and contains all potential elements (tools and other complexities) for the pilot project and face the problems head on, because doing so will provide much data about how to implement the SCM system and SCM tool in other modules or subsystems. So in the case of large projects, you should choose the module that is most difficult and complex as the pilot because of all of the difficulties that could be encountered and solved during the pilot project phase.

Also during the pilot project phase, because the SCM implementation team, the SCM experts, and the tool vendor's representatives will be concentrating on one project, the problems could be solved more effectively and efficiently. In large projects, it is better to have the SCM system in place from the initial phases onward. So if the pilot implementation can be done in a simulated environment in which all of the tools and other elements representative of the project in question are present, this will give developers the opportunity to understand the problems, solve them, and then implement the SCM system and the tools in the project from the initial phase.

20.3.3   Distributed, concurrent, and parallel development

Large projects are characterized by their distributed nature, where concurrent and parallel development is commonplace. At any given time, many people will be working on the same programs or different variants of it. So the SCM tool that is used in a large project should be good at managing variants (branches that will not be merged) and temporary branches (branches that will be merged).

The merging capabilities of these tools also have to be good. Any tool that is used in a large project should be capable of supporting distributed development. Now development teams work from different continents, creating different subsystems or modules of a software product. To treat these physically distributed systems as a single logical entity and to manage them so that project managers are not bothered with the underlying complexities is a must for a tool used in a large project.

20.3.4 Change management

In large projects, change management activities cannot be handled by a single change controlboard (CCB), so there will be multiple CCBs and in many cases multilevel CCBs. Change initiation, change request routing, and change disposition can be automated using SCM tools, but people are needed to make decisions, so the CCB members should be trained to use the technology.

Because there are many CCBs of equal status and priority, a super CCB (SCCB) should be authorized to resolve conflicts among the multiple CCBs. The guidelines for the functioning of the CCBs and how to resolve conflicts should be well documented, and if required they can be automated (a rule-based system) so the SCM tool can take appropriate actions without human intervention. For example, you need to consider what to do if there is a tie among the members during a vote. Should the problem be escalated to the higher-level CCB or should the members be informed about the poll result and asked to vote again or to attend a physical CCB meeting? These rules can be coded into the system and many procedures can be automated, thus making the best and most effective use of the CCB members' time and reducing the time required for the disposition of change requests.

20.3.5 Status accounting

Status accounting is the function that documents and reports the information related to configuration items to everyone involved in the project. The status accounting function should also be able to answer ad hoc queries. In a large project, creating and distributing reports, even routine reports, as hard copy is expensive and an administrative nightmare. So in this kind of project, it is better to publish and post these reports on the corporate intranet and inform staff that the reports are available via e-mail or any other messaging system tthe project is using.

For ad hoc querying, it is better to assign roles, such as developer, tester, and manager, and give selective access to the people who fit these roles. For example, a developer could be given access to query the table that contains information about the configuration items of his module, whereas a manager could be given access to query any table in the database. This kind of electronic distribution of the status accounting information is necessary for a large project, because the other option of having hard copies is a burden on the SCM budget.

20.3.6 System building

In the case of large products, system building can take many hours or even days, so the frequency of the builds is important because much time and money is involved with each build. Therefore, a build strategy must be developed.

There are two types of build: clean and nonclean. A clean build is the process of starting with only the source items and then building the entire system step by step from those source items. A nonclean build uses some derived items as inputs for the build process. For example, in the case of a nonclean build, all subsystems that were not changed could be used as is for system building, whereas in the case of a clean build, even the subsystems or modules that were not changed would be built again from the source components. In the case of large projects, having a clean build every time is neither practical nor needed. The system could be built using derived components or subsystems that were not changed. This will save a lot of time, especially during the integration testing and alpha and beta testing phases.

For the final release, a clean build is best. As we saw earlier, SCM tools are used for large projects. The build capabilities of the tool should be adequate enough to produce accurate and reliable builds.

20.3.7 Skill inventory database

We discussed the skill inventory database in Chapter 15. This kind of database is an absolute must in a large project. The two main reasons are that (1) there will be a huge demand for people to do change evaluation, impact analysis, auditing, and so on; and (2) in a large project, the skills and availability of all the people involved with the project are difficult to remember and should therefore be recorded somewhere. So the best, fastest, and easiest method for finding the right people to get the job done is to store the details about the people in a database.

20.3.8 Training

In a large project, SCM training of the team members is an important issue. Because these projects span many years, many different people will be involved. So once the team member training that is done during the implementation phase is over, a system should be put in place to train new members who join the project at a later date.

All large projects have induction programs, which the new members have to undertake. These programs usually give a general idea about the project, the major components, the different functions, and other necessary information so that the person will get an overview of the project. This is important because the big picture is required in order to understand the consequences of individual actions in a module or subsystem. The SCM and SCM tool training should be a part of the induction program, so that all new members will be trained in that also.

20.3.9   Help desks and other knowledge-sharing systems

As we have seen, the team in a large project is transient. Hence, it is important for all events in a project to be recorded: how a problem was identified, how it was fixed, how a bug escaped the testing phase, what points developers should be aware of when using a tool, and other pertinent data. This information should be captured in a knowledge base or help desk and made available to team members.

This knowledge capturing and sharing function is important in a large project because the chances of problems recurring and people reinventing the wheel are enhanced. If all experiences are documented (perhaps an expert system could be used), much time could be saved and development productivity improved. These help desks are also invaluable to the technical support teams and system maintenance personnel.

20.3.10   SCM costs

It is difficult to estimate the cost, effort, time, or size of large systems with a high degree of accuracy. Even in small- and medium-sized projects, the hidden costs of SCM implementation that were discussed in Chapter 18 apply. In large projects, SCM implementation costs will be even more difficult to predict, because many factors are difficult to estimate as a result of uncertain project duration. Estimating what the scenario will be five years down the road is quite difficult.

Being able to foresee the future with unerring accuracy is not a task that is easily accomplished by people or even machines. Also, the real world does not stand still while large systems are developed; new products and processes are discovered, underlying assumptions are invalidated, new laws are passed, and developers learn new things. So any estimates about SCM implementation and postimplementation will have to be reevaluated frequently in the case of large projects, so that estimates and budgets can be updated.

20.4   Concurrent and parallel development

The days of one-at-a-time modifications to configuration items are a thing of the past. Today's SCM tools have the capability to support parallel branches for concurrent development and variant development. In the case of parallel branches that are used for concurrent development, the sophisticated tools allow more than one user to modify the same file(s) and then the tool merges those parallel versions. The merging capabilities of the SCM tools are increasing, and that makes the life of the person doing the merging a lot easier. Now the tools can compare the different parallel versions against a common ancestor and highlight the areas where they are different and where the changes have been made. According to Burrows [2], the capability of modern merge tools is now so strong that users are tempted to accept the tools' automatic resolutions and omit essential testing processes, which is not recommended.

20.5   Web site management

Web design and development is a totally different scenario from the normal software development process. In order to attract visitors and encourage them to come back, Web sites have to change their content and offerings frequently. An advantage of having a Web site is that up-to-the-minute information can be provided to users. So managing the changes to a Web site is more difficult than that of a software product, because of the rate at which the contents of the Web site changes. Not only the contents change, but in order to make the pages attractive and catchy, the presentation styles, design elements, and layout are also changed often.

Another factor that makes Web development different from software development is the number of configuration items that must be managed. Even a medium-sized company's Web site has more than 1,000 pages, each containing various objects and elements, such as downloads, pictures, and movie clips. So we are talking about thousands of objects. Even though some of the modern full-fledged SCM tools can handle a huge number of configuration items, the traditional SCM tools were never designed to manage a project of this size and, even if they do, it will be at the cost of performance.

Another capability that is required to manage Internet sites is the ability to re-create the Web page as it was on a particular day or time. Because the rate at which the contents change is extremely rapid (in many cases, almost on a daily basis, and in some cases—weather, stocks, airlines, etc.—the content changes more often than once a minute), the information required for the build management tools is phenomenal. So ensuring repeatable and reliable rebuilds of the thousands of versions of the Web site is quite a challenge. Therefore, configuration management of Web sites and Internet sites requires different skills than those used for software management. According to Burrows [2], configuration management support for Web and particularly intranet pages and their embedded objects is creating an important new market for the vendors of configuration management tools, which in time could exceed the size of the market for managing software development.

20.6   SCM in integrated development environments

An integrated development environment (IDE) is a programming environment integrated into an application. So an IDE is a set of programs that runs from a single user interface. Some of the most popular IDEs include Visual C++, PowerBuilder, and Visual Basic.

The advantage of using an IDE is that you can design, develop, test, debug, and run the applications without leaving the development environment. So when using an IDE, it is natural to assume that even for SCM functions one does not have to leave the development environment. Today's SCM tools do integrate with IDEs such as Visual C++, Visual Basic, and PowerBuilder so that the developer need not go outside the IDE for SCM functions. The same is true with CASE tools, in which the SCM tools share information from the CASE repository. Many of today's SCM tools integrate seamlessly with IDEs, so that they become part of the environment. Therefore, when carrying out SCM functions, the developer does not have to leave the development environment. Some examples of tools are Continnus CM integrating with Visual C++, PVCS integrating with Power-Builder, and Visual SourceSafe integrating with Microsoft's IDEs. Thus, these tools make the configuration management process in an IDE more intuitive and painless.

In the future, we will see seamless integration (integration without interfaces and interface packages) of the SCM tools, and IDEs and CASE tools will incorporate SCM functionality. Thus, the development environment becomes truly integrated. The day is not far off when SCM tools will supply information or merge with project management tools, thus enabling seamless information integration and easier and more efficient project management.

20.7 SCM in distributed environments

Today the development of a software system is done by many teams distributed across different parts of the globe. Different teams working from different locations develop a software product or system. This situation is ideal for SCM because lack of control can lead to chaos and result in project failures. With the advancements in telecommunications and networking technologies, distributed computing is becoming easier. The capability to manage distributed development is now being offered by many tools. As communications and information technology make rapid strides forward, distributed development is going to be commonplace, and the distributed development capabilities of SCM tools are going to get increasingly better.

Today, project teams that are thousands of miles apart can work as if they share the same office. SCM tools have evolved to incorporate these technologies. Today's SCM tools are capable of supporting distributed development, parallel and concurrent development, and so on. The capabilities and features of the modern SCM tools are so advanced that users do not have to bother about the complexities involved. The system will manage issues such as networking, communication, security, and concurrency management.

20.8 SCM and CASE tools

CASE tools provide automated methods for designing and documenting traditional structured programming techniques. The ultimate goal of CASE is to provide a language for describing the overall system that is sufficient to generate all necessary programs. Thus, a CASE tool is a software package that is used to develop an information system. It is used in all phases of software development: analysis, design, programming, testing, and so on. For example, data dictionaries and programming tools aid in the analysis and design phase, while application generators help speed the programming phase. Automated testing tools and test data generators help in the testing phase.

Most CASE tools store project information in their repositories, and they use this information for code generation, test plan creation, test data generation, and so on. Because a CASE tool uses the information from its repository to generate the application code, the information stored in a CASE tool's repository is detailed. For example, many CASE tools use the entity-relation models as a starting point for analysis. So their repositories will contain details about the various entities, their attributes, and so on. These repositories also contain information about the interdependencies of the various objects and programs, because this type of information is required for application generation and testing.

We have seen that SCM systems also use the same information (but maybe not to the detail as that of CASE tools) to function. So a CASE tool's repository contains the information that is needed for an SCM system. Many CASE tools have rudimentary SCM functions built into them. For example, CASE tools can manage changes, keep an audit trail of modifications to the changes to an item, and other SCM-related tasks.

CASE tools do not, however, have the full functionality of an SCM tool, but they do provide the inputs required by the SCM system. Thus, if the CASE tools and SCM systems can be integrated, so that the SCM systems draw information from the CASE tools and then perform the SCM functions, much time and effort that would otherwise be spent on information gathering can be saved. The ideal solution to this scenario is that of a CASE tool that is so tightly integrated with an SCM tool that they share the same repository, and hence users could perform all SCM functions without leaving the CASE environment.

20.9   Summary

In this chapter, we looked at some of the special situations in which SCM is practiced. The basic SCM concepts are the same irrespective of the situation in which they are used. Only the application of these concepts varies. The degree of formalism, the presence or absence of certain procedures, and the structure of the SCM organization will vary depending on the situation. As technology makes rapid strides and new and more efficient methods of developing software are emerging and becoming popular, the way in which SCM is practiced is also changing. SCM tools are also evolving to support these new development paradigms and methodologies.

Reference

[1] Dart, S., "Not All Tools Are Created Equal," *Application Development Trends*, Vol. 3, No. 9, 1996, pp. 45–48.

[2] Burrows, C., "Configuration Management: Coming of Age in the Year 2000," *Crosstalk: The Journal of Defense Software Engineering*, Mar. 1999, pp. 12–16.

Selected bibliography

Babich, W. A., *Software Configuration Management: Coordination for Team Productivity*, Boston, MA: Addison-Wesley, 1986.

Ben-Menachem, M., *Software Configuration Guidebook*, London: McGraw-Hill International, 1994.

Berlack, H. R., *Software Configuration Management*, New York: John Wiley & Sons, 1992.

Bersoff, E. H., V. D. Henderson, and S. G. Siegel, *Software Configuration Management: An Investment in Product Integrity*, Englewood Cliffs, NJ: Prentice-Hall, 1980.

Burrows, C., and I. Wesley, *Ovum Evaluates: Configuration Management*, London: Ovum Limited, 1998.

Conradi, R. (ed.), *Software Configuration Management: ICSE'97 SCM-7 Workshop Proc.*, Berlin: Springer-Verlag, 1997.

Denning, D. E., *Information Warfare and Security*, Reading, MA: Addison Wesley Longman, 1999.

Heiman, R. V., S. Garone, and S. D. Hendrick, "Development Life-Cycle Management: 1999 Worldwide Markets and Trends," Technical Report, Framingham, MA: International Data Corporation, June 1999.

Magnusson, B. (ed.), *System Configuration Management: ECOOP'98 SCM-8 Symp. Proc.*, Berlin: Springer-Verlag, 1998.

Pressman, R. S., *Software Engineering: A Practitioner's Approach*, New York: McGraw-Hill, 2001.

Sommerville, I., *Software Engineering*, Reading, MA: Addison-Wesley, 2001.

Whitgift, D., *Methods and Tools for Software Configuration Management*, Chichester, England: John Wiley & Sons, 1991.

SCM Resources on the Internet

Organizations and Institutes

- American National Standards Institute (ANSI), *www.ansi.org*

- Association for Computing Machinery, *www.acm.org*

- Association for Configuration and Data Management (ACDM), *www.acdm.org*

- Configuration Management, Inc. (CMI), *www.cmi.com*

- Configuration Management Specialist Group of British Computer Society (CMSG), *www.bcs-cmsg.org.uk*

- Institute of Configuration Management—The home of CM II, *www.icmhq.com/index.html*

- Institute of Electrical and Electronics Engineers, Inc. (IEEE), *www.ieee.org*

- International Organization for Standardization (ISO), *www.iso.ch*

- International Society for Configuration Management, *www.iscmus.com*

- National Aeronautics & Space Administration (NASA), *www.nasa.gov*

- Software Engineering Institute—SCM Home Page, *www.sei.cmu.edu/ legacy/scm/scmHomePage.html*

- Software Technology Support Center (STSC) Home Page, *www.stsc.hill.af.mil/home.asp*

- The Configuration Management Information Center, *www.pdmic.com/ cmic*

Resource Pages

- CM Crossroads: The Configuration Management Community, *www.cmcrossroads.com*

- Brad Appleton's Software Configuration Management Links, *www.cmcrossroads.com/bradapp/links/scm-links.html*

- CMII Key Articles Index Page, *www.icmhq.com/key/keyarticles.html*

- Configuration Management Yellow Pages, *www.cmcrossroads.com/yp/index.php?oldpage=configuration_management.html*

- Pascal Molli's CM Bubbles, *www.loria.fr/~molli/cm-index.html*

- SCM Links by Mária Bieliková, *www.dcs.elf.stuba.sk/~bielik/scm/links.html*

- Steve Easterbrook's CM Resource Guide On-Line, *www.cmiiug.com/Sites.htm*

Commercial Research Organizations

- Butler Group, *www.butlergroup.com*

- International Data Corporation (IDC), *www.idc.com*

- Ovum Ltd., *www.ovum.com*

Digital/Online Libraries

- ACM Digital Library, *http://portal.acm.org/dl.cfm*

- IEEE Computer Society Digital Library, *www.computer.org/publications/dlib*

- IEEE Publications Online, *www.ieee.org/products/onlinepubs*

Magazines and Periodicals

- ACM Computing Reviews, *www.acm.org/reviews*

- ACM Computing Surveys, *www.acm.org/surveys*

- ACM Transactions on Software Engineering and Methodology, *www.acm.org/tosem*

- Application Development Trends, *www.adtmag.com*

- Communications of the ACM, *www.acm.org/cacm*

- Cross Talk Home, *www.stsc.hill.af.mil/CrossTalk/index.asp*

> ‣ IEEE Annals of the History of Computing, *www.computer.org/annals*

> ‣ IEEE Computer, *www.computer.org/computer*

> ‣ IEEE Computing in Science & Engineering, *www.computer.org/cse*

> ‣ IEEE IT Professional, *www.computer.org/itpro*

> ‣ IEEE Software, *www.computer.org/software*

> ‣ IEEE Spectrum, *www.spectrum.ieee.org*

> ‣ IEEE Transactions on Computers, *www.computer.org/tc*

> ‣ IEEE Transactions on Software Engineering, *www.computer.org/tse*

> ‣ Journal of the ACM, *www.acm.org/jacm*

General Sites

> ‣ comp.software.config-mgmt FAQ: Configuration Management Tools Summary, *www.cis.ohio-state.edu/hypertext/faq/usenet/sw-config-mgmt/cm-tools/faq.html*

> ‣ comp.software.config-mgmt FAQ: General Questions, *www.cis.ohio-state.edu/hypertext/faq/usenet/sw-config-mgmt/faq/faq.html*

> ‣ comp.software.config-mgmt FAQ: Problem Management Tools Summary, *www.cis.ohio-state.edu/hypertext/faq/usenet/sw-config-mgmt/prob-mgt-tools/faq.html*

> ‣ Cross Talk Articles on Configuration Management, *http://stsc.hill.af.mil/CM/cmxtlk.asp*

> ‣ Department of Defense Single Stock Point (DODSSP) for Military Specifications, Standards, and Related Publications, *http://dodssp.daps.mil*

> ‣ Hal Render's Bibliography on Software Configuration Management, *http://liinwww.ira.uka.de/bibliography/SE/scm.html*

> ‣ Ken Rigby's Configuration Management Glossary, *www.airtime.co.uk/users/wysywig/gloss.htm*

> ‣ Ken Rigby's Configuration Management Plan—Model Text, *www.airtime.co.uk/users/wysywig/cmp.htm*

> ‣ List of the 20 most popular CM standards by Software Engineering Process Technology (SEPT), *www.12207.com/test.htm*

> ‣ Military Standards Collection, *www-library.itsi.disa.mil*

> ‣ NASA Software Configuration Management Guidebook, *http://satc.gsfc.nasa.gov/GuideBooks/cmpub.html*

▶ NASA's Software Assurance Technology Center (SATC), *http://satc.gsfc.nasa.gov*

▶ SEI Summary of Available CM-Related Documents, *www.sei.cmu.edu/ legacy/scm/scmDocSummary.html*

▶ Software Configuration Management Index, *www.faqs.org/faqs/sw-config-mgmt*

▶ Sources for Standards Documents, *www-library.itsi.disa.mil/org/ std_src.html*

▶ SPAWAR Systems Center San Diego Software Engineering Process Office (SEPO) documentation, *http://sepo.nosc.mil/Docs.html*

Major SCM Tools

▶ AccuRev/CM, *www.accurev.com*

▶ AllChange, *www.intasoft.net/default.asp*

▶ AllFusion Harvest Change Manager, *www3.ca.com/Solutions/ Product.asp?ID=255*

▶ assyst, *www.axiossystems.com*

▶ ChangeMan, *http://serena.com/Products/changeman/home.asp*

▶ ClearCase, *www-306.ibm.com/software/rational/offerings/scm.html*

▶ Dimensions, *www.merant.com*

▶ ISPW, *www.ispw.com*

▶ KONGIG CM, *www.auto-trol.com*

▶ MKS Source Integrity, *www.mks.com/products/sie*

▶ Razor, *www.visible.com/Products/Razor*

▶ Spectrum SCM, *www.spectrumscm.com*

▶ StartTeam, *www.borland.com/starteam/index.html*

▶ SYNERGY/CM, *www.telelogic.com*

▶ Teamcenter, *www.ugs.com/products/teamcenter*

▶ TRUEChange, *www.mccabe.com/true_tc.htm*

Note: This list contains only the most popular high-end SCM tools. For a comprehensive list, users are requested to check the following site, which is regularly updated: *www.cmcrossroads.com/yp/Tools/index.php*.

Appendix B

SCM Bibliography

Abu-Shakra, M., and G. L. Fisher, "Multi-grain Version Control in the Historian System," in B. Magnusson (ed.), *System Configuration Management: ECOOP'98 SCM-8 Symposium Proc.*, Berlin: Springer-Verlag, 1998, pp. 46–56.

ACM Staff (ed.), *Proc. 3rd Int. Workshop on Software Configuration Management*, New York: Association for Computing Machinery, 1991.

ACM Staff (ed.), *2nd Int. Workshop: Software Configuration Management Proc.*, New York: Association for Computing Machinery, 1989.

Adams, C., "Why Can't I Buy an SCM Tool?" in J. Estublier (ed.), *Software Configuration Management: ICSE SCM 4 and SCM 5 Workshops, (Selected Papers)*, Berlin: Springer-Verlag, 1995, pp. 278–281.

Adams, P., and M. Solomon, "An Overview of the CAPITAL Software Development Environment," in J. Estublier (ed.), *Software Configuration Management: ICSE SCM 4 and SCM 5 Workshops, (Selected Papers)*, Berlin: Springer-Verlag, 1995, pp. 1–34.

Adams, R. J., and S. Eslinger, "Lessons Learned from Using COTS Software on Space Systems," *Crosstalk: The Journal of Defense Software Engineering*, June 2001, pp. 25–30.

Alain Abran, A., and J. W. Moore (eds.), *SWEBOK: Guide to the Software Engineering Body of Knowledge (Trial Version)*, Los Alamitos, CA: IEEE Computer Society, 2001.

Alder, P. S., and A. Shenhar, "Adapting Your Technological Base: The Organizational Challenge," *Sloan Management Review*, Fall 1990, pp. 25–37.

Alder, R. S., "Today's Software Complexity Demands Good CM," *Crosstalk: The Journal of Defense Software Engineering*, February 1998, pp. 2.

Allen, L., et al., "ClearClase MultiSite: Supporting Geographically Distributed Software Development," in J. Estublier (ed.), *Software Configuration Management: ICSE SCM 4 and SCM 5 Workshops, (Selected Papers)*, Berlin: Springer-Verlag, 1995, pp. 194–214.

Ambriola, V., and L. Bendix, "Object-Oriented Configuration Control," in ACM Staff (ed.), *2nd Int. Workshop: Software Configuration Management Proc., Princeton, NJ, October 1989*, New York: Association for Computing Machinery, 1989, pp. 135–136.

Andriole, S. J., *Managing Systems Requirements: Methods, Tools, and Cases*, New York: McGraw-Hill, 1996.

Angstadt, B. L., "SCM: More than Support and Control," *Crosstalk: The Journal of Defense Software Engineering*, March 2000, pp. 26–27.

ANSI/IEEE Std-1028-1988—*Standard for Software Reviews and Audits*, 1988.

ANSI/IEEE Std-1042-1987—*IEEE Guide to Software Configuration Management*, 1987.

ANSI/IEEE Std-730.1-1995—*IEEE Guide for Software Quality Assurance Planning*, 1995.

ANSI/IEEE Std-730-1998—*IEEE Standard for Software Quality Assurance Plans*, 1998.

Aquilino, D., et al., "Supporting Reuse and Configuration: A Port Based SCM Model," in ACM Staff (ed.), *Proc. 3rd Int. Workshop on Software Configuration Management, Trondheim, Norway, June 1991*, New York: Association for Computing Machinery, 1991, pp. 62–67.

Asklund, U., and B. Magnusson, "A Case-study of Configuration Management with ClearCase in an Industrial Environment," in R. Conradi (ed.), *Software Configuration Management: ICSE'97 SCM-7 Workshop Proc., Boston, MA, May 1997*, Berlin: Springer-Verlag, 1997, pp. 201–221.

Atkins, D. L., "Version Sensitive Editing Change History as a Programming Tool," in B. Magnusson (ed.), System Configuration Management: ECOOP '98 *SCM-8 Symposium Proc.*, Berlin: Springer-Verlag, 1998, pp. 146–157.

Auer, A., and J. Taramaa, "Experience Report on the Maturity of Configuration Management of Embedded Software," in I. Sommerville, (ed.), *Software Configuration Management: ICSE'96 SCM-6 Workshop, Berlin, Germany, March 1996, (Selected Papers)*, Berlin: Springer-Verlag, 1996, pp. 187–197.

Ayer, S., and F. S. Patrinostro, *Documenting the Software Development Process: A Handbook of Structured Techniques*, New York: McGraw-Hill, 1992.

Ayer, S., and F. S. Patrinostro, *Software Configuration Management: Identification, Accounting, Control, and Management*, New York: McGraw-Hill, 1992.

Baalbergen, E. H., K. Verstoep, and A. S. Tanenbaum, "On the Design of the Amoeba Configuration Manager," in ACM Staff (ed.), *2nd Int. Workshop: Software Configuration Management Proc., Princeton, NJ, October 1989*, New York: Association for Computing Machinery, 1989, pp. 15–22.

Babich, W.A., *Software Configuration Management: Coordination for Team Productivity*, Boston, MA: Addison-Wesley, 1986.

Bays, M. E., *Software Release Methodology*, Englewood Cliffs, NJ: Prentice-Hall PTR, 1999.

Belanger, D., D. Korn, and H. Rao, "Infrastructure for Wide-area Software Development," in I. Sommerville (ed.), *Software Configuration Management: ICSE'96 SCM-6 Workshop, Berlin, Germany, March 1996, (Selected Papers)*, Berlin: Springer-Verlag, 1996, pp. 154–165.

Bendix, L., "Fully Supported Recursive Workspaces," in I. Sommerville (ed.), *Software Configuration Management: ICSE'96 SCM-6 Workshop, Berlin, Germany, March 1996, (Selected Papers)*, Berlin: Springer-Verlag, 1996, pp. 256–261.

Bendix, L., et al., "CoEd—A Tool for Versioning of Hierarchical Documents," in B. Magnusson (ed.), *System Configuration Management: ECOOP'98 SCM-8 Symposium Proc.*, Berlin: Springer-Verlag, 1998, pp. 174–187.

Ben-Menachem, M., *Software Configuration Guidebook*, London: McGraw-Hill International (UK) Limited, 1994.

Berczuk, S., and Appleton, B., *Software Configuration Management Patterns: Effective Teamwork, Practical Integration*, Boston, MA: Addison-Wesley, 2003.

Berlack, H. R., "Evaluation and Selection of Automated Configuration Management Tools," *Crosstalk: The Journal of Defense Software Engineering*, November 1995.

Berlack, H. R., *Software Configuration Management*, New York: John Wiley & Sons, 1992.

Berrada, K., F. Lopez, and R. Minot, "VMCM, A PCTE Based Version and Configuration Management System," in ACM Staff (ed.), *Proc. 3rd Int. Workshop on Software Configuration Management, Trondheim, Norway, June 1991*, New York: Association for Computing Machinery, 1991, pp. 43–52.

Bersoff, E. H., V. D. Henderson, and S. G. Siegel, *Software Configuration Management, An Investment in Product Integrity*, Englewood Cliffs, NJ: Prentice-Hall, 1980.

Bielikova, M., and P. Navrat, "Modeling Versioned Hypertext Documents," in B. Magnusson (ed.), *System Configuration Management: ECOOP'98 SCM-8 Symposium Proc.*, Berlin: Springer-Verlag, 1998, pp. 188–197.

Black, R., *Managing the Testing Process*, Redmond, WA: Microsoft Press, 1999.

Blanchard, B. S., *System Engineering Management*, New York: John Wiley & Sons, 1991.

Bochenski, B., "Managing It All: Good Management Boosts C/S Success", *Software Magazine Client/Server Computing Special Edition*, November 1993, pp. 98.

Boehm, B. W., "A Spiral Model for Software Development and Enhancement," *IEEE Computer*, Vol. 21, No. 5, 1988, pp. 61–72.

Boehm, B. W., and P. N. Papaccio, "Understanding and Controlling Software Costs," *IEEE Transactions on Software Engineering*, Vol. 14, No. 10, 1988, pp. 1462–1477.

Bohem, B. W., *Software Engineering Economics*, Englewood Cliffs, NJ: Prentice-Hall, 1981.

Bouldin, B. M., *Agents of Change: Managing the Introduction of Automated Tools*, Englewood Cliffs, NJ: Yourdon Press, 1989.

Bounds, N. M., and S. Dart, "CM Plans: The Beginning to Your CM Solution," Technical Report, Software Engineering Institute, Carnegie-Mellon University, 1998.

Brereton, P., and P. Singleton, "Deductive Software Building," in J. Estublier (ed.), *Software Configuration Management: ICSE SCM 4 and SCM 5 Workshops, (Selected Papers)*, Berlin: Springer-Verlag, 1995, pp. 81–87.

Brooks, F. P., "No Silver Bullet: Essence and Accidents of Software Engineering", *IEEE Computer*, Vol. 20, No. 4, 1987, pp.10–19.

Brooks, F. P., *The Mythical Man-Month*, New York: Addison Wesley Longman, 1995.

Brown, A., et al., "The State of Automated Configuration Management," Technical Report, Software Engineering Institute, Carnegie-Mellon University, 1991.

Brown, W. J., *Antipatterns and Patterns in Software Configuration Management*, New York: John Wiley & Sons, 1999.

Buckle, J. K., *Software Configuration Management*, Basingstoke, England: Macmillan, 1982.

Buckley, F. J., *Implementing Configuration Management: Hardware, Software, and Firmware*, Los Alamitos, CA: IEEE Computer Society Press, 1996.

Buffenbarger, J., "Syntactic Software Merging," in J. Estublier (ed.), *Software Configuration Management: ICSE SCM 4 and SCM 5 Workshops, (Selected Papers)*, Berlin: Springer-Verlag, 1995, pp. 153–172.

Buffenbarger, J., and K. Gruell, "What have you done for me lately? (Branches, Merges and Change Logs)," in R. Conradi (ed.), *Software Con-*

figuration Management: ICSE'97 SCM-7 Workshop Proc., Boston, MA, May 1997, Berlin: Springer-Verlag, 1997, pp. 18–24.

Burrows, C., "Configuration Management: Coming of Age in the Year 2000," *Crosstalk: The Journal of Defense Software Engineering*, March 1999, pp. 12–16.

Burrows, C., and I. Wesley, *Ovum Evaluates: Configuration Management*, London: Ovum Limited, 1998.

Burrows, C., S. Dart, and G. W. George, *Ovum Evaluates: Software Configuration Management*, London: Ovum Limited, 1996.

Burton, T., "Software Configuration Management Helps Solve Year 2000 Change Integration Obstacles," *Crosstalk: The Journal of Defense Software Engineering*, January 1998, pp. 7–8.

Butler, T., et al, "Software Configuration Management: A Discipline with Added Value," *Crosstalk: The Journal of Defense Software Engineering*, July 2001, pp. 4–8.

Cagan, M., and D. W. Weber, "Task-Based Software Configuration Management: Support for "Change Sets" in Continuus/CM," Technical Report, Continuus Software Corporation, 1996.

Cagan, M., "Untangling Configuration Management," in J. Estublier (ed.), *Software Configuration Management: ICSE SCM 4 and SCM 5 Workshops, (Selected Papers)*, Berlin: Springer-Verlag, 1995, pp. 35–52.

Caputo, K., *CMM Implementation Guide*, Reading, MA: Addison-Wesley, 1998.

Casavecchia, D. E., "Reality Configuration Management," *Crosstalk: The Journal of Defense Software Engineering*, November 2002, pp. 17–21.

Cave, W. C., and G. W. Maymon, *Software Lifecycle Management: The Incremental Method*, Basingstoke, England: Macmillan, 1984.

Choi, S. C., and W. S. Scacchi, "Assuring the Correctness of Configured Software Descriptions," in ACM Staff (ed.), *2nd Int. Workshop: Software Configuration Management Proc., Princeton, NJ, October 1989*, New York: Association for Computing Machinery, 1989, pp. 66–75.

Chris, A. "Why Can't I Buy an SCM Tool?" in J. Estublier (ed.), *Software Configuration Management: ICSE SCM 4 and SCM 5 Workshops, (Selected Papers)*, Berlin: Springer-Verlag, 1995, pp. 278–281.

Christensen, A., and T. Egge, "Store—A System for Handling Third-Party Applications in a Heterogeneous Computer Environment," in J. Estublier (ed.), *Software Configuration Management: ICSE SCM 4 and SCM 5 Workshops, (Selected Papers)*, Berlin: Springer-Verlag, 1995, pp. 263–276.

Christensen, H. B., "Experiences with Architectural Software Configuration Management in Ragnarok," in B. Magnusson (ed.), *System Configuration*

Management: ECOOP'98 SCM-8 Symposium Proc., Berlin: Springer-Verlag, 1998, pp. 67–74.

Ci, J. X., et al., "ScmEngine: A Distributed Software Configuration Management Environment on X.500," in R. Conradi (ed.), *Software Configuration Management: ICSE'97 SCM-7 Workshop Proc., Boston, MA, May 1997,* Berlin: Springer-Verlag, 1997, pp. 108–127.

Clemm, G. M., "Replacing Version-Control with Job-Control," in ACM Staff (ed.), *2nd Int. Workshop: Software Configuration Management Proc., Princeton, NJ, October 1989,* New York: Association for Computing Machinery, 1989, pp. 162–169.

Clemm, G. M., "The Odin System," in J. Estublier (ed.), *Software Configuration Management: ICSE SCM 4 and SCM 5 Workshops, (Selected Papers),* Berlin: Springer-Verlag, 1995, pp. 241–262.

Coallier, F., "International Standardization in Software and Systems Engineering," *Crosstalk: The Journal of Defense Software Engineering,* February 2003, pp. 18–23.

Compton, S. B., and G. R. Conner, *Configuration Management for Software,* New York: Van Nostrand Reinhold, 1994.

Conradi, R., (ed.), *Software Configuration Management: ICSE'97 SCM-7 Workshop Proc.,* Berlin: Springer-Verlag, 1997.

Conradi, R., and B. Westfechtel, "Configuring Versioned Software Products," in I. Sommerville (ed.), *Software Configuration Management: ICSE'96 SCM-6 Workshop, Berlin, Germany, March 1996, (Selected Papers),* Berlin: Springer-Verlag, 1996, pp. 88–109.

Conradi, R., and B. Westfechtel, "Towards a Uniform Version Model for Software Configuration Management," in R. Conradi (ed.), *Software Configuration Management: ICSE'97 SCM-7 Workshop Proc., Boston, MA, May 1997,* Berlin: Springer-Verlag, 1997, pp. 1–17.

Conradi, R., and C. R. Malm, "Cooperating Transactions against the EPOS Database," in ACM Staff (ed.), *Proc. 3rd Int. Workshop on Software Configuration Management, Trondheim, Norway, June 1991,* New York: Association for Computing Machinery, 1991, pp. 98–101.

Continuus Software Corporation, "Change Management for Software Development," Continuus Software Corporation, 1998.

Continuus Software Corporation, "Distributed Code Management for Team Engineering," Continuus Software Corporation, 1998.

Continuus Software Corporation, "Problem Tracking and Task Management for Team Engineering," Continuus Software Corporation, 1998.

Continuus Software Corporation, "Software Configuration Management for Team Engineering," Continuus Software Corporation, 1998.

Continuus Software Corporation, "Task-Based Configuration Management: A New Generation of Software Configuration Management," Continuus Software Corporation, 1997.

Cook, D. A., "Laws of Software Motion," *Crosstalk: The Journal of Defense Software Engineering*, February 2004, pp. 31.

Cook, D. A., "Software Process Improvement—A Good Idea for Other People," *Crosstalk: The Journal of Defense Software Engineering*, April 2004, pp. 31.

Crnkovic, I., "Experience of Using a Simple SCM Tool in a Complex Development Environment," in I. Sommerville (ed.), *Software Configuration Management: ICSE'96 SCM-6 Workshop, Berlin, Germany, March 1996, (Selected Papers)*, Berlin: Springer-Verlag, 1996, pp. 262–263.

Crnkovic, I., "Experience with Change-Oriented SCM Tool," in R. Conradi (ed.), *Software Configuration Management: ICSE'97 SCM-7 Workshop Proc., Boston, MA, May 1997*, Berlin: Springer-Verlag, 1997, pp. 222–234.

Crnkovic, I., and P. Willfor, "Change Measurements in an SCM Process," in B. Magnusson (ed.), *System Configuration Management: ECOOP'98 SCM-8 Symposium Proc.*, Berlin: Springer-Verlag, 1998, pp. 26–32.

Daniels, M. A., *Principles of Configuration Management*, Annandale, VA: Advanced Application Consultants, Inc., 1985.

Dart, S., "Content Change Management: Problems for Web Systems," *Crosstalk: The Journal of Defense Software Engineering*, January 2000, pp. 1–7.

Dart, S., "Achieving the Best Possible Configuration Management Solution," *Crosstalk: The Journal of Defense Software Engineering*, September 1996.

Dart, S., "Adopting an Automated Configuration Management Solution," Technical Paper, STC'94 (Software Technology Center), Utah, April 12, 1994.

Dart, S., "Best Practice for a CM Solution," in I. Sommerville (ed.), *Software Configuration Management: ICSE'96 SCM-6 Workshop, Berlin, Germany, March 1996, (Selected Papers)*, Berlin: Springer-Verlag, 1996, pp. 239–255.

Dart, S., "Concepts in Configuration Management Systems," in ACM Staff (ed.), *Proc. 3rd Int. Workshop on Software Configuration Management, Trondheim, Norway, June 1991*, New York: Association for Computing Machinery, 1991, pp. 1–18.

Dart, S., "Concepts in Configuration Management Systems," Technical Report, Software Engineering Institute, Carnegie-Mellon University, 1994.

Dart, S., "Configuration Management Bibliography," Technical Report, Software Engineering Institute, Carnegie-Mellon University, 1992.

Dart, S., "Containing the Web Crisis Using Configuration Management", Web Engineering Workshop at the Conference on Software Engineering (ICSE'99), May 16–17, 1999, Los Angeles, USA.

Dart, S., "Content Change Management: Problems for Web Systems," Int. Symp. System Configuration Management SCM9, Toulouse, France, September 5–7, 1999.

Dart, S., "Not All Tools are Created Equal," *Application Development Trends*, Vol. 3, No. 9, 1996, pp. 45–48.

Dart, S., "Parallels in Computer-Aided Design Framework and Software Development Environment Efforts," Technical Report, Software Engineering Institute, Carnegie-Mellon University, 1994.

Dart, S., "Past, Present and Future of CM Systems," Technical Report, Software Engineering Institute, Carnegie-Mellon University, 1992.

Dart, S., "Spectrum of Functionality in Configuration Management Systems," Technical Report, Software Engineering Institute, Carnegie-Mellon University, 1990.

Dart, S., "The Agony and Ecstasy of Configuration Management (Abstract)," in B. Magnusson (ed.), *System Configuration Management: ECOOP'98 SCM-8 Symposium Proc.*, Berlin: Springer-Verlag, 1998, pp. 204–205.

Dart, S., "Tool Configuration Assistant," in ACM Staff (ed.), *2nd Int. Workshop: Software Configuration Management Proc., Princeton, NJ, October 1989*, New York: Association for Computing Machinery, 1989, pp. 110–113.

Dart, S., and J. Krasnov, *"Experiences in Risk Mitigation with Configuration Management,"* 4th SEI Risk Conference, November 1995.

Dart, S., *Configuration Management: The Missing Link in Web Engineering*, Boston, MA: Artech House, 2000.

Dart, S., "To Change or Not to Change," *Application Development Trends*, Vol. 4, No. 6, 1997, pp. 55–57.

Dart, S., "WebCrisis.Com: Inability to Maintain," *Software Magazine*, September 1999.

Davis, A., and P. Sitaram, "A Concurrent Process Model for Software Development," *Software Engineering Notes*, Vol. 19, No. 2, pp. 38–51.

Davis, A. M., *201 Principles of Software Development*, New York: McGraw-Hill, 1995.

Dehforooz, A., and F. J. Hudson, *Software Engineering Fundamentals*, New York: Oxford University Press, 1996.

DeMillo, R. A., et al., *Software Testing and Evaluation*, Benjamin Cummings Publishing, 1987.

Deustsch, M. S., *Software Verification and Validation: Realistic Project Approaches*, Englewood Cliffs, NJ: Prentice-Hall, 1982.

Dinsart, A., et al., "Object Derivation and Validation from a Data Base Definition," in ACM Staff (ed.), *2nd Int. Workshop: Software Configuration Management Proc., Princeton, NJ, October 1989*, New York: Association for Computing Machinery, 1989, pp. 170–178.

Dix, A., T. Rodden, and I. Sommerville, "Modeling the Sharing of Versions," in I. Sommerville (ed.), *Software Configuration Management: ICSE'96 SCM-6 Workshop, Berlin, Germany, March 1996, (Selected Papers)*, Berlin: Springer-Verlag, 1996, pp. 282–290.

DOD-STD-2167A—*Defense System Software Development*, 1988.

DOD-STD-2168—*Defense System Software Quality Program*, 1988.

Donald, R. M., and D. Bollinger, "Transitioning From SA-CMM to CMMI in the Special Operations Forces Systems Program Office," *Crosstalk: The Journal of Defense Software Engineering*, February 2002, pp. 12–14.

Donaldson, S. E., and S. G. Siegel, *Cultivating Successful Software Development: A Practitioner's View*, Englewood Cliffs, NJ: Prentice-Hall PTR, 1997.

Dyer, M., *The Cleanroom Approach to Quality Software Development*, New York: John Wiley & Sons, 1992.

Eggerman, W. V., *Configuration Management Handbook*, Blue Ridge Summit, PA: TAB Books, 1990.

Eidnes, H., D. O. Hallsteinsen, and D. H. Wanvik, "Separate Compilation in CHIPSY," in ACM Staff (ed.), *2nd Int. Workshop: Software Configuration Management Proc., Princeton, NJ, October 1989*, New York: Association for Computing Machinery, 1989, pp. 42–45.

Eilfield, P., "Configuration Mangement as 'Gluware' for Development of Client/Server Applications on Heterogeneous and Distributed Environments," in I. Sommerville (ed.), *Software Configuration Management: ICSE'96 SCM-6 Workshop, Berlin, Germany, March 1996, (Selected Papers)*, Berlin: Springer-Verlag, 1996, pp. 264–271.

Estublier, J. (ed.), *Software Configuration Management: ICSE SCM 4 and SCM 5 Workshops, (Selected Papers)*, Berlin: Springer-Verlag, 1995.

Estublier, J., "Workspace Management in Software Engineering Environments," in I. Sommerville (ed.), *Software Configuration Management: ICSE'96 SCM-6 Workshop, Berlin, Germany, March 1996, (Selected Papers)*, Berlin: Springer-Verlag, 1996, pp. 127–138.

Estublier, J., and R. Casallas, "Three Dimensional Versioning," in J. Estublier (ed.), *Software Configuration Management: ICSE SCM 4 and SCM 5 Workshops, (Selected Papers)*, Berlin: Springer-Verlag, 1995, pp. 118–135.

Estublier, J., J. Favre, and P. Morat, "Toward SCM/PDM Integration?" in B. Magnusson (ed.), *System Configuration Management: ECOOP'98 SCM-8 Symposium Proc.*, Berlin: Springer-Verlag, 1998, pp. 75–94.

Estublier, J., S. Dami, and M. Amiour, "High Level Process Modeling for SCM Systems," in R. Conradi (ed.), *Software Configuration Management: ICSE'97 SCM-7 Workshop Proc., Boston, MA, May 1997*, Berlin: Springer-Verlag, 1997, pp. 81–97.

Evans, M. W., Abela, A. M., and Beltz, T., "Seven Characteristics of Dysfunctional Software Projects," *Crosstalk: The Journal of Defense Software Engineering*, April 2002, pp. 16–20.

Evans, M. W., *Productive Software Test Management*, Chichester, England: John Wiley & Sons, 1984.

Falkerngerg, B., "Configuration Management for a Large (SW) Development," in ACM Staff (ed.), *2nd Int. Workshop: Software Configuration Management Proc., Princeton, NJ, October 1989*, New York: Association for Computing Machinery, 1989, pp. 34–37.

Feiler, P. H., "Software Configuration Management: Advances in Software Development Environments," Technical Report, Software Engineering Institute, Carnegie-Mellon University, 1990.

Feiler, P. H., and G. F. Downey, "Tool Version Management Technology: A Case Study," Technical Report, Software Engineering Institute, Carnegie-Mellon University, 1990.

Feiler, P. H., and G. F. Downey, "Transaction-Oriented Configuration Management: A Case Study," Technical Report, Software Engineering Institute, Carnegie-Mellon University, 1990.

Feiler, P. H., "Managing Development of Very Large Systems: Implications for Integrated Environment Architectures", Technical Paper, Software Engineering Institute, Carnegie-Mellon University, 1988.

Feiler, P. H., "Configuration Management Models in Commercial Environments," Technical Report, Software Engineering Institute, Carnegie-Mellon University, 1991.

Feiler, P. H., "Software Configuration Management: Advances in Software Development Environments," Technical Paper, Software Engineering Institute, Carnegie-Mellon University, 1990.

Florence, A., "Reducing Risks Through Proper Specification of Software Requirements," *Crosstalk: The Journal of Defense Software Engineering*, April 2002, pp. 13–15.

Frohlich, P., and W. Nejdl, "WebRC: Configuration Management for a Cooperation Tool," in R. Conradi (ed.), *Software Configuration Management: ICSE'97 SCM-7 Workshop Proc., Boston, MA, May 1997*, Berlin: Springer-Verlag, 1997, pp. 175–185.

Gallagher, K., "Conditions to Assure Semantically Consistent Software Merges in Linear Time," in ACM Staff (ed.), *Proc. 3rd Int. Workshop on Software Configuration Management, Trondheim, Norway, June 1991*, New York: Association for Computing Machinery, 1991, pp. 80–83.

Gardy, R. B., *Successful Software Process Improvements*, Englewood Cliffs, NJ: Prentice-Hall PTR, 1997.

Gentleman, W. M., S. A. MacKay, and D. A. Stewart, "Commercial Real-Time Software Needs Different Configuration Management," in ACM Staff (ed.), *2nd Int. Workshop: Software Configuration Management Proc., Princeton, NJ, October 1989*, New York: Association for Computing Machinery, 1989, pp. 152–161.

Gilb, T., *Principles of Software Engineering Management*, New York: Addison-Wesley, 1988.

Gill, T., "Stop-Gap Configuration Management," *Crosstalk: The Journal of Defense Software Engineering*, February 1998, pp. 3–5.

Glass, R. L., *Software Runaways*, Englewood Cliffs, NJ: Prentice-Hall, 1998.

Godart, C., et al., "About Some Relationships Between Configuration Management, Software Process and Cooperative Work: COO Environment," in J. Estublier (ed.), *Software Configuration Management: ICSE SCM 4 and SCM 5 Workshops, (Selected Papers)*, Berlin: Springer-Verlag, 1995, pp. 173–178.

Gowen, L. D., "Predicting Staff Sizes to Maintain Networks," *Crosstalk: The Journal of Defense Software Engineering*, November 2001, pp. 22–26.

Grosjean, S., "Building a CM Database: Nine Years at Boeing," *Crosstalk: The Journal of Defense Software Engineering*, January 2000, pp. 8–10.

Grossman, R., "Defect Management: A Study in Contradictions," *Crosstalk: The Journal of Defense Software Engineering*, September 2003, pp. 28–30.

Gulla, P., and J. Gorman, "Experiences with the Use of a Configuration Language," in I. Sommerville (ed.), *Software Configuration Management: ICSE'96 SCM-6 Workshop, Berlin, Germany, March 1996, (Selected Papers)*, Berlin: Springer-Verlag, 1996, pp. 198–219.

Gustavsson, A., "Maintaining the Evolution of Software Objects in an Integrated Environment," in ACM Staff (ed.), *2nd Int. Workshop: Software Configuration Management Proc., Princeton, NJ, October 1989*, New York: Association for Computing Machinery, 1989, pp. 114–117.

Hall, R. S., D. Heimbigner, and A. L. Wolf, "Requirements for Software Deployment Languages and Schema," in B. Magnusson (ed.), *System Configuration Management: ECOOP'98 SCM-8 Symposium Proc.*, Berlin: Springer-Verlag, 1998, pp. 198–203.

Haque, S., "Introducing Process into Configuration Management," *Crosstalk: The Journal of Defense Software Engineering*, June 1996.

Haque, T., "Process-Based Configuration Management: The Way to Go to Avoid Costly Product Recalls," *Crosstalk: The Journal of Defense Software Engineering*, April 1997.

Haque, T., "The F-16 Software Test Station Program: A Success Story in Process Configuration Management," *Crosstalk: The Journal of Defense Software Engineering*, November 1997.

Hass, A. M. J., *Configuration Management: Principles and Practice*, Boston, MA: Addison-Wesley, 2003.

Haug, M., et al, *Managing the Change: Software Configuration and Change Management*, Berlin: Springer-Verlag, 2001.

Hedin, G., L. Ohlsson, and J. McKenna, "Product Configuration using Object-Oriented Grammars." in B. Magnusson (ed.), *System Configuration Management: ECOOP'98 SCM-8 Symposium Proc.*, Berlin: Springer-Verlag, 1998, pp. 107–126.

Heiman, R. V., and E. Quinn, "Software Configuration Management Meets the Internet," Technical Report, Framingham, MA: International Data Corporation, November 1997.

Heiman, R. V., et al., "Programmer Development Tools: 1997 Worldwide Markets and Trends," Technical Report, Framingham, MA: International Data Corporation, July 1997.

Heiman, R. V., S. Garone, and S. D. Hendrick, "Development Life-Cycle Management: 1999 Worldwide Markets and Trends," Technical Report, Framingham, MA: International Data Corporation, June 1999.

Heiman, R. V., S. Garone, and S. D. Hendrick, "Development Life-Cycle Management: 1998 Worldwide Markets and Trends," Technical Report, Framingham, MA: International Data Corporation, May 1998.

Heiman, R. V., "The Growing Market for Software Configuration Management Tools," Technical Report, Framingham, MA: International Data Corporation, September 1997.

Heimbigner, D., and A. L. Wolf, "Post-Deployment Configuration Mangement," in I. Sommerville (ed.), *Software Configuration Management: ICSE'96 SCM-6 Workshop, Berlin, Germany, March 1996, (Selected Papers)*, Berlin: Springer-Verlag, 1996, pp. 272–276.

Hoek, A., D. Heimbigner, and A. L. Wolf, "Does Configuration Management Research have a Future?" in J. Estublier (ed.), *Software Configuration Management: ICSE SCM 4 and SCM 5 Workshops, (Selected Papers)*, Berlin: Springer-Verlag, 1995, pp. 305–309.

Hoek, A., D. Heimbigner, and A. L. Wolf, "System Modeling Resurrected," in B. Magnusson (ed.), *System Configuration Management: ECOOP'98 SCM-8 Symposium Proc.*, Berlin: Springer-Verlag, 1998, pp. 140–145.

Hoek, A., et al., "Software Deployment: Extending Configuration Mangement Support into the Field," *Crosstalk: The Journal of Defense Software Engineering*, February 1998, pp. 9–13.

Holdsworth, J., *Software Process Design: Out of the Tar Pit*, London: McGraw-Hill International (UK) Ltd., 1994.

Humphrey, W. S., *Managing the Software Process*, New York: Addison-Wesley, 1989.

Hunt, J. J., et al., "Distributed Configuration Management via Java and the World Wide Web," in R. Conradi (ed.), *Software Configuration Management: ICSE'97 SCM-7 Workshop Proc., Boston, MA, May 1997*, Berlin: Springer-Verlag, 1997, pp. 161–174.

Hunt, J. J., K. Vo, and W. F. Tichy, "An Empirical Study of Delta Algorithms," in I. Sommerville (ed.), *Software Configuration Management: ICSE'96 SCM-6 Workshop, Berlin, Germany, March 1996, (Selected Papers)*, Berlin: Springer-Verlag, 1996, pp. 49–66.

IEEE Std-610.12-1990—*IEEE Standard Glossary of Software Engineering Terminology*, 1990.

IEEE Std-828-1998—*IEEE Standard for Software Configuration Management Plans*, 1998.

IEEE, *IEEE Software Engineering Standards Collection: 1999 Edition*, New Jersey: IEEE, 1999.

Ince, D., *An Introduction to Software Quality Assurance and Its Implementation*, London: McGraw-Hill International (UK) Ltd., 1994.

Ince, D., *ISO 9001 and Software Quality Assurance*, London: McGraw-Hill International (UK) Ltd., 1994.

Ingram, P., Burrows, C., and Wesley, I., *Configuration Management Tools: A Detailed Evaluation*, London: Ovum Limited, 1993.

Intersolv, "Cost Justifying Software Configuration Management," PVCS Series for Configuration Management, White Paper, Intersolv, Inc., 1998.

Intersolv, "Software Configuration Management for Client/Server Development Environments: An architecture guide," White Paper, Intersolv, Inc., 1998.

Intersolv, "Software Configuration Management: A primer for development teams and managers," White Paper, Intersolv, Inc., 1997.

ISO 10007: 199—*Quality Management: Guidelines for Configuration Management*, 1995.

ISO 9000-3: 1997—*Guidelines for the Application of ISO 9001:1994 to the Development, Supply, Installation and Maintenance of Computer Software*, 1997.

ISO 9001: 1994—*Quality Systems: Model for Quality Assurance in Design, Development, Production, Installation and Servicing*, 1994.

Jackelen, G., "Verification and Validation People Can Be More Than Technical Advisors," *Crosstalk: The Journal of Defense Software Engineering*, February 2004, pp. 26–29.

Jacobson, I., M. Griss, and P. Jonsson, *Software Reuse: Architecture, Process, and Organization for Business Success*, New York: ACM Press, 1997.

Jenner, M.G., *Software Quality Measurement and ISO 9001: How to Make Them Work for You*, New York: John Wiley & Sons, 1995.

Jones, C., *Software Quality: Analysis and Guidelines for Success*, London: International Thompson Press, 1997.

Jones, C. T., *Estimating Software Costs*, New York: McGraw-Hill. 1998.

Jones, G. W., *Software Engineering*, New York: John Wiley & Sons, 1990.

Jordan, M., "Experiences in Configuration Management for Modula-2," in ACM Staff (ed.), *2nd Int. Workshop: Software Configuration Management Proc., Princeton, NJ, October 1989*, New York: Association for Computing Machinery, 1989, pp. 126–128.

Kaiser, G. W., "Modeling Configuration as Transactions," in ACM Staff (ed.), *2nd Int. Workshop: Software Configuration Management Proc., Princeton, NJ, October 1989*, New York: Association for Computing Machinery, 1989, pp. 133–134.

Kasse, T., "Software Configuration Management for Project Leaders," Technical Paper, Institute for Software Process Improvement, Inc., Belgium, 1998.

Kasse, T., and McQuaid, P. A., "Factors Affecting Process Improvement Initiatives," *Crosstalk: The Journal of Defense Software Engineering*, August 2000, pp. 4–7.

Kelly, M. V., *Configuration Management: The Changing Image*, New York: McGraw-Hill, 1995.

Kenefick, S., *Real World Software Configuration Management*, Berkeley, CA: Apress, 2003.

Keyes, J., *Software Configuration Management*, Boca Raton, FL: Auerbach Publications, 2004.

Keyes, J., *Software Engineering Productivity Handbook*, New York: McGraw-Hill, 1993.

Kilpi, T., "Product Management Requirements for SCM Discipline," in R. Conradi (ed.), *Software Configuration Management: ICSE'97 SCM-7 Workshop Proc., Boston, MA, May 1997*, Berlin: Springer-Verlag, 1997, pp. 186–200.

Kinball, J., and A. Larson, "Epochs, Configuration Schema, and Version Cursors in the KBSA Framework CCM Model," in ACM Staff (ed.), *Proc. 3rd Int. Workshop on Software Configuration Management, Trondheim, Norway, June 1991*, New York: Association for Computing Machinery, 1991, pp. 33–42.

Kingsbury, J., "Adopting SCM Technology," *Crosstalk: The Journal of Defense Software Engineering*, March 1996.

Kirzner, R., "Managing Content: The Key to Success in Web Business," Technical Report, Framingham, MA: International Data Corporation, June 1999.

Kolvik, S., "Introducing Configuration Management in an Organization," in I. Sommerville (ed.), *Software Configuration Management: ICSE'96 SCM-6 Workshop, Berlin, Germany, March 1996, (Selected Papers)*, Berlin: Springer-Verlag, 1996, pp. 220–230.

Korel, B., et al., "Version Management in Distributed Network Environment," in ACM Staff (ed.), *Proc. 3rd Int. Workshop on Software Configuration Management, Trondheim, Norway, June 1991*, New York: Association for Computing Machinery, 1991, pp. 161–166.

Kramer, S. A., "History Management System," in ACM Staff (ed.), *Proc. 3rd Int. Workshop on Software Configuration Management, Trondheim, Norway, June 1991*, New York: Association for Computing Machinery, 1991, pp. 140–143.

Lacroix, M., and P. Lavency, "The Change Request Process," in ACM Staff (ed.), *2nd Int. Workshop: Software Configuration Management Proc., Princeton, NJ, October 1989*, New York: Association for Computing Machinery, 1989, pp. 122–125.

Lacroix, S. M. J., D. Roelants, and J. E. Waroquier, "Flexible Support for Cooperation in Software Development," in ACM Staff (ed.), *Proc. 3rd Int. Workshop on Software Configuration Management, Trondheim, Norway, June 1991*, New York: Association for Computing Machinery, 1991, pp. 102–108.

Lago, P., and R. Conradi, "Transaction Planning to Support Coordination," in J. Estublier (ed.), *Software Configuration Management: ICSE SCM 4 and SCM 5 Workshops, (Selected Papers)*, Berlin: Springer-Verlag, 1995, pp. 145–151.

Lange, R., and R. W. Schwanke, "Software Architecture Analysis: A Case Study," in ACM Staff (ed.), *Proc. 3rd Int. Workshop on Software Configuration Management, Trondheim, Norway, June 1991*, New York: Association for Computing Machinery, 1991, pp. 19–28.

Larson, J., and H. M. Roald, "Introducing ClearCase as a Process Improvement Experiment," in B. Magnusson (ed.), *System Configuration Management: ECOOP'98 SCM-8 Symposium Proc.*, Berlin: Springer-Verlag, 1998, pp. 1–12.

Leblang, D. B., "Managing the Software Development Process with Clear-Guide," in R. Conradi (ed.), *Software Configuration Management: ICSE'97 SCM-7 Workshop Proc., Boston, MA, May 1997*, Berlin: Springer-Verlag, 1997, pp. 66–80.

Leblang, D. B., and P. H. Levine, "Software Configuration Management: Why Is It Needed and What Should It Do?" in J. Estublier (ed.), *Software Configuration Management: ICSE SCM 4 and SCM 5 Workshops, (Selected Papers)*, Berlin: Springer-Verlag, 1995, pp. 53–60.

Lee, T., P. Thomas, and V. Lowen, "An Odyssey Towards Best SCM Practices: The Big Picture," in I. Sommerville (ed.), *Software Configuration Management: ICSE'96 SCM-6 Workshop, Berlin, Germany, March 1996, (Selected Papers)*, Berlin: Springer-Verlag, 1996, pp. 231–238.

Lehman, M. M., "Software Engineering, the Software Process and Their Support," *Software Engineering Journal*, Vol. 6, No. 5, 1991, pp. 243–258.

Lehman, M. M., and L. Belady, "A Model of Large Program Development," *IBM Systems Journal*, Vol. 15. No. 3, 1976, pp. 225–252.

Lehman, M. M., and L. Belady, *Program Evolution: Processes of Software Change*, London: Academic Press, 1985.

Leishman, T. R., and D. A. Cook, "But I Only Changed One Line of Code!" *Crosstalk: The Journal of Defense Software Engineering*, January 2003, pp. 20–23.

Leishman, T. R., and D. A. Cook, "Lessons Learned from Software Engineering Consulting," *Crosstalk: The Journal of Defense Software Engineering*, February 2004, pp. 4–6.

Leishman, T. R., and D. A. Cook, "Requirements Risks Can Drown Software Projects," *Crosstalk: The Journal of Defense Software Engineering*, April 2002, pp. 4–8.

Leishman, T. R., and D. A. Cook, "Risk Factor: Confronting the Risks That Impact Software Project Success," *Crosstalk: The Journal of Defense Software Engineering*, May 2004, pp. 31–34.

Lie, A., et al., "Change Oriented Versioning in a Software Engineering Database," in ACM Staff (ed.), *2nd Int. Workshop: Software Configuration Man-*

agement Proc., Princeton, NJ, October 1989, New York: Association for Computing Machinery, 1989, pp. 56–65.

Lientz, B. P., and E. B. Swanson, *Software Maintenance Management,* Reading, MA: Addison-Wesley, 1980.

Lin, Y., and S. P. Reiss, "Configuration Management in Terms of Modules," in J. Estublier (ed.), *Software Configuration Management: ICSE SCM 4 and SCM 5 Workshops, (Selected Papers),* Berlin: Springer-Verlag, 1995, pp. 101–117.

Lindsay, P., and O. Traynor, "Supporting Fine-grained Traceability in Software Development Environments," in B. Magnusson (ed.), *System Configuration Management: ECOOP'98 SCM-8 Symposium Proc.,* Berlin: Springer-Verlag, 1998, pp. 133–139.

Lubkin, D., "Heterogeneous Configuration Management with DSEE," in ACM Staff (ed.), *Proc. 3rd Int. Workshop on Software Configuration Management, Trondheim, Norway, June 1991,* New York: Association for Computing Machinery, 1991, pp. 153–160.

Lundholm, P., "Design Management in Base/OPEN," in ACM Staff (ed.), *2nd Int. Workshop: Software Configuration Management Proc., Princeton, NJ, October 1989,* New York: Association for Computing Machinery, 1989, pp. 38–41.

Lyn, F., *Change Control During Computer Systems Development,* Englewood Cliffs, NJ: Prentice-Hall, 1991.

Lyon, D. D., *Practical CM,* Pittsfield, MA: Raven Publishing, 1994.

MacKay, S. A., "Changesets Revisited and CM of Complex Documents," in I. Sommerville (ed.), *Software Configuration Management: ICSE'96 SCM-6 Workshop, Berlin, Germany, March 1996, (Selected Papers),* Berlin: Springer-Verlag, 1996, pp. 277–281.

MacKay, S. A., "The State-of-the-art in Concurrent Distributed Configuration Management," J. in Estublier (ed.), *Software Configuration Management: ICSE SCM 4 and SCM 5 Workshops, (Selected Papers),* Berlin: Springer-Verlag, 1995, pp. 180–193.

Mack-Crane, B., and A. Pal, "Conflict Management in a Source Version Management System," in ACM Staff (ed.), *2nd Int. Workshop: Software Configuration Management Proc., Princeton, NJ, October 1989,* New York: Association for Computing Machinery, 1989, pp. 149–151.

Magnusson, B. (ed.), *System Configuration Management: ECOOP'98 SCM-8 Symposium Proc.,* Berlin: Springer-Verlag, 1998.

Magnusson, B., and U. Asklund, "Fine Grained Version Control of Configurations in COOP/Orm," in I. Sommerville (ed.), *Software Configuration Management: ICSE'96 SCM-6 Workshop, Berlin, Germany, March 1996, (Selected Papers),* Berlin: Springer-Verlag, 1996, pp. 31–48.

Marciniak, J. J. (ed.), *Encyclopedia of Software Engineering*, 2nd ed., New York: John Wiley & Sons, 2002.

Marshall, A. J., "Demystifying Software Configuration Management," *Crosstalk: The Journal of Defense Software Engineering*, May 1995.

Marshall, A. J., "Software Configuration Management: Function or Discipline?" *Crosstalk: The Journal of Defense Software Engineering*, October 1995.

Martin, J., and C. McClure, *Software Maintenance: The Problem and its Solutions*, Englewood Cliffs, NJ: Prentice-Hall, 1983.

Martin, J., *Rapid Application Development*, Englewood Cliffs, NJ: Prentice-Hall, 1991.

McCann, R. T., "How Much Code Inspection Is Enough?" *Crosstalk: The Journal of Defense Software Engineering*, July 2001, pp. 9–12.

McClure, C., *Software Reuse Techniques: Adding Reuse to the System Development Process*, Englewood Cliffs, NJ: Prentice-Hall, 1997.

McClure, S., "Web Development Life-Cycle Management Software," Technical Report, Framingham, MA: International Data Corporation, June 1999.

McConnel, S., *Code Complete*, 2nd ed., Redmond, WA: Microsoft Press, 2004.

McConnel, S., *Software Project Survival Guide*, Redmond, WA: Microsoft Press, 1998.

McDermid, J.A., (ed.), *Software Engineer's Reference Book*, Boca Raton, FL: CRC Press, 1994.

McDonald, J., P. N. Hilfinger, and L. Semenzato, "PRCS: The Project Revision Control System," in B. Magnusson (ed.), *System Configuration Management: ECOOP'98 SCM-8 Symposium Proc.*, Berlin: Springer-Verlag, 1998, pp. 33–45.

McKnight, W. L., "What Is Information Assurance?" *Crosstalk: The Journal of Defense Software Engineering*, July 2002, pp. 4–6.

Meiser, K., "Software Configuration Management Terminology," *Crosstalk: The Journal of Defense Software Engineering*, January 1995.

Micallef, J., and G. M. Clemm, "The Asgard System: Activity-based Configuration Management," in I. Sommerville (ed.), *Software Configuration Management: ICSE'96 SCM-6 Workshop, Berlin, Germany, March 1996, (Selected Papers)*, Berlin: Springer-Verlag, 1996, pp. 175–186.

Mikkelsen, T., and S. Pherigo, *Practical Software Configuration Management: The Latenight Developer's Handbook*, Upper Saddle River, NJ: Prentice-Hall PTR, 1997.

Milewski, B., "Distributed Source Control System," in R. Conradi (ed.), *Software Configuration Management: ICSE'97 SCM-7 Workshop Proc., Boston, MA, May 1997*, Berlin: Springer-Verlag, 1997, pp. 98–107.

Miller, D. B., R. G. Stockton, and C. W. Krueger, "An Inverted Approach to Configuration Management," in ACM Staff (ed.), *2nd Int. Workshop: Software Configuration Management Proc., Princeton, NJ, October 1989*, New York: Association for Computing Machinery, 1989, pp. 1–4.

Miller, T. C., "A Schema for Configuration Management," in ACM Staff (ed.), *2nd Int. Workshop: Software Configuration Management Proc., Princeton, NJ, October 1989*, New York: Association for Computing Machinery, 1989, pp. 26–29.

MIL-STD-1521B—*Technical Reviews and Audits for Systems, Equipment and Computer Programs*, 1985.

MIL-STD-480B—*Configuration Control Engineering Changes, Deviations and Waivers*, 1988.

MIL-STD-481B—*Configuration Control Engineering Changes (Short Form), Deviations and Waivers*, 1988.

MIL-STD-482A—*Configuration Status Accounting Data Elements and Related Features*, 1974.

MIL-STD-483A—*Configuration Management Practices for Systems, Equipment, Munitions and Computer Programs*, 1985.

MIL-STD-490A—*Specification Practices*, 1985.

MIL-STD-973—*Configuration Management*, 1995.

Molli, P., "COO-Transaction: Supporting Cooperative Work," in R. Conradi (ed.), *Software Configuration Management: ICSE'97 SCM-7 Workshop Proc., Boston, MA, May 1997*, Berlin: Springer-Verlag, 1997, pp. 128–141.

Moore, J.W., *Software Engineering Standards: A User's Road Map*, New Jersey: IEEE, 1997.

Mosley, V., et al., "Software Configuration Management Tools: Getting Bigger, Better, and Bolder," *Crosstalk: The Journal of Defense Software Engineering*, January 1996, pp. 6–10.

Munch, B. P., "HiCoV—Managing the Version Space," in I. Sommerville (ed.), *Software Configuration Management: ICSE'96 SCM-6 Workshop, Berlin, Germany, March 1996, (Selected Papers)*, Berlin: Springer-Verlag, 1996, pp. 110–126.

Musa, J. D., "Software Engineering: The Future of a Profession," *IEEE Software*, Vol. 22, No. 1, 1985, pp. 55–62.

Narayanaswamy, K., "A Text-Based Representation for Program Variants," in ACM Staff (ed.), *2nd Int. Workshop: Software Configuration Management*

Proc., Princeton, NJ, October 1989, New York: Association for Computing Machinery, 1989, pp. 30–33.

NASA, *NASA Software Configuration Management Guidebook*, Technical Report SMAP-GB-A201, NASA, 1995.

Newbery, F. J., "Edge Concentration: A Method for Clustering Directed Graphs," in ACM Staff (ed.), *2nd Int. Workshop: Software Configuration Management Proc., Princeton, NJ, October 1989*, New York: Association for Computing Machinery, 1989, pp. 76–85.

Nicklin, P. J., "Managing Multi-Variant Software Configuration," in ACM Staff (ed.), *Proc. 3rd Int. Workshop on Software Configuration Management, Trondheim, Norway, June 1991*, New York: Association for Computing Machinery, 1991, pp. 53–57.

Nierstrasz, "Component-Oriented Software Development," *Communications of the ACM*, Vol. 35, No. 9, 1992, pp. 160–165.

Noll, J., and W. Scacchi, "Supporting Distributed Configuration Management in Virtual Enterprises," in R. Conradi (ed.), *Software Configuration Management: ICSE'97 SCM-7 Workshop Proc., Boston, MA, May 1997*, Berlin: Springer-Verlag, 1997, pp. 142–160.

Ochuodho, S. J., and A. W. Brown, "A Process-Oriented Version and Configuration Management Model for Communications Software," in ACM Staff (ed.), *Proc. 3rd Int. Workshop on Software Configuration Management, Trondheim, Norway, June 1991*, New York: Association for Computing Machinery, 1991, pp. 109–120.

Opperthauser, D., "Defect Management in an Agile Development Environment," *Crosstalk: The Journal of Defense Software Engineering*, September 2003, pp. 21–24.

Pakstas, A., "Aladdin/Lamp: Configuration Management Tools for Distributed Computer Control Systems," in ACM Staff (ed.), *2nd Int. Workshop: Software Configuration Management Proc., Princeton, NJ, October 1989*, New York: Association for Computing Machinery, 1989, pp. 141–144.

Parker, K., "Customization of a Commercial CM System to Provide Better Management Mechanisms," in J. Estublier (ed.), *Software Configuration Management: ICSE SCM 4 and SCM 5 Workshops, (Selected Papers)*, Berlin: Springer-Verlag, 1995, pp. 289–292.

Peach, R. W. (ed.), *The ISO 9000 Handbook*, New York: McGraw-Hill, 1997.

Perry, D. E., "Dimensions of Consistency in Source Versions and System Compositions," in ACM Staff (ed.), *Proc. 3rd Int. Workshop on Software Configuration Management, Trondheim, Norway, June 1991*, New York: Association for Computing Machinery, 1991, pp. 29–32.

Perry, D. E., "System Compositions and Shared Dependencies," in I. Sommerville (ed.), *Software Configuration Management: ICSE'96 SCM-6 Work-*

shop, Berlin, Germany, March 1996, (Selected Papers), Berlin: Springer-Verlag, 1996, pp. 139–153.

Persson, A., "Experiences of Customization and Introduction of a CM Model," in J. Estublier (ed.), *Software Configuration Management: ICSE SCM 4 and SCM 5 Workshops, (Selected Papers)*, Berlin: Springer-Verlag, 1995, pp. 293–303.

Petersen, G., "The Weakest Geek," *Crosstalk: The Journal of Defense Software Engineering*, July 2001, pp. 31.

Pfleeger, S. L., *Software Engineering: Theory and Practice*, Englewood Cliffs, NJ: Prentice-Hall, 1998.

Phillips, M., "CMMI Version1.1: What Has Changed?" *Crosstalk: The Journal of Defense Software Engineering*, February 2002, pp. 4–6.

Platinum, "Configuration Management and Software Testing," White Paper, Platinum Technology, Inc., 1999.

Platinum, "Controlling Application Development Costs using Software Configuration Management (CM)," White Paper, Platinum Technology, Inc., 1999.

Platinum, "How to Evaluate a CM Tool for Client/Server Environments?" White Paper, Platinum Technology, Inc., 1999.

Platinum, "Strategic Thinking About Software Change Management," White Paper, Platinum Technology, Inc., 1999.

Platinum, "The Expanding Role of Software Change and Configuration Management (CM)," White Paper, Platinum Technology, Inc., 1999.

Platinum, "What is CM?" White Paper, Platinum Technology, Inc., 1999.

Ploedereder, E., and A. Fergany, "The Data Model of the Configuration Management Assistant (CMA)," in ACM Staff (ed.), *2nd Int. Workshop: Software Configuration Management Proc., Princeton, NJ, October 1989*, New York: Association for Computing Machinery, 1989, pp. 5–14.

Potter, N., and Sakry, M., "The Documentation Diet," *Crosstalk: The Journal of Defense Software Engineering*, October 2003, pp. 21–24.

Powers, J., *Configuration Management Procedures*, Santa Ana, CA: Global Engineering Documents, 1984.

Pressman, R. S., *Software Engineering: A Practitioner's Approach*, 5th ed., New York: McGraw-Hill, 2001.

Pressman. R. S., *A Manager's Guide to Software Engineering*, New York: McGraw-Hill, 1993.

Rahikkala, T., J. Taramma, and A. Valimaki, "Industrial Experiences from SCM Current State Analysis," B. Magnusson (ed.), *System Configuration*

Management: ECOOP'98 SCM-8 Symposium Proc., Berlin: Springer-Verlag, 1998, pp. 13–25.

Rawlings, J. H., *SCM for Network Development Environments*, New York: McGraw-Hill, 1994.

Ray, R. J., "Experiences with a Script-based Software Configuration Management System," in J. Estublier (ed.), *Software Configuration Management: ICSE SCM 4 and SCM 5 Workshops, (Selected Papers)*, Berlin: Springer-Verlag, 1995, pp. 282–287.

Reichberger, C., "Orthogonal Version Management," in ACM Staff (ed.), *2nd Int. Workshop: Software Configuration Management Proc., Princeton, NJ, October 1989*, New York: Association for Computing Machinery, 1989, pp. 137–140.

Reichenberger, C., "Delta Storage for Arbitrary Non-Text Files," in ACM Staff (ed.), *Proc. 3rd Int. Workshop on Software Configuration Management, Trondheim, Norway, June 1991*, New York: Association for Computing Machinery, 1991, pp. 144–152.

Reichenberger, C., "VOODOO—A Tool for Orthogonal Version Management," in J. Estublier (ed.), *Software Configuration Management: ICSE SCM 4 and SCM 5 Workshops (Selected Papers)*, Berlin: Springer-Verlag, 1995, pp. 61–79.

Render, H., and R. Campbell, "An Object-Oriented Model of Software Configuration Management," in ACM Staff (ed.), *Proc. 3rd Int. Workshop on Software Configuration Management, Trondheim, Norway, June 1991*, New York: Association for Computing Machinery, 1991, pp. 127–139.

Reps, T., and T. Bricker, "Illustrating Interference in Interfering Versions of Programs," in ACM Staff (ed.), *2nd Int. Workshop: Software Configuration Management Proc., Princeton, NJ, October 1989*, New York: Association for Computing Machinery, 1989, pp. 46–55.

Reuter, J., et al., "Distributed Version Control via the WWW," in I. Sommerville (ed.), *Software Configuration Management: ICSE'96 SCM-6 Workshop, Berlin, Germany, March 1996, (Selected Papers)*, Berlin: Springer-Verlag, 1996, pp. 166–174.

Rice, R. W., "Surviving the Top 10 Challenges of Software Test Automation," *Crosstalk: The Journal of Defense Software Engineering*, May 2002, pp. 26–29.

Rich, A., and M. Solomon, "A Logic-Based Approach to System Modeling," in ACM Staff (ed.), *Proc. 3rd Int. Workshop on Software Configuration Management, Trondheim, Norway, June 1991*, New York: Association for Computing Machinery, 1991, pp. 84–93.

Rigg, W., C. Burrows, and P. Ingram, *Ovum Evaluates: Configuration Management Tools*, London: Ovum Limited, 1995

Rosenblum, D. S., and B. Krishnamurthy, "An Event-Based Model of Software Configuration Management," in ACM Staff (ed.), *Proc. 3rd Int. Workshop on Software Configuration Management, Trondheim, Norway, June 1991*, New York: Association for Computing Machinery, 1991, pp. 94–97.

Royce, W. "Managing the Development of Large Software Systems: Concepts and Techniques," IEEE, WESCON, 1970.

Royce, W., *Software Project Management: A Unified Framework*, Reading, MA: Addison Wesley Longman, 1998.

Rustin, R. (ed.), *Debugging Techniques in Large Systems*, Englewood Cliffs, NJ: Prentice-Hall, 1971.

Samaras, T. T., and F. Czerwinski, *Fundamentals of Configuration Management*, Chichester, England: John Wiley & Sons, 1971.

Samaras, T. T., *Configuration Management Deskbook: Vol. 1*, Annandale, VA: Advanced Application Consultants, Inc., 1988.

Samaras, T. T., *Configuration Management Deskbook: Vol. 2, Instruction Supplement*, Annandale, VA: Advanced Application Consultants, Inc., 1988.

Schach, S. R., *Software Engineering*, Boston, MA: Richard D. Irwin, 1990.

Schmerl, B. R., and C. D. Maralin, "Designing Configuration Management Facilities for Dynamically Bound Systems," in J. Estublier (ed.), *Software Configuration Management: ICSE SCM 4 and SCM 5 Workshops, (Selected Papers)*, Berlin: Springer-Verlag, 1995, pp. 88–100.

Schmerl, B. R., and C. D. Maralin, "Versioning and Consistency for Dynamically Composed Configurations," in R. Conradi (ed.), *Software Configuration Management: ICSE'97 SCM-7 Workshop Proc., Boston, MA, May 1997*, Berlin: Springer-Verlag, 1997, pp. 49–65.

Schroeder, U., "Incremental Variant Control," in ACM Staff (ed.), *2nd Int. Workshop: Software Configuration Management Proc., Princeton, NJ, October 1989*, New York: Association for Computing Machinery, 1989, pp. 144–148.

Schulmeyer, G. G., and J. I. McManus, *Handbook of Software Quality Assurance*, London: International Thompson Press, 1996.

Schwanke, R. W., and M. A. Platoff, "Cross References are Features," in ACM Staff (ed.), *2nd Int. Workshop: Software Configuration Management Proc., Princeton, NJ, October 1989*, New York: Association for Computing Machinery, 1989, pp. 86–95.

SEI, Carnegie-Mellon University, "A Quick Guide to Information about Software Environments, Configuration Management, and CASE," Technical Report, Software Engineering Institute, 1995.

SEI, Carnegie-Mellon University, *The Capability Maturity Model: Guidelines for Improving the Software Process*, Reading, MA: Addison Wesley Longman, 1994.

Seiwald, C., "Inter-file Branching—A Practical Method for Representing Variants," in I. Sommerville (ed.), *Software Configuration Management: ICSE'96 SCM-6 Workshop, Berlin, Germany, March 1996, (Selected Papers)*, Berlin: Springer-Verlag, 1996, pp. 67–75.

Sheard, S. A., "How Do I Make My Organization Comply With Yet Another New Model?" *Crosstalk: The Journal of Defense Software Engineering*, February 2002, pp. 15–20.

Sheedy, C., "Sorceress: A Database Approach to Software Configuration Management," in ACM Staff (ed.), *Proc. 3rd Int. Workshop on Software Configuration Management, Trondheim, Norway, June 1991*, New York: Association for Computing Machinery, 1991, pp. 121–126.

Simmonds, I., "Configuration Management in the PACT Software Engineering Environment," in ACM Staff (ed.), *2nd Int. Workshop: Software Configuration Management Proc., Princeton, NJ, October 1989*, New York: Association for Computing Machinery, 1989, pp. 118–121.

Simmonds, I., "Duplicates: A Convention for Defining Configurations in PCTE-Based Environments," in ACM Staff (ed.), *Proc. 3rd Int. Workshop on Software Configuration Management, Trondheim, Norway, June 1991*, New York: Association for Computing Machinery, 1991, pp. 58–61.

Sodhi, J., and P. Sodhi, *Software Reuse: Domain Analysis and Design Process*, New York: McGraw-Hill, 1999.

Sommerville, I. (ed.), *Software Configuration Management: ICSE'96 SCM 6 Workshop, Berlin, Germany, March 1996, (Selected Papers)*, Berlin: Springer-Verlag, 1996.

Sommerville, I. *Software Engineering*, 6th ed., Reading, MA: Addison-Wesley, 2001.

Sorensen, R., "The CM Database: To Buy or to Build?" *Crosstalk: The Journal of Defense Software Engineering*, January 2000, pp. 11–12.

Sorensen, R., "CCB—An Acronym for "Chocolate Chip Brownies"? *Crosstalk: The Journal of Defense Software Engineering*, March 1999, pp. 3–6.

Starbuck, R. A., "A Beginner's Look at Process Improvement Documentation," *Crosstalk: The Journal of Defense Software Engineering*, March 2004, pp. 18–20.

Starbuck, R. A., "A Configuration Manager's Perspective," *Crosstalk: The Journal of Defense Software Engineering*, July 2000, pp. 12–14.

Starbuck, R. A., "Software Configuration Management by MIL-STD-498," *Crosstalk: The Journal of Defense Software Engineering*, June 1996.

Starbuck, R. A., "Software Configuration Management: Don't Buy a Tool First," *Crosstalk: The Journal of Defense Software Engineering*, November 1997.

Starbuck, R. A., "Using CM to Recapture Baselines for Y2K Compliance Efforts," *Crosstalk: The Journal of Defense Software Engineering*, March 1999, pp. 7–11.

Thomas, I., "Version and Configuration Management on a Software Engineering Database," in ACM Staff (ed.), *2nd Int. Workshop: Software Configuration Management Proc., Princeton, NJ, October 1989*, New York: Association for Computing Machinery, 1989, pp. 23–25.

Thompson, K., "People Projects: Psychometric Profiling," *Crosstalk: The Journal of Defense Software Engineering*, April 2003, pp. 18–23.

Thomson, R., and I. Sommerville, "Configuration Management Using SySL," in ACM Staff (ed.), *2nd Int. Workshop: Software Configuration Management Proc., Princeton, NJ, October 1989*, New York: Association for Computing Machinery, 1989, pp. 106–109.

Tibrook, D., "An Architecture for a Construction System," in I. Sommerville (ed.), *Software Configuration Management: ICSE'96 SCM-6 Workshop, Berlin, Germany, March 1996, (Selected Papers)*, Berlin: Springer-Verlag, 1996, pp. 76–87.

Tichy, W.F., *Configuration Managment*, New York: John Wiley & Sons, 1994.

Tryggeseth, E., B. Gulla, and R. Conardi, "Modeling Systems with Variability Using the PROTEUS Configuration Language," in J. Estublier (ed.), *Software Configuration Management: ICSE SCM 4 and SCM 5 Workshops, (Selected Papers)*, Berlin: Springer-Verlag, 1995, pp. 216–240.

Vacca, J., *Implementing a Successful Configuration Change Management Program*, Information Systems Management Group, 1993.

Van De Vanter, M. L., "Coordinated Editing of Versioned Packages in the JP Programming Environment," in B. Magnusson (ed.), *System Configuration Management: ECOOP'98 SCM-8 Symposium Proc.*, Berlin: Springer-Verlag, 1998, pp. 158–173.

Ventimiglia, B., "Effective Software Configuration Management," *Crosstalk: The Journal of Defense Software Engineering*, February 1998, pp. 6–8.

Viskari, J., "A Rationale for Automated Configuration Status Accounting," in J. Estublier (ed.), *Software Configuration Management: ICSE SCM 4 and SCM 5 Workshops, (Selected Papers)*, Berlin: Springer-Verlag, 1995, pp. 138–144.

Wallnau, K. C., "Issues and Techniques of CASE Integration with Configuration Management," Technical Report, Software Engineering Institute, Carnegie-Mellon University, 1992.

Watts, F. B., *Engineering Documentation Control Handbook*, 2nd ed., Park Ridge, NJ: Noyes Publications, 2000.

Watts, F.B., *Engineering Documentation Control Handbook: Configuration Management for Industry*, Park Ridge, NJ: Noyes Publications, 1993.

Weatherall, B., "A Day in the Life of a PVCS Road Warrior: Want to Get PVCS Organized Quickly in a Mixed-Platform Environment?" Technical Paper, Synergex International Corporation, 1997.

Weber, D. W., "Change Sets Versus Change Packages: Comparing Implementations of Change-Based SCM," in R. Conradi (ed.), *Software Configuration Management: ICSE'97 SCM-7 Workshop Proc., Boston, MA, May 1997*, Berlin: Springer-Verlag, 1997, pp. 25–35.

Weber, D. W., *"Change-based SCM Is Where We're Going,"* Continuus Software Corporation, 1997.

Wein, M., et al., "Evolution is Essential for Software Tool Development," Position Paper, Institution of Information Technology, National Research Council Canada, 1995.

Weinberg, G. M., "Destroying Communication and Control in Software Development," *Crosstalk: The Journal of Defense Software Engineering*, April 2003, pp. 4–8.

Westfechtek, B., "Revision Control in an Integrated Software Development Environment," in ACM Staff (ed.), *2nd Int. Workshop: Software Configuration Management Proc., Princeton, NJ, October 1989*, New York: Association for Computing Machinery, 1989, pp. 96–105.

Westfechtel, B., "Structure-Oriented Merging of Revisions of Software Documents," in ACM Staff (ed.), *Proc. 3rd Int. Workshop on Software Configuration Management, Trondheim, Norway, June 1991*, New York: Association for Computing Machinery, 1991, pp. 68–79.

Westfechtel, B., and R. Conradi, "Software Configuration Management and Engineering Data Management: Differences and Similarities," in B. Magnusson (ed.), *System Configuration Management: ECOOP'98 SCM-8 Symposium Proc.*, Berlin: Springer-Verlag, 1998, pp. 95–106.

Whitgift, D., *Methods and Tools for Software Configuration Management*, Chichester, England: John Wiley & Sons, 1991.

Wingerd, L., and C. Seiwald, "Constructing a Large Product with Jam," in R. Conradi (ed.), *Software Configuration Management: ICSE'97 SCM-7 Workshop Proc., Boston, MA, May 1997*, Berlin: Springer-Verlag, 1997, pp. 36–48.

Appendix C

SCM Glossary and Acronyms

Abend   Abbreviation for abnormal end (i.e., termination of a process before completion).

Acceptance testing   Testing conducted to determine whether a system or product is acceptable to the customer, user, or client.

Adaptive maintenance   Software maintenance performed to make a computer program work in an environment that is different from the one for which it was originally designed.

AEA   American Electronics Association

AIA   Aerospace Industries Association

Allocated baseline   Allocated baseline is the initial approved specifications governing the development of configuration items that are part of a higher-level configuration item.

Allocated configuration identification   The current approved specifications governing the development of configuration items that are part of a higher-level configuration item.

Allocation   The process of distributing requirements, resources, or other entities among the components of a system or program.

ANSI   American National Standards Institute

Application software   Software designed to fulfill the specific needs of a user or client.

Approval   The agreement that an item is complete and suitable for its intended use.

Approved data   Data that has been approved by an appropriate authority and is the official (identified) version of the data until replaced by another approved version.

Archived data   Released or approved data that is to be retained for historical purposes.

Attributes   Performance, functional, and physical characteristics of a product.

Audit   An independent examination or review conducted to assess whether a product or process or set of products or processes are in compliance with specifications, standards, contractual agreements, or some other criteria.

Baseline   A specification or product that has been formerly reviewed and agreed upon and that serves as a basis for further development, which can be changed only through change management procedures. Baselines can be defined at various parts of the development life cycle.

Baseline management   The application of technical and administrative direction to designate the documents and changes to those documents that formerly identify and establish baselines at specific times during the life cycle of a configuration item. In other words, the set of activities performed to establish and maintain the different baselines in a project.

Bug   An error, defect, fault, or problem.

Build   The process (or the final result of the process) of generating an executable, testable system from source code.

CA   Configuration Audit

CASE   Computer-Aided Software Engineering. CASE is the use of computers to aid in the software engineering process. This can include the application of software tools to software design, requirements analysis, code generation, testing, documentation, and other software engineering activities.

CCA   Configuration Control Authority. Another name for CCB.

CCB   Configuration Control Board (also known as Change Control Board). A group of people responsible for evaluating and approving or disapproving changes to configuration items.

Certification   A written guarantee that a system or component complies with its specified requirements and is acceptable for operational use.

Change control   See *configuration control.*

Change request form   A change request form (paper or electronic) used to initiate a change and containing the details of the change, such as the name of the change originator, item to be changed, and other details.

CI   Configuration Item. An aggregation of hardware or software or both that is designated for configuration management and treated as a single entity in the configuration management process.

CM   Configuration Management

CMM   Capability Maturity Model

Configuration   The functional and/or physical characteristics of a hardware or software item as set forth in the technical documentation and achieved in a product.

Configuration   (1) The performance, functional, and physical attributes of an existing or planned product or a combination of products. (2) One of a series of sequentially created variations of a product.

Configuration audit   Product configuration verification accomplished by inspecting documents, products, and records and reviewing procedures, processes, and systems of operation to verify that the product has achieved its required attributes (performance requirements and functional constraints) and that the product's design is accurately documented.

Configuration control   Configuration control is the element of configuration management consisting of the evaluation, coordination, approval or disapproval, and implementation of changes to configuration items after formal establishment of their configuration identification.

Configuration documentation   Technical information, the purpose of which is to identify and define a product's performance, functional, and physical attributes (e.g., specifications, drawings).

Configuration identification   The configuration management activity that encompasses selecting configuration documents; assigning and applying unique identifiers to a product, its components, and associated documents; and maintaining document revision relationships to product configurations.

Configuration management   A management process for establishing and maintaining consistency of a product's performance, functional, and physical attributes with its requirements, design, and operational information throughout its life.

Configuration status accounting   The configuration management activity concerning capture and storage of, and access to, configuration information needed to manage products and product information effectively.

Configuration verification   The action verifying that the product has achieved its required attributes (performance requirements and functional constraints) and the product's design is accurately documented.

Contract   As used herein, denotes the document (e.g., contract, memorandum of agreement or understanding, purchase order) used to implement an agreement between a customer (buyer) and a seller (supplier).

Corrective maintenance   Maintenance performed to correct faults in software.

COTS software   Commercial off-the-shelf software.

CPC   Computer Program Component

CPCI   Computer Program Configuration Item

CR   Change Request. A request to make a change or modification.

Crash   The sudden and complete failure of a computer system or component.

Criticality   The degree of impact that a requirement, module, error, fault, or failure has on the development or operation of a system. Synonymous with *severity*.

CSC   Computer Software Component. A functionally or logically distinct part of a computer software configuration item.

CSCI   Computer Software Configuration Item. A software item that is identified for configuration management.

Data   Recorded information of any nature (including administrative, managerial, financial, and technical), regardless of medium or characteristics.

Debug   To detect, locate, and correct faults in a computer program.

Delta   A technique to store versions by storing only the differences between versions as opposed to storing each version in its entirety. Forward deltas store the original version in its entirety and later versions as deltas. Reverse deltas store the most recent version in its full form and previous versions as deltas.

Design information   Technical information resulting from translating requirements for a product into a complete description of the product.

Design phase   The period of time in the software development life cycle during which the designs for architecture, software components, interfaces, and data are created, documented, and verified to satisfy requirements.

Design standard   A standard that describes the characteristics of a design or design description of data or program components.

Detailed design   The process of refining and expanding the preliminary design of a system or component to the extent that the design is sufficiently complete to be implemented.

Development testing   The testing conducted during the development of a system or component. This kind of testing is usually done in the development environment by the developer.

Developmental configuration   The software and associated technical documentation that define the evolving configuration of a computer software configuration item during development.

Disapproval   Conclusion by the appropriate authority that an item submitted for approval is either incomplete or not suitable for its intended use.

Document representation   A set of digital files that collectively represent a complete digital document.

ECMI   European Computer Manufacturers Institute

ECP   Engineering Change Proposal. A proposed engineering change and the documentation by which the change is described and suggested.

EIA   Electronics Industries Alliance

Engineering change   An alteration in the configuration of a configuration item after formal establishment of its configuration identification.

EPRI   Electric Power Research Institute

ERP   Enterprise Resource Planning

ESA   European Space Agency

Evaluation   The process of determining whether an item or activity meets specified criteria.

FAA   Federal Aviation Authority

Failure   The inability of a component or system to perform its required functions within specified performance requirements.

FCA   Functional Configuration Audit. FCA is an audit conducted to verify that the development of a configuration item has been completed satisfactorily, that the item has achieved the performance and functional characteristics specified in the functional and allocated configuration identification, and that its operational and support documents are complete and satisfactory.

Firmware   The combination of a hardware device and computer instructions or computer data that reside as read-only software on the hardware device. The software cannot be readily modified under program control.

Fit   The ability of a product to interface or interconnect with or become an integral part of another product.

Form   The shape, size, dimensions, and other physically measurable parameters that uniquely characterize a product. For software, form denotes the language and media.

Form, fit, and function   The configuration comprising the physical and functional characteristics of an item as an entity, but not including any characteristics of the elements making up the item.

Formal specification   A specification written and approved in accordance with established standards and guidelines.

Formal testing   Testing conducted in accordance with test plans and procedures that have been reviewed and approved by a customer, user, or designated approving authority.

FQR   Formal Qualification Review. The test or inspection by which a group of configuration items comprising a system is verified to have met specific contractual performance requirements.

FR   Fault Report. Same as *problem report*.

Function   The action or actions that a product is designed to perform.

Functional attributes   Measurable performance parameters, including reliability, maintainability, and safety.

Functional baseline   The initial approved technical documentation for a configuration item. Also known as *requirements baseline*.

Functional specification   A document that specifies the functions that a system or component must perform.

Functional testing   The testing process that ignores the internal mechanism of a system or component and focuses solely on the outputs generated in response to selected inputs and execution conditions. Also known as *black-box testing*.

Hardware   Devices or machines that are capable of accepting and storing computer data, executing a systematic sequence of operations on computer data, or producing control outputs. Such devices can perform substantial interpretation, computation, communication, control, or other logical functions.

HWCI   Hardware Configuration Item

IDE   Integrated Development Environment. An environment in which the user can design, develop, debug, test, and run the application is developed. Some popular IDEs are Visual C++, PowerBuilder, and Delphi.

IEEE   Institute of Electrical and Electronics Engineers

Incremental development   A software development methodology in which requirements definition, design, implementation, and testing occur in an overlapping and interactive manner, resulting in incremental completion of the overall software product.

Informal testing   Testing conducted in accordance with test plans and procedures that have not been reviewed and approved by a customer, user, or designated approving authority.

INPO   Institute of Nuclear Power Operations

Inspection   A static analysis technique that relies on visual examination of development products to detect errors and faults.

Integration testing   The testing process in which the software components, hardware components, or both are combined and tested to evaluate the interaction between them and how they perform in combination.

Integrity   The degree to which a system or component prevents unauthorized access to or modifications of computer programs or data.

Interchangeable   A product that possesses such functional and physical attributes as to be equivalent in performance to another product of similar or identical purposes and is capable of being exchanged for the other product without selection for fit or performance, and without alteration of the products themselves or of adjoining products, except for adjustment.

Interface   A shared boundary across which information is passed.

Interface control   The process of identifying all functional and physical characteristics relevant to the interfacing of two or more configuration items provided by one or more organizations and ensuring that the proposed changes to these characteristics are evaluated and approved before implementation.

Interface documentation   Interface control drawing or other documentation that depicts physical, functional, and test interfaces of related or co-functioning products.

Interface   The performance, functional, and physical attributes required to exist at a common boundary.

ISO   International Organization for Standardization

IV&V   Independent Verification and Validation. Verification and validation that is performed by an organization that is technically, managerially, and financially independent of the development organization.

JCL   Job Control Language. A language used to identify a sequence of jobs, describe their requirements to an operating system, and control their execution.

Life cycle   A generic term relating to the entire period of conception, definition, building, distribution, operation, and disposal of a product.

Maintenance   The process of modifying a software system or component after delivery to correct faults, improve performance or another attribute, or adapt to a changed environment.

Metrics   Measures used to indicate progress or achievement.

MMI   Man-Machine Interface

NASA   National Aeronautics and Space Administration

NATO   North Atlantic Treaty Organization

NIRMA   Nuclear Information & Records Management Association

Nonconformance   Nonfulfillment of a specified requirement operational information

Information that supports the use of a product (e.g., operation maintenance and user's manuals or instructions, procedures, and diagrams).

NOR   Notice of Revision. A form used in configuration management to propose revisions to a drawing or list and, after approval, to notify users that the drawing or list has been or will be revised accordingly.

NSIA   National Security Industrial Association

Object-oriented design   A software development technique in which a system or component is built using objects and connections between those objects.

Operational testing   Testing conducted to evaluate the performance of a system or component in its operational environment.

Original   The current design activity's document or digital document representation and associated source data file(s) of record (i.e., for legal purposes.)

Patch   A modification made to a source program as a last-minute fix.

PCA   Physical Configuration Audit. An audit conducted to verify that a configuration item, as built, conforms to the technical documentation that defines it.

Perfective maintenance   Software maintenance performed to improve the performance, maintainability, or other attributes of a computer program.

Performance   A quantitative measure characterizing a physical or functional attribute relating to the execution of an operation or function. Performance attributes include quantity (how many or how much), quality (how well), coverage (how much area, how far), timeliness (how responsive, how frequent), and readiness (availability, mission/operational readiness). Performance is an attribute for all systems, people, products, and processes, including those for development, production, verification, deployment, operations, support, training, and disposal. Thus, supportability parameters, manufacturing process variability, reliability, and so forth are all performance measures.

Performance specification   A document that specifies the performance characteristics that a system or component must possess.

Performance testing   Testing conducted to evaluate the compliance of a system or component with specified performance requirements.

Physical attributes   Quantitative and qualitative expressions of material features, such as composition, dimensions, finishes, form, fit, and their respective tolerances.

PR   Problem Report. A report of a problem found in the software system or documentation that needs to be corrected.

Preliminary design   The process of analyzing design alternatives and defining the architecture, components, interfaces, and timing and sizing estimates for a system or component.

Preventive maintenance   Maintenance performed to prevent problems before they occur.

Product   Anything that is used or produced to satisfy a need (e.g., facilities, systems, hardware, software, firmware, data, processes, materials, or services).

Product baseline   The product baseline is the initial approved technical documentation (including source code, object code, and other deliverables) defining a configuration item during the production, operation, maintenance. and logistic support of its life cycle.

Product information   Information related to a product, including configuration documentation and other information that is derived from configuration documentation (e.g., instruction manuals, manufacturing instructions, catalogs).

Product support   The act of providing information, assistance, and training to install and make the software operational in its intended environment.

QA   Quality Assurance. A planned and systematic pattern of all actions necessary to provide adequate confidence that an item or product conforms to established technical requirements.

QC   Quality Control. A set of activities designed to evaluate the quality of a developed product. In the case of QC, the focus is to find the defect, whereas in QA the focus is to prevent the defect from occurring.

Query language   A language used to access information stored in a database.

Rapid prototyping   A type of prototyping in which emphasis is placed on developing prototypes early in the development process to permit early feedback and analysis in support of the development process.

Regression testing   The process of testing a software system, again usually using the original test plan and test data to ensure that the modifications that were carried out have not caused unintended effects and that the system or component still complies with its specified requirements.

Release   A configuration management action whereby a particular version of software is made available for a specific purpose.

Released data   (1) Data that has been released after review and internal approvals. (2) Data that has been provided to others outside the originating group or team for use (as opposed to for comment).

Requirements analysis   The process of studying user needs to arrive at a definition of system, hardware, or software requirements.

Requirements phase   The period of time in the software development life cycle during which the requirements of a software product are defined and documented.

Requirements specification   A document that specifies the requirements for a system or component. Also known as Requirements Definition Document (RDD).

Requirements   Specified essential attributes.

Response time   The elapsed time between the end of an inquiry or command to an interactive computer system and the beginning of the system's response.

Retirement   Permanent removal of a system or component from its operational environment.

Retirement phase   The period of time in the software development life cycle during which the support for a software product is terminated.

Retrofit   The incorporation of new design parts or software code, resulting from an approved engineering change to a product's current approved product configuration documentation, into products already delivered to and accepted by customers.

Reusability   The degree to which a software component can be used in more than one computer program or system.

Rework   A procedure applied to a product to eliminate a nonconforming attribute.

RFD   Requests for Deviations

RFW   Requests for Waiver

SAE   Society of Automotive Engineers

SCM   Software Configuration Management. The set of methodologies, procedures, and techniques to manage and control change in the software development process and to ensure that the products that are developed satisfy the requirements. IEEE defines SCM as a discipline applying technical and administrative direction and surveillance to identify and document the functional and physical characteristics of a configuration item, control changes to those characteristics, record and report change processing and implementation status, and verify compliance with specified requirements.

SCM tool   Software used to automate SCM functions such as change management, problem tracking, version management, build management, and status accounting, which would otherwise have to be performed manually.

SCMP   Software Configuration Management Plan. The SCM plan documents what SCM activities are to be done, how they are to be done, who is responsible for doing specific activities, when they are to happen, and what resources are required.

SCN   Specification Change Notice. A document used in configuration management to propose, transmit, and record changes to a specification.

SDLC   Software Development Life Cycle. The period of time that begins when a software product is conceived and ends when the software is no longer available for use. The SDLC typically includes phases such as analysis, design, development, testing, release, and maintenance.

Software   Computer programs, procedures, and associated documentation and data pertaining to the operation of a computer system.

Software development process   The set of actions required to efficiently transform the user's need into an effective software solution.

Software engineering   The application of a systematic, disciplined, and quantifiable approach to the development, operation, and maintenance of software. The practice of software engineering is a discipline, with a well-defined process (or system) that produces a product (e.g., the software, documentation) and has a set of (automated) tools to improve the productivity and quality of work.

Software product   The set of computer programs, procedures, and possibly associated documentation and data.

Software program A combination of computer instructions and data definitions that enable computer hardware to perform computational or control functions.

Software tool A computer program used in the development, testing, analysis, or maintenance of a program or its documentation.

Software unit A separately compliable piece of code.

Source code Computer instructions and data definitions expressed in a form suitable for input to an assembler, compiler, or other translator.

Specification A document that explicitly states essential technical attributes and requirements for a product and procedures to determine that the product's performance meets its requirements and attributes.

Spiral model A model of the software development process in which the constituent activities, typically requirements analysis, preliminary and detailed design, coding, integration, and testing, are performed interactively until the software is complete.

SPR Software Problem Report. Same as *problem report*.

SQA Software Quality Assurance. The discipline of applying the quality assurance principles to the software development process.

SQAP Software Quality Assurance Plan. The document in which the procedures and guidelines for practicing software quality assurance are recorded.

Submitted data Released data that has been made available to customers.

Support equipment Equipment and computer software required to maintain, test, or operate a product or facility in its intended environment.

System testing Testing conducted on the complete system to evaluate whether it meets the specified requirements.

Unit One of a quantity of items (products, parts, etc.).

Unit testing The testing of individual units in a software system.

U.S. DoD United States Department of Defense

Usability The ease with which a user can learn to operate, prepare inputs, and interpret outputs of a system or component.

Variance; deviation; waiver; departure A specific written authorization to depart from a particular requirement(s) of a product's current approved configuration documentation for a specific number of units or a specified time period. (A variance differs from an engineering change in that an approved engineering change requires corresponding revision of the product's current approved configuration documentation, whereas a variance does not.).

Variant Versions that are functionally equivalent but designed for different hardware and software environments.

Verification   The act of validating that a requirement has been fulfilled.

Version   An initial release or re-release of a configuration item. It is an instance of the system that differs in some way from the other instances. New versions of the system may have additional functionality or different functionality. Their performance characteristics may be different, or they may be the result of fixing a bug that was found by the user or customer.

Version identifier   A supplementary identifier used to distinguish a changed body or set of computer-based data (software) from the previous configuration with the same primary identifier. Version identifiers are usually associated with data (such as files, databases, and software) used by, or maintained in, computers.

Waterfall model   A model of the software development model in which the different phases, requirements, analysis, design, coding, testing, and implementation, are performed in that order, without any overlap or interaction.

Working data   Data that has not been reviewed or released; any data that is currently controlled solely by the originator, including new versions of data that was released, submitted, or approved.

WWW   World Wide Web

Selected bibliography

Configuration Management Practices for Systems, Equipment, Munitions and Computer Programs (MIL-STD-483).

Configuration Management Standards (MIL-STD-973).

Defense System Software Development Standards (DOD-STD-2167A).

Freedman, A., *The Computer Glossary: The Complete Illustrated Dictionary,* 8th ed., New York: Amacom, 1998.

IEEE Standard for Software Configuration Management Plans (IEEE Std-828-1998).

IEEE Standard Glossary of Software Engineering Terminology (IEEE Std-610.12-1990).

Margolis, P. E., *Computer and Internet Dictionary,* 3rd ed., New York: Random House, 1999.

National Consensus Standard for Configuration Management (EIA-649).

Author Biography

Alexis Leon is the co-founder and managing director of L & L Consultancy Services Pvt. Ltd., a company specializing in software engineering, Web design and development, groupware and workflow automation, software procedures, management and industrial engineering, Internet/intranet development, and client/server application development.

He graduated from Kerala University with first rank and distinction in industrial engineering in 1989. In 1991, he earned his master's degree (M.Tech.) in industrial engineering with distinction also from the same university. His areas of specialization include software engineering, database management systems, workflow automation, groupware, ergonomics, and industrial engineering.

He has written more than 35 books on topics including CICS, DB2, Oracle, PowerBuilder, Developer/2000, mainframes, year 2000 solutions, the Internet, information technology, SQL, ERP, SCM, e-business, database systems, and business computing. Two of his books have been translated into Mandarin by McGraw-Hill Taiwan. His books on ERP, the Internet, Oracle, information technology, database management systems, and others are prescribed textbooks in many universities and training institutes in India, Sri Lanka, Nepal, Taiwan, China, Nigeria, Ethiopia, and other countries around the world.

Before starting his own company, he worked with Pond's India Ltd. as an industrial engineer, Tata Consultancy Services as a software consultant, and Cybernet Software Systems as the technical director. You can contact him via e-mail at *aleon@acm.org*.

Index

A

Acceptance testing, 28–29
    defined, 28–29
    tasks, 29
    See also Software development life cycle
        (SDLC)
Adaptive maintenance, 50
Adaptive software development, 18
Ad hoc queries, 139–40
Administrative support team, 291
Administrators, 220
Aerospace Industries Association (AIA), 166
Agile methods, 18
AllFusion Harvest CM, 116
American National Standards Institute (ANSI),
    166
ANSI/IEEE Std-730-2002, 177
ANSI/IEEE Std-828-1998, 200
ANSI/IEEE Std-1028-1988, 177
ANSI/IEEE Std-1042-1987, 176–77, 200
Assigners, 220
Auditing, 11
    activity, 147–48
    configuration, 71, 212
    SCM system, 150–51
Audits
    benefits, 143, 144
    to be performed, 212
    conducting, 148–49
    defined, 147
    during, 149
    functional configuration (FCA), 148, 149–50
    objective, 144
    operations, 310
    performance, 146
    physical configuration (PCA), 148, 150
    procedures, 212
    SCM plan, 204–5
    SCM team role in, 151
    SCM tools and, 151–52, 237

B

Baselines, 57–60
    approaches, 58
    change control, 115
    configuration control and, 95
    controlling number of, 60
    defined, 58, 94
    deliverables, 96
    design, 59, 95
    establishing, 59, 95, 96
    importance, 57
    product, 59, 96, 150
    requirements, 59, 95
BOOTSTRAP, 191–92
    defined, 191
    maturity levels, 192
    process model, 192
Branches
    extending, 63
    multiple, 63
    numbering scheme, 62
    version numbers, 62
Brook's law, 35
Budgets, 87, 279
Bug fixes, 52
Build managers, 220

C

Capability Maturity Model (CMM), 188
Capability Maturity Model Integration (CMMI),
    189–90
    configuration management definition, 189
    defined, 189
    goals, 190

Practical Guide to Software Quality Management, Second Edition,
John W. Horch

Practical Insight into CMMI®, Tim Kasse

A Practitioner's Guide to Software Test Design, Lee Copeland

The Requirements Engineering Handbook, Ralph R. Young

Risk-Based E-Business Testing, Paul Gerrard and Neil Thompson

Secure Messaging with PGP and S/MIME, Rolf Oppliger

Software Configuration Management, Second Edition, Alexis Leon

Software Fault Tolerance Techniques and Implementation, Laura L. Pullum

Strategic Software Production with Domain-Oriented Reuse, Paolo Predonzani,
Giancarlo Succi, and Tullio Vernazza

Successful Evolution of Software Systems, Hongji Yang and Martin Ward

Systematic Process Improvement Using ISO 9001:2000 and CMMI®,
Boris Mutafelija and Harvey Stromberg

Systematic Software Testing, Rick D. Craig and Stefan P. Jaskiel

Testing and Quality Assurance for Component-Based Software, Jerry Zeyu Gao,
H. -S. Jacob Tsao, and Ye Wu

*Workflow Modeling: Tools for Process Improvement and Application
Development,* Alec Sharp and Patrick McDermott

For further information on these and other Artech House titles, including previously considered out-of-print books now available through our In-Print-Forever® (IPF®) program, contact:

Artech House	Artech House
685 Canton Street	46 Gillingham Street
Norwood, MA 02062	London SW1V 1AH UK
Phone: 781-769-9750	Phone: +44 (0)20 7596-8750
Fax: 781-769-6334	Fax: +44 (0)20 7630-0166
e-mail: artech@artechhouse.com	e-mail: artech-uk@artechhouse.com

Find us on the World Wide Web at: www.artechhouse.com